KALLIS' iBT TOEFL® PATTERN

Reading 3

KALLIS' iBT TOEFL® Pattern Reading 3

KALLIS EDU, INC.
7490 Opportunity Road, Suite 203
San Diego, CA 92111
(858) 277-8600
info@kallisedu.com
www.kallisedu.com

ISBN-10: 1-4953-1764-1
ISBN-13: 978-1-4953-1764-4

iBT TOEFL® Pattern - Reading III is the third
of our three-level iBT TOEFL® Reading Exam
preparation book series.

Our **iBT TOEFL® Pattern Reading** series helps
students understand the *context* of each question
and provides numerous types of *practice* to
master test-taking skills. **Hacking Strategies**
and **Quick Looks** break down each question
type seen on the official exam so that students
have a better understanding of what they are
asked to look for in each question. *Practice*
includes **Warm Up** questions, **Quick Practice**
for focusing on particular question types, and an
Actual Test that combines all question types.

KALLIS

KALLIS'

TOEFL® iBT

PATTERN

READING 3

SPECIALIST

Getting Started

A study guide should familiarize the reader with the material found on the test, develop unique methods that can be used to solve various question types, and provide practice questions to challenge future test-takers. *KALLIS' iBT TOEFL® Pattern Series* aims to accomplish all these study tasks by presenting iBT TOEFL® test material in an organized, comprehensive, and easy-to-understand way.

KALLIS' iBT TOEFL® Pattern Reading Series presents the ten different types of questions that you can expect to encounter on the reading component of the iBT TOEFL test. An entire chapter is devoted to each type of question, allowing you to easily discover which question types you find most challenging and then develop an individual strategy for each type of question. Each chapter uses unique techniques of presenting the reading test material in order to make the practice questions as easy to understand as possible.

Putting the Question into Context

▶ The beginning of each chapter provides a definition of the type of questions that you will learn to master throughout the chapter.

▶ The *Question Model* section located below the definition provides an example question that is then solved in a step-by-step process using the **Hacking Strategy**.

▶ The *Question Formats* section presents the specific wording used to ask each question.

▶ The *Tips* section provides helpful hints so that you know the features of a correct answer and how to identify incorrect answers.

Hacking Strategy

- **Hacking Strategy** provides a step-by-step visualization of how to approach each question.

- Because dealing with so many different types of questions can be confusing, the **Example Breakdown** that follows the **Hacking Strategy** develops a common process to assist you in properly analyzing the text and selecting the most logical answer.

Quick Look

- **Quick Look** provides necessary information to understand how to solve the practice questions.

- The hints given in **Quick Look** can be utilized to learn new aspects of English grammar, and they can be used to brush up on concepts that may already be familiar to you.

- For the more difficult types of questions that are presented in later chapters, **Quick Look** combines visual representations and written descriptions to illuminate what you need to find within each question.

Enhancing Test-Taking Skills with Numerous Practice Questions

Though understanding test-taking strategies will greatly improve your success on the reading test, the best way to improve your skills is through practice. Thus, *KALLIS' iBT TOEFL® Pattern Reading Series* includes a variety of practice questions with varying levels of difficulty.

Warm Up

- The **Warm Up** provides practice questions that are simplified versions of the problem types that you will spend much of your time solving on the actual iBT TOEFL test.

Quick Practice

- Each chapter contains **Quick Practice**, which is composed of ten practice passages with questions that elaborate on the skills developed during the **Quick Look** and **Warm Up**.
- At the end of each chapter, you will be challenged with a **Pop Quiz** that tests your vocabulary skills using words found throughout the passages in the corresponding chapter.

Actual Practice

- Located in Chapter 11, the **Actual Practice** provides passages with multiple question types that require the reader to combine skills developed throughout the book.
- This section is meant to be more challenging and should be attempted only after you understand the types of questions presented in Chapters 1 through 10.

Actual Test

- The **Actual Test** will familiarize you with the format of the official TOEFL reading test and includes types of questions from each chapter.
- A scaled scoring chart is located at the beginning of the test so that you can grade yourself and get an idea of how you might score on the official TOEFL reading test.
- After the **Actual Test**, you will find **Actual TOEFL Vocabulary**, which contains hundreds of the most commonly employed vocabulary words from TOEFL reading tests.

In Case You Need Help

▶ Toward the back of this book, you will find the **Answer Key**, which provides the correct answer to each question and includes explanations.
▶ If you do not want to repeatedly flip to the back of the book for answers, simply cut out the **Simple Answers** at the very back of the book. **Simple Answers** provides a quick reference so you can confirm that all your answers are correct.

Are you ready to become a specialist?

Table of Contents

Reading **3**

Specialist

I. What Is a Vocabulary Question?

Vocabulary in Context

The vocabulary question asks you to define a vocabulary word or a phrase as it is used within a sentence. Everything surrounding the vocabulary word is called its *context*. Since many English words can have several meanings, the definition of the vocabulary word or the phrase is determined by its context.

A. VOCABULARY QUESTION MODEL

The Roman emperor Diocletian had a massive palace complex built for himself on a peninsula in Croatia, where he retired in 304 CE. "Diocletian's Palace," as the complex is still known, was so well built that even 300 years after its construction, it served as a fortress for residents fleeing a military invasion. A small town emerged within the palace walls, and it has remained inhabited ever since. Today, the estate features **antiquated** structures from the Roman era, the Middle Ages, the Renaissance, and later periods.

1. The word "**antiquated**" in the passage means

   (A) colorful

   (B) aged

   (C) sentimental

   (D) special

B. VOCABULARY QUESTION FORMATS

The word/phrase is closest in meaning to _____.

The word/phrase means _____.

The word/phrase _____ probably means _____.

What does the word/phrase _____ mean?

In stating _____, the author means that _____.

C. TIPS

1. To identify the correct meaning of the word in context, take a close look at the sentence and grammatical structure, the usage of punctuation marks, and the meanings of surrounding words.

2. In some cases, you can figure out the meaning of a word simply based on your understanding of the passage's main idea.

3. On the official TOEFL test, some unusual or technical terms have hyperlinked definitions. In this book, such terms are defined at the end of the passage. Because the definition is provided, these words will not appear as questions.

II. Hacking Strategy

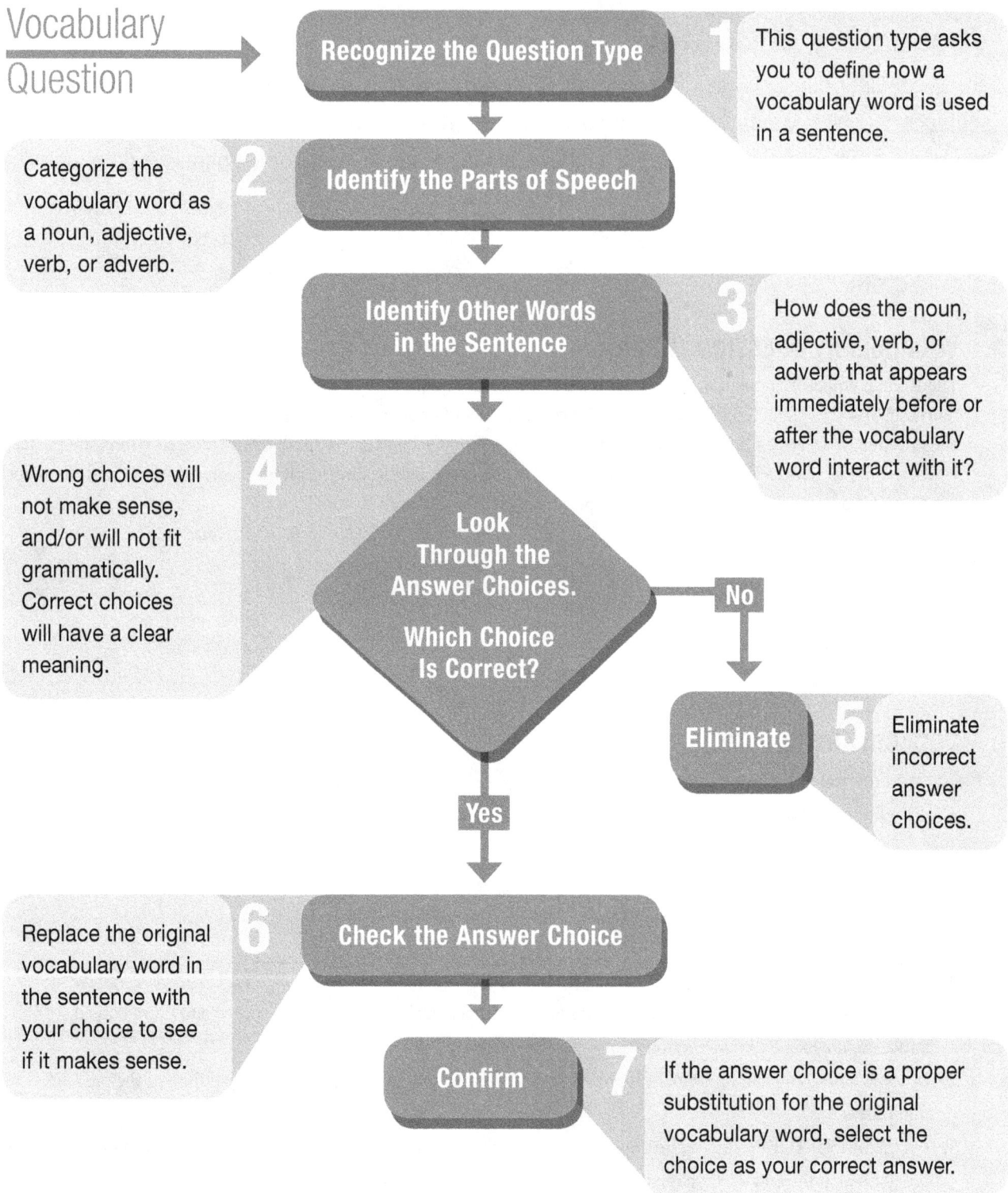

Vocabulary Question →

Recognize the Question Type

1 This question type asks you to define how a vocabulary word is used in a sentence.

2 Categorize the vocabulary word as a noun, adjective, verb, or adverb.

Identify the Parts of Speech

Identify Other Words in the Sentence

3 How does the noun, adjective, verb, or adverb that appears immediately before or after the vocabulary word interact with it?

4 Wrong choices will not make sense, and/or will not fit grammatically. Correct choices will have a clear meaning.

Look Through the Answer Choices.

Which Choice Is Correct?

No

Eliminate

5 Eliminate incorrect answer choices.

Yes

6 Replace the original vocabulary word in the sentence with your choice to see if it makes sense.

Check the Answer Choice

Confirm

7 If the answer choice is a proper substitution for the original vocabulary word, select the choice as your correct answer.

1 The Roman emperor Diocletian had a massive palace complex built for himself on a peninsula in Croatia, where he retired in 304 CE. "Diocletian's Palace," as the complex is still known, was so well built that even 300 years after its construction, it served as a fortress for residents fleeing a military invasion. A small town emerged within the palace walls, and it has remained inhabited ever since. Today, the estate features **antiquated** structures from the Roman era, the Middle Ages, the Renaissance, and later periods.

The word "**antiquated**" in the passage means
(A) colorful
(B) aged
(C) sentimental
(D) special

2 **Antiquated** is an adjective describing *structures*.

3 Today, the estate features **antiquated** structures from the *Roman era*, *the Middle Ages*, *the Renaissance*, and later periods.

The sentence mentions different periods that are now represented architecturally by the structures. Because the time periods are in past centuries, the word **antiquated** must be a synonym for *old*.

4 (A) colorful
(B) aged
(C) sentimental
(D) special

The correct choice will be an adjective and probably means *old*.

5
• Eliminate **Choice A** because *colorful* has nothing to do with age, and we are looking for a synonym for *old*.
• Eliminate **Choice C** because *sentimental* has to do with emotion, so it is not a synonym for *old*.
• Eliminate **Choice D** because *special* has nothing to do with age or being *old*.

6 Today, the estate features *aged* structures from the Roman era, the Middle Ages, the Renaissance, and later periods.

This makes sense because *aged* is a synonym for *old*, or **antiquated**.

7 Select the correct answer — **Choice B**.

III. Quick Look

Word Prefixes, Suffixes, Roots

Prefix, Suffix or Root	Meaning	Example and Definition
agri, agro	pertaining to fields or soil	**agri**culture: agri (field) + culture (tend to) = *the production of crops* **agro**industry: agro (field) + industry = *the large-scale production of food*
ambi	both	**ambi**dextrous: ambi (both) + dexter (right-handed) + ous (relating to) = *able to use both hands well* **ambi**lateral: ambi (both) + lateral (side) = *relating to both sides*
ante	before	**ante**room: ante (before) + room (chamber) = *waiting room* **ante**date: ante (earlier) + date = *precede in time*
anti, antico	old	**anti**que: anti (old) + que (suffix) = *an old and collectible thing* **anti**quate: anti (old) + quate (to make) = *to make old-fashioned*
ate	quality of, state, office, function	candid**ate**: candid (honest, outspoken) + ate (quality of) = *a person seeking to be elected* elector**ate**: elector (a person who elects) + ate (quality of) = *the body of all qualified voters*
aud, audi, audio, aur	to hear, listen	**audi**ence: audi (to hear) + ence (state of) = *those who are listening or watching* **audio**visual: audio (to hear) + visual (to see) = *involving both hearing and sight*
belli	war	**belli**gerent: belli (war) + ger (to conduct) + ent (one who causes) = *warlike* **belli**cose: belli (war) + cose (like) = *eager to fight*
bibl, bible, biblio	book	**biblio**phile: biblio (book) + phile (one who loves) = *a person who loves books* **biblio**graphy: biblio (book) + graphy (writing) = *a list of books or references*
bio, bi	life	**bio**graphy: bio (life) + graphy (writing) = *an account of a person's life by another* **bio**logy: bio (life) + logy (to study) = *the study of a living organism*
chrom, chrome, chromo	color	**chromo**some: chromo (color) + some (body) = *a threadlike body of DNA* poly**chrome**: poly (many) + chrome (colored) = *being of many colors*
chron	time around	**chron**ology: chron (time) + ology (to study) = *the sequential order* **chron**ometer: chron (time) + meter (measure) = *any timepiece designed for accuracy*
circum	around	**circum**navigate: circum (around) + navigate (voyage) = *to travel completely around* **circum**flex: circum (around) + flex (to bend) = *to bend around*

Prefix, Suffix or Root	Meaning	Example and Definition
co, cog, col, coll, com, con, cor	with, together	**co**llaborate: col (together) + labor (work) + ate (state of) = *join together to work on something* **con**temporary: con (with) + temporary (of time) = *of the current time*
cogn, cogni, gnos, gnosis	to know	**recogn**ize: re (again) + cogn (to know) + ize (to cause) = *to identify something already known* **diagnosis**: dia (thorough) + gnosis (suffix) = *identification of disease or injury*
corp	body	**corp**oral: corp (body) + or (activity) + al (result of) = *physical* **corp**ulent: corp (body) + ulent (full of) = *fat*
dem, demo	people, populace, population	**dem**ocracy: demo (common people) + cracy (rule) = *government by the people or elected representatives* **dem**ography: demo (people) + graphy (writing) = *the scientific study of human populations*
dic, dict, dicta, dit	say, speak	**dict**ionary: diction (words) + ary (related to) = *collection of words and phrases* **dicta**phone: dicta (speak) + phone (speech, sound) = *dictating machine*
domin	rule, master, that which is under control	**domin**ate: domin (master) + ate (state of) = *control* **domin**ant: domin (ruling) + ant (suffix) = *overbearing*
dorm	sleep	**dorm**ant: dorm (to sleep) + ant (suffix) = *inactive* **dormi**tory: dormi (sleep) + tory (suffix) = *sleeping place or building with rooms, as at a college*
eco	household, environment	**eco**logy: eco (environment) + logy (study) = *the study of the relationship between living organisms and environments* **eco**spheres: eco (environment) + sphere (globe) = *physiological atmosphere*
erg, ergo	work, effect	**ergo**meter: ergo (work) + meter (measure) = *a device to measure muscle power* **ergo**phobia: ergo (work) + phobia (fear) = *a fear of work*
fac, fact, facture, fas, fea, fec, fect, fic	do, make	manu**facture**: manu (hand) + facture (to make) = *build* arti**fact**: arti (using art or skill) + fact (something made) = *object crafted by people in the past*
fix	repair, attach	**fix**ture: fix (repair) + ture (condition of) = *something securely attached* pre**fix**: pre (before) + fix (attach) = *to put before*
flect, flex	bend	re**flect**: re (again) + flect (bend) = *to cast back from a surface* circum**flex**: circum (around) + flex (bend) = *bending around*

Prefix, Suffix or Root	Meaning	Example and Definition
flu, fluc, fluv, flux	flow	***flu**x*: in (in, into) + flux (flow) = *flowing in* ***reflu**x*: re (again) + flux (flow) = *a flowing back*
fract, frag, frai	break	***fract**ure*: fract (break) + ure (suffix) = *the act of breaking* ***frag**ile*: frag (break) + ile (ability) = *easily broken*
geo	earth	***geo**graphy*: geo (earth) + graphy (to write) = *the study of natural features of earth* ***geo**logy*: geo (earth) + logy (to study) = *the scientific study of the earth*
giga, gigas	billion, giant	***giga**byte*: giga (billion) + byte (split) = *a unit of computer memory* ***giga**ntic*: gigas (giant) + ic (having the nature of) = *very large*
grat, grate	pleasing	*in**grate***: in (not) + grate (pleasing) = *ungrateful* *con**grat**ulate*: con (together) + grat (pleasing) + ate (state of) = *to express pleasure*
hema, hemo	blood	***hemo**rrhage*: hemo (blood) + rrhage (burst) = *to bleed profusely* ***hemo**globin*: hemo (blood) + globin (globule) = *the protein in red blood cells*
her, here, hes	stick	*ad**here***: ad (toward) + here (stick) = *stick to* *co**here***: co (together) + here (stick) = *to stick together*
hetero	other, different	***hetero**dox*: hetero (different) + dox (opinion) = *other opinion* ***hetero**dyne*: hetero (different) + dyne (power) = *to mix with a different frequency*
hydr, hydra, hydro	water	*de**hydr**ate*: de (away from) + hydr (water) + ate (state of) = *to deprive of water* ***hydro**phobia*: hydro (water) + phobia (fear) = *a fear of water*
gen, geny, gene	birth, race	***gen**ealogy*: genea (generation, race) + logy (student of) = *the study of family ancestries* *pro**geny***: pro (forth) + geny (birth, to produce) = *a descendant*
infra	beneath, below	***infra**sonic*: infra (below) + sonic (sound) = *sound waves* ***infra**structure*: infra (below) + structure (building) = *foundation, basic equipment, services, facilities*
intra	within, during, between layers, underneath	***intra**mural*: intra (within) + mural (walls) = *involving only students at the same school* ***intra**net*: intra (within) + net (network) = *internal network*
intro	into, within, inward	***intro**vert*: intro (inward) + vert (to turn) = *a shy person* ***intro**spection*: intro (within) + spec (look) + tion (noun suffix) = *self-examination*
ist	person or member	*podiat**rist***: podiatry (foot care) + ist (noun: person) = *a person who treats foot conditions* *nove**list***: novel + ist (noun: person) = *a person who writes a novel*

Prefix, Suffix or Root	Meaning	Example and Definition
jac, ject	throw	**re***ject*: re (again) + ject (throw) = *refuse* **pro***ject*: pro (forward) + ject (throw) = *to propose or set forth*
liber, liver	free	**de***liver*: de (away) + liver (free) = *to give or transfer* **liber**ty: liber (free) + ty (state of) = *freedom*
magn, magni	great	***magn***animous: magn (great) + anim (spirit) + ous (suffix) = *generous in being forgiving* ***magni***tude: magni (great) + tude (state of) = *great size or importance*
mal	bad, badly	***mal***function: mal (bad) + func (performed) + tion (quality of) = *failure to function correctly* dis***mal***: dis (days) + mal (bad) = *gloomy; dreary*
mand, manda	command	***manda***tory: manda (command) + tory (relating to) = *required* re***mand***: re (again) + mand (command) = *to send back*
matri	mother	***matri***mony: matri (mother) + mony (state) = *marriage* ***matri***archate: matri (mother) + arch (rule) + ate (state of) = *a family under female domination*
meter	measure	volta***meter***: volt + meter (measure) = *an instrument measuring voltage and amperage* baro***meter***: baro (weight) + meter (measure) = *an instrument measuring atmospheric pressure*
migra	wander, move	**e***migra*nt: e (out) + migra (move) + ant (a person who) = *a person who moves somewhere else* im***migra***te: im (go into) + migra (move) + ate (state of) = *to move into somewhere*
miss, mit	send	re***mit***: re (again) + mit (send) = *return* sub***mit***: sub (under) + mit (send) = *to send; to comply*
neo	new	***neo***lithic: neo (new) + lithic (stone) = *the later Stone age* ***neo***phyte: neo (new) + phyte (plant) = *a beginner*
neur, neuro	nerve	***neur***itis: neur (nerve) + itis (disease) = *inflammation of a nerve* ***neuro***pathic: neuro (nerve) + path (suffering) + ic (pertaining to) = *disease of the nervous system*
oct, octa, octo	eight	***octo***pus: octo (eight) + pus (foot) = *name of a type of eight-limbed cephalopod* ***octa***gon: octa (eight) + gon (angle) = *a polygon having eight sides*
nym, onym	name	an***onym***ous: an (without) + onym (name) + ous (full of) = *without a name* pseud***onym***: pseudo (false) + nym (name) = *alias*

Prefix, Suffix or Root	Meaning	Example and Definition
ped, pede, pedes	foot, having a foot	**im*ped*e**: im (not) + pede (foot) = *to obstruct or hinder* ***pede*strian**: pedes (one who goes on foot) + train (a person) = *one who walks*
pel, puls	drive, push, urge	**com*pel***: com (together) + pel (drive) = *to force or drive* **dis*pel***: dis (away) + pel (drive) = *to rid of, especially by scattering*
phobia, phobos	fear	**claustro*phobia***: claustro (place shut in) + phobia (fear) = *a fear of small spaces* **acro*phobia***: acro (the top) + phobia (fear) = *a fear of being at a great height*
pod, pus	foot, feet	***pod*iatry**: pod (foot) + diatry (healing) = *the care of the human foot* **tri*pod***: tri (three) + pod (foot) = *a stand with three legs*
poly	many	***poly*theist**: poly (many) + the (god) + ist (person who) = *a believer of more than one god* ***poly*gon**: poly (many) + gon (angle) = *a figure having more than three sides*
prim, prime, prin, princip	first	***princip*al**: princip (first) + al (relating to) = *first* ***prime*val**: prim (first) + eval (age) = *of the first age*
proto	first	***proto*type**: proto (first) + type (impression) = *an original model* ***proto*col**: proto (first) + col (glue) = *a formal process; a draft of document*
psych	mind, soul	***psych*iatry**: psych (mind) + iatry (healing) = *the science of diagnosing mental disorders* ***psych*ology**: psycho (mind) + logy (to study) = *the scientific study of all forms of human and animal behavior*
retro	backward, back	***retro*rocket**: retro (backward) + rocket = *a small rocket engine* ***retro*spect**: retro (back) + spect (look at) = *a survey of past time*
rupt	break	**inter*rupt***: inter (between) + rupt (break) = *to stop* **ab*rupt***: ab (off) + rupt (break) = *sudden*
sanct	holy	***sanct*uary**: sanct (holy) + uary (place) = *shrine* ***sanct*imonious**: sancti (holy) + moni (state of) + ous (full of) = *making a display of holiness*
sci, scient scientia, scio, scious	know	**con*scious***: con (with) + scious (know) = *aware* **omni*scient***: omni (all) + scient (know) = *having unlimited knowledge*
scrib, script	write	**in*scrib*e**: in (preposition) + scribe (write) = *to address informally to a person; to write* **sub*scrib*e**: sub (underneath) + scribe (write) = *to agree to by giving a signature*

Prefix, Suffix or Root	Meaning	Example and Definition
se	apart, move away from	**se**cede: se (apart) + cede (to go) = *to withdraw formally* **se**duce: se (apart) + duce (to lead) = *allure*
sign, signi, signia	sign, mark, seal sleep	de**sign**: de (out) + sign (mark) = *plan* in**signia**: in (into) + signia (mark) = *a mark or badge of honor*
somn	wise	in**somn**ia: in (not) + somnia (sleep) = *inability to fall asleep* **somn**ambulist: somn (sleep) + nambul (to walk) + ist (person who) = *sleepwalking person*
soph, sopho	build	**sopho**more: sopho (wise) + more (fool) = *a student in the second year of college* philo**soph**y: philo (loving) + sophy (wisdom) = *the rational investigation of the truth of the being*
story, stru, struct, stry	touch	con**struct**: con (together) + struct (build) = *to build* de**struct**ion: de (pull down) + struct (build) + tion (state of) = *in ruins*
tact, tag, tang, tig, ting	distance, far,	con**tact**: con (together) + tact (touch) = *the act of touching* in**tang**ible: in (not) + tang (touch) + ible (able to) = *incapable of being touched*
tele	from, afar	**tele**phone: tele (far) + phone (sound) = *a system for transmission of sound* **tele**graph: tele (far) + graph (written) = *a system for transmitting messages*
tem, tempo	time	ex**tempo**raneously: ex (out of) + temporaneous (relating to time) + ly (in what manner) = *impromptu* con**tempo**rary: con (together) + temporary (relating to time) = *of the current time*
vict, vinc, vince	conquer, overcome	con**vict**: con (jointly) + vict (conquer) = *to prove guilty of an offense* con**vince**: con (together) + vince (overcome) = *to make one believe*
vita, viv, vive, vivi	alive, life	re**vive**: re (again) + vive (alive) = *bring back to life* sur**vive**: sur (super) + vive (alive) = *to stay alive*
voc, voke	call	con**voc**ation: con (together) + voc (to call) + ation (state of) = *a gathering or assembly* in**voc**ation: in (into) + voc (to call) + ation (state of) = *the act of calling upon a deity*
vor	eat greedily	carni**vor**ous: carni (flesh) + vor (eat greedily) + ous (full of) = *meat-eating* omni**vor**ous: omni (all) + vor (eat greedily) + ous (full of) = *eating both animals and plant foods*

IV. Warm Up

Circle the vocabulary word that correctly completes each sentence.

1. Passing an electric current through water causes (**subsistent** / **subsequent**) reactions that produce hydrogen and oxygen.

2. Trying to sustain a high level of alertness can be stressful when one is engaged in a (**monotonous** / **monopolistic**) task.

3. *Pacifists*, who reject violence under any circumstances, object to the (**unreliable** / **unreasonable**) and destructive elements of war.

4. Jasper Johns is an American artist famous for his (**abstract** / **abridged**) paintings of objects such as flags, targets, numbers, and maps.

5. One of the reasons that human beings create art is to (**translate** / **transmit**) culture from generation to generation.

6. Scientists use Doppler Radar to (**forecast** / **forestall**) the strength and movement patterns of tornadoes and hurricanes.

7. A crossword puzzle is a popular game commonly played on a (**dialogue** / **diagram**) of black and white squares.

8. The two countries made a (**bilingual** / **bilateral**) agreement not to fish in one another's ocean waters.

9. Children with learning (**diseases** / **disabilities**) have a normal range of intelligence, but cannot use information sent by the senses to the brain as accurately as other children.

10. Plants (**descend** / **derive**) energy from the Sun by means of a process called *photosynthesis*.

11. Delivered to Congress in 1823, the Monroe Doctrine protected independent nations of the Western Hemisphere from European (**convention** / **intervention**).

12. In his famous poem "The Raven," Edgar Allan Poe uses sound and imagery to create a (**vivid** / **vital**) impression in the reader's mind.

13. A *circus* is a live production that features a (**spectator** / **spectacle**) of acrobats, aerial artists, clowns, and other performers.

14. A(n) (**inscription** / **description**) on the Franklin D. Roosevelt Memorial reads, "The only thing we have to fear is fear itself," which was one of his most famous sayings.

15. One way that an airplane's wings keep it airborne by (**reflecting** / **deflecting**) air downward toward the ground.

16. One goes to see a career counselor in order to learn how to (**instruct** / **construct**) a career for oneself.

17. When people join the military, they must take an oath of (**confidence** / **fidelity**) to defend their country under all circumstances.

18. In December of 2000, Al Gore (**proceeded** / **conceded**) the U.S. presidential election to George W. Bush after six weeks of vote recounting in Florida.

19. At the end of the autobiography, there is a detailed (**anachronism** / **chronology**) of the author's life.

20. The classic films *Gone With the Wind* and *The Wizard of Oz* were both released in 1939, when the Technicolor filming process was still a (**novice** / **novelty**).

V. Quick Practice

Practice #1

Read the passage and choose the best answer to each question.

Copyright is the *right* to prevent **unauthorized** *copying*. Copyright laws exist in the artistic community to **guarantee** that artistic people have the opportunity to make money from their artistic expressions. For example, if a person writes a book or composes a symphony, he or she can copyright the work. **Henceforth**, it will be his or her intellectual property – **that is**, an expression that has become a product. Someone who "steals" the property may face fines and/or jail time.

However, society seeks to ensure that cultural treasures, such as beloved plays, images, or songs, can be **feasibly** accessed by the general public. Therefore, copyright coverage extends for only a limited time. United States copyright laws usually safeguard intellectual property for 70 years after the death of the work's creator. Many other countries have fixed terms for copyright protection. Of course, **disparate** circumstances affect this **duration** or whether a creative work is protected. For example, copyright protection may differ if the artist is **anonymous** or if he or she creates works for an employer.

1) The word "**unauthorized**" in Paragraph 1 means
   (A) not written
   (B) not approved
   (C) not specific
   (D) not proven

2) The word "**guarantee**" in Paragraph 1 is closest in meaning to
   (A) realize
   (B) exhibit
   (C) deny
   (D) promise

3) The word "**Henceforth**" in Paragraph 1 is closest in meaning to
   (A) hereafter
   (B) accordingly
   (C) therefore
   (D) consequently

4) The phrase "**that is**" in Paragraph 1 means
   (A) noticeably
   (B) on the other hand
   (C) to be exact
   (D) apparently

5) The word "**feasibly**" in Paragraph 2 is closest in meaning to
   (A) easily
   (B) instantaneously
   (C) profusely
   (D) intentionally

6) The word "**disparate**" in Paragraph 2 is closest in meaning to
   (A) specific
   (B) desperate
   (C) restrictive
   (D) different

7) The word "**duration**" in Paragraph 2 means
   (A) distance
   (B) span
   (C) intensity
   (D) endurance

8) The word "**anonymous**" in Paragraph 2 is closest in meaning to
   (A) identical
   (B) enigmatic
   (C) unidentified
   (D) unqualified

Practice #2

Read the passage and choose the best answer to each question.

The *rumba* is a ballroom dance that has its roots in Afro-Cuban dances. Introduced in America around 1913, the rumba did not immediately become popular, possibly because its **hyperbolic** hip movements **scandalized** the American public. In the early 1930s, attitudes began shifting, partly due to a wildly popular rumba song called "Peanut Vendor." A number of years later, in 1947, an influential London dance teacher known as "Monsieur Pierre" went to Cuba to learn a more **authentic** version of the rumba, which he practiced **strenuously** and then refined and **standardized** for social dance competition. A small group of dance specialists established an examination system and syllabus for all levels of dancers; this syllabus gradually became the **cornerstone** for teaching and competition in Latin American dancing.

The rumba, like most Cuban social dances, calls for taking three steps for every four beats of music, resulting in a quick-quick-slow rhythm. Steps are small, and the bending and straightening of the knees results in a **swaying** hip motion. Rumba dancers also keep their upper bodies fairly still and **sustain** eye contact with each other. Percussive instruments create a tempo that is slow compared with many other Latin dances.

9) The word "**hyperbolic**" in Paragraph 1 is closest in meaning to
   (A) exaggerated
   (B) systematic
   (C) elegant
   (D) hypocritical

10) The word "**scandalized**" in Paragraph 1 is closest in meaning to
    (A) sickened
    (B) invited
    (C) shocked
    (D) gratified

11) The word "**authentic**" in Paragraph 1 means
    (A) ambiguous
    (B) efficient
    (C) diverse
    (D) genuine

12) The word "**strenuously**" in Paragraph 1 is closest in meaning to
    (A) possibly
    (B) intensively
    (C) primarily
    (D) cynically

13) The word "**standardized**" in Paragraph 1 is closest in meaning to
    (A) specialized
    (B) homogenized
    (C) improved
    (D) dissolved

14) The word "**cornerstone**" in Paragraph 1 is closest in meaning to
    (A) foundation
    (B) method
    (C) regulation
    (D) performance

15) The word "**swaying**" in Paragraph 2 means
    (A) tossing
    (B) sheltering
    (C) rolling
    (D) jerking

16) The word "**sustain**" in Paragraph 2 is closest in meaning to
    (A) impose
    (B) promote
    (C) avoid
    (D) maintain

Practice #3

Read the passage and choose the best answer to each question.

From the time Europeans first landed along the Atlantic Coast of what is now the United States, they began moving west. Initially the westward movement was slow, as settlers needed to be near European ships arriving with cargo. **Enticed** by fertile farmlands, settlers gradually moved inland along **navigable** rivers. It was not until the 1840s that Americans began to eye the Pacific Coast as a **covetable** destination, but they feared crossing **rugged** mountains and vast deserts. Furthermore, other peoples, including Native American tribes and Spanish settlers, already lived there.

Two events **spurred** Americans to overcome their fears of the westward journey. One was the 1848 victory in the Mexican-American War, which gave the U.S. most of the territory that now **constitutes** its western states. But what abruptly motivated people, both **affluent** and poor, to move was the California Gold Rush beginning in 1849. It attracted **droves** of fortune-seeking Americans as well as immigrants from Asia, South America, and many other regions of the world.

17) The word "**Enticed**" in Paragraph 1 means
    (A) repulsed
    (B) defeated
    (C) snared
    (D) lured

18) The word "**navigable**" in Paragraph 1 is closest in meaning to
    (A) accessible
    (B) visible
    (C) mobile
    (D) divisible

19) The word "**covetable**" in Paragraph 1 means
    (A) paramount
    (B) indigenous
    (C) obvious
    (D) desirable

20) The word "**rugged**" in Paragraph 1 is closest in meaning to
    (A) extensive
    (B) extraordinary
    (C) rocky
    (D) unknown

21) The word "**spurred**" in Paragraph 2 means
    (A) kicked
    (B) encouraged
    (C) advised
    (D) frightened

22) The word "**constitutes**" in Paragraph 2 means
    (A) comprises
    (B) supplements
    (C) publishes
    (D) retains

23) The word "**affluent**" in Paragraph 2 is closest in meaning to
    (A) indifferent
    (B) prosperous
    (C) humane
    (D) problematic

24) The word "**droves**" in Paragraph 2 is closest in meaning to
    (A) vehicles
    (B) rivers
    (C) crowds
    (D) lines

Practice #4

Read the passage and choose the best answer to each question.

Microwaves are a range of electromagnetic waves that have become useful because their wavelengths and frequencies are **conducive** to transmitting information over long distances. With the ability to bounce off metal surfaces, microwaves were first produced for radar systems by the British military to spot enemy planes during World War II. Microwave technology has nonmilitary applications as well: to cook food using a microwave oven, to **convey** information for satellite and spacecraft communication systems, to broadcast radio and TV signals, and even to clean up polluted soil.

Microwaves are produced by an electron tube called a *magnetron*. In a microwave oven, the magnetron **channels** the microwaves into the oven, where they bounce **haphazardly** off the metal sides of the oven to **bombard** and penetrate the food. When a microwave heats food that contains water molecules, which have oppositely charged **poles** called *dipoles*, the dipolar molecules are affected by the positive and negative fields of the microwaves. This interaction causes the molecules to **pivot** as they are magnetically pulled toward opposite electric charges, and then to bump into other molecules. This movement, or *kinetic* energy, is essentially heat. Thus, the food's own water molecules cause the food to cook. The more water molecules there are in the food, the more **efficacious** the heating process is.

25) The word "**conducive**" in Paragraph 1 means
(A) suitable
(B) relative
(C) respective
(D) portable

26) The word "**convey**" in Paragraph 1 is closest in meaning to
(A) suppress
(B) transmit
(C) scrutinize
(D) restore

27) The word "**channels**" in Paragraph 2 means
(A) reduces
(B) opens
(C) stores
(D) directs

28) The word "**haphazardly**" in Paragraph 2 means
(A) adequately
(B) consistently
(C) randomly
(D) impartially

29) The word "**bombard**" in Paragraph 2 means
(A) undertake
(B) consume
(C) curtail
(D) strike

30) The word "**poles**" in Paragraph 2 is closest in meaning to
(A) tips
(B) pores
(C) tubes
(D) circles

31) The word "**pivot**" in Paragraph 2 is closest in meaning to
(A) jump
(B) rotate
(C) change
(D) expand

32) The word "**efficacious**" in Paragraph 2 means
(A) regular
(B) intense
(C) approximate
(D) effective

Practice #5

Read the passage and choose the best answer to each question.

Boasting deep historical roots and an evolving contemporary status, the quilt is an **ingenious** product. *Quilts* are extra-warm blankets consisting of two layers of cloth that **wrap** a thick layer of insulation such as wool. The layers of cloth are **fastened** together with many tiny stitches over the entire surface. While functional, the stitching may be decorative as well. Similarly, most finished quilts are **utilitarian**, but some are highly prized as art and hang in museums.

Quilters often produce colorful geometric patterns and shapes on the top layer, and may **embroider** or overlay cloth cutouts of flowers, animals, people, or symbols. Sometimes quilts **commemorate** a **compelling** family or historical event. Sometimes they are rather chaotically **pieced together** from scraps of worn-out clothing so that each piece has an association with a person who wore it.

33) The word "**ingenious**" in Paragraph 1 means
(A) clever
(B) convenient
(C) historical
(D) celebrated

34) The word "**wrap**" in Paragraph 1 means
(A) release
(B) permit
(C) surround
(D) moderate

35) The word "**fastened**" in Paragraph 1 means
(A) displayed
(B) observed
(C) described
(D) attached

36) The word "**utilitarian**" in Paragraph 1 means
(A) practical
(B) trivial
(C) frugal
(D) prolific

37) The word "**embroider**" in Paragraph 2 means
(A) belittle
(B) harm
(C) decorate
(D) scour

38) The word "**commemorate**" in Paragraph 2 means
(A) honor
(B) assist
(C) memorize
(D) summon

39) The word "**compelling**" in Paragraph 2 means
(A) inconsequential
(B) inspiring
(C) irrelevant
(D) interesting

40) The phrase "**pieced together**" in Paragraph 2 is closest in meaning to
(A) repaired
(B) assembled
(C) found
(D) planned

Practice #6

Read the passage and choose the best answer to each question.

Geological faults are **fractures** in land where rock on either side has slipped, moved apart, or pushed together. They occur because the Earth's crust incorporates numerous **non-pliable** plates that move continuously – though very, very slowly. For example, the San Andreas Fault stretches 1,300 kilometers along the length of California. It is the boundary where the North American Plate and the Pacific Plate meet and push against each other. Because the plates move an average of 5 or 6 centimeters annually, geologists **postulate** that in about 25 million years California will be quite different, perhaps **ruptured** completely.

Even now, the activity of the plates does not always seem gradual to people on Earth's surface. When tension along the fault builds up like a coiled spring, the stored-up energy can cause rock to suddenly crack and slide, resulting in an earthquake. Many earthquakes are **minute**, but several earthquakes of **colossal magnitude** have occurred along the San Andreas Fault in the last two centuries, including the San Francisco earthquake of 1906. The **turbulence** of the 1906 earthquake was felt even in Oregon, Nevada, and south of Los Angeles.

41) The word "**fractures**" in Paragraph 1 is closest in meaning to
(A) fractions
(B) cracks
(C) walls
(D) rivers

42) The word "**non-pliable**" in Paragraph 1 means
(A) overlapping
(B) gigantic
(C) fragile
(D) rigid

43) The word "**postulate**" in Paragraph 1 means
(A) hypothesize
(B) notice
(C) expect
(D) assure

44) The word "**ruptured**" in Paragraph 1 means
(A) split
(B) disrupted
(C) changed
(D) raised

45) The word "**minute**" in Paragraph 2 is closest in meaning to
(A) gigantic
(B) small
(C) streamlined
(D) sharp

46) The word "**colossal**" in Paragraph 2 means
(A) ample
(B) astonishing
(C) enormous
(D) potential

47) The word "**magnitude**" in Paragraph 2 means
(A) size
(B) might
(C) magnet
(D) energy

48) The word "**turbulence**" in Paragraph 2 means
(A) sedimentation
(B) disorder
(C) agitation
(D) consequence

Practice #7

Read the passage and choose the best answer to each question.

Elizabeth Bishop was a 20th century American poet known for her precision. She won **a myriad of** awards in her lifetime, including the Pulitzer Prize for poetry in 1956. The **motifs** in Bishop's poetry did not reveal intimate details about her life. Rather, her imagery expresses deep emotional **undercurrents**. For example, in her poem "At the Fishhouses," Bishop describes a decaying fishing wharf that shines with silvery light because it is covered with light-reflecting fish scales. But underneath the glittery wharf, there is "the heavy surface of the sea / **swelling** slowly as if considering spilling over...." A seal appears, which makes the narrator imagine being **immersed** in the water. The unseen underwater environment becomes a metaphor for the ever-changing nature of knowledge: "dark, salt, clear, moving, utterly free, / ...and since / our knowledge is historical, flowing, and flown."

Although Bishop was a celebrated poet, she published only 101 poems during her lifetime, and she was **meticulous** with these works, often spending years revising a single poem. As a child, Bishop lost both of her parents and moved between relatives and boarding school. In her adult life, she loved to travel, drawing on a **bequest** from her father. Such circumstances may explain why many of Bishop's poems **dwelt on** the search for a sense of belonging.

49) The phrase "**a myriad of**" in Paragraph 1 is closest in meaning to
(A) unintentional
(B) reputable
(C) exceptional
(D) numerous

50) The word "**motifs**" in Paragraph 1 means
(A) themes
(B) arguments
(C) statements
(D) rhythms

51) The word "**undercurrents**" in Paragraph 1 means
(A) disappointments
(B) surprises
(C) suspicions
(D) implications

52) The word "**swelling**" in Paragraph 1 means
(A) tumbling
(B) receding
(C) curving
(D) rising

53) The word "**immersed**" in Paragraph 1 is closest in meaning to
(A) enveloped
(B) liberated
(C) dispersed
(D) steadfast

54) The word "**meticulous**" in Paragraph 2 means
(A) painstaking
(B) inconstant
(C) obsessive
(D) gracious

55) The word "**bequest**" in Paragraph 2 is closest in meaning to
(A) background
(B) property
(C) inheritance
(D) business

56) The phrase "**dwelt on**" in Paragraph 2 means
(A) arrived on
(B) commented on
(C) worked on
(D) focused on

Read the passage and choose the best answer to each question.

Western South Dakota is home to Wind Cave, which in 1903 was the first cave in the world to be designated as a national park. The cave has so many long passages that it has not yet been fully explored. Because the cave is so **extensive** and has only a few small openings, **drafts** of air rush out of it when the air pressure inside the cave is higher than the air pressure outside, hence the name *Wind Cave*. The Lakota Sioux consider the cave to be sacred ground. According to their mythology, the cave is the **portal** where the Lakota people originally blew into the world on a **gust** of wind **emanating** from the underworld.

Geologists say that the cave developed as water dissolved limestone over more than 300 million years. As a result, the cave's walls are **adorned** with rare calcite formations known as *boxwork*. Featuring complex geometric **configurations**, boxwork is formed by minerals that once filled cracks in rocks until the rocks **eroded**, leaving behind the boxwork. Wind Cave is also famous for its *frostwork*, or delicate, needle-like crystal formations.

57) The word "**extensive**" in Paragraph 1 means
(A) complicated
(B) impermeable
(C) large
(D) tall

58) The word "**drafts**" in Paragraph 1 is closest in meaning to
(A) bits
(B) currents
(C) tons
(D) shocks

59) The word "**portal**" in Paragraph 1 is closest in meaning to
(A) opening
(B) dock
(C) palace
(D) temple

60) The word "**gust**" in Paragraph 1 means
(A) explosion
(B) rush
(C) breeze
(D) outlet

61) The word "**emanating**" in Paragraph 1 means
(A) replenishing
(B) originating
(C) entailing
(D) existing

62) The word "**adorned**" in Paragraph 2 is closest in meaning to
(A) appreciated
(B) decorated
(C) amazed
(D) understood

63) The word "**configurations**" in Paragraph 2 means
(A) arrangements
(B) appearances
(C) ornaments
(D) orientations

64) The word "**eroded**" in Paragraph 2 means
(A) sharpened
(B) disintegrated
(C) exploded
(D) decayed

Practice #9

Read the passage and choose the best answer to each question.

A *near-Earth object*, known as an NEO, is an asteroid, comet, or meteorite in some kind of orbit that brings it into **proximity** with Earth. Currently, researchers in many countries are cooperating on projects to monitor NEOs and find ways to deflect them if they seem likely to **collide with** Earth. Scientists also are considering the possibilities of **dispatching** spacecraft to some of the larger NEOs, and possibly even mining them for resources.

NEOs caught the science world's interest in 1980 when a father-and-son science team, Luis and Walter Alvarez, published their "Alvarez Hypothesis." The Alvarez team suggested that a huge **depression** in Mexico's Yucatan Peninsula was the spot where an asteroid struck 65 million years ago. This event, they said, could have raised **opaque** dust clouds that **obstructed** sunlight, leading to mass extinctions of organisms, including dinosaurs. More recent NEOs have mostly landed in wilderness areas or **combusted** long before hitting land, but on February 15, 2013, a meteor exploded just 25 kilometers above Chelyabinsk Oblast in Russia. The explosion caused shock waves that **demolished** buildings and injured about 1,500 people.

65) The word "**proximity**" in Paragraph 1 means
(A) contact
(B) orbit
(C) space
(D) nearness

66) The phrase "**collide with**" in Paragraph 1 is closest in meaning to
(A) communicate with
(B) crash into
(C) change into
(D) cast light upon

67) The word "**dispatching**" in Paragraph 1 is closest in meaning to
(A) sending
(B) informing
(C) convincing
(D) intercepting

68) The word "**depression**" in Paragraph 2 means
(A) mountain
(B) hole
(C) extension
(D) alteration

69) The word "**opaque**" in Paragraph 2 means
(A) significant
(B) breakable
(C) equivalent
(D) impenetrable

70) The word "**obstructed**" in Paragraph 2 is closest in meaning to
(A) blocked
(B) reflected
(C) occupied
(D) resembled

71) The word "**combusted**" in Paragraph 2 is closest in meaning to
(A) replaced
(B) burst
(C) disappeared
(D) melted

72) The word "**demolished**" in Paragraph 2 means
(A) discharged
(B) supported
(C) destroyed
(D) promoted

Practice #10

Read the passage and choose the best answer to each question.

In the field of literature, the *Lost Generation* identifies a group of writers who became adults during World War I. Some of these **scribes** served as soldiers or medics in the war and rose to **prominence** in the 1920s. Specifically, the Lost Generation **roster** usually includes Ernest Hemingway, John Dos Passos, F. Scott Fitzgerald, T.S. Eliot, and Erich Remarque. Many of them lived in Paris as **expatriates** after World War I.

The Lost Generation writers felt **disillusioned** by the principles for which they had fought and wanted to create literature that was blunt, honest, and free of romantic clichés. Hemingway wrote that his friend, writer Gertrude Stein, had **coined the term** *Lost Generation* when she said to him that "all of you young people who served in the war...you are all a lost generation."

Hemingway used Stein's quote as an epigraph to his novel *The Sun Also Rises*, which is about aimless young Americans living in Paris. However, the book's title is taken from the biblical book *Ecclesiastes*' poetic commentary on continuity, which **underscores** Hemingway's hopeful view that the world will endure, the Sun will rise every day, and his generation will be **resilient**.

73) The word "**scribes**" in Paragraph 1 means
(A) nobles
(B) writers
(C) interpreters
(D) adolescents

74) The word "**prominence**" in Paragraph 1 means
(A) wisdom
(B) control
(C) wealth
(D) fame

75) The word "**roster**" in Paragraph 1 means
(A) fatality
(B) participant
(C) obligation
(D) list

76) The word "**expatriates**" in Paragraph 1 is closest in meaning to
(A) exiles
(B) fugitives
(C) residents
(D) experts

77) The word "**disillusioned**" in Paragraph 2 means
(A) disenchanted
(B) distrusted
(C) invisible
(D) intrigued

78) The expression "**coined the term**" in Paragraph 2 means
(A) decided the phrase
(B) created the phrase
(C) captured the phrase
(D) understood the phrase

79) The word "**underscores**" in Paragraph 3 means
(A) exaggerates
(B) conceals
(C) emphasizes
(D) indicates

80) The word "**resilient**" in Paragraph 3 is closest in meaning to
(A) irrepressible
(B) silent
(C) temporary
(D) defeated

Select the vocabulary word or phrase that has the closest meaning.

6. attitude
A. altitude
B. viewpoint
C. fundamental
D. frequency

7. authentic
A. genuine
B. durable
C. effective
D. accustomed

8. gratified
A. extreme
B. imperative
C. impaired
D. delighted

9. overcome
A. go over
B. get over
C. look over
D. come over

10. abruptly
A. absolutely
B. adequately
C. suddenly
D. cautiously

16. curtail
A. differ
B. efface
C. measure
D. lessen

17. boast
A. exhibit
B. compensate
C. keep
D. encourage

18. evolve
A. heighten
B. entitle
C. eliminate
D. develop

19. contemporary
A. exquisite
B. current
C. sporadic
D. alien

20. association
A. delegation
B. contention
C. relationship
D. impediment

26. belonging
A. beginning
B. access
C. tendency
D. affiliation

27. suspicion
A. speck
B. consumption
C. delegation
D. supposition

28. delicate
A. wretched
B. specific
C. fragile
D. acceptable

29. impermeable
A. inadequate
B. impervious
C. tenable
D. indigent

30. entail
A. involve
B. exert
C. gather
D. construct

1. prevent
A. boost
B. reflect
C. hesitate
D. impede

2. fine
A. penalty
B. beauty
C. primacy
D. money

3. differ
A. foster
B. depict
C. conjure
D. vary

4. profusely
A. pleasantly
B. abundantly
C. properly
D. incredibly

5. catch on
A. is available
B. lack approval
C. become popular
D. reach people

11. repulse
A. repel
B. cheer
C. erect
D. deprive

12. paramount
A. momentous
B. steadfast
C. comprehensive
D. supreme

13. suppress
A. restrain
B. surprise
C. determine
D. propel

14. scrutinize
A. abstain
B. amend
C. probe
D. endeavor

15. impartially
A. dramatically
B. frequently
C. hesitantly
D. equitably

21. trivial
A. trifling
B. lenient
C. innocent
D. repetitive

22. disrupt
A. disturb
B. maneuver
C. exclude
D. detest

23. astonishing
A. courageous
B. moody
C. deadly
D. startling

24. reveal
A. overwhelm
B. divulge
C. enclose
D. attach

25. vivid
A. obscure
B. lucid
C. extensive
D. firm

31. decay
A. corrupt
B. offend
C. pile
D. corrode

32. deflect
A. reflect
B. emit
C. divert
D. surmount

33. endure
A. restrict
B. survive
C. suspect
D. antagonize

34. participant
A. partaker
B. roamer
C. protagonist
D. murderer

35. conceal
A. appeal
B. intrigue
C. resist
D. camouflage

I. What Is a Referent Question?

Referent

The referent question asks you to locate a referent, which is a noun or a noun phrase that another word, usually a pronoun, refers. A correct referent should be able to replace the pronoun in the paragraph or passage. It must also agree with the pronoun in number and gender (examples: philosophy → it; phenomena → they).

A. REFERENT QUESTION MODEL

Kabuki is an ancient form of Japanese drama that follows a very specific format. Kabuki actors must convey the play's story with movement because the dialogue uses an old-fashioned form of Japanese that contemporary audiences may not comprehend. Kabuki was originally performed exclusively by women, but during the Edo Period their participation was forbidden. Since that time, only males have been allowed to perform. **They** portray both the male and female characters.

2. The word "**They**" in the passage refers to:

(A) actors

(B) audiences

(C) women

(D) males

B. REFERENT QUESTION FORMATS

The word/phrase _____ refers to _____.

The word/phrase _____ in the passage refers to _____.

What does the word/phrase _____ refer to?

Which of the following does the word/phrase _____ refer to?

C. TIPS

1. A pronoun's referent normally appears before the pronoun, but occasionally the referent will appear after the pronoun.

2. The referent can show up within the same sentence of the pronoun or in a different sentence.

3. In some cases, you may have to locate the referent of a term or phrase instead of a pronoun.

4. Understanding the meaning of the sentence and the role of the pronoun within the sentence can lead you to the referent.

5. Unless a specific gender is indicated, an animal is usually referred to as "it."

II. Hacking Strategy

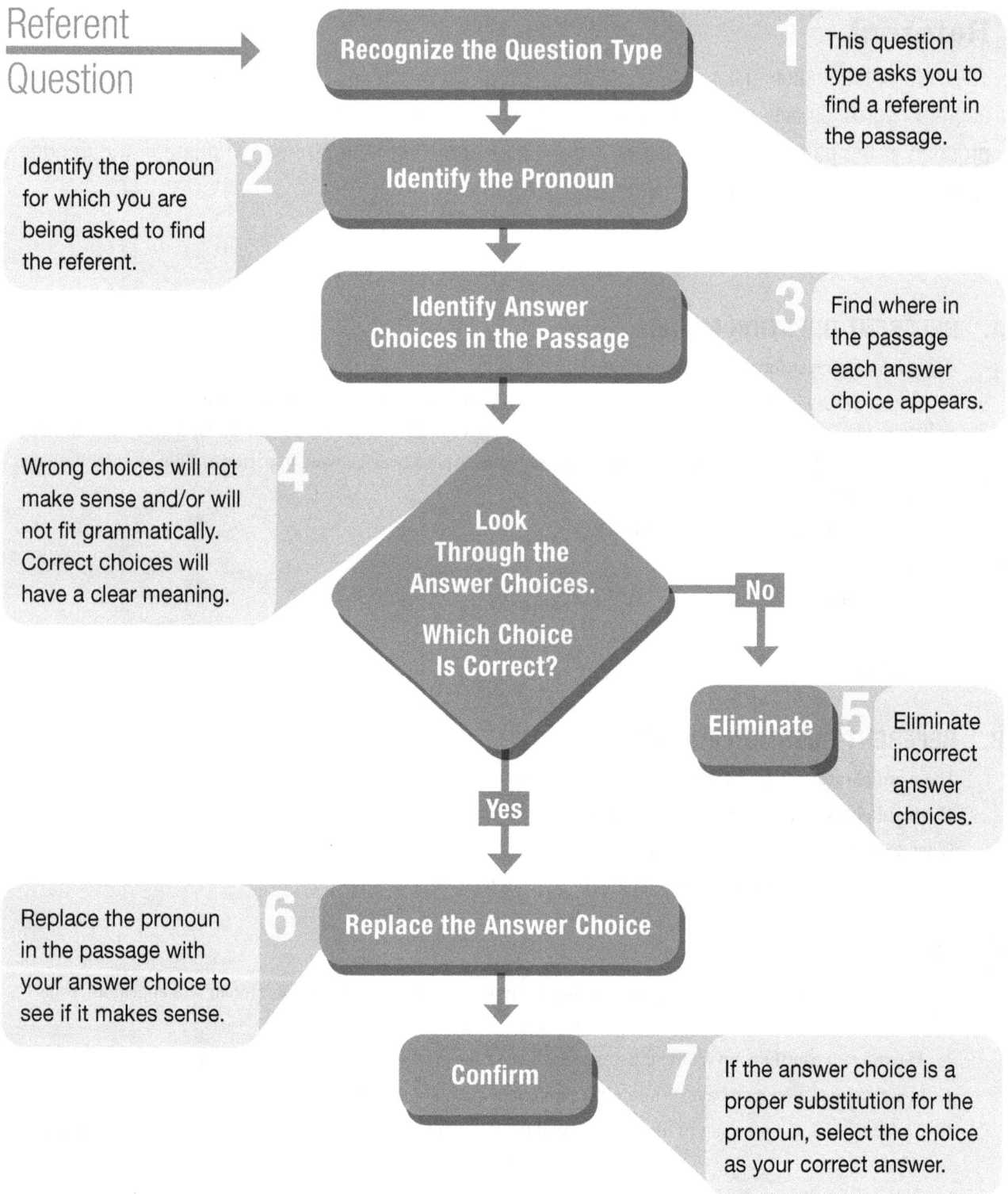

Referent Question →

Recognize the Question Type

1   This question type asks you to find a referent in the passage.

Identify the Pronoun

2   Identify the pronoun for which you are being asked to find the referent.

Identify Answer Choices in the Passage

3   Find where in the passage each answer choice appears.

Look Through the Answer Choices.

Which Choice Is Correct?

4   Wrong choices will not make sense and/or will not fit grammatically. Correct choices will have a clear meaning.

No → **Eliminate**

5   Eliminate incorrect answer choices.

Yes ↓

Replace the Answer Choice

6   Replace the pronoun in the passage with your answer choice to see if it makes sense.

Confirm

7   If the answer choice is a proper substitution for the pronoun, select the choice as your correct answer.

1

Kabuki is an ancient form of Japanese drama that follows a very specific format. Kabuki actors must convey the play's story with movement because the dialogue uses an old-fashioned form of Japanese that contemporary audiences may not comprehend. Kabuki was originally performed exclusively by women, but during the Edo Period their participation was forbidden. Since that time, only males have been allowed to perform. **They** portray both the male and female characters.

The word "**They**" in the passage refers to
(A) actors
(B) audiences
(C) women
(D) males

2

They is the pronoun that you are being asked to find the referent for. Notice that **They** is a plural pronoun.

3

Kabuki is an ancient form of Japanese drama that follows a very specific format. Kabuki <u>actors</u> must convey the play's story with movement because the dialogue uses an old-fashioned form of Japanese that contemporary <u>audiences</u> may not comprehend. Kabuki was originally performed exclusively by <u>women</u>, but during the Edo Period their participation was forbidden. Since that time, only <u>males</u> have been allowed to perform. **They** portray both the male and female characters.

4

(A) actors
(B) audiences
(C) women
(D) males

Check the choices for grammatical fit and logical meaning.

5

Determine which choices to eliminate by replacing the pronoun with each answer choice:
• Eliminate **Choice A** because "Actors portray both the male and female characters" makes sense, but the referent actors is too far from the pronoun and is too general.
• Eliminate **Choice B** because "Audiences portray both the male and female characters" does not make sense.
• Eliminate **Choice C** because "Women portray both the male and female characters" contradicts information presented in preceding sentences.

6

Replace **They** with **Choice D** to test if it is correct.

Males portray both male and female characters.

This makes sense!

7

Select the correct answer — **Choice D**.

III. Quick Look

Pronouns Used in Referent Questions

Subject Pronouns	he	she	you	it	they	we	one
Object Pronouns	him	her	you	it	them	us	one
Possessive Adjectives	his	her	your	its	their	our	one's
Demonstrative Pronouns	this	these	that	those			
Relative Pronouns	who	whom	which/ that	whose			
Other Pronouns	some	most	many	any	one(s)	another	(a) few
	the other	others	all	both	none	several	(a) little
	either	neither	each	the first	the last	the former	the latter

Example

Q: **Who** is giving the flower to **whom**?
  Subject   Object

A: John (**he**) is giving it to Sarah (**her**).
   Subject   Object

Q: **Whose** was it?
  Possessive

A: It was John's (**his**).
   Possessive

IV. Warm Up

Circle the noun or pronoun that correctly completes each sentence.

1. People eat carrots in different ways; (**they** / **these**) may eat them raw, steamed, dried, or ground up.

2. When an academic journal is peer-reviewed, several scholars in the field evaluate (**all** / **any**) articles before publication.

3. An organism's response to stimuli depends on instincts, habits, and other ways of acting that (**he** / **it**) has learned.

4. Part of Thomas Edison's success was due to the many research assistants he hired to help (**it** / **him**) conduct experiments in the lab.

5. Television stations often survey viewers to discover (**which** / **whose**) types of programs they watch regularly.

6. Using forks for dining was common in Turkey and the Middle East by the 10th century; (**its** / **their**) common use in Europe occurred about 600 years later.

7. "Mark Twain" was a measurement of river depth in the 19th century; author Samuel Clemens took (**the term** / **the process**) as his pen name.

8. Dolphins live in the oceans and in fresh water, and they are threatened by human activity in (**most** / **both**) environments.

9. Michael Jordan played professional basketball and baseball, but it is for (**the former** / **the other**) that he is most famous.

10. Although not every member on the board agreed to the proposal, (**several** / **both**) have given their consent.

11. Ramen is a popular Japanese noodle dish, and many variants of (**one** / **it**) incorporate different meats and vegetables.

12. Humorist Erma Bombeck once advised, "Never go to a doctor (**whose** / **which**) office plants have died."

13. *Bindis* are red dots that many women in South Asia traditionally apply to their foreheads for religious purposes; today some women may wear (**some** / **them**) to be fashionable.

14. Bald eagles usually mate with one partner for their entire lives, except in the case where one of them dies, and then (**the other** / **other**) may seek another mate.

15. *The Nutcracker* is a classic Russian ballet that is performed frequently in the U.S. around Christmas because (**his** / **its**) story takes place on Christmas Eve.

16. *Macabre art* emphasizes death, uses skulls and bones, or has a grim and gruesome quality; examples of these (**emphases** / **contrasts**) are visual allegories of the "Dance of Death" that decorate some medieval European churches.

17. In 1930 the chef at the Toll House Inn was attempting to bake chocolate cookies and accidentally invented the chocolate-chip cookie, (**a mistake** / **an inventor**) that is now a well-loved American sweet.

18. The professional basketball team of Boston, Massachusetts, is the *Celtics*, which is not surprising considering that (**much** / **many**) of the population traces its ancestry to Ireland.

19. Although the cowboy image is often thought of as purely American, (**it** / **he**) originally derived from Spain, with Islamic influences.

20) American pediatricians generally discourage parents from feeding regular cows' milk or goats' milk to their infants under the age of one, as both products contain too much protein, sodium, chloride, and potassium for (**their** / **any**) bodies to process.

V. Quick Practice

Practice #1

Read the passage and choose the best answer to each question.

Census figures indicate that the United States is home to one of the largest Hispanic populations in the world, second only to Mexico, and that this population is growing. One in four children in the U.S. is Hispanic. The term *Hispanic* describes people whose primary language is Spanish and those **who** are descended from Spanish-speakers. Many Hispanics are also *Latinos*, or people from *Latin America*, which refers to Mexico, Central America, and South America. Representing such **diversity**, Latinos may speak Spanish, but they may also speak Portuguese, French, or a regional language such as Nahuatl.

Hispanic immigration into the U.S. over many years is one reason for the large Hispanic population. However, there is **another**. Some Hispanics are descended from Spanish-speaking settlers in areas that were once Spanish or Mexican before they were taken over by the U.S. **These** include some of the nation's oldest cities, such as St. Augustine, Florida. Until 1848, Mexico encompassed what is now Texas, New Mexico, Arizona, California, Nevada, Utah, and western Colorado.

1) The word "**who**" in Paragraph 1 refers to
   (A) people
   (B) population
   (C) children
   (D) Spanish-speakers

2) The word "**diversity**" in Paragraph 1 refers to
   (A) Spanish-speakers or descendants of Spanish-speakers
   (B) Hispanics who are also Latinos
   (C) Mexico, Central America, and South America
   (D) Brazil and Caribbean islands

3) The word "**another**" in Paragraph 2 refers to
   (A) Hispanic immigration to the United States
   (B) Hispanic immigration over many years
   (C) descending from Spanish-speaking settlers
   (D) reason for the large U.S. Hispanic population

4) The word "**These**" in Paragraph 2 refers to
   (A) areas once claimed by Spain or Mexico
   (B) descendants of Spanish-speaking settlers
   (C) areas claimed by the United States
   (D) some of the nation's oldest cities

Practice #2

Read the passage and choose the best answer to each question.

Rap music usually emphasizes rhymed lyrics spoken at a quick rhythmic pace. In rap recordings, the rap artist may intersperse his or her "raps" with hip-hop music elements, such as repeated melodic segments, special sound effects, and collaborations with other artists. **He or she** may speak playfully, angrily, boastfully, or in many other tones. A few artists have used long silent intervals for dramatic effect. The underlying formula for **most** includes a strong beat, personal lyrics, and a repeating mix of sounds.

The rap genre began developing in the 1970s in New York City. *Block parties*, or outdoor parties in neighborhoods where a street was *blocked off*, often featured disc jockeys, or DJs, playing records on loud sound systems. Influenced by Jamaican dub styles, the DJs played soul songs, isolated the percussive breaks, and then used two turntables to extend **them**. **This technique** created a rhythmic base that the artists could rap over, with lyrics springing from their economic, political, and social realities.

5) The words "**He or she**" in Paragraph 1 refer to
   (A) rap music
   (B) pace
   (C) rap artist
   (D) another artist

6) The word "**most**" in Paragraph 1 refers to
   (A) tones
   (B) intervals
   (C) artists
   (D) principles

7) The word "**them**" in Paragraph 2 refers to
   (A) DJs
   (B) percussive breaks
   (C) soul songs
   (D) two turntables

8) The phrase "**This technique**" in Paragraph 2 refers to
   (A) the blocking of a street
   (B) a loud sound system
   (C) a Jamaican dub style
   (D) an isolation-and-extension method

Practice #3

Read the passage and choose the best answer to each question.

Astrobiologists take many approaches to searching for life in space. One approach is to make hypotheses about the physical and chemical conditions in which life developed here on Earth, and then to look for those conditions elsewhere. For example, the presence of water is the single condition required for all life forms on Earth, so it is reasonable to assume that water was present for life's origins here. **This assumption** has permeated thinking about the importance of determining whether other planets have or once had water.

Another approach is the search for signs of *microbes*, or microorganisms including bacteria, fungi, protozoa, and viruses. On Earth, people are surrounded by billions of microbes, and these simple organisms play key roles in sustaining life. One of **these** is to break down organic matter into nutrients for plants or animals, a **process** without which nothing could live. Because researchers have found that some microbes on Earth flourish in extreme conditions – boiling hot, freezing cold, toxic, airless, and so on – **they** have deduced that even apparently barren planets with conditions that seem hostile to life could nevertheless harbor microbes.

9) The phrase "**This assumption**" in Paragraph 1 refers to
   (A) conditions existing elsewhere
   (B) water being required by all life on Earth
   (C) water being present for life's origins
   (D) water permeating thinking

10) The word "**these**" in Paragraph 2 refers to
    (A) people
    (B) microbes
    (C) organisms
    (D) roles

11) The word "**process**" in Paragraph 2 refers to
    (A) being surrounded by
    (B) breaking down
    (C) playing key roles
    (D) sustaining life

12) The word "**they**" in Paragraph 2 refers to
    (A) researchers
    (B) microbes
    (C) conditions
    (D) planets

Practice #4

Read the passage and choose the best answer to each question.

The ancient Greeks loved athletic competitions. Although it may seem peculiar, the first occasions for formal contests of athletic skill may have been funerals of high-ranking people. Ancient Greeks also held athletic competitions to honor particular gods at festivals. By the sixth century BCE, there were regular competitions throughout Greece. The most important and prestigious of **these** was held at the temple complex known as Olympia. City-states sent athletes to Olympia for many reasons, including honoring Zeus, the powerful god associated with Olympia; gaining prestige through winning; and maintaining friendly relations with other city-states. The **convergence of purposes** made the Olympic games indispensable. Even when they were at war with each other, city-states respected a truce throughout the games' duration.

The ancient Olympics were open to any contestants from anywhere in the Greek realm, as long as **they** were male, not enslaved, and ethnically Greek. Athletic events included foot races, boxing, wrestling, javelin, and long jump. Equestrian events such as chariot racing took place in specially constructed sports facilities. Fans were welcome to cheer from the sidelines, but contestants competed nude, a **factor** that led to married women being excluded from watching.

13) The word "**these**" in Paragraph 1 refers to
   (A) ancient Greeks
   (B) particular gods
   (C) religious festivals
   (D) regular competitions

14) The phrase "**convergence of purposes**" in Paragraph 1 refers to
   (A) many reasons
   (B) representatives
   (C) friendly relations
   (D) prestige through winning

15) The word "**they**" in Paragraph 2 refers to
   (A) Olympics
   (B) contestants
   (C) city-states
   (D) males

16) The word "**factor**" in Paragraph 2 refers to
   (A) competing nude
   (B) excluded from watching
   (C) cheering from the sidelines
   (D) specially constructed sports facilities

Read the passage and choose the best answer to each question.

People often misuse the term "centrifugal force." In Latin, *centri-* means "center" and *-fugal* means "to flee," so *centrifugal* means "to flee from the center." An instance of centrifugal force can be seen when two people holding hands and spinning around suddenly let go. They would both fall outward, or "flee from the center." Any object that is orbiting and then flies out of rotation is exhibiting **the same phenomenon**. Prehistoric people made use of centrifugal force with weapons called *slings*. **They** nestled a rock in a leather pouch, swung the pouch in a circle, and let go of one end, launching the rock with deadly force.

More precisely, centrifugal force is *the effect of a lack* of force. In the case of two people spinning while holding hands, the true force is in the strength of their hands, which *prevents* them from flying outward. The force that keeps an object *in* rotation is called *centripetal*. In Latin **the term** means "to seek the center." Centripetal force causes an object to move in a curved path rather than to fly away in a straight path. The curved path can be maintained because something is holding the object, such as a strong hand, a sling, or gravity, or because something is stopping **it**, such as a curved wall against which a skateboarder turns.

17) The phrase "**the same phenomenon**" in Paragraph 1 refers to
   (A) holding on
   (B) spinning around
   (C) centrifugal force
   (D) orbiting about

18) The word "**They**" in Paragraph 1 refers to
   (A) two people
   (B) prehistoric people
   (C) weapons
   (D) slings

19) The phrase "**the term**" in Paragraph 2 refers to
   (A) *effect*
   (B) *prevents*
   (C) *in*
   (D) *centripetal*

20) The word "**it**" in Paragraph 2 refers to
   (A) object
   (B) hand
   (C) sling
   (D) gravity

Practice #6

Read the passage and choose the best answer to each question.

With advances in telecommunications, transportation, and the Internet, the last decades of the 20th century saw a steep increase in *globalization*; people around the world exchanged more goods, knowledge, and ideas. Most people consider more connection to the outside world desirable, yet as a consequence of **this**, society experiences nearly infinite contradictions. Jobs move to or away from certain workers more often, or workers **themselves** move. Natural resources are more exploited, or sometimes more protected. Illnesses are more easily spread, yet more illnesses are treated. Cultures gain access to variety, but also lose some of their own unique features.

With globalization, for example, there are more incentives than ever to learn other languages and increase the frequency and ease of global communication. The majority of people in the world are multilingual; they speak their native language and at least one more, sometimes **several**. Because English dominates the Internet and also factors largely in the world's business, entertainment, and academic communication, it has become a *lingua franca*, or common language. But the **trend** is also leading to the extinction of thousands of languages spoken by smaller populations.

21) The word "**this**" in Paragraph 1 refers to
   (A) last decades of the 20th century
   (B) more connection
   (C) a steep increase
   (D) people around the world

22) The word "**themselves**" in Paragraph 1 refers to
   (A) people
   (B) contradictions
   (C) jobs
   (D) workers

23) The word "**several**" in Paragraph 2 refers to
   (A) incentives
   (B) people
   (C) frequency and ease
   (D) other languages

24) The word "**trend**" in Paragraph 2 refers to
   (A) learning another language
   (B) dominating the Internet
   (C) having a *lingua franca*
   (D) factoring largely in entertainment

Practice #7

Read the passage and choose the best answer to each question.

In the late 1940s, fear of the Soviet Union was becoming rampant in the United States. In Congress, a young Representative Richard M. Nixon gained a seat on the House Committee on Un-American Activities, also known as HUAC. He turned **its** attention to a scandalous accusation. A former member of the U.S. Communist Party testified that a highly ranked government official was also secretly a Communist. The accused official was Alger Hiss, a well-respected lawyer who had worked for the State Department. Hiss went before HUAC and denied the accusation as well as any involvement in spying for the Soviets.

In a later trial, the accuser produced evidence that supposedly showed that Hiss had passed secret government documents to **him**. Because the alleged spying had taken place in the 1930s, too much time had passed for Hiss to be tried for **it**. Instead, in 1949 prosecutors brought him to trial for the crime of *perjury*, or lying to HUAC. A jury eventually found Hiss guilty, and he went to prison, but he maintained his claim of innocence. In 1991, when the Soviet Union dissolved, both the elderly Hiss and the elderly Nixon wrote letters inquiring about old Soviet intelligence records **there**. Russian researchers provided documents that left room for debate about the case, but many historians have concluded that Hiss was, in fact, a spy.

25) The word "**its**" in Paragraph 1 refers to
   (A) House Committee on Un-American Activities
   (B) Congress
   (C) Soviet Union
   (D) United States

26) The word "**him**" in Paragraph 2 refers to
   (A) Richard M. Nixon
   (B) government official
   (C) accuser
   (D) Alger Hiss

27) The word "**it**" in Paragraph 2 refers to
   (A) perjury
   (B) spying
   (C) accusation
   (D) evidence

28) The word "**there**" in Paragraph 2 refers to
   (A) HUAC
   (B) court
   (C) prison
   (D) Soviet Union

Practice #8

Read the passage and choose the best answer to each question.

Most people have probably had the frustrating experience of trying – without success – to remember a name, an event, or an important fact that they have read. Through a few novels and films, people can vicariously experience having *photographic memories*, or the ability to recall an image and "see" every detail of it whenever they want. Some characters with supernatural memories are geniuses, such as Sherlock Holmes, while **others** are superheroes, such as Professor X from X-Men. However, among real humans the existence of comprehensive photographic memory has never been proven in **anyone**. The few documented cases of photographic memory were confined to one type of image, such as the configurations on a chess board.

Researchers have documented cases of young children who demonstrated *short-term photographic memory*. These children could look at an image for a few seconds and then provide a precise description, as though they were referring to a photograph inside their minds. However, after a few minutes passed, they remembered **less of it**. As the children grew older and developed more abstract thinking abilities around the age of six, the **unusual ability** faded.

29) The word "**others**" in Paragraph 1 refers to
   (A) people
   (B) characters
   (C) geniuses
   (D) memories

30) The word "**anyone**" in Paragraph 1 refers to
   (A) characters
   (B) superheroes
   (C) Professor X
   (D) humans

31) The phrase "**less of it**" in Paragraph 2 refers to
   (A) image
   (B) photograph
   (C) description
   (D) memory

32) The phrase "**unusual ability**" in Paragraph 2 refers to
   (A) short-term photographic memory
   (B) precise description
   (C) abstract thinking
   (D) referring to a photograph

Practice #9

Read the passage and choose the best answer to each question.

In the current era, Impressionist and post-Impressionist paintings from the 19th century are among the most highly valued and beloved paintings. The Musée d'Orsay, or Orsay Museum, opened in Paris in 1986 with the largest collection of Impressionist paintings in the world. Around 4 million visitors flock to see **it** annually. Prints and posters of Impressionist paintings are ubiquitous in the United States. Other measures of the style's popularity include the high prices paid for the **originals**. Paul Cézanne's post-Impressionist masterpiece, *The Card Players*, broke records when it sold for $250 million in 2012.

The reception was quite different in the 1870s when some artists in Paris first began painting and exhibiting Impressionist works together. By the conventional criteria of **the time**, the Impressionists lacked skills and had strange notions. For example, Claude Monet had the "radical" idea of painting outdoors in order to capture movement and the play of natural light. Monet also went against tradition when he used little or no black paint and created shadows only with blue tints. He also applied paint without waiting for underlying layers to dry. **The practice** resulted in soft, intermingled edges that only took on a form when viewers moved back. Art critics ridiculed Monet and other Impressionists for exhibiting art that was "unfinished."

33) The word "**it**" in Paragraph 1 refers to
(A) Paris
(B) Musée d'Orsay
(C) collection
(D) world

34) The word "**originals**" in Paragraph 1 refers to
(A) 4 million people
(B) high prices
(C) Impressionist paintings
(D) prints and posters

35) The phrase "**the time**" in Paragraph 2 refers to
(A) 19th century
(B) 1986
(C) 2012
(D) 1870s

36) The phrase "**The practice**" in paragraph 2 refers to
(A) painting outdoors
(B) capturing movement and light
(C) using little or no black tints
(D) applying fresh paint to wet layers

Read the passage and choose the best answer to each question.

Some semi-arid places can support crops in most years even without irrigation if farmers use age-old *dry farming* techniques. The techniques can be highly successful; dry farming produces grain in the drought-prone southern Russia and the Ukraine that makes these areas the "breadbasket" for the Eurasian continent. Other regions that rely on dry farming include Spain, Australia, Argentina, and the Middle East. Generally, **the method** will work in locations that receive at least 250 mm of rainfall a year and have types of soil that retain moisture.

Dry farming aims to capture and conserve any moisture that the climate provides. Farmers collect as much rainfall and snow as possible by digging terraces into hillsides. They may plant trees as a windbreak and spread hay or leave crop stubble on fallow fields to hold down and shade the soil. When they select crops, dry farmers must choose deep-rooted and drought-tolerant **varieties** and space them far apart. Good candidates for **these** include winter wheat, grapes, olives, tomatoes, and garbanzo beans. Many dry farmers believe that their products are tastier and more nutritious than **those** of wetter regions, though dry-farm yields may be smaller.

37) The phrase "**the method**" in Paragraph 1 refers to
   (A) supporting crops
   (B) dry farming
   (C) producing grain
   (D) retaining moisture

38) The word "**varieties**" in Paragraph 2 refers to
   (A) trees
   (B) hay or stubble
   (C) soil
   (D) crops

39) The word "**these**" in Paragraph 2 refers to
   (A) good candidates
   (B) dry farmers
   (C) deep-rooted and drought-tolerant plants
   (D) winter wheat, grapes, olives, tomatoes, and garbanzo beans

40) The word "**those**" in Paragraph 2 refers to
   (A) products
   (B) dry farmers
   (C) dryer regions
   (D) wetter regions

Select the vocabulary word or phrase that has the closest meaning.

6. **isolate**
   A. deplete
   B. hinder
   C. segregate
   D. transact

7. **hypothesis**
   A. conclusion
   B. experimentation
   C. study
   D. theory

8. **origins**
   A. resources
   B. sources
   C. beginnings
   D. adaptations

9. **permeate**
   A. pervade
   B. baffle
   C. enter
   D. expand

10. **barren**
    A. empty
    B. flat
    C. dry
    D. cracked

11. **honor**
    A. recognize
    B. dictate
    C. award
    D. sustain

12. **prestigious**
    A. massive
    B. accurate
    C. distinguished
    D. astute

13. **indispensable**
    A. unnecessary
    B. popular
    C. mandated
    D. essential

14. **truce**
    A. contact
    B. armistice
    C. exchange
    D. consensus

15. **equestrian**
    A. cart competitions
    B. horse riding
    C. foot racing
    D. acrobatic shows

16. **rotate**
    A. cycle
    B. reverse
    C. turn
    D. launch

17. **curved**
    A. fascinated
    B. reverse
    C. squeaking
    D. crooked

18. **steep**
    A. rigid
    B. precipitous
    C. gradual
    D. durable

19. **infinite**
    A. valid
    B. boundless
    C. vague
    D. wide

20. **incentives**
    A. reasons
    B. changes
    C. possibilities
    D. requirements

21. **dominate**
    A. govern
    B. tame
    C. exalt
    D. deprive

22. **rampant**
    A. challenging
    B. pervasive
    C. competitive
    D. certifiable

23. **accusation**
    A. gadget
    B. denunciation
    C. conviction
    D. misbelief

24. **perjury**
    A. falsehood
    B. pirate
    C. robbery
    D. jewelry

25. **vicarious**
    A. crude
    B. indirect
    C. capricious
    D. evident

26. **configuration**
    A. concern
    B. scheme
    C. diagram
    D. layout

27. **fade**
    A. disappear
    B. tremble
    C. revive
    D. burst

28. **ubiquitous**
    A. favored
    B. priceless
    C. liquidated
    D. prevalent

29. **conventional**
    A. necessary
    B. methodical
    C. standard
    D. fashionable

30. **capture**
    A. manage
    B. represent
    C. assemble
    D. cripple

31. **intermingle**
    A. intermix
    B. interrupt
    C. intersect
    D. interpret

32. **ridicule**
    A. attack
    B. disappoint
    C. deride
    D. refurbish

33. **retain**
    A. preserve
    B. produce
    C. inflate
    D. remind

34. **terraces**
    A. slopes
    B. walls
    C. gardens
    D. platforms

35. **fallow**
    A. plowed
    B. uncultivated
    C. sophisticated
    D. harvested

1. **primary**
   A. routine
   B. main
   C. coherent
   D. potential

2. **diversity**
   A. variety
   B. dispersal
   C. ordeal
   D. trend

3. **descendant**
   A. offspring
   B. parachute
   C. forebear
   D. maintenance

4. **emphasize**
   A. exhaust
   B. mend
   C. accentuate
   D. germinate

5. **influence**
   A. impact
   B. tighten
   C. generate
   D. familiarize

I. What Is a Fact and Detail Question?

Fact and Detail

The fact and detail question asks you to identify a fact or detail from the passage.

- A **fact** is something that can be proven when it agrees with an experience or observation.
- A **detail** is a piece of information used to support the main idea of a passage.
- Facts and details are directly stated in the passage.

A. FACT AND DETAIL QUESTION MODEL

Clownfish have adapted to survive among the stinging tentacles of sea anemones. An even more interesting adaptation is their *sequential hermaphroditism*: they start their lives as males and may later change into females. The largest clownfish in any group is a female, and all the other fish in the group are male. When the dominant female dies, the largest male fish gains weight and changes into a female to rule the group around its particular sea anemones.

3. According to the passage, what happens to some male clownfish?

    (A) They undergo a transformation of gender.

    (B) They die violently during battles for dominance.

    (C) They challenge the female with displays of strength.

    (D) They rule over the smaller female clownfish.

B. FACT AND DETAIL QUESTION FORMATS

What _____?   Which _____?   Why _____?   Where _____?   When _____?   How _____?

Which statement BEST describes _____?   What does the author say about _____?

What is the main cause of _____?   Which of the following is an example of _____?

Which of the following is true?

C. TIPS

1. The correct answer may be a paraphrase* of the passage's information.

    Paraphrase: the restatement of information in a different form

2. Incorrect answers may:

    • restate information from the passage without correctly answering the question

    • state information from the passage incorrectly

    • be false according to the information from the passage

    • be unnecessary or not mentioned in the passage

II. Hacking Strategy

Fact and Detail
Question

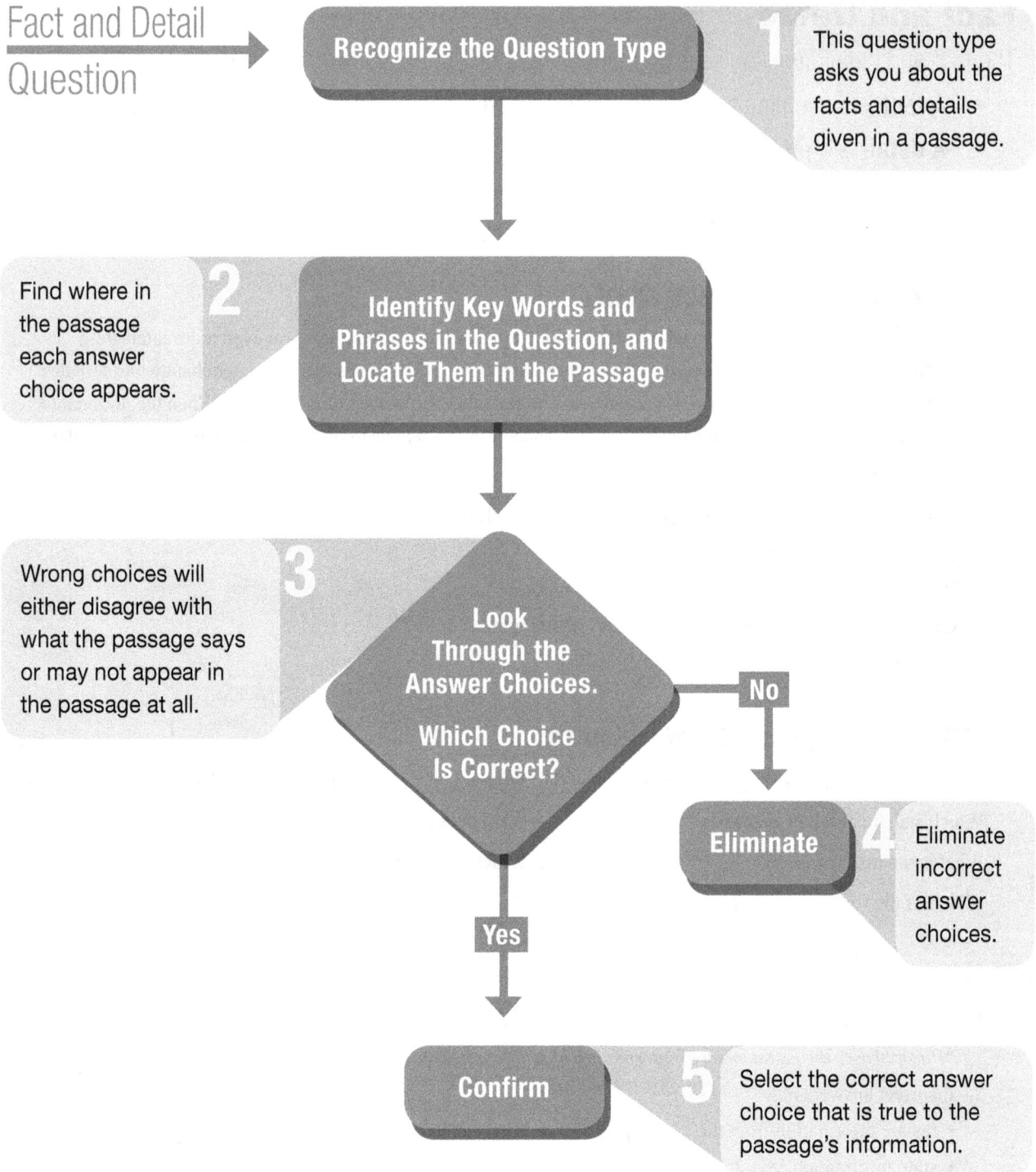

Recognize the Question Type

1 This question type asks you about the facts and details given in a passage.

Find where in the passage each answer choice appears.

2 **Identify Key Words and Phrases in the Question, and Locate Them in the Passage**

Wrong choices will either disagree with what the passage says or may not appear in the passage at all.

3 **Look Through the Answer Choices.**

Which Choice Is Correct?

No

Eliminate

4 Eliminate incorrect answer choices.

Yes

Confirm

5 Select the correct answer choice that is true to the passage's information.

1 Clownfish have adapted to survive among the stinging tentacles of sea anemones. An even more interesting adaptation is their *sequential hermaphroditism*: they start their lives as males and may later change into females. The largest clownfish in any group is a female, and all the other fish in the group are male. When the dominant female dies, the largest male fish gains weight and changes into a female to rule the group around its particular sea anemones.

According to the passage, what happens to some male clownfish?
(A) They undergo a transformation of gender.
(B) They die violently during battles for dominance.
(C) They challenge the female with displays of strength.
(D) They rule over the smaller female clownfish.

2 According to the passage, **what happens to some male clownfish**?

Clownfish have adapted to survive among the stinging tentacles of sea anemones. An even more interesting adaptation is their *sequential hermaphroditism*: they start their lives as males and may later change into females. The largest clownfish in any group is a female, and all the other fish in the group are male. When the dominant female dies, the largest male fish gains weight and changes into a female to rule the group around its particular sea anemone.

According to the passage, what happens to some male clownfish?
(A) They undergo a transformation of gender.
(B) They die violently during battles for dominance.
(C) They challenge the female with displays of strength.
(D) They rule over the smaller female clownfish.

3 By looking at the key words and phrases, we see that our answer is in the second sentence. Even though we believe that we've found the right answer, it is still a good idea to look further in the passage to be sure. Check thoroughly.

- Select **Choice A** because the passage states that clownfish "start their lives as males and... later change into females," or *undergo a transformation of gender*.

4
- Eliminate **Choice B** because neither *violent deaths* nor *battles* are mentioned in the passage.
- Eliminate **Choice C** because *displays of strength* are not mentioned in the passage.
- Eliminate **Choice D** because *ruling over the smaller female clownfish* is not mentioned in the passage.

5 Select the correct answer — **Choice A**.

III. Quick Look

Transitions Used to Introduce Facts and Details

Illustrating	*provides description*				
	For example	Next	Such	For instance	To illustrate	Such as

Explaining	*tells more to provide better understanding*				
	At this point	Furthermore	In fact	Because	How	In this case

Adding	*gives more supporting information*				
	Also	Finally	Moreover	Another	Furthermore	Too

Giving Reasons	*tells why something is*				
	As a result of	Because of	One reason is	Because	Due to	Since

Contrasting	*gives information that is different from what was provided before*				
	Although	Instead	Rather	However	Nevertheless	Like / Unlike

Comparing	*notes how things are similar to or different from/than each other*				
	Both	Like	Similarly	Equally important	The same	Similar to

Showing Results	*tells the outcome*				
	Accordingly	Consequently	Therefore	Thus	Otherwise	As a result of

Limiting	*puts boundaries on the information's scope or reach*				
	Although	Except for	However	But	Even though	Yet

Emphasizing	*highlights important information*				
	Clearly	In fact	Surely	Certainly	Indeed	Most important

IV. Warm Up

Identify each sentence and indicate whether it contains a fact (F) or an opinion (O).

1. If the company baseball team has a better coaching staff, the team will definitely win the tournament next week. _____

2. Listening to violent rap and rock music lyrics leads to violent behavior in young people. _____

3. When people exercise, the body expends more energy than it does while in a resting state. _____

4. Research indicates that listening to music while exercising increases endurance. _____

5. Had they been able to see, keyboardist Stevie Wonder and pianist Ray Charles would not have been great musicians. _____

6. In order to grow, crops need water and the proper ratio of nutrients in the soil where they are planted. _____

7. Raw foods are more desirable for good health than cooked foods are. _____

8. Making a financial profit is the goal of most people who invest money in the stock market. _____

9. Before the invention of airplanes, boats and ships were the only means of traveling long distances at sea. _____

10. Wars are a natural part of human behavior, and it is quite likely that wars will persist as long as the human species exists. _____

11. If a person wants to lose weight, eating a healthy diet will most certainly make him or her achieve that goal. _____

12. Living organisms are sustained by chemical reactions within their cells that are catalyzed by enzymes. _____

13. Tides occur due to a number of natural phenomena, including the rotation of Earth. _____

14. Gemologists consider rubies one of the world's four precious gemstones; the others are sapphires, emeralds, and diamonds. _____

15. Parents find it impossible to keep up with their children's use of digital technology and social media. _____

16. If the air temperature is below freezing and water molecules fall from clouds, then the water molecules change into snow. _____

17. There is little chance of discovering life in the universe outside of Earth, and funds spent pursuing such a discovery are wasted. _____

18. In writing or speaking, *logical appeal* is a method of persuasion that relies on reasoning to convince the audience. _____

19. An emotional appeal is most effective when it creates fear in the audience. _____

20. Men usually do not harbor concern about their own appearance as much as women do. _____

V. Quick Practice

Practice #1

Read the passage and choose the best answer to each question.

Modern schools for children under the age of seven began developing in 1837 when educator Friedrich Froebel opened his first "play and activity center" for young children in Germany. Froebel recognized the impact of early childhood learning on later academic development and believed that teachers must take into account children's natural activity levels. He later began calling his school a *kindergarten*, which is German for "garden of children." This symbolized his contention that children, like plants, need to be given the time, nurturing, and resources to develop on their own.

Daily routines at Froebel's kindergarten included time for singing, dancing, gardening, and playing with toys. Many kindergarten teachers who received training from Froebel started their own schools. Froebel's other accomplishments included publishing a book of nursery songs and activities for parents to use with their children. He began manufacturing and selling toys as well, especially carved wooden blocks; thus, he virtually created the educational toy market. His school and toys were instrumental in the childhoods of many people, including architect Frank Lloyd Wright and physicist Albert Einstein.

1) According to Paragraph 1, what belief motivated Froebel to invent kindergarten?
   (A) Schools should provide structure for society's youngest members.
   (B) The most important preparation for school is learning.
   (C) Early learning improves subsequent achievement.
   (D) High-energy activity for young children is most beneficial to learning.

2) In Paragraph 1, Froebel used the term "garden of children" to indicate
   (A) how young children should be treated
   (B) the importance of the natural world for the very young
   (C) why young children should be left alone
   (D) the way the school and playground should look

3) What were the practical applications of Froebel's philosophies, according to Paragraph 2?
   (A) A typical day at the school was unstructured.
   (B) Adults at the school supervised children but did not converse with them.
   (C) There was more socializing than independent exploration.
   (D) Children had chances to interact and do many hands-on activities.

4) By what means did Froebel influence his era, according to Paragraph 2?
   (A) He inspired parents to send their children to kindergarten.
   (B) He trained teachers to help younger children learn.
   (C) He created the virtual toy market.
   (D) He provided insight into human achievement.

Practice #2

Read the passage and choose the best answer to each question.

When Spanish explorers first arrived in Central and South America in the 16th century, they noticed that indigenous tribes and civilizations were using an interesting stretchy material. The material was formed from white fluid known as *caoutchouc*, or "crying wood," that native people extracted from rubber trees. People shaped products by smoothing the white fluid over molds or their feet and letting the substance dry. The natives utilized the rubber-tree sap to create bouncing balls, containers, and waterproof shoes.

In 1736, French scientist Charles Marie de la Condamine traveled throughout what is now Ecuador and sent home samples of *caoutchouc*, or "rubber" as it came to be called in English. In Europe and America there was great interest in the material, but people found that latex products became sticky in hot weather and stiff in cold. By the early 1800s, Charles Goodyear, an American son of a manufacturing businessman, began experimenting with rubber. Goodyear worked for years, enduring extreme poverty and repeated confinement in debtors' prison. In 1839, he discovered how to produce weather-resistant rubber by accidentally dropping a rubber-sulfur solution on a hot stove.

5) According to Paragraph 1, what was one invention preceding Spanish contact?
(A) Elastic fabric
(B) Molded basins
(C) Impermeable footwear
(D) Wooden structure

6) Paragraph 1 describes *caoutchouc* as
(A) a milky substance from a tropical plant
(B) an opaque liquid from complex trade network
(C) a sticky fluid from soaking timber
(D) a supple material from one location only

7) What mainly hampered wide-scale use of rubber, according to Paragraph 2?
(A) It was "discovered" by both the Spanish and French.
(B) It was not useful at temperature extremes.
(C) It was difficult to obtain in the heat and the cold.
(D) It was not cultivated at Europe's latitude.

8) In Paragraph 2, why was Charles Goodyear able to invent rubber production?
(A) He hypothesized and used a process of elimination.
(B) He prepared and retried formulas.
(C) He persevered and was eventually lucky.
(D) He investigated and used conjecture.

Practice #3

Read the passage and choose the best answer to each question.

The brain's billions of *neurons* or nerve cells send signals to each other using electrochemical impulses. The continuous electrical activity of neurons occurs in patterns that can be thought of as brain *waves*. Clinicians and researchers can measure these patterns with instruments called *electroencephalographs*, or more commonly, EEGs. The data recorded during an EEG session is called an *electroencephalogram*. The EEG can provide information about both normal brain activity and irregularities caused by disease or injury.

A patient or research subject undergoing an EEG has electrodes attached to his or her head. The electrodes connect to the EEG device, which records data digitally or on a long roll of paper. The resulting data takes the form of spiky or wavy lines showing the *frequency* of the brain waves – how frequently the patterns occur. Generally, taxing mental activities or stressful situations produce high frequency brain waves called *beta waves*, while on the other hand relaxing activities produce low frequency brain waves called *alpha waves*.

9) According to Paragraph 1, how does an EEG work?
   (A) It changes electrochemical impulses with devices.
   (B) It detects cycles in electrical activity from neurons.
   (C) It interprets the neuron communication.
   (D) It redirects electrical signals between neurons.

10) What are the practical uses of an EEG, according to Paragraph 1?
   (A) It can stimulate the brain to heal from disease or injury.
   (B) It may identify brain problems as well as healthy functioning.
   (C) It usually helps doctors diagnose abnormal thought processes.
   (D) It can show evidence of sleep disorders such as insomnia.

11) Paragraph 2 defines a brain wave frequency as
   (A) how nervous or calm a subject is
   (B) how a waking state is categorized
   (C) how short or tall the electric wave is
   (D) how often an electric pattern occurs

12) According to Paragraph 2, what can EEGs reveal about subjects?
   (A) Their ability to learn effectively at a given moment
   (B) Their heartbeat and ability to react quickly
   (C) Their level of alertness or calmness
   (D) Their state of mental health

Practice #4

Read the passage and choose the best answer to each question.

Clouds, wind, rain, and temperature are all affected by the pressure of the air. Air pressure in the atmosphere is a measure of how much the air's weight is pressing down on the Earth's surface. When there are more molecules in a unit of air, the air weight is heavier and therefore will exert more downward pressure. Thus, dense air creates *high pressure*. If the number of molecules decreases, the lighter air will exert *low pressure*.

Jet stream winds that flow high above Earth's surface can cause differences in air pressure. Like water flowing in a stream, the jet stream can be forced to bend, and molecules pile up as a result; or the jet stream can be unblocked, allowing air molecules to radiate out. When the jet stream is spreading out, air pressure is low, and air molecules from the ground rise up to fill the empty spaces. Rising air frequently forms clouds, which are more likely to bring rain. Clouds also act as a shade during the day and a blanket at night for Earth, keeping surface temperatures more stable. Conversely, high air pressure forces air closer to the surface of the Earth and inhibits clouds. High-pressure tends to create clear skies, dry weather, and extreme temperatures.

13) According to Paragraph 1, air pressure is a measure of
  (A) how strong the air is
  (B) how windy the air is
  (C) how heavy the air is
  (D) how polluted the air is

14) According to Paragraph 2, what causes the differences in air pressure?
  (A) Air molecules are either destroyed or diffused by the jet stream.
  (B) Wind movement causes air molecules to converge or disperse.
  (C) The jet stream can collect behind an obstacle, drying the air.
  (D) Currents of air at a high altitude cause air molecules to scatter in all directions.

15) Why does low air pressure frequently bring rain, according to Paragraph 2?
  (A) Water molecules are not pressed out of the area by dense air molecules.
  (B) When air molecules ascend, they form rain clouds.
  (C) More stable temperatures create conditions for precipitation.
  (D) Air molecules rise, allowing in low clouds from surrounding areas.

16) Besides rain, how do clouds affect weather, according to Paragraph 2?
  (A) They reflect solar heat and retain surface warmth.
  (B) They take on different roles to balance out rainfall.
  (C) They act as a barrier for winds and affect air pressure.
  (D) They provide a mechanism for temperature change.

Practice #5

Read the passage and choose the best answer to each question.

Humor is an inherently social phenomenon. Social research illustrates that people are 30 times more likely to laugh when they are with others than when they are alone. People are more likely to laugh at humorous material if they hear someone else reading it aloud than if they read it silently to themselves. Humor is also contagious; audience members are more likely to smile and laugh during a performance when others laugh, even if the laughter of other people is delivered via a "laugh track" with recordings of people laughing.

The principle for what makes something humorous is fairly simple. The requirements are a non-serious context followed by a social incongruity in which someone does or says something unexpected. For example, an audience may laugh when it sees a clown in performance who is walking and then suddenly slips on a banana peel.

Humor may not seem crucial to human survival. However, it may be, as evolution seems to have favored it. The *social brain hypothesis* claims that the brains of social animals developed to adapt to social demands and form beneficial bonds between the members of the species. Laughter fits into this hypothesis because people in virtually all cultures value humor and give positive attention and admiration to jocular individuals. Humans begin to laugh as infants when something unthreatening and unpredictable happens, such as tickling and peek-a-boo games. Apes also laugh when playing, usually because of non-serious attacks and lighthearted chasing.

17) According to Paragraph 1, humor is
   (A) tenaciously irrepressible and catching
   (B) basically relative and interconnected
   (C) intrinsically communal and infectious
   (D) normally verbal and anonymous

18) Why do people think that something is amusing rather than upsetting, according to Paragraph 2?
   (A) People perceive that it is lighthearted.
   (B) Peers supply a comforting presence.
   (C) Laughter helps one overcome fears.
   (D) The social atmosphere is sincere.

19) What does Paragraph 2 identify as the reason something is funny?
   (A) It is unique to an individual's cultural outlook.
   (B) It involves people doing or saying nonsensical things.
   (C) It focuses on serious situations that might have different outcomes.
   (D) It is inconsistent with expectations based on previous experiences.

20) What evidence does Paragraph 3 give that humor is important?
   (A) Babies of human and other primate species enjoy playing.
   (B) Humor is appreciated and encouraged globally.
   (C) Laughing socially is cross-cultural, innate, and cross-species.
   (D) Reacting to surprise may be an important survival technique.

Practice #6

Read the passage and choose the best answer to each question.

Jenny Holzer is an American artist who attempts to bring messages to a wide audience outside of museums through printed and electronic signs. She has been described as a member of the "conceptual art" movement. Some conceptual artists view traditional art as irrelevant. They believe that an idea or a *concept* is the principle element in an art object. However, they may use traditional art materials to articulate a thought.

Holzer uses textual "truisms" in her work, often in public spaces. She has projected declassified government documents on walls of the New York University Library, produced inscribed marble benches, and created signs with electric LED lighting. One of her works was an inscription painted on a race car, saying "Protect me from what I want." She has inscribed silver spoons with the phrase "Money creates taste." These approaches grew out of her artistic beginnings in the 1970s, when she put up posters with clichés, philosophical sayings, and controversial comments around her neighborhood in New York City.

21) What are Jenny Holzer's artistic goals, according to Paragraph 1?
   (A) To provide art for people who never go to museums
   (B) To spread sociopolitical statements in unexpected places
   (C) To directly reach a broad spectrum of people with written commentary
   (D) To lift the public's spirits in urban centers

22) Paragraph 1 describes *conceptual artists* as artists who
   (A) place more emphasis on meaning than on appearance
   (B) rarely use traditional media such as paint
   (C) center their work around a significant text
   (D) focus on the process of art rather than the finished piece

23) Based on Paragraph 2, what kinds of messages does Holzer exhibit?
   (A) Slogans and papers that reveal an institution's dullness
   (B) Statements and documents that provoke thinking
   (C) Only textual facts and true statements
   (D) Abstract and concrete ideas for a particular occasion

24) What are some of the media for Holzer's work mentioned in Paragraph 2?
   (A) Walls, ceilings, floors, posters, paint
   (B) Spoons, film, a car, buildings, markers
   (C) Racetrack, sidewalk, foil, concrete wall, marble sculpture
   (D) Posters, projectors, dining utensils, stone seating, LED lighting

Practice #7

Read the passage and choose the best answer to each question.

When Europeans began arriving in the Americas, they brought with them the deadliest of passengers: the smallpox virus. This disease causes blisters on its victims that, if broken open, secrete infectious fluid. The virus can then spread to other surfaces and can also become airborne, entering new victims when they inhale it. Individuals who come in contact with an infected person, who is contagious for approximately 12 days, may also contract the virus.

Historians believe that smallpox was brought to the mainland on a Spanish ship from Cuba around 1520. Because people who were native to the Americas had never been exposed to the virus, they had not developed immunity to it. Estimates are that 90 to 95 percent of the native population, perhaps as many as 20 million people, died from smallpox and other Eurasian diseases.

In the 1600s, English colonists in the Americas also suffered from diseases, including smallpox, scurvy, influenza, malaria, and typhoid. In an attempt to cure these maladies, European medicine of the era made use of *bloodletting*, or draining blood from the patient. The practice was based on the belief that sickness was caused by an imbalance of the body's *humors*, or fluids. However, bloodletting often caused more harm than help. Therefore, the colonists in the New World often turned to Native Americans or Africans for home medicines, usually made of certain barks, herbs, or roots.

25) According to Paragraph 1, how does the smallpox virus spread?
    (A) Via trans-oceanic travel
    (B) Via hidden, secretive blisters on the skin
    (C) Via breathing near coughing victims
    (D) Via physical contact and breathing air around infected people

26) According to Paragraph 2, what was the effect of Eurasian viruses on the Americas?
    (A) Depopulation
    (B) Genocide
    (C) Famine
    (D) Toxicity

27) In Paragraph 3, what were English settlers' strategies for coping with illness?
    (A) They tried to get back to doctors in England.
    (B) They asked others about the healing properties of unfamiliar plants.
    (C) They grew special crops and orchards for medicinal use.
    (D) They made special cuts in their clothing.

28) According to Paragraph 3, why did Europeans believe physicians should drain blood from patients?
    (A) To rid the immune system of viruses
    (B) To revitalize the patients' blood supply
    (C) To redistribute disease-fighting properties in the body
    (D) To reduce a fluid that was out of proportion

Practice #8

Read the passage and choose the best answer to each question.

A handful of healthy soil is not only a collection of minerals but a complex, interactive food web, full of microscopic organisms, or *microbes*. Even one gram of soil may contain billions of microbes. The greatest in number are *bacteria*, or one-celled organisms without a nucleus. There are also types of fungi, algae, and protozoa. The latter are one-celled organisms that eat bacteria.

Microbes as a whole produce substances that hold soil together, even when the soil is watered. The most important role of microbes, however, is *mineralization*. The organisms digest organic materials like dead leaves and produce inorganic elements such as carbon, nitrogen, phosphorus, and sulfur. Plants depend on these elements for nutrients.

The area around a plant's roots is called a *rhizosphere*. In this region, the roots release nutrients for microbes, increasing the microbial population, and in return the microbes mineralize nutrients for the plant. However, man-made products have varying impacts on the ability of microbes to mineralize nutrients in the rhizosphere. Man-made fertilizers bypass the microbes by supplying the minerals directly to the plants. *Herbicides*, or poisons used to kill weeds, can usually be broken down quickly by microbes, but some *pesticides*, or poisons used to kill insects, cannot.

29) According to Paragraphs 1 and 2, what kind of natural system is present in soil?
(A) Competition for limited sources of food
(B) Microbial communities that collect at the surface
(C) Types of organisms that form web-like structures
(D) A complex network of producers and consumers

30) In Paragraph 2, why are soil microbes important?
(A) Their digestive systems are good.
(B) They detract from the soil through mineralization.
(C) They create plant nutrients by eating organic waste.
(D) They have two specific roles in plant growth.

31) According to Paragraph 3, a rhizosphere is a place where
(A) microbes hold the soil together
(B) plants can grow roots in essential ways
(C) plant roots provide pesticides to microbes
(D) microbes and plants benefit each other

32) According to Paragraph 3, what is true about certain man-made substances?
(A) Microbes can break down some more easily than others.
(B) Herbicides do not affect microbes, but pesticides do.
(C) Fertilizers tend to kill off microbial life.
(D) Some poisons never break down in the environment.

Practice #9

Read the passage and choose the best answer to each question.

Feng shui is the ancient Chinese art of arranging a particular space to promote the inhabitants' happiness and health. The practice is based on the belief that a powerful energy or life-force called *chi* flows into and out of all matter, including people and things. However, according to feng shui, the flow of chi can be blocked or misguided in a space, which can be destructive to humans.

To attain freely flowing energy, according to feng shui teachings, a balance must be maintained among the five crucial but common "elements," which are water, wood, fire, earth, and metal. Each element has associations with specific colors and shapes. For example, fire is associated with triangles and red, orange, and pink. Of course, a candle or a fireplace is a fire object, but so is a bright light, a red wall, or a red vase.

Direction and placement of an object are important in feng shui practices. The discipline addresses where and how a structure should be built, as well as its interior design. Planning may range from serious structural decisions, such as which direction the front door should face, to simple decorating decisions regarding the best color for a particular pillow.

33) According to Paragraph 1, what is feng shui?
   (A) A Chinese art of object placement for free energy flow
   (B) An ancient Chinese philosophy and religious practice
   (C) A way to ensure joy and physical well-being
   (D) A type of movement that helps people feel better

34) According to Paragraph 1, feng shui philosophy warns against what problem?
   (A) Destructive spirits
   (B) Unbalanced or blocked energy
   (C) Unbalanced *chi* in furniture
   (D) Misguided decorating plans

35) How does Paragraph 2 define the five elements in feng shui?
   (A) They are parts of the primitive world.
   (B) They are simple but essential materials or phenomena.
   (C) They are what must be incorporated in structures.
   (D) They are the foundations of life.

36) According to Paragraphs 2 and 3, practical applications of feng shui include
   (A) considering an object's balance of shape, color, and materials
   (B) discovering which elements an object mainly represents
   (C) learning how to master all the elemental forces of nature
   (D) recognizing an object's major element and placing it appropriately

Practice #10

Read the passage and choose the best answer to each question.

During the financially devastating Great Depression, Hollywood provided the moviegoing public with a diversion: a monstrously giant gorilla. The 1933 black-and-white film *King Kong*, full of trick photography and exotic settings, was a smash success, and its images became iconic.

The story follows a film producer who sets off by ship to make a film on the little-known Skull Island, bringing his lead actress, Ann, with him. During the journey, the ship's first mate, Jack, seems to be attracted to Ann. The film producer talks to Jack privately and tries to persuade him to forget about her. He talks about the fairy tale "Beauty and the Beast" in which a "beast" becomes "soft" and gentle once he falls in love with a "beauty."

On the island, native people capture Ann and offer her as a sacrifice to Kong, a colossal gorilla. However, Kong is fascinated with the beautiful lady and wants to protect her. Eventually the film producer and ship's crew rescue Ann, and they sedate Kong so that they can take him to New York. Once in New York, Kong escapes because he thinks that Ann is in danger. He abducts and carries her to the top of the Empire State Building. Fighter planes swarm around him, and, after placing Ann on a low ledge of the skyscraper, he falls to his death. Watching from below, the film producer makes the comment that it was not the planes that killed the beast; it was the beauty.

37) In Paragraph 1, what was the historical context in which *King Kong* was released?
   (A) Americans were involved in a war.
   (B) Americans were struggling economically.
   (C) Americans were unaccustomed to movies.
   (D) Americans were culturally isolated.

38) According to Paragraph 1, what were some popular aspects of *King Kong?*
   (A) Glamorous leading actors playing likable characters
   (B) Suspenseful action leading to chase scenes
   (C) Unpredictable plot twists and an evil villain
   (D) Special effects and intriguing locales

39) In Paragraph 2, what is the context of the film's first reference to "Beauty and the Beast"?
   (A) Advice to a tough sailor not to fall in love
   (B) A warning that acting like a beast is unwise
   (C) A hint to a crew member that pretty ladies can be cruel
   (D) A film producer's description of a movie that he wants to make

40) According to Paragraph 3, what ironic action does Kong take?
   (A) He instinctively climbs up.
   (B) He inadvertently endangers his beloved.
   (C) He compels his captors to regret their actions.
   (D) He undermines his full strength.

Select the vocabulary word or phrase that has the closest meaning.

6. **opaque**
   A. probable
   B. nontransparent
   C. ostentatious
   D. annoying

7. **pliant**
   A. harsh
   B. bitter
   C. lavish
   D. supple

8. **diagnose**
   A. cause
   B. determine
   C. encompass
   D. cure

9. **exert**
   A. force
   B. exercise
   C. undergo
   D. surpass

10. **pile up**
    A. cumulate
    B. translate
    C. reproduce
    D. assist

1. **take into account**
   A. welcome
   B. consider
   C. affect
   D. confirm

2. **contention**
   A. satisfaction
   B. assertion
   C. impetus
   D. increment

3. **subsequent**
   A. adverse
   B. spontaneous
   C. later
   D. unlimited

4. **insight**
   A. viewpoint
   B. scenery
   C. understanding
   D. improvement

5. **elastic**
   A. valuable
   B. cautious
   C. ultimate
   D. pliable

11. **conversely**
    A. obliquely
    B. contrarily
    C. uncannily
    D. chronically

12. **precipitation**
    A. storm
    B. fog
    C. rainfall
    D. typhoon

13. **inherently**
    A. cordially
    B. confidently
    C. naturally
    D. voluntarily

14. **contagious**
    A. urgent
    B. strategic
    C. transmittable
    D. serious

15. **crucial**
    A. remarkable
    B. permanent
    C. moderate
    D. imperative

16. **jocular**
    A. friendly
    B. numerous
    C. normal
    D. jolly

17. **tenaciously**
    A. probably
    B. realistically
    C. persistently
    D. sufficiently

18. **intrinsically**
    A. essentially
    B. mercilessly
    C. consciously
    D. distinctly

19. **innate**
    A. convenient
    B. forcible
    C. inborn
    D. indifferent

20. **irrelevant**
    A. ambiguous
    B. immaterial
    C. trite
    D. facile

21. **articulate**
    A. enunciate
    B. demonstrate
    C. relish
    D. dissolve

22. **utensil**
    A. implement
    B. illustration
    C. hostility
    D. antagonist

23. **airborne**
    A. haphazard
    B. aerial
    C. zealous
    D. substantial

24. **cope with**
    A. contend
    B. tolerate
    C. detect
    D. adhere

25. **depend on**
    A. focus on
    B. live on
    C. rely on
    D. work on

26. **in return**
    A. inversely
    B. reciprocally
    C. contrastively
    D. baldly

27. **destructive**
    A. constructive
    B. affirmative
    C. confirmative
    D. damaging

28. **address**
    A. adobe
    B. undertake
    C. repair
    D. exchange

29. **appropriately**
    A. judiciously
    B. affordably
    C. currently
    D. deliberately

30. **diversion**
    A. admission
    B. selection
    C. description
    D. amusement

31. **exotic**
    A. unusual
    B. delinquent
    C. complicated
    D. compulsory

32. **colossal**
    A. repetitive
    B. tiresome
    C. impartial
    D. enormous

33. **glamorous**
    A. enormous
    B. miserable
    C. attractive
    D. ridiculous

34. **villain**
    A. robber
    B. barbarian
    C. criminal
    D. monk

35. **intriguing**
    A. blemish
    B. fascinating
    C. unyielding
    D. majestic

1B 2B 3C 4C 5D 6B 7D 8B 9A 10A 11B 12C 13C 14C 15D 16D 17C 18A 19C
20B 21A 22A 23B 24A 25C 26B 27D 28B 29A 30D 31A 32D 33C 34C 35B

I. What Is a Negative Fact Question?

Negative Fact

The negative fact question asks you to identify the answer choice that is not described in the passage or is not true according to the passage.

A. NEGATIVE FACT QUESTION MODEL

Northern Thailand is home to the Kayan people, whose women wear brass coils around their necks from the time they are five. As a Kayan girl matures, her family adds longer coils with more turns, and by the time she is an adult, her neck appears to be elongated. In truth, a Kayan woman's neck does not lengthen; the weight of the brass coils pushes her collarbone down and compresses her rib cage. Although the historical reasons for wearing the coils are obscured, the Kayan people consider the result to be feminine and beautiful.

4. According to the passage, all of the following statements about brass coils worn around the neck are true EXCEPT:

(A) The coils produce an effect that is aesthetically appealing in Kayan culture.

(B) Coils eventually create the illusion of a long neck through body manipulation.

(C) Coils change the skeletal and muscular structure of a woman's neck.

(D) In Kayan culture, girls typically start wearing the coils when they are very young.

B. NEGATIVE FACT QUESTION FORMATS

Which of the following is NOT mentioned in the passage?

What is NOT mentioned as _____?

What is NOT given as a reason for _____?

All are examples of _____ EXCEPT _____.

All describe _____ EXCEPT _____.

All statements are true EXCEPT _____.

All are mentioned EXCEPT _____.

_____ involves all EXCEPT _____.

C. TIPS

1. When you see questions with words EXCEPT or NOT, three of the answer choices will be true.

2. Remember, you are looking for an answer that is untrue or is not included in the passage.

II. Hacking Strategy

Negative Fact Question

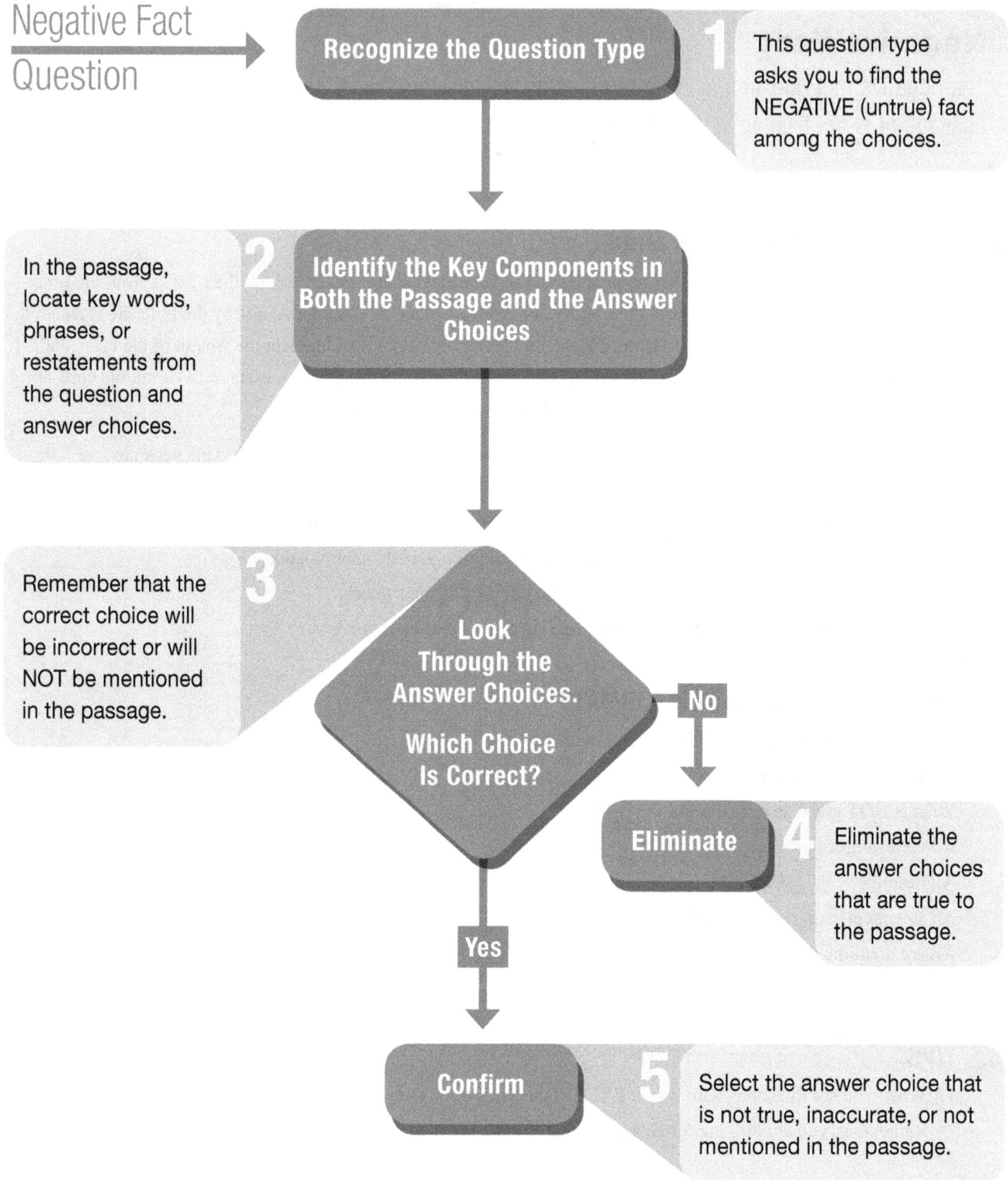

Recognize the Question Type

1 This question type asks you to find the NEGATIVE (untrue) fact among the choices.

In the passage, locate key words, phrases, or restatements from the question and answer choices.

2 Identify the Key Components in Both the Passage and the Answer Choices

Remember that the correct choice will be incorrect or will NOT be mentioned in the passage.

3 Look Through the Answer Choices.

Which Choice Is Correct?

No

Eliminate

4 Eliminate the answer choices that are true to the passage.

Yes

Confirm

5 Select the answer choice that is not true, inaccurate, or not mentioned in the passage.

1

Northern Thailand is home to the Kayan people, whose women wear brass coils around their necks from the time they are five. As a Kayan girl matures, her family adds longer coils with more turns, and by the time she is an adult, her neck appears to be elongated. In truth, a Kayan woman's neck does not lengthen; the weight of the brass coils pushes her collarbone down and compresses her rib cage. Although the historical reasons for wearing the coils are obscured, the Kayan people consider the result to be feminine and beautiful.

According to the passage, all of the following statements about brass coils worn around the neck are true EXCEPT:

(A) The coils produce an effect that is aesthetically appealing in Kayan culture.

(B) Coils eventually create the illusion of a long neck through body manipulation.

(C) Coils change the skeletal and muscular structure of a woman's neck.

(D) In Kayan culture, girls typically start wearing the coils when they are very young.

2

(A) The coils produce an effect that is <u>aesthetically appealing in Kayan culture</u>.

(B) Coils eventually create the <u>illusion</u> of a long neck through <u>body manipulation</u>.

(C) Coils change the skeletal and muscular structure of a woman's neck.

(D) In Kayan culture, girls typically start wearing the coils <u>when they are very young</u>.

Northern Thailand is home to the Kayan people, whose <u>women wear brass coils around their necks from the time they are five</u>. As a Kayan girl matures, her family adds longer coils with more turns, and by the time she is an adult, her neck appears to be elongated. <u>In truth, a Kayan woman's neck does not lengthen; the weight of the brass coils pushes her collarbone down and compresses her rib cage.</u> Although the historical reasons for wearing the coils are obscured, <u>the Kayan people consider the result to be feminine and beautiful</u>.

3

Which choice is NOT something the passage says?

• Select **Choice C** because the passage states that the "neck does not lengthen," which proves that **Choice C** is NOT true.

4

• Eliminate **Choices A** and **B** because they identify qualities of brass coils that are mentioned in the passage.

• Eliminate **Choice D** because it describes the users of brass coils that are mentioned in the passage.

5

Select the correct answer — **Choice C**.

III. Quick Look

Negative Fact Questions

Look at the images below. Then select which answer choice is a negative fact.

A. This device yields light that can brighten a place, such as a room.
B. This device was invented by Thomas Edison in 1879.
C. This device dispenses ideas that people can utilize.
D. This device operates with electricity.

Choice C is the negative fact because although a light bulb is used as a symbol for an idea, it does not actually give people ideas (false information).

A. This creature has a body of a lion and a face of a woman.
B. This creature is known for its riddles and cruel punishments for those who could not answer them correctly.
C. This creature is sculpted in large scale in Egypt.
D. This creature is an animal that became extinct because of overexploitation.

Choice D is the negative fact because the Sphinx is a mythical creature that never existed; therefore, it cannot be extinct (false information).

IV. Warm Up

Choose the answer choice that does NOT belong in each group.

1. (A) touching
    (B) hearing
    (C) speaking
    (D) tasting
    (E) seeing

2. (A) algebra
    (B) physics
    (C) geometry
    (D) trigonometry
    (E) calculus

3. (A) novel
    (B) dictionary
    (C) encyclopedia
    (D) thesaurus
    (E) almanac

4. (A) jellyfish
    (B) lobster
    (C) crab
    (D) shrimp
    (E) crayfish

5. (A) enormous
    (B) gigantic
    (C) abnormal
    (D) colossal
    (E) massive

6. (A) comedy
    (B) narration
    (C) drama
    (D) mystery
    (E) horror

7. (A) cheese
    (B) milk
    (C) tofu
    (D) butter
    (E) yogurt

8. (A) hard drive
    (B) pop-up ads
    (C) search engine
    (D) email
    (E) website

9. (A) create
    (B) generate
    (C) contain
    (D) form
    (E) produce

10. (A) bees
    (B) wasps
    (C) flies
    (D) moths
    (E) bats

11. (A) perfume
    (B) lipstick
    (C) bracelet
    (D) eyeliner
    (E) hair spray

12. (A) harp
    (B) violin
    (C) cello
    (D) harmonica
    (E) viola

13. (A) copper
    (B) silver
    (C) carbon
    (D) gold
    (E) nickel

14. (A) cactus
    (B) maple
    (C) chestnut
    (D) aspen
    (E) pine

15. (A) century
    (B) year
    (C) decade
    (D) calendar
    (E) month

16. (A) heart
    (B) stomach
    (C) lungs
    (D) skeleton
    (E) kidney

17. (A) illustration
    (B) beauty
    (C) image
    (D) portrayal
    (E) depiction

18. (A) preserve
    (B) tunnel
    (C) guard
    (D) shelter
    (E) protect

19. (A) flavorful
    (B) delicious
    (C) aromatic
    (D) appetizing
    (E) savory

20. (A) permit
    (B) voucher
    (C) receipt
    (D) ticket
    (E) recipe

V. Quick Practice

Practice #1

Read the passage and choose the best answer to each question.

Speed reading is a technique used to increase a person's ability to read text quickly, yet still comprehend its meaning. Evelyn Wood, a teacher of remedial reading in Utah, first coined the term in the 1950s. Wood studied the habits of naturally fast readers and found that faster readers actually retained more information. She developed a methodology for teaching people to read two to five times faster.

Wood identified bad reading habits that could be overcome and good habits that could be acquired with practice. She established Evelyn Wood speed-reading schools throughout the United States and other English-speaking countries, and her system met with acclaim. At least three U.S. presidents used the technique and sent members of their cabinets to study it.

Ineffective habits that the Evelyn Wood Program addresses include stumbling on long words, even if the reader knows the words; *vocalizing*, or "saying" each word mentally; and *regressing*, or rereading a sentence or phrase, even if the reader comprehends it at the first reading. Effective habits identified by the program include setting a purpose for reading, such as learning something in particular; focusing completely; and looking at groups of words rather than reading word by word.

1) According to Paragraph 1, all of the following are true about Evelyn Wood EXCEPT:
   (A) She originally specialized in reteaching poor readers.
   (B) She analyzed how fast readers proceeded.
   (C) She formulated a new term for a new concept.
   (D) She believed reading speed was immutable.

2) Which of the following do Paragraphs 1 and 2 NOT say about speed reading?
   (A) It makes it possible for some people to at least double their reading rate.
   (B) It necessitates sacrificing some amount of comprehension.
   (C) It requires practicing effective reading skills.
   (D) It improves how much textual information readers remember.

3) What is a bad reading habit that is NOT mentioned in Paragraph 3?
   (A) Skipping unimportant sentences or sections
   (B) Reading lengthy words with difficulty
   (C) Internally "pronouncing" each word
   (D) Needlessly looking back at what one just read

4) Faster readers, according to Paragraph 3, tend to do all of the following EXCEPT
   (A) establish a reason for reading a text
   (B) concentrate fully on textual material
   (C) read only the topic sentence of each paragraph
   (D) move their eyes between clusters of words

Practice #2

Read the passage and choose the best answer to each question.

Model ships are scaled-down versions of seafaring vessels. The ship-building industry creates models to test designs and train ship pilots. Hobbyists make decorative model ships for enjoyment, and toymakers design boats that can be floated in tubs. Indeed, since prehistoric times, model-ship making appears to have served multiple purposes.

Archaeologists find model ships in excavations of many ancient and prehistoric nautical communities. Model ships probably helped people plan and test boat designs then as they do now. Model ships also appear to have served as toys, decorative lamps, and funerary offerings. Europeans have placed model ships in churches from at least the 12th century to signify their prayers for safe sea travel.

Depending on their purpose, model ships may range from matchbook-sized to just large enough for a person to board. Some are models of particular ships in which every measurement has been painstakingly converted to a smaller scale. Crafters in the 18th century – possibly bored sailors on long journeys – devised an even more challenging method of producing model ships inside narrow-necked bottles. Usually the models were built with hinges and then inserted in the bottle and pulled upright with a pre-attached thread.

5)   What is NOT a reason given in Paragraph 1 for making model ships?
(A) To keep a record of great ships in a particular era
(B) To try out certain designs before building a big version
(C) To divert oneself during spare time
(D) To create an object to decorate the home

6)   According to Paragraph 2, which of the following did ancient people probably NOT do with ship models?
(A) Use them in rites or burial for the dead
(B) Make use of them during prayer or daily life
(C) Use them to plan and navigate sea voyages
(D) Give them to children for play and amusement

7)   All of these descriptions of model ships are true according to Paragraph 3 EXCEPT:
(A) Some can hold a person.
(B) Some are used for transportation.
(C) Some are exact replicas of existing ships.
(D) Some are only a few centimeters long.

8)   Which of the following statements about ships in bottles is NOT true, according to Paragraph 3?
(A) They always require more meticulous work than any other model.
(B) They are usually constructed outside the bottle.
(C) They include tiny hinges for vertical pieces.
(D) They may have been invented by nautical crews.

Practice #3

Read the passage and choose the best answer to each question.

Ethnography is the study of a given community's customs and other aspects of its culture. It is used in both anthropology and sociology. Ethnographers aim to produce not just a journalistic description but a systematic record of a culture. The study is usually in written form, accompanied by photography or video images. Field work for ethnographical studies usually requires the researcher to live with the group, participate in daily life, speak the language, and engage in conversation. Today, ethnographic methodology takes a step further and regards members of the observed group as *participants* rather than *subjects* of study.

In addition to providing information about a particular culture, ethnological data can also be used to identify cross-cultural thematic comparisons, such as child-rearing practices. Ethnographers usually attempt to reveal meaningful insights, balancing fact with interpretation and explanation. To strike such a balance, an ethnographer must maintain an objective viewpoint, and at the same time must interact closely with the group's members.

Some ethnographic studies focus on a single ethnic community, such as the influential 1922 work *Argonauts of the Pacific* by Bronislaw Malinowski, which focuses on the Trobriand people of the Kiriwina Islands. Other ethnographies may focus on a group within a larger society, such as Paul Willis' study of working-class youths in Britain, detailed in his 1977 book *Learning to Labour*.

9) All of the following statements agree with Paragraph 1's description of ethnography EXCEPT:
   (A) It is used in more than one academic field.
   (B) It mainly chronicles parenting strategies.
   (C) It transcends simple narrative description.
   (D) It usually includes visual representation.

10) What is NOT a typical ethnographic procedure, according to Paragraph 1?
    (A) Becoming a leader of the community
    (B) Taking part in the group's routines
    (C) Becoming fluent in the local dialect
    (D) Residing with the group under study

11) According to Paragraph 2, which of the following is NOT important to most ethnographic research?
    (A) Objectivity with familiarity
    (B) Factuality with elucidation
    (C) Specificity with criticism
    (D) Impartiality with empathy

12) Which of the following is NOT a method of ethnography mentioned in the passage?
    (A) Analyzing a subset of a people within a larger set
    (B) Studying a people's way of life without their knowledge
    (C) Documenting cultural practices of a particular aggregate of people
    (D) Identifying study subjects as collaborators in creating records

Practice #4

Read the passage and choose the best answer to each question.

Several species of river dolphins live in freshwater lakes and rivers in Asia and South America. River dolphins are mammals and resemble their saltwater cousins, marine dolphins. However, while marine dolphins must actively navigate in the open oceans, river dolphins lead more circumscribed lives.

River dolphins spend their days swimming along muddy rivers looking for fish and diving to the bottom to forage for shrimp, other crustaceans, and even turtles. They have smaller eyes than marine dolphins, possibly because vision is not helpful in more sediment-filled river water. Their snouts may be 30 centimeters long, about four times longer than the snouts of marine dolphins, and their necks are flexible, helping them turn and nab prey in a smaller setting. However, like marine dolphins, they rely on echolocation.

In most cases, river dolphins live in waterways that are bordered by vast human populations, which has made them vulnerable to extinction. Dams, pollution, overfishing, and noise hinder their survival. While the *baiji* dolphin, which lived in the Yangtze River in China, is thought to be extinct, river dolphin species still exist in the Indus and Ganges Rivers in southern Asia and in several rivers in South America, including the Amazon. One rare species, the *La Plata* dolphin, lives only in estuaries* along the southern Atlantic coast of South America.

Estuary: the mouth of a river where the river's current flows into the ocean

13) River dolphins have the following characteristics compared to marine dolphins according to Paragraph 2 EXCEPT
    (A) smaller brain cavities
    (B) smaller eye openings
    (C) more pliable necks
    (D) longer nose and mouth structures

14) Paragraph 3 does NOT mention which of the following threats to river dolphins?
    (A) Toxins draining into the habitat
    (B) Sounds that interfere with hearing
    (C) Competition from other species
    (D) Constructed barriers to natural flow

15) Based on Paragraph 3, what is NOT true about the locations of river dolphins?
    (A) One type lives where rivers and the sea meet.
    (B) A species disappeared from one river.
    (C) Most species live where human populations are dense.
    (D) In general, they prefer rivers near the equator.

16) According to the passage, all of the following statements about river dolphins are true EXCEPT:
    (A) There is not just one species.
    (B) They live in waterways on two continents.
    (C) Their movement is restricted relative to sea-going species.
    (D) They are indistinguishable from marine dolphins.

Practice #5

Read the passage and choose the best answer to each question.

Ambrose Bierce was a late-19th century American journalist and writer. He published works in many genres, including satire, short fiction, and poetry. Nicknamed "Bitter Bierce," he took pride in being an outspoken cynic and harsh critic. In spite of his negativity, he was extremely popular for his wit, irreverence, and style. A number of books and films have focused on Bierce himself because at the age of 71, while traveling in Mexico with Mexican rebels, he disappeared.

Bierce's cynical viewpoint may have been forged in his youth. Born in Ohio in 1842, Bierce fought on the side of the Union during the Civil War and participated in some of its most violent battles, possibly fueling his disillusionment with political leaders. Many years after the war, he published a collection of short fiction based on his experiences, *Tales of Soldiers and Civilians*. His most famous story, "An Occurrence at Owl Creek Bridge," is told from the point of view of a Confederate sympathizer who is about to be hung from a bridge by Union soldiers.

For many years, Bierce wrote and edited for various newspapers in San Francisco. He specialized in satire, and in 1881, while editing a newspaper called the *Wasp*, he began writing a column focused on satirical word definitions. One entry includes the definition: *Conservative: (n.) A statesman who is enamored of existing evils, as distinguished from the Liberal, who wishes to replace them with others.* Another example is *Peace: (n.) In international affairs, a period of cheating between two periods of fighting.* Hundreds of his definitions were eventually collected and published in 1906 as the *Cynic's Word Book* and later renamed *The Devil's Dictionary*.

17) According to Paragraph 1, which of the following is NOT a reason for Ambrose Bierce's fame?
   (A) He wrote in a comic way to make serious points.
   (B) The public appreciated his writing style.
   (C) He inspired many people with his hopefulness.
   (D) His ultimate fate is unknown.

18) According to Paragraph 2, all of the following may have been effects of the U.S. Civil War on Ambrose Bierce EXCEPT:
   (A) He became distrustful of politicians.
   (B) He witnessed and took part in violence.
   (C) He never escaped his nostalgia for his youth.
   (D) He was able to imagine the war from opposing perspectives.

19) Paragraph 3 does NOT provide examples of
   (A) literature that Bierce criticized
   (B) writings from a newspaper that Bierce edited
   (C) material that Bierce published
   (D) jobs that Bierce held

20) In Paragraph 3, examples of satirical definitions do NOT indicate that
   (A) Bierce was hostile about politicians
   (B) Bierce was a political conservative
   (C) Bierce tended to doubt the honesty of leaders
   (D) Bierce did not speculate about prospects for peace

Practice #6

Read the passage and choose the best answer to each question.

Physics uses math to illuminate the nature of matter and the workings of the universe. A fundamental and crucial aspect of physics was formulated in the 20th century by physicists including Albert Einstein. They theorized about the *atom*, the basic building block in different elements, and the particles that make up the atom, including neutrons, protons, and electrons. Attention then turned to particles called *quarks* that make up neutrons and protons. Physicists also have thought that the fundamental forces in the universe, including electromagnetism and gravity, rely on fundamental particles – the photon and the graviton, respectively – acting as carriers. Historically, particles were often depicted as dots.

String theory revolutionized the theoretical framework of particle physics. The string model proposes that all matter and force come from different oscillations of tiny strings or loops. Thus, what *appears* to be an electron is a string oscillating in a particular manner, while what *appears* to be a photon is an *identical* string oscillating in a different manner; thus, everything is the back-and-forth movement of identical lines.

One reason that string theory is difficult to "picture" without mathematics is the size of the hypothesized strings. According to the theory, a string is a millionth of a billionth of a billionth of a billionth of a centimeter. String theory is also difficult to envision because it hypothesizes strings oscillating in a manner outside of normal experience. Rather than just height, width, depth, and time, string theory predicts that strings move in 11 dimensions. Just as puzzling, the theory describes the strings themselves as one-dimensional, or having length but not width or depth.

21) According to Paragraph 1, what is NOT true about physics?
   (A) It makes use of formulas to describe nature.
   (B) It originated with the discoveries of Albert Einstein.
   (C) It attempts to penetrate the mysteries of outer space.
   (D) It discerns processes at the subatomic level.

22) As described in Paragraph 1, particle physics has NOT hypothesized that
   (A) gravity is dependent on particles
   (B) forces such as magnetism look like dots
   (C) forces at work in the world operate via particles
   (D) basic building blocks of the world include quarks and electrons

23) String theory, as described in Paragraphs 2 and 3, suggests all of the following EXCEPT:
   (A) There are different types of strings that make up different materials.
   (B) Matter and force are caused by infinitesimal filaments.
   (C) Elemental particles only appear to be different from one another.
   (D) Different movements, not different materials, comprise matter.

24) Paragraph 3 gives the following factors for string theory being difficult to visualize EXCEPT
   (A) dimensions that people cannot sense
   (B) objects that are neither two-dimensional nor three-dimensional
   (C) strings that are incomprehensibly slight
   (D) oscillating movement that is too rapid to detect

Practice #7

Read the passage and choose the best answer to each question.

The prairie state of Wisconsin is perhaps best known for its dairy products, but it is not usually associated with the mining industry. However, mining for lead in its southwestern hills and bluffs is what brought the first wave of European settlement to the area. By 1829, about 4,000 miners in Wisconsin produced nearly 6 million kilograms of lead, which was in demand for use in products such as paint, pipes, and ammunition. Prospectors looking for lead did not have time to settle down and build homes, so they sometimes slept in their shallow mines or dug out holes in the sides of hills to sleep in. People gave the miners the nickname "badgers" because the badger is a solitary animal that sleeps in burrows.

Badgers are in the same family as otters, weasels, and skunks. They are brisk diggers, seeming to sink into the soil as they pursue rodents. The animals do not generally attack humans, but badgers may try to scare humans away from their burrows by growling ferociously. Their growls reportedly sound like snoring.

The University of Wisconsin adopted the badger as its mascot in 1889, even though by that time lead mining had faded out. The university still uses the feisty character "Bucky Badger" as its mascot. In 1955, Wisconsin prohibited hunting badgers and in 1957 named the badger its official state animal. As a result, Wisconsin is frequently called the *Badger State*.

25) According to Paragraph 1, all of the following statements are true about Wisconsin EXCEPT:
   (A) Farmers were not the first Europeans there.
   (B) It is renowned for its farmers' milk and cheese.
   (C) The majority of its natural terrain is mountainous.
   (D) It once had large deposits of a sought-after metal.

26) Paragraph 1 does NOT mention which of the following about lead miners?
   (A) They tended to bring their families and settle in one place.
   (B) They immigrated to Wisconsin in the 19th century by the thousands.
   (C) Their circumstances did not make construction practical.
   (D) They acquired a special name because of their lifestyle.

27) What is NOT true about badgers, according to Paragraphs 1 and 2?
   (A) They sleep alone in subterranean homes.
   (B) They are placid and serene in temperament.
   (C) Their expertise is predatory digging.
   (D) They defend themselves with clamorous threats.

28) According to the passage, what is NOT a way the badger is used as a symbol?
   (A) It represents an institution of higher education.
   (B) It signifies laborers in a specific industry and era.
   (C) It is an emblem for a specific province.
   (D) It stands for European-American colonists.

Practice #8

Read the passage and choose the best answer to each question.

Titan is the largest of the 62 moons orbiting the planet Saturn. It has a diameter of 5,150 kilometers, making it the second-largest satellite* in the solar system after one of Jupiter's moons. Titan is even larger than the planet Mercury. Until recently, however, not much has been known about Titan. One problem was that it has a thick atmosphere that cloaks the surface.

In 2005, a consortium of international agencies engaging in a mission to Saturn sent a probe to Titan. The probe parachuted down through the hazy orange atmosphere. At an altitude of about 30 kilometers above the surface, the haze cleared, allowing the probe to capture photographs. The images sent back to Earth revealed a landscape of pale hills, darker features that looked like riverbeds, and a dark plain. These features appear to result from erosion caused by rains of liquid methane.

Scientists now suspect that Titan has an unusual composition: rock and ice at the center, surrounded by a liquid water ocean, which is completely covered by a hard crust. Moreover, in spite of the freezing surface temperature of -179 degrees Celsius, more liquid exists on Titan's surface, where scientists have identified oily lakes of liquid methane and ethane. Titan is the only space object known to have liquid on its surface. It is also the only moon known to have a thick atmosphere, with nitrogen gas making up almost the entire atmosphere. At the surface of Titan, the atmospheric pressure is about 1.45 times greater than that found on Earth.

Satellite: a natural or man-made object that orbits a planet

29) According to Paragraph 1, what is NOT true of Titan?
   (A) It circles around another planet.
   (B) Its size surpasses that of a planet.
   (C) It is one of the moons of Jupiter.
   (D) It features a gaseous cover.

30) According to Paragraph 2, all of the following statements are true about the probe sent to Titan EXCEPT:
   (A) The collaborative mission gave humans a first view of the surface.
   (B) The probe was propelled to the surface with rocket technology.
   (C) Foggy gases did not extend all the way to the ground.
   (D) There was enough light for the probe's cameras to take pictures.

31) According to Paragraph 2, photographs of Titan did NOT show which of the following?
   (A) Nitrogen snow
   (B) Geographic evidence of precipitation
   (C) Lighter-colored slopes
   (D) Dark, flat land and dry channels

32) According to Paragraph 3, researchers do NOT think that Titan
   (A) has air consisting of mainly one element
   (B) has liquids on its surface
   (C) has extremely low temperatures
   (D) has a liquid core

Practice #9

Read the passage and choose the best answer to each question.

From the 1830s to the mid-1850s, the two main American political parties were the Democrats, many of whom were small farmers, and the modernizing Whigs. However, during these decades both parties were divided within themselves over the issue of slavery. The tension grew as the United States acquired additional rich farmland to the west. Congress struggled to resolve the question of whether to permit slavery in the new western territories.

The *Free Soil Party* formed in 1848 in New York as a third party with a single ambition: to prevent the expansion of slavery into new territories. Members of both major political parties were attracted to join the upstart party. The Free Soil Party did not actively work to outlaw existing slavery in the South; its pragmatic message was that slavery would create unfair economic competition in new territories. In the 1848 presidential election, the Free Soil candidate received 10 percent of the popular vote.

Both the Free Soil Party and the Whig Party started to dissolve in the early 1850s as compromise on the issue of slavery was reached. Then, in 1854, Congress abruptly opened the door to slavery in Kansas and Nebraska. The act outraged and energized both those who opposed slavery and those who feared that rich slaveholders would monopolize the new land. The net result was that some former members from all three parties were motivated to form the Republican Party, which firmly opposed allowing slavery in new territories. In 1860, the Republican Party nominated Abraham Lincoln for president, and he won. With compromise no longer possible, civil war loomed.

33) What point does Paragraph 1 NOT make about U.S. politics in the 1830s to the 1850s?
   (A) Democratic processes were largely dominated by a two-party system.
   (B) Leaders were pressured to establish laws in covetable new lands.
   (C) Major political groups were splintering over a single controversy.
   (D) Elected officials in each faction found it impossible to negotiate at all.

34) According to Paragraph 2, all of the following statements about the Free Soil Party are true EXCEPT:
   (A) It was mainly a disgruntled segment of the Whig Party.
   (B) It failed to advocate an end to slavery nationwide.
   (C) Its goal was to ensure a free labor force in certain areas.
   (D) One out of 10 voters cast their ballots for it at one point.

35) Paragraph 3 describes all of the following political shifts EXCEPT:
   (A) Congress created a political backlash with its decision about two new regions.
   (B) Anti-slavery advocates founded a new political party.
   (C) Voters in the new western territories indicated that they opposed slavery.
   (D) Abraham Lincoln's election signaled that confrontation was impending.

36) Which of the following points does Paragraph 3 NOT make about the early Republican Party?
   (A) Its members all wanted land in the new territories.
   (B) It disapproved of spreading a system of forced labor.
   (C) It launched a successful presidential campaign.
   (D) It attracted voters from across the political spectrum.

Practice #10

Read the passage and choose the best answer to each question.

No one knows when people first got the idea of communicating across long distances with beams of light, or *beacons*. However, historical evidence reveals that people have set fires on high places for millennia to warn faraway friends about the approach of invaders. The Great Wall of China, constructed in different periods from the seventh century BCE through the 17th century CE, made use of beacons to relay signals from one watch tower to another across many kilometers. Beacons on hilltops appear in the ancient Greek epic the *Iliad*, and they were commonly used in castles and on hills in the British Isles.

People also have long used onshore beacons to alert ships of rocky or shallow areas and to guide them into safe harbors. Egypt built the first known lighthouse in the world, the *Pharos*, in the third century BCE. At about 45 stories high, it was one of the tallest buildings on Earth in its time. Using a large curved mirror to reflect sunlight and firelight, the Pharos guided ships into the port at Alexandria for about 1,500 years.

Before Europeans arrived in the Caribbean region, the indigenous Mayan people built shrines that appear to have doubled as lighthouses for canoes. In colonial America, the first lighthouse was built near the Boston Harbor in 1716 and utilized candle light and a cannon that was regularly fired for auditory signaling in foggy weather.

37) All of the following information about beacons are mentioned in Paragraph 1 EXCEPT:
   (A) They were generally fueled by wood.
   (B) They were optical long-distance communication systems.
   (C) Sentries could use them to warn comrades.
   (D) They have been widely used since ancient times.

38) According to Paragraph 2, which of the following statements is NOT true about the Pharos?
   (A) It does not seem to have had predecessors.
   (B) Its purpose was to indicate treacherous seas at Alexandria.
   (C) It made use of reflection as well as incandescence.
   (D) It was distinctive in its height.

39) What does Paragraph 3 NOT state about the lighthouse in Boston?
   (A) It was the initial lighthouse in what is now the United States.
   (B) It was constantly obscured by atmospheric vapor.
   (C) The light source was from candle light.
   (D) It utilized an alternative type of signal when necessary.

40) The passage does NOT mention the historic use of beacons
   (A) as part of a barrier in ancient China
   (B) in religious settings along the Caribbean coast
   (C) in various regions of Great Britain
   (D) along an important trade route in the Pacific Ocean

Select the vocabulary word or phrase that has the closest meaning.

6. **influential**
A. imposing
B. important
C. notorious
D. vociferous

7. **elucidation**
A. brightness
B. compliment
C. assumption
D. explanation

8. **empathy**
A. compassion
B. apprehension
C. accomplishment
D. rejection

9. **circumscribed**
A. concerned
B. plentiful
C. confined
D. circular

10. **forage**
A. improve
B. seek
C. describe
D. feed

1. **formulate**
A. stipulate
B. devise
C. astonish
D. compensate

2. **immutable**
A. speechless
B. fluent
C. fixed
D. straightforward

3. **nautical**
A. seafaring
B. neutral
C. undue
D. fervent

4. **amusement**
A. teasing
B. delight
C. smash
D. component

5. **meticulous**
A. competitive
B. excessive
C. thorough
D. agile

11. **vulnerable**
A. voluntary
B. realistic
C. susceptible
D. unanimous

12. **hinder**
A. deliver
B. plead
C. hamper
D. organize

13. **equatorial**
A. equational
B. applicable
C. countable
D. tropical

14. **irreverence**
A. argumentation
B. defeat
C. disrespect
D. adversity

15. **illuminate**
A. screen
B. induce
C. explain
D. overlook

16. **turn to**
A. drop by
B. count on
C. focus on
D. comply with

17. **envision**
A. exclude
B. disrupt
C. visualize
D. summon

18. **oscillate**
A. remit
B. vibrate
C. undertake
D. suppress

19. **ferociously**
A. discreetly
B. cautiously
C. fiercely
D. accurately

20. **feisty**
A. boring
B. critical
C. unnoticeable
D. lively

21. **placid**
A. upset
B. calm
C. abrupt
D. bleak

22. **subterranean**
A. solitude
B. courageous
C. underground
D. abrupt

23. **temperament**
A. temperature
B. curiosity
C. character
D. confirmation

24. **clamorous**
A. vociferous
B. admiring
C. delicate
D. discreet

25. **cloak**
A. yearn
B. hesitate
C. conceal
D. refute

26. **consortium**
A. profusion
B. conformation
C. scarcity
D. conglomerate

27. **surpass**
A. provide
B. exceed
C. elevate
D. approach

28. **outrage**
A. dependence
B. indignation
C. support
D. tragedy

29. **disgruntled**
A. considered
B. disclosed
C. startled
D. annoyed

30. **advocate**
A. encourage
B. oppose
C. fulfill
D. admit

31. **impending**
A. imminent
B. controversial
C. religious
D. severe

32. **auditory**
A. impaired
B. authentic
C. acoustic
D. rigorous

33. **optical**
A. optional
B. visual
C. urgent
D. worthless

34. **distinctive**
A. stern
B. sympathetic
C. merciful
D. unique

35. **obscured**
A. followed
B. hidden
C. stopped
D. observed

I. What Is a Coherence Question?

Coherence

The coherence question asks you to create a more logical or coherent passage by adding a new sentence that will improve the overall information.

A. COHERENCE QUESTION MODEL

A Contrary to popular perception, the emperors of Japan have often been venerated as symbolic leaders rather than power holders. **B** The most notable of these were the Tokugawa Shogunate, which formalized hierarchical class distinctions, consolidated and exerted control over the unified land, and answered to no one during the Edo Period, from 1603 until 1868. **C** Positioned in Edo Castle, the Tokugawa Shogunate directed the military and ruled during a peaceful era. **D**

5. Look at the squares [■] that indicate where the following sentence could be added:

   The actual power resided with the *shogunate*, military governments led by a general, who was known as the *shogun*.

   Where would the sentence best fit?
   Circle the square [■] to add the sentence.

B. COHERENCE QUESTION FORMATS

Look at the squares [■] and indicate where the following sentence could be added.

(A bold-faced sentence)

Where would the sentence best fit?
Circle the square [■] to add the sentence.

C. TIPS

1. When taking the official, Internet-based TOEFL test, you will be asked to click on the correct answer choice rather than circle it.
2. Understanding the purpose of the passage will help you identify the correct placement of the new sentence.
3. Look for transitions to indicate what kind of information should come next if the given information seems unrelated.
4. Check that all of the pronouns have referents. If a referent is missing, that omission can give you a clue as to where the new sentence should be placed.
5. An incorrect answer may:
   - stop the logical continuation of ideas between sentences
   - conflict with the function of the transitions
   - disrupt the relationship between a pronoun and its referent

CHAPTER 5

COHERENCE QUESTION

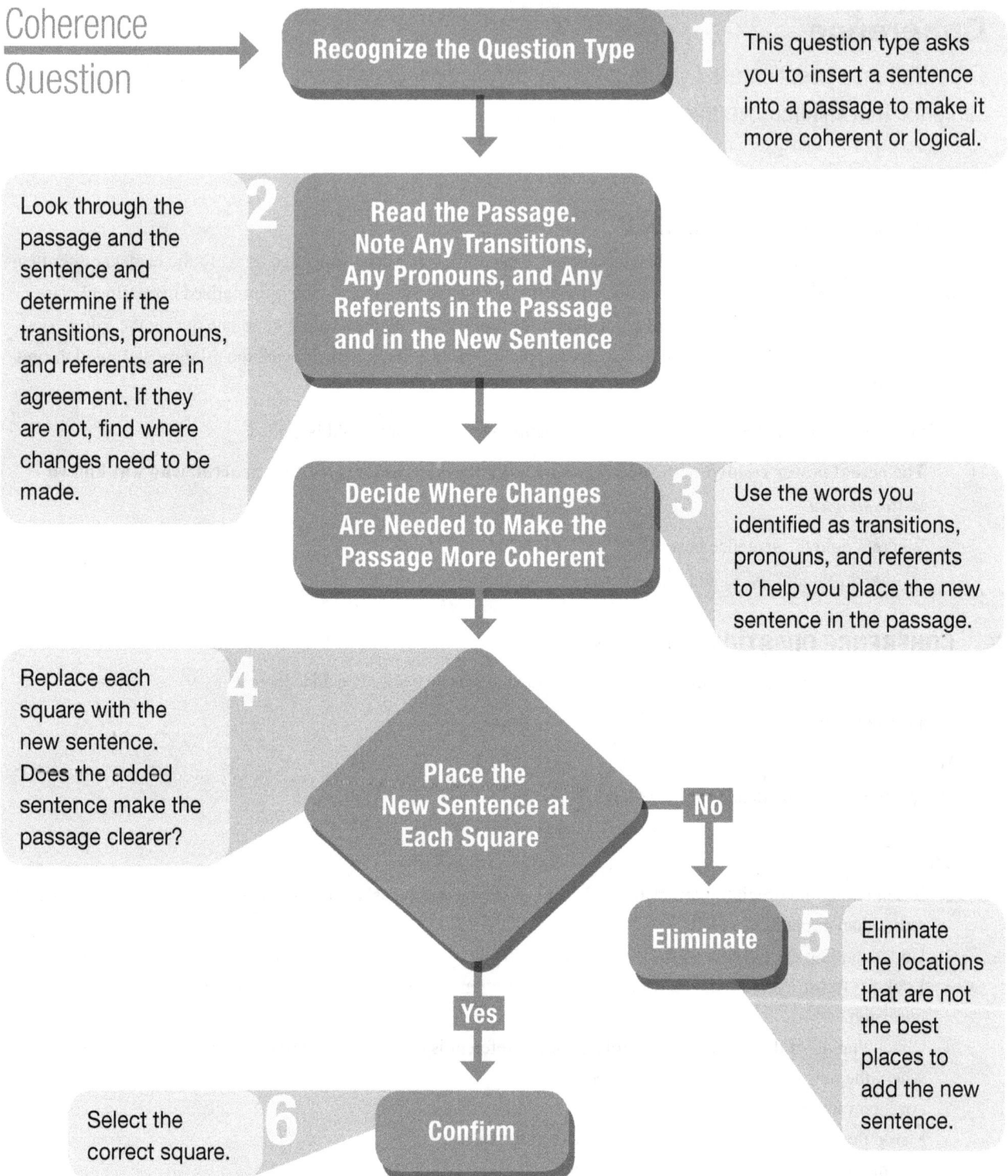

II. Hacking Strategy

Coherence Question →

Recognize the Question Type

1 This question type asks you to insert a sentence into a passage to make it more coherent or logical.

2 Look through the passage and the sentence and determine if the transitions, pronouns, and referents are in agreement. If they are not, find where changes need to be made.

Read the Passage. Note Any Transitions, Any Pronouns, and Any Referents in the Passage and in the New Sentence

Decide Where Changes Are Needed to Make the Passage More Coherent

3 Use the words you identified as transitions, pronouns, and referents to help you place the new sentence in the passage.

4 Replace each square with the new sentence. Does the added sentence make the passage clearer?

Place the New Sentence at Each Square

No → **Eliminate**

5 Eliminate the locations that are not the best places to add the new sentence.

Yes ↓

6 Select the correct square.

Confirm

◖EXAMPLE

1

A Contrary to popular perception, the emperors of Japan have often been venerated as symbolic leaders rather than power holders. **B** The most notable of these were the Tokugawa Shogunate, which formalized hierarchical class distinctions, consolidated and exerted control over the unified land, and answered to no one during the Edo Period, from 1603 until 1868. **C** Positioned in Edo Castle, the Tokugawa Shogunate directed the military and ruled during a peaceful era. **D**

Look at the squares [■] that indicate where the following sentence could be added:

The actual power resided with the *shogunate*, military governments led by a general, who was known as the *shogun*.

Where would the sentence best fit?
Circle the square [■] to add the sentence.

2

A **Contrary** to popular perception, the emperors of Japan have often been venerated as symbolic leaders rather than power holders. **B** The most notable of **these** were the Tokugawa Shogunate, which formalized hierarchical class distinctions, consolidated and exerted control over the unified land, and answered to no one during the Edo Period, from 1603 until 1868. **C** **Positioned** in Edo Castle, the Tokugawa Shogunate directed the military and presided over a peaceful era. **D**

3

The first sentence says that the emperor did not traditionally have much power, but the second sentence refers to a group of powerful leaders, "the most notable of these," without explanation. This is not coherent.

4 & 5

Place the new sentence in each square, and eliminate incorrect squares.

The definition of shogunate is accomplished partly by the contrast with emperors mentioned in the opening statement. The rest of the paragraph focuses on a particular example of a shogunate. Therefore, the paragraph becomes more coherent with the definition of the shogunate inserted at square "B," so that the reader can understand the details that follow.

A Contrary to popular perception, the emperors of Japan have often been venerated as symbolic leaders rather than power holders. **The actual power resided with the *shogunate*, military governments led by a general, who was known as the *shogun*.** The most notable of these were the Tokugawa Shogunate,....

The passage is more coherent with the definition inserted at square "B."

6

Select the correct square — **B** — by circling it.

III. Quick Look

Transitions Used in Coherence Questions

1. Addition Signals that more information similar to the previous sentence is going to be introduced.

Also   Another   Other   First, Second, etc.   And so on

Topic: Painting

Choices

2. Contrast Signals that information contrasting to the previous sentence is going to follow.

Although   However   In contrast   While   But

Topic: Contrast

HELP!

Choices

3. Cause / Result Signals that information that describes the results of the information in the previous sentence is going to follow.

Because / Since   Consequently   Therefore   Thus   To conclude

Topic: Actions

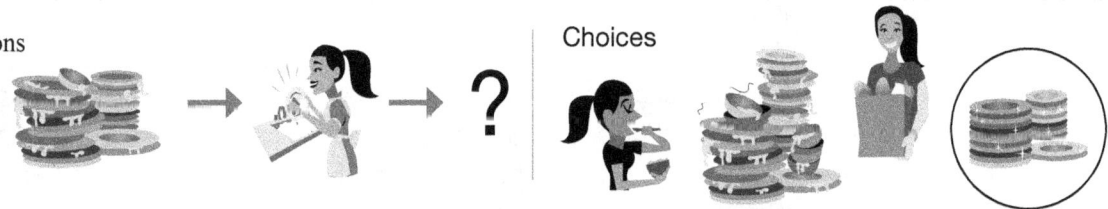

Choices

4. Example Signals that a supporting example is going to follow.

For example   For instance   Including   Such as   First, Second, etc.   In conclusion

Topic: Flags of countries

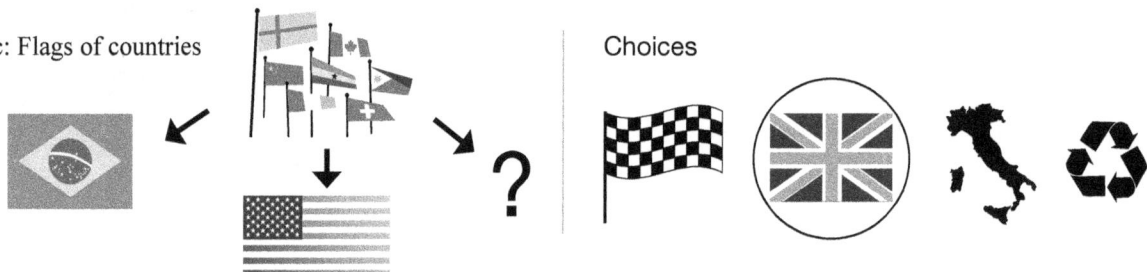

Choices

IV. Warm Up

Read each sentence below. Then put the sentences in the correct sequence by labeling each choice as 1, 2, or 3.

1. _____ For example, Hippocrates, an ancient Greek physician, proposed that there were four fluids in the body called *humors* that influenced a person's health and behavior.
   _____ There have been many different theories concerning the nature and development of personality.
   _____ According to this theory, people with calm personalities have one dominant humor while more excitable people have a different dominant humor.

2. _____ One basic pattern of socialization stresses individual accomplishment, exploration, and risk-taking, and another stresses cooperation, responsibility, and group accomplishment.
   _____ Patterns of socialization can often fit into one of two broad cultural categories.
   _____ All parents and communities consciously and unconsciously socialize with children in ways that encourage certain attributes.

3. _____ Ohio is also called the "Buckeye State" because of the buckeye trees that once grew plentifully there.
   _____ The state of Ohio adopted the name because the river forms the state's southeastern and southern borders.
   _____ The Iroquois word *ohio*, which translates as "great river," is also the name of an American state.

4. _____ By the end of the 1800s, music publishing centered in an area around 28th Street in New York City that came to be known as Tin Pan Alley.
   _____ The area got its name from the noise of the cheap pianos in song publishers' offices.
   _____ Musicians sometimes called these pianos "tin pans" because of the way they sounded.

5. _____ A major National Institutes of Health study of different medical approaches to treating Raynaud's found that a vasodilator drug alleviated symptoms in many sufferers.
   _____ People whose fingers, toes, ears, and noses seem to become "bloodless" and cold easily may suffer from an ailment known as Raynaud's phenomenon.
   _____ Raynaud's, which probably is caused by spasms in blood vessels, may affect around 5 percent of women, who find it very difficult to cope with cold weather.

6. _____ In order to function efficiently, radio stations need program planners, announcers, newscasters, technicians, and maintenance workers.
   _____ An employee of a small radio station may be called on to do any of these jobs at one time or another.
   _____ Therefore, a job in a small station provides excellent experience for a person starting a radio career.

7. _____ People come into contact with the plant resin by brushing against any slightly bruised leaf or stem of the plant, or by touching clothing or animal fur that has brushed against it.
   _____ Rinsing with plenty of cold water or applying rubbing alcohol may break down and remove the oily resin and reduce its effect on the skin.
   _____ *Urushiol resin*, found in poison oak, poison ivy, and the Japanese lacquer tree, causes painful and itchy allergic reactions in human skin.

8. _____ At that time, federal marshals collected the data.
   _____ Later, as the country grew, censuses gathered more information and the government created a permanent agency responsible for the census.
   _____ During the late 18th century, U.S. censuses were simple population tallies.

9. _____ Grizzly bears can occasionally grow 3 meters long and weigh 680 kg, and they can bite with deadly strength.
   _____ Efforts to save the endangered species are hampered by a grizzly's territorial requirements of thousands of square kilometers.
   _____ Despite their size, human deforestation and land development have greatly reduced the grizzly bear population.

10. _____ These preserves remain largely unknown; many people associate Southern California with palm trees, but in fact much of it was originally covered with oak, walnut, sycamore, and willow.
    _____ Furthermore, shrubs along the southern coast, such as various types of sages, sagebrush, and buckwheat, tend to be brown and dry but highly aromatic in the summer.
    _____ California's native plant communities exist today in only slivers of protected space.

V. Quick Practice

Practice #1

Read the passage and choose the best answer to each question.

A Indoor air in homes and businesses can be polluted even if there are no detectable signs. **B** Some sources of indoor air pollution may be obvious, such as tobacco smoke, visible mold, or strong-smelling pesticides or cleansers. **C** A three-pronged attack can bring about healthier air: controlling the source of the pollutant, ventilating with outdoor air to dilute toxins, and ensuring proper air filtration. **D**

    E Air filters are devices that pull air through a filter made of wool, cotton, or cellulose. **F** They can collect large amounts of dust, which harbors molds, bacteria, and other contaminants. **G** Some air filters can be washed, and some are disposable. **H** Carpets and rugs also act as air filters and must be cleaned frequently. House plants can absorb some toxins, but also may increase mold by increasing humidity.

1) In Paragraph 1, look at the four squares [■] that indicate where the following sentence can be added.

   Examples of less noticeable sources include pressed-wood furniture, which may emit formaldehyde, and leaky gas stoves or space heaters, which may emit toxic gases.

   Where would the sentence best fit?
   Circle the square [■] to add the sentence to the passage.

2) In Paragraph 2, look at the four squares [■] that indicate where the following sentence can be added.

   But large amounts of such substances can clog filter pores, disturbing the filter's effectiveness.

   Where would the sentence best fit?
   Circle the square [■] to add the sentence to the passage.

Practice #2

Read the passage and choose the best answer to each question.

Atoms and molecules can have electric charges, in which case they are called *ions*. **A** Ions are charged because they have an unequal number of protons and electrons. **B** Ions rarely exist by themselves because they are immediately attracted to ions with opposite charges, creating new molecules. **C** For example, table salt forms when positively charged sodium ions attach to negatively charged chlorine ions. **D** The result is an electrically neutral compound, sodium chloride.

Acids and bases are substances which, when added to water, produce particular ions. **E** Acids produce ions with extra hydrogen protons while bases produce ions that lack hydrogen protons. Thus, bases and acids can balance each other. **F** One common base is sodium bicarbonate, commonly known as *baking soda*. **G** When baking soda is added to water with an acid, hydrogen ions combine in processes that produce neutralized compounds. **H**

3) In Paragraph 1, look at the four squares [■] that indicate where the following sentence can be added.

More electrons than protons create a negative charge, while more protons than electrons create a positive one.

Where would the sentence best fit?
Circle the square [■] to add the sentence to the passage.

4) In Paragraph 2, look at the four squares [■] that indicate where the following sentence can be added.

For this reason, people sometimes drink baking soda mixed with water to neutralize excess stomach acid.

Where would the sentence best fit?
Circle the square [■] to add the sentence to the passage.

Practice #3

Read the passage and choose the best answer to each question.

A One way to make something desirable is to make it rare, such as a name-brand purse, or to make it temporarily unavailable, such as the latest smartphone. **B** In fact, the less of something there is, the more people will compete for it. **C** Psychologists have theorized several reasons that people may yearn for what is just out of their reach. **D** One is that when people perceive that something is difficult to obtain because it is scarce or is denied to them, they simply pay more attention to it.

E In order for people to truly yearn for something, psychologists say, they have to feel that the object of desire is real and within the realm of possibility. **F** If something is easily obtainable, such as an inexpensive pair of shoes at a local store, people do not need to think about it. **G** However, they may feel that the opportunity to buy a pair of designer shoes in a faraway metropolis is an *incomplete project*. **H** As they have not "finished" the task of obtaining the shoes, the task demands additional attention. The activity also requires further investments of their time and energy, so as they begin the task, the time investment itself feels valuable.

5) In Paragraph 1, look at the four squares [■] that indicate where the following sentence can be added.

Marketing managers know that people often want what they cannot have.

Where would the sentence best fit?
Circle the square [■] to add the sentence to the passage.

6) In Paragraph 2, look at the four squares [■] that indicate where the following sentence can be added.

They may feel that the shoes have already been given to them, in a sense.

Where would the sentence best fit?
Circle the square [■] to add the sentence to the passage.

Practice #4

Read the passage and choose the best answer to each question.

The term *Gothic* describes the architectural style prevalent in Europe from the 12th to the 16th centuries. **A** The term was not used at the time but was applied later during the Renaissance by critics of the style. **B** The critics felt that Gothic style was an uncivilized abandonment of Greek and Roman styles, and blamed its use on the *Goths*, or northern Germanic tribes that overran Rome in 410. **C** Gothic style also was most likely influenced by contact with the Muslim world and the Middle East. **D**

The most important change associated with Gothic architecture was the way roofs were constructed. **E** The Gothic style makes use of a series of pointed arches holding up the roof, reminiscent of the ribs of a skeleton, hence the term *ribbed vault*. **F** Because the arches rather than the walls hold the weight of the roof, the walls can be thinner and have many more windows. **G** Such roofs make it possible to create taller buildings with vast, well-lit spaces inside. **H**

7) In Paragraph 1, look at the four squares [■] that indicate where the following sentence can be added.

However, researchers now believe that Gothic architecture evolved naturally out of engineering innovations.

Where would the sentence best fit?
Circle the square [■] to add the sentence to the passage.

8) In Paragraph 2, look at the four squares [■] that indicate where the following sentence can be added.

The arches gain extra support from bars that stick out or seem to "fly" out to the sides, known as *flying buttresses*.

Where would the sentence best fit?
Circle the square [■] to add the sentence to the passage.

Practice #5

Read the passage and choose the best answer to each question.

Landlords are property owners who rent out or lease space to *tenants*, or renters of property. **A** When landlords force tenants to move out, the process is called *eviction*. **B** Laws concerning eviction differ among communities and states. **C** Generally, however, a landlord must provide written notice to the tenant, allowing time for locating a new property. **D** In most states, it is illegal for the landlord to turn off the utilities, such as water and electricity, or change the locks until the tenant has moved out.

Landlords have a legal right to evict tenants "for cause," such as nonpayment of rent. In most areas, they also can ask tenants to move out for no reason other than wanting to use the space for something else. At the same time, tenants also have legal rights. **E** Most jurisdictions have laws requiring rental space to be "fit for habitation," or in other words, reasonably clean and safe. **F** Tenants should inform landlords of any problems and allow a reasonable amount of time for repairs. **G** If a landlord does not take any action, a tenant should make the request in writing. A tenant also can contact local government agencies to inquire about building code enforcement. **H**

9) In Paragraph 1, look at the four squares [■] that indicate where the following sentence can be added.

If the tenant refuses to vacate the premises, the landlord must then file a lawsuit and allow the courts and law enforcement officers to handle the case.

Where would the sentence best fit?
Circle the square [■] to add the sentence to the passage.

10) In Paragraph 2, look at the four squares [■] that indicate where the following sentence can be added.

For example, if the water is unsafe to drink, there is no heat in winter, or there is a leak in the ceiling, the space may be considered "unfit."

Where would the sentence best fit?
Circle the square [■] to add the sentence to the passage.

Practice #6

Read the passage and choose the best answer to each question.

The United States Federal Reserve System controls key aspects of the U.S. economy. **A** The "Fed," as it is called informally, determines the country's monetary policy, such as its money supply. **B** It also supervises banks, provides financial services to the U.S. government, and conducts research. **C** The Fed is a combination of public and private sectors. **D**

In 1790, Secretary of the Treasury Alexander Hamilton proposed that Congress charter a national bank. **E** The bank would be private but would be under the Secretary of the Treasury's supervision. **F** Hamilton, a northerner, thought that the bank would clear up currency issues, establish order, and make credit available. **G** Southern leaders such as Thomas Jefferson opposed the idea. **H** Southerners also believed that a national bank would benefit merchants in the industrial North much more than the agricultural South. In the end, the proposal passed, and President George Washington, a southerner, signed it. Still, the issue was not completely settled for more than 100 years.

11) In Paragraph 1, look at the four squares [■] that indicate where the following sentence can be added.

Its unique structure resulted from a compromise between those who wanted a national bank and those who did not, a debate that had been going on since the nation's very beginning.

Where would the sentence best fit?
Circle the square [■] to add the sentence to the passage.

12) In Paragraph 2, look at the four squares [■] that indicate where the following sentence can be added.

They said that it would be unconstitutional, as well as financially risky, to centralize banking power.

Where would the sentence best fit?
Circle the square [■] to add the sentence to the passage.

Practice #7

Read the passage and choose the best answer to each question.

In traditional medicine, *poultices* are pastes, often made of mashed grains, plants, or clay. They are usually heated and applied to the skin for a short time, often over a layer of thin cloth. **A** Used alone, poultices can have the effect of increasing blood circulation in a particular spot. **B** But they also can be mixed with medicines to enhance their effect. **C** For example, a paste of ground mustard seeds, flour, and warm water can be applied to the chest for chest colds; the mustard causes tiny blood vessels to open wider, increasing blood flow and helping to open up the lungs. **D**

Modern medicine's version of the poultice is the *transdermal patch*, or a small medication-packed square that attaches to the skin. **E** When they can be used, patches have an important advantage over shots or pills. The body absorbs the medicine in patches slower than it does from alternative methods. **F** Therefore, they are ideal for some pain relievers, hormones, and other medicines that work best in small, regular doses. **G** In 1981, a patch for motion sickness became the first approved transdermal medication available in the United States. **H**

13) In Paragraph 1, look at the four squares [■] that indicate where the following sentence can be added.

Many traditional cultures have used poultices to increase healing to wounded or aching parts of the body.

Where would the sentence best fit?
Circle the square [■] to add the sentence to the passage.

14) In Paragraph 2, look at the four squares [■] that indicate where the following sentence can be added.

It can only be used with medications that have molecules small enough to penetrate the skin's barriers.

Where would the sentence best fit?
Circle the square [■] to add the sentence to the passage.

Practice #8

Read the passage and choose the best answer to each question.

A Comedic puppet shows featuring the classic characters Punch and Judy have been appearing at outdoor markets and festivities in Great Britain for centuries. **B** The mischievous Mr. Punch usually has a bent back and an enormous nose, and speaks in a strange-sounding voice. **C** Originally the puppets were *marionettes*, or dolls dangling from strings, but over time they became hand-held puppets, enabling them to engage in more robust physical humor. **D**

E Generally, Punch behaves in an outrageous manner, provoking shock and laughter from the audience. **F** He may unexpectedly hit his wife Judy with a "slapstick," and she may hit him back. He may be talking while the audience can see a crocodile sneaking up behind him or another character stealing something. **G** Punch usually gets in trouble with the law, but always manages to escape punishment and exclaim, "Now *that's* the way to do it!" **H** Although all the characters' behavior is often violent, audiences tend to find the action silly rather than serious.

15) In Paragraph 1, look at the four squares [■] that indicate where the following sentence can be added.

His character evolved from a tricky character in a 16th-century Italian comedy, *Pulcinella*.

Where would the sentence best fit?
Circle the square [■] to add the sentence to the passage.

16) In Paragraph 2, look at the four squares [■] that indicate where the following sentence can be added.

Each Punch and Judy show is different, as there is no set plot.

Where would the sentence best fit?
Circle the square [■] to add the sentence to the passage.

Practice #9

Read the passage and choose the best answer to each question.

The most common heart disease is caused by narrowing of the *arteries*, or tubes that carry oxygen-rich blood away from the heart. **A** The disease starts when the inner walls of the arteries become coated with *plaque*, a hard material made up of fats, inflamed cells, or other matter. **B** Sometimes the plaque *ruptures* – bursts or breaks open. A blood clot can form around the plaque rupture, filling the artery and blocking the flow of blood. **C** Deprived of its regular supply of blood and oxygen, the heart begins to die, and the event is known as a *heart attack*. **D**

For most of human history, people had little insight into how the heart functioned. **E** It was not until 1628 that English physician William Harvey first described the heart's role in circulating blood through the body. **F** In the 20th and 21st centuries, researchers made enormous advances in preventing and treating heart disease, but it remains the top cause of death in many developed nations. **G** Rather, treatment may focus more on gene therapy and nanotechnology, which may include the manipulation of atoms. **H**

17) In Paragraph 1, look at the four squares [■] that indicate where the following sentence can be added.

Depending on the size of the artery and the speed of treatment, the patient may recover and the heart may rebuild cells.

Where would the sentence best fit?
Circle the square [■] to add the sentence to the passage.

18) In Paragraph 2, look at the four squares [■] that indicate where the following sentence can be added.

Some people predict that in the future, heart treatment may be less focused on surgery and mechanical devices than it is now.

Where would the sentence best fit?
Circle the square [■] to add the sentence to the passage.

Practice #10

Read the passage and choose the best answer to each question.

A The cells of plants are very similar to the cells of animals. **B** However, most animal and plant cells have a few fundamental differences. **C** One is that while animal cells tend to be smaller and round, plant cells tend to be larger and square or rectangular. **D** Plant cells also have an extra cell wall, mostly made up of *cellulose*, a tough material that gives plant stems and tree branches their strength.

However, the biggest differentiation between plant and animal cells is that unlike animals, plants have *chloroplasts* in their cells. **E** These usually contain a green pigment called *chlorophyll*, which is necessary for photosynthesis. **F** The reactions provide the energy necessary to disassemble carbon dioxide molecules from the atmosphere and water molecules from the soil to form a carbon-based molecule, a sugar. **G** The plant thus creates its own food, which it can then "burn," or convert back into energy for growth. **H**

19) In Paragraph 1, look at the four squares [■] that indicate where the following sentence can be added.

Each has a cell membrane, a nucleus, and many of the same organelles.

Where would the sentence best fit?
Circle the square [■] to add the sentence to the passage.

20) In Paragraph 2, look at the four squares [■] that indicate where the following sentence can be added.

When light hits the chlorophyll in a plant's leaves, each chlorophyll molecule absorbs one photon, causing the loss of one electron and a number of resulting chemical reactions.

Where would the sentence best fit?
Circle the square [■] to add the sentence to the passage.

Select the vocabulary word or phrase that has the closest meaning.

6. **perceive**
   A. deem
   B. flourish
   C. displace
   D. stimulate

7. **scarce**
   A. fearful
   B. thrifty
   C. thirsty
   D. lacking

8. **yearn**
   A. yawn
   B. bear
   C. long
   D. submit

9. **realm**
   A. domain
   B. acclaim
   C. evaporation
   D. majority

10. **prevalent**
    A. convenient
    B. genuine
    C. widespread
    D. fresh

1. **detectable**
   A. indigenous
   B. valid
   C. discernible
   D. ominous

2. **obvious**
   A. soaked
   B. aspire
   C. confidential
   D. apparent

3. **dilute**
   A. weaken
   B. fulfill
   C. initiate
   D. unveil

4. **noticeable**
   A. subjective
   B. considerable
   C. notable
   D. furious

5. **emit**
   A. permit
   B. encompass
   C. discharge
   D. remain

11. **abandonment**
    A. division
    B. relinquishment
    C. maxim
    D. hospitality

12. **reminiscent**
    A. evocative
    B. informative
    C. remarkable
    D. irrelevant

13. **naturally**
    A. methodically
    B. normally
    C. thoroughly
    D. liberally

14. **reasonable**
    A. acceptable
    B. fiscal
    C. extroverted
    D. jovial

15. **enforcement**
    A. commerce
    B. implementation
    C. jurisdiction
    D. evacuation

16. **vacate**
    A. mar
    B. notify
    C. leave
    D. attach

17. **supervise**
    A. improvise
    B. consume
    C. relish
    D. oversee

18. **propose**
    A. suggest
    B. exaggerate
    C. promote
    D. impair

19. **charter**
    A. perish
    B. subside
    C. surrender
    D. authorize

20. **establish**
    A. grow
    B. create
    C. augment
    D. validate

21. **mashed**
    A. sudden
    B. temperate
    C. crushed
    D. affluent

22. **enhance**
    A. amplify
    B. confirm
    C. cede
    D. protrude

23. **approved**
    A. refined
    B. clogged
    C. proposed
    D. authorized

24. **dangling**
    A. dubious
    B. enterprising
    C. hanging
    D. vague

25. **robust**
    A. vigorous
    B. valuable
    C. dubious
    D. feeble

26. **outrageous**
    A. miscellaneous
    B. brazen
    C. voluminous
    D. undue

27. **provoke**
    A. tease
    B. convince
    C. arouse
    D. disregard

28. **unexpectedly**
    A. abruptly
    B. aggressively
    C. adversely
    D. apparently

29. **inflamed**
    A. suspicious
    B. docile
    C. irritated
    D. expendable

30. **rupture**
    A. report
    B. burst
    C. roar
    D. achieve

31. **advances**
    A. experimentations
    B. improvements
    C. provisions
    D. treatments

32. **manipulation**
    A. control
    B. modification
    C. illustration
    D. enthusiasm

33. **depending on**
    A. dwelling on
    B. going on
    C. working on
    D. contingent on

34. **fundamental**
    A. cardinal
    B. inconvenient
    C. lenient
    D. nominal

35. **disassemble**
    A. appraise
    B. dismantle
    C. transform
    D. adjust

I. What Is an Inference Question?

Inference

The inference question asks you to assume or "infer" an idea about a passage based on the information presented. In an inference question, you must be aware that an author does not directly state an idea but rather implies it. The author will state specific facts and details that will lead you to the unstated idea.

A. INFERENCE QUESTION MODEL

African-American men were granted the right to vote in the United States when the 15th Amendment to the U.S. Constitution was ratified in 1870. *Women's suffrage*, or women's right to vote, was achieved nationally in 1920 when the 19th Amendment was passed. Interestingly, both the quest for women's suffrage and the pursuit of voting rights for African-American men began in the second half of the 1800s.

Two prominent women's organizations crusaded for women's suffrage but diverged on the best method to attain the goal. The American Woman Suffrage Association (AWSA) strongly supported the effort to pass the 15th Amendment, believing that it would help pave the way for women's voting rights. Conversely, the National Woman Suffrage Association (NWSA) opposed the amendment because it did not specifically encompass women's suffrage.

6. What can be inferred about the social climate of the United States in the late 19th and early 20th centuries?

   (A) Segments of American society held racist and sexist views.
   (B) Many African-American men supported women's suffrage.
   (C) Few individuals understood the importance of voting rights.
   (D) African-American women's rights would not be addressed until much later.

B. INFERENCE QUESTION FORMATS

What can be inferred about _____?

Which statement is MOST LIKELY true about _____?

What PROBABLY occurred after/before/during _____?

Which MOST ACCURATELY reflects the author's opinion?

It can be inferred from _____ that _____.

What can be inferred from Paragraph _____?

What is a probable belief of the author?

C. TIPS

1. An inference can be made from just one sentence or from the entire passage.
2. Often the answer choices paraphrase the ideas of the passage, so it is important to understand the passage well.
3. An incorrect answer may:
   • be too broad or unclear
   • be off-topic or unrelated to the passage
   • be false or not be supported by the stated information in the passage
   • restate the information directly given in the passage

II. Hacking Strategy

Inference
Question →

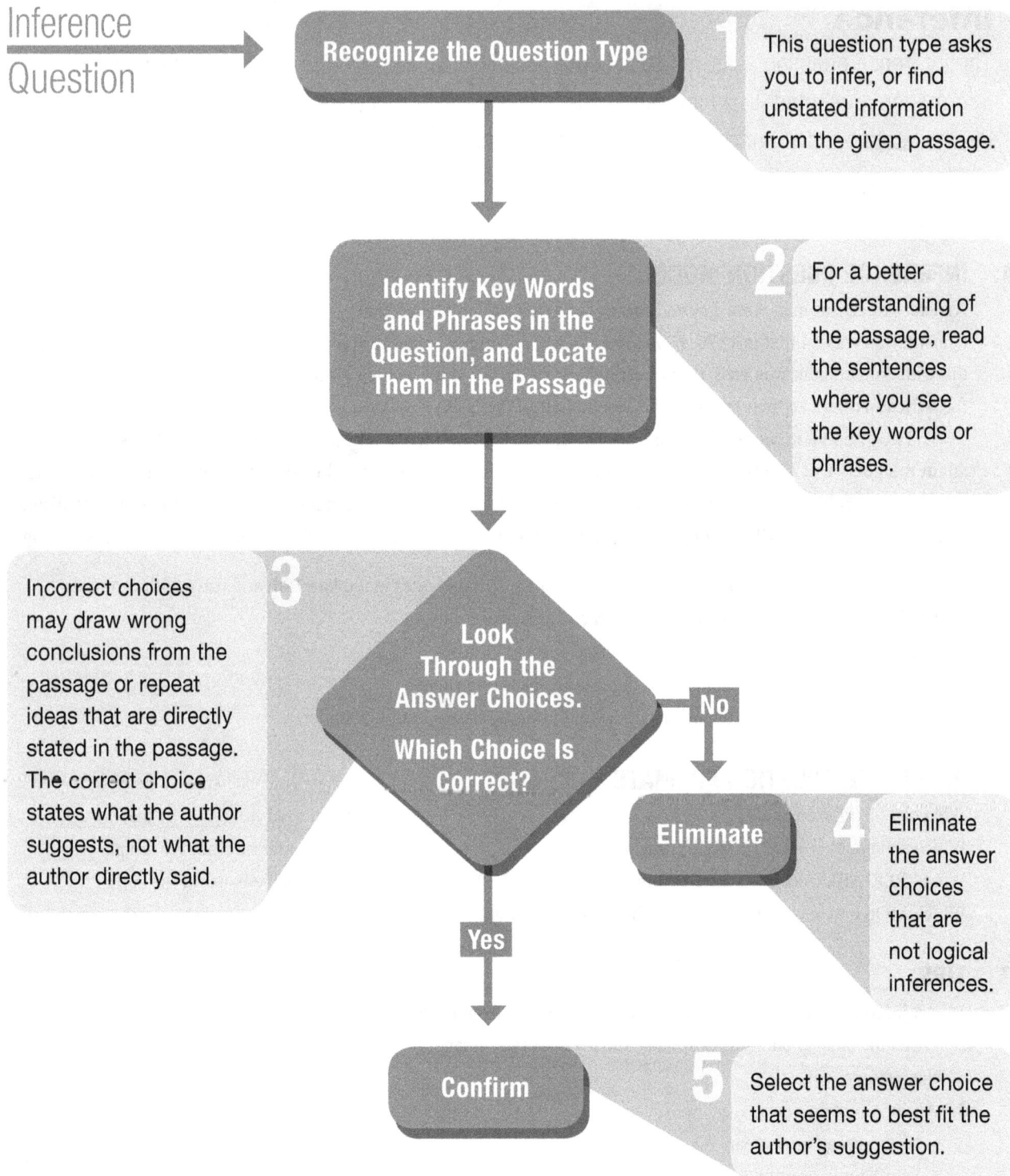

Recognize the Question Type

1 This question type asks you to infer, or find unstated information from the given passage.

↓

Identify Key Words and Phrases in the Question, and Locate Them in the Passage

2 For a better understanding of the passage, read the sentences where you see the key words or phrases.

↓

Incorrect choices may draw wrong conclusions from the passage or repeat ideas that are directly stated in the passage. The correct choice states what the author suggests, not what the author directly said.

3 **Look Through the Answer Choices. Which Choice Is Correct?**

No →

Eliminate

4 Eliminate the answer choices that are not logical inferences.

Yes ↓

Confirm

5 Select the answer choice that seems to best fit the author's suggestion.

1

African-American men were granted the right to vote in the United States when the 15th Amendment to the U.S. Constitution was ratified in 1870. *Women's suffrage,* or women's right to vote, was achieved nationally in 1920 when the 19th Amendment was passed. Interestingly, both the quest for women's suffrage and the pursuit of voting rights for African-American men began in the second half of the 1800s.

Two prominent women's organizations crusaded for women's suffrage but diverged on the best method to attain the goal. The American Woman Suffrage Association (AWSA) strongly supported the effort to pass the 15th Amendment, believing that it would help pave the way for women's voting rights. Conversely, the National Woman Suffrage Association (NWSA) opposed the amendment because it did not specifically encompass women's suffrage.

What can be inferred about the social climate of the United States in the late 19th and early 20th centuries?
(A) Segments of American society held racist and sexist views.
(B) Many African-American men supported women's suffrage.
(C) Few individuals understood the importance of voting rights.
(D) African-American women's rights would not be addressed until much later.

2

African-American men were granted the right to vote in the United States when the 15th Amendment to the U.S. Constitution was ratified in 1870. *Women's suffrage*, or women's right to vote, was achieved nationally in 1920 when the 19th Amendment was passed. Interestingly, both the quest for women's suffrage and the pursuit of voting rights for African-American men began in the second half of the 1800s.

Two prominent women's organizations crusaded for women's suffrage but diverged on the best method to attain the goal. The American Woman Suffrage Association (AWSA) strongly supported the effort to pass the 15th Amendment, believing that it would help pave the way for women's voting rights. Conversely, the National Woman Suffrage Association (NWSA) opposed the amendment because it did not specifically encompass women's suffrage.

What can be inferred about the social climate of the United States in the late 19th and early 20th centuries?
(A) Segments of American society held racist and sexist views.
(B) Many African-American men supported women's suffrage.
(C) Few individuals understood the importance of voting rights.
(D) African-American women's rights would not be addressed until much later.

3

Which choice is NOT STATED in the passage but is SUGGESTED?
• Select **Choice A** because women and African Americans originally did not have the right to vote in America, so some people must have *held racist and sexist views*.

4

• Eliminate **Choice B**; the passage does not mention African-American men's relationship to women's suffrage.
• Eliminate **Choice C**; the passage emphasizes that many sought voting rights, so people must have realized voting's importance.
• Eliminate **Choice D**; African-American women's rights are not specifically mentioned anywhere in the passage, so we cannot infer this.

5

Select the correct answer — **Choice A**.

III. Quick Look

Making Inferences

Inference: An *inference* is an idea that you create on your own BASED ON the information that is directly stated in the passage.

1.

Choices

2.

Choices

3.

Choices

IV. Warm Up

Choose the MORE LIKELY inference from each of the following sentences.

1. Except for brief periods, the Medici family ruled Florence, Italy, from the early 1400s to 1737.
   - (A) Florence split into several different cities after 1737.
   - (B) Much of the Medici Family was ambitious and politically savvy.

2. Ruling Florence from 1434 to 1464, Cosimo Medici was the first member of his family to gain fame, giving large amounts of money to sponsor the arts in Florence.
   - (A) Many painters and sculptors visited Florence during the 1400s.
   - (B) Cosimo Medici believed that all powerful people should be artists.

3. Stamp collecting has been called the "king of hobbies and the hobby of kings."
   - (A) Stamp collecting can be an expensive hobby.
   - (B) Stamp collecting is practiced by many different kinds of people.

4. A group of United States airmail stamps was issued in 1918 with the airplane depicted on the stamp mistakenly appearing upside down, and they are now very valuable to stamp collectors.
   - (A) Stamp collectors appreciate items that are rare and hard to find.
   - (B) Stamp collectors are interested in flight-related stamps.

5. In American football, a team uses strategy and force to get into "enemy" territory, overcome the "enemy's" defenses, and score points by infiltrating the "enemy's" zone.
   - (A) American football has become popular because of its strategies and violence.
   - (B) American football is a metaphorical battle.

6. During a game of ice hockey, players can skate at speeds upward of 30 kilometers per hour, and they can sometimes send the tiny puck shooting across the ice at 160 kilometers per hour.
   - (A) Hockey is an extremely fast-moving game.
   - (B) Hockey players are ranked based on their skating speeds.

7. An intriguing figure in Russian folklore is the terrifying witch with iron teeth, Baba Yaga; when not eating people, she occasionally proves helpful to them.
   - (A) Baba Yaga helps people so that she can eat them.
   - (B) Baba Yaga is a slightly ambiguous character.

8. The Sirens of Greek mythology are part woman and part bird creatures, and they sing beautifully in order to lure sailors to fatal crashes on the Sirens' rocky island.
   - (A) Sirens represent the dangers of allure.
   - (B) Birds always represented danger in Greek mythology.

9. A prehistoric surgical treatment, an operation called *trephining*, involved using a stone instrument to cut a hole in the patient's skull, and it appears to have been done in a religious setting.
   - (A) Prehistoric people mostly had problems with their skulls.
   - (B) Ancient people sometimes intertwined medical treatment with spiritual beliefs.

10. More than 2,000 years ago, the ancient Chinese developed medical practices that remain almost unchanged to this day.
    - (A) Ancient medicine developed in China is still considered successful for many ailments.
    - (B) Practices and treatment methods in traditional Chinese medicine are unreliable.

11. Speaking at the 1988 Democratic convention, the Reverend Jesse Jackson said that in the United States most poor people actually do work hard, and in fact they "catch the early bus."
    (A) Jackson was refuting claims that poor people are lazy.
    (B) Jackson was supporting more funding of public transportation.

12. United States President Ronald Reagan told an audience at Moscow State University in 1988 that the free market succeeds because millions of individual entrepreneurs learn from failure.
    (A) Reagan wanted the audience to experience failure.
    (B) Reagan was explaining the merits of taking risks.

13. Dominant animals in hierarchical groups often develop threatening displays of strength so that they can avoid actual physical confrontations.
    (A) Animals in hierarchical groups always conserve their strength for clashes with outsiders.
    (B) Dodging conflicts when possible may be an adaptive trait for survival among hierarchical animals.

14. Researchers in social psychology say that most people view those who are physically above them as dominant, perhaps because of childhood memories of parents being taller than them.
    (A) Humans draw many conclusions subconsciously.
    (B) Humans who are tall are always able to dominate others.

15. Antarctica, the coldest continent on Earth with temperatures as low as -89 degrees Celsius and mile-thick ice over 98% of its surface, went generally unexplored during the 19th century after it was first sighted and still has no permanent residents; only research personnel are stationed there.
    (A) A country claimed Antarctica as its own and prohibited other nations from exploring Antarctica during the 19th century.
    (B) The uninhabitable conditions in Antarctica prohibit populations from settling on the continent.

16. In 1957, United States Senator Strom Thurmond spoke for more than 24 hours in front of the U.S. Senate to delay the passage of anti-discrimination legislation.
    (A) Thurmond strongly opposed federally enforced racial integration.
    (B) Thurmond's actual goal was to enter the record books for giving the longest speech.

17. Web-spinning spiders construct their webs with both sticky thread for trapping insects and non-sticky thread for the spiders' own pathways.
    (A) Spiders could possibly get stuck in their own webs.
    (B) Spiders can predict the pathways of prey.

18. Black widow spiders tend to build webs that look like messy clumps, but they are actually protective homes and three-dimensional systems for detecting vibrations from prey.
    (A) Black widows cause their webs to vibrate, which lures unsuspecting prey.
    (B) Black widow spiders rely on feeling movements in their webs to know when an insect is caught.

19. An exciting ballet move is the *grand jeté*, in which a dancer runs and takes a big leap from one foot, does a complete stretch of the legs in mid-air, and lands quietly on the other foot.
    (A) Ballet dancers must practice landing leaps without making sound.
    (B) Few ballet dancers have been able to master the difficult *grand jeté* move.

20. Dancers making a series of turns can avoid feelings of dizziness by *spotting*, or looking at one spot in front of them for as long as possible before whipping their heads around.
    (A) Choreographers can challenge dancers by having them turn in different directions.
    (B) Learning how to not become dizzy and not lose balance is crucial for dancers.

V. Quick Practice

Practice #1

Read the passage and choose the best answer to each question.

In 1912, an amateur British archaeologist named Charles Dawson seemed to have found the "missing link" in the evolution of humans from apes. Dawson first wrote to a geologist at the British Natural History Museum to describe fossilized pieces of a human skull from the village of Piltdown in England. Later, Dawson claimed to have found a fossilized ape-like jaw bone and two teeth in Piltdown as well. Based on these findings, the museum geologist presented scientific papers about the "Piltdown Man," an early hominid* who had lived an estimated 500,000 years before, with the brain of a human and the jaw of an ape.

Some archaeologists were skeptical of Piltdown Man from the beginning, saying that the jaw was not a human's. Then in 1915, Dawson "discovered" even more Piltdown-type fossils at another English location, and public doubt seemed to dissipate. There was excitement that early human remains had finally been found in English soil, as they had been in Germany and France. Some scientists also felt that the Piltdown fossils proved their theory that human brains developed before other human features, rather than after. However, some forty years later, researchers proved that the Piltdown Man was a hoax – the jawbone was from an orangutan and the skull from the Medieval period.

Hominid: the family of bipedal primates that includes modern humans and their extinct ancestors

1) In Paragraph 1, what can be inferred about Charles Dawson?
   (A) He was highly motivated to find a "missing link" in evolution.
   (B) He made use of an expert's reputation to validate his claims.
   (C) He was a laborer who worked in the gravel pits at Piltdown.
   (D) He was very critical of previous "missing link" discoveries.

2) Based on Paragraph 2, what is PROBABLY true about Dawson finding more fossils in 1915?
   (A) He dedicated years of his life to searching for scientific answers.
   (B) Clever tricksters were able to deceive him more than once.
   (C) His archaeological skills became stronger over time.
   (D) He contrived a second finding to quiet scientific challenges to his first finding.

3) According to the passage, it is LIKELY that the British Natural History Museum's geologist
   (A) trusted everyone who claimed a discovery
   (B) was very meticulous with his work
   (C) had little expertise in zoology
   (D) was correct about some aspects of the fossils

4) According to the passage, which of the following is the probable belief of the passage's author about the initial acceptance of Piltdown Man?
   (A) The British scientific community was partly influenced by national pride.
   (B) The hoax could not have been detected without more modern technology.
   (C) The British scientific community made a mistake because of Dawson's stellar reputation.
   (D) Many scientists later mistrusted the British Natural History Museum.

Practice #2

Read the passage and choose the best answer to each question.

A dog's nose provides the animal's major source of sensory information. The wet nose tip helps capture odors and determine their source. A dog even can identify which nostril is receiving a smell. When dogs inhale, part of the air is diverted to an *olfactory recess*, or a special chamber in the snout that sorts out odor molecules and sends messages to the brain. The highly developed olfactory lobe in a dog's brain is 40 times larger than that in a human, and its olfactory recess may contain 125 to 220 million scent receptors. For comparison, humans have only 5 million scent receptors.

Detection dogs are trained to alert their human handlers – often by sitting down – when they smell a particular substance. Because dogs can smell parts per trillion, they can be trained to quickly scan for extremely subtle scents. As a result, scientists are increasingly relying on dogs to help with endangered species monitoring. Dogs can thoroughly and safely search a large wilderness area for indications of an elusive animal, such as its den, nest, or waste materials. Dogs even accompany some marine biologists on boats because dogs can be taught to detect small amounts of whale feces floating hundreds of meters away. The feces can then be collected and analyzed to learn a great deal about the whale, including its stress level.

5) From Paragraph 1, what can be inferred about dog noses?
(A) Their anatomical structures evolved to process minute olfactory information.
(B) They have greater lung capacity and can inhale more air than humans.
(C) They are one of a few species to have a developed olfactory recess.
(D) Their nose tips and olfactory systems are relatively incompatible with one another.

6) Which of the following is PROBABLY true about dog brains, according to Paragraph 1?
(A) They are usually larger than human brains.
(B) Most of the dog's brain is devoted to processing scents.
(C) They can process many strong odors that humans cannot.
(D) The area that analyzes scent information is more effective than that in humans.

7) From Paragraph 2, what can be inferred about why dogs are beneficial in field research?
(A) They can search a wide area for dangerous animal species.
(B) They can sense when an animal is frightened or wounded.
(C) They can indicate where an animal has been even after it has moved on.
(D) They can trace a wide diversity of organisms at one time.

8) What can be inferred from Paragraph 2 about dogs searching for whales?
(A) Dogs can use their swimming and scent abilities to track whales from boats.
(B) Dogs and whales share a similar sense of smell.
(C) Dogs can alert humans when whales are experiencing stress.
(D) Dogs can learn to indicate where a whale has been.

Practice #3

Read the passage and choose the best answer to each question.

American Gothic, a 1930 portrait of a man and a woman standing in front of a farmhouse, has become an iconic American image. The man is holding a pitchfork and seems to be looking at the viewer. The woman, who is younger, wears a 19th-century style dress and looks to her left. Artist Grant Wood completed the scene in his home state of Iowa. He got the idea after noticing a farmhouse with a window that looked like it belonged in a Gothic cathedral in Europe. Wood added the people to the painting after the house, recruiting his sister to model as the woman and basing the image of the man on his dentist.

The painting won a minor award in an art contest at the Art Institute of Chicago, which purchased it for $300. Then newspapers began to print it, garnering a range of reactions. Some art critics assumed that because Wood had studied art in Europe, he was satirizing rural American life, depicting the unsmiling people in the picture as old-fashioned and narrow-minded. Others believed that he was honoring the work ethic and tough character of American Midwesterners. Some perceived the scene as an expression of grief because Wood's father had died when Wood was a child. Wood went on to create many more figurative paintings of rural scenes until his death in 1942.

9) In Paragraph 1, to what is the painting's title *American Gothic* PROBABLY referring?
   (A) The funereal and ghostly mood that is depicted
   (B) The odd, ambiguous juxtaposition of the Gothic window and the simple farm
   (C) The paradox of young America and old Europe
   (D) The artist's viewpoint that American farm life was uncivilized

10) From Paragraph 1, what can be inferred about the actual people pictured in the painting?
   (A) Neither of them led the life that the painting depicts.
   (B) Wood thought that they embodied his most important values.
   (C) Wood exaggerated features of their faces to obtain a certain look.
   (D) They had to go to the farmhouse to model for the painting.

11) What can be inferred about Wood's career from Paragraph 2?
   (A) He was the only artist to focus on America's Midwest at the time.
   (B) *American Gothic* was an extension of his already well-known motifs.
   (C) He was keenly interested in characteristics of abstract painting.
   (D) *American Gothic* helped establish Wood professionally.

12) What is LIKELY true about the painting based on Paragraph 2?
   (A) Wood intended the painting to be a parody of farmers with fancy houses.
   (B) Most Americans felt that the painting validated their beliefs.
   (C) The subjects' expressions could be interpreted in many ways.
   (D) The painting became popular in Europe for its romanticization of American rural life.

Practice #4

Read the passage and choose the best answer to each question.

Star Trek was a network television series that premiered in the United States in 1966, when America was confronting domestic and international conflicts. The weekly episodes focused on the interplanetary crew of a "star ship" that was exploring space in the future. The crew encountered humanoid life forms and usually helped them solve a problem, such as war or discrimination. *Star Trek* had a low budget and was canceled after three seasons. Then, during the 1970s, it was rerun* frequently during afternoons and early evenings, reaching a younger generation. The show became a *cult classic*, or a series with intensely loyal supporters. *Star Trek* eventually spawned many movies and other series.

The original *Star Trek* was unusual for its time because it presented a multiethnic cast. The actors portrayed a team of cooperative professionals from many countries. One of the characters, Uhura, was the first African-American woman character on television with science-related profession.

A number of astronauts and other scientists have said that watching *Star Trek* affected their career choices when they were young. In addition, some inventors have said that the imaginary technology on *Star Trek* gave them ideas for desirable and innovative devices. For example, cell phones, Bluetooth technology, flat-screen television, and computer tablets are among the many inventions that resemble *Star Trek*'s fictional technology.

*Rerun: showing an episode after its original broadcast date

13) Based on Paragraph 1, which of the following can be inferred about the original *Star Trek* themes?

(A) They tended to be about tragic circumstances and events.

(B) They were socially and politically relevant to Americans in the 1960s.

(C) They were mainly focused on what the imaginary technology could do.

(D) They exposed the many terrifying problems of the future.

14) According to Paragraph 1, what can be inferred about *Star Trek* fans?

(A) They were people who already loved science and technology.

(B) Many were exposed to the show through reruns.

(C) They all watched the show as children in the 1970s.

(D) Many held religious beliefs based on the show.

15) Based on Paragraphs 1 and 2, what is the LIKELY way that the original *Star Trek* influenced people's views?

(A) It raised expectations that people would be able to do what the characters did.

(B) It created a backlash because it only featured one African-American character.

(C) It made Americans less apt to fund space programs.

(D) It increased optimism about peace and international cooperation in the future.

16) According Paragraph 3, it is PROBABLY true that some inventors of technological products

(A) stole engineering designs from *Star Trek* producers

(B) have already surpassed the devices from the original series

(C) set out to try to create devices that they remembered from *Star Trek*

(D) had already patented products that were first showcased on *Star Trek*

Practice #5

Read the passage and choose the best answer to each question.

In the late 19th and early 20th centuries, a movement known as *Modernism* transformed the culture and arts in many countries by rejecting the idea of certainty. For example, Modernist art does not try to present a "truthful" image of a person or a scene. For Modernists, there can never be a truthful image because what seems like objective reality is actually a *subjective viewpoint*, or one person's way of seeing. Thus, painters such as Pablo Picasso concentrated on how they, themselves, saw shape and color rather than on how a scene "really" looks. In music, composers embraced atonal* sounds that interested them. In literature, writers tried reproducing the highly personal way an individual thinks.

Postmodernists of the late 20th century felt that Modernism did not go far enough in emphasizing multiple perspectives. For example, Postmodernists pointed to the way that Modernist urban planners attempted to solve urban problems with massive, uniform developments, not taking into account the differing desires of the intended inhabitants. Postmodernism focuses on variety, multiculturalism, and audience personalization. A Postmodern artist and an art viewer are co-constructors of the viewing experience; the artist does not presume to control it.

Atonal: pertaining to music lacking a distinct key

17) Based on Paragraph 1, what can be inferred about Modernism?
   (A) It considered most classical works to be lying about life.
   (B) It was not very influential because people found it disconcerting.
   (C) It questioned principles that had always seemed obvious.
   (D) It presented art as an unbiased representation of reality.

18) Based on Paragraph 1, Modernist expression PROBABLY had which of the following primary goals?
   (A) Create societal distrust of all science and art
   (B) Promote self-reflection about truthfulness
   (C) Astonish the public with unusual works
   (D) Explore the artist's unique perspective

19) According to Paragraph 2, which of the following MOST ACCURATELY reflects a primary aim of Postmodernist culture?
   (A) To be more interactive with the audience
   (B) To increase conceptual complexity
   (C) To de-emphasize individualism in philosophical questions
   (D) To better appreciate imagination and fantasy

20) Based on Paragraph 2, which of the following would LIKELY be categorized as Postmodern?
   (A) A symphony based on a classic story
   (B) A symphony that completely rejects traditional sounds
   (C) A symphony that incorporates music from many cultures
   (D) A symphony that appears on television

Practice #6

Read the passage and choose the best answer to each question.

The name "America" derives from the name of an Italian, Amerigo Vespucci, who was a merchant in Spain at the end of the 15th century. Vespucci was a supplier for at least one of the voyages of Italian explorer Christopher Columbus, who believed that he was traveling back and forth to Asia, or "the Indies." Hoping to find a lucrative trade route, Vespucci joined several Spanish and Portuguese expeditions across the treacherous Atlantic Ocean between 1497 and 1504, less than a decade after Columbus made his first trans-Atlantic voyage to the Americas. Because of Vespucci's interest in navigation, he studied the stars, estimated longitude, and recorded details about much of what he observed during these voyages.

Two of Vespucci's letters describing his voyages were published. The first was titled *Mundus Novas*, or *New World*, because unlike Columbus, Vespucci realized that the land he was seeing was not India or any other part of Asia, but another continent altogether. The letters described the people he encountered and their cultural customs. The letters created a sensation among Europeans, outselling Columbus' journals. In 1507, a German *cartographer*, or mapmaker, published 1,000 copies of the first world map showing a Western Hemisphere. The cartographer included a landmass that he labeled *America*, which was a Latin form of Amerigo. He also published a book containing a Latin translation of "The Four Voyages of Amerigo Vespucci," purportedly one of Vespucci's own letters.

21) Which of the following can be inferred about Amerigo Vespucci from Paragraph 1?
   (A) He could foresee the exciting changes about to happen in Spain.
   (B) He was willing to risk his safety to increase his trading opportunities.
   (C) He developed a professional rivalry with Christopher Columbus.
   (D) He made spontaneous decisions about joining risky journeys.

22) What can be inferred from Paragraph 1 about Amerigo Vespucci's voyages?
   (A) He knew that he wanted to publish his travel records later.
   (B) He kept records of what the ship's crew said and did.
   (C) He applied astronomy and geometry to discern his ships' locations.
   (D) He was the first European to keep records of the New World.

23) The letters described in Paragraph 2 PROBABLY "created a sensation" because the European public
   (A) felt shocked and amazed that a large, unknown landmass existed
   (B) was divided between those who agreed and those who did not
   (C) panicked about the possibility of one country's ownership over the new lands
   (D) became uneasy about unfamiliar peoples and cultures

24) What can be inferred from Paragraph 2 about the German cartographer?
   (A) He did not know anything about Christopher Columbus.
   (B) He was influenced by Amerigo Vespucci's published letters.
   (C) He was a colleague of Amerigo Vespucci.
   (D) He knew that his decision would have vast consequences.

Practice #7

Read the passage and choose the best answer to each question.

The *Anglo-Saxon Chronicle* is an unusual historical record of England. It was started during the reign of Alfred the Great around 890 CE. Alfred launched a number of projects to stimulate education and literacy in his Anglo-Saxon kingdom of Wessex. After years of Danish attacks, in which monasteries had been pillaged, few people were able to read or write Latin. Therefore, Alfred advocated writing in the Anglo-Saxon language of the day, now called *Old English*. During this period of intellectual revival, an anonymous scribe compiled a year-by-year list of events in English history. The record indicates that the Roman invasion occurred in 60 BCE and identifies events up to the scribe's own time nearly 1,000 years later.

Nine copies of the manuscript were made by hand and carried to different monasteries around the kingdom. From that point on, generations of monastery scribes contributed to the manuscripts by listing lunar and solar eclipses, battles, and actions of kings and church officials. Historians can thus compare independent versions of the same events. Some of the manuscripts' entries end fairly soon after their distribution to the monasteries, but one was continued for 264 years, well after the Anglo-Saxons had been conquered by the Normans in 1066 CE. Additionally, the chronicle provides insights into the development of the English language, as one part of the chronicle shows the transformation of Old English into Middle English during the 12th century.

25) From Paragraph 2, what can be inferred about the events listed in the chronicle?
(A) Most monks who served as scribes were personally familiar with kings.
(B) Anglo-Saxon society was war-like and barbaric.
(C) The temporary blocking out of the Sun or Moon was seen as important.
(D) Guidelines in the manuscripts controlled topics that scribes could include.

26) Based on Paragraph 2, what is one LIKELY reason that the *Anglo-Saxon Chronicle* is significant to modern scholars?
(A) It provides records of older forms of the English language.
(B) It covers every aspect of English history during the Middle Ages.
(C) It offers insight into common people's daily life in England during the era.
(D) It explains why societal leaders took certain actions.

27) What can be inferred about the Anglo-Saxons from the passage?
(A) Most of their literature was stored in monasteries.
(B) Danish raids on Wessex completely devastated local populations.
(C) Rulers such as Alfred did not read Latin.
(D) They lived in a relatively peaceful territory.

28) Based on the passage, the Anglo-Saxons PROBABLY copied and distributed the chronicles in order to
(A) declare Alfred's accomplishments and victories
(B) force people to write and read in a particular language
(C) provide intellectuals with material to read
(D) increase the chances of preserving Anglo-Saxon history

Practice #8

Read the passage and choose the best answer to each question.

Changes in one population in an ecosystem can impact virtually every other population in the ecosystem. One example is the fluctuation of the deer population on the Kaibob Plateau, a high, forested area in Arizona. In the late 1800s, the deer population suffered due to food competition with domestic animals brought to the area. In 1906, President Theodore Roosevelt led a campaign to protect deer on the plateau from hunters. At the same time, federal rangers began to kill species at the "top" of the food chain such as wolves, mountain lions, and bobcats. With few human or natural predators, the deer population boomed. However, after overgrazing the plant populations, the deer began to starve in huge numbers. In 1939, the state of Arizona began to allow some deer hunting while reducing the hunting of the deer's natural predators.

Another example comes from the north Pacific Ocean. In recent decades, increasingly efficient fishing boats have overharvested certain fish populations there, which decreased a food source for seals and sea lions, causing their populations to decrease. Usually seals and sea lions comprise most of the diet of *orcas*, also known as killer whales. Because seals and sea lions became scarce, orcas began to consume the much smaller sea otters. As a result, the sea otter population declined, leaving its favorite prey, sea urchins, with no predators. The unchecked sea urchin population overconsumed *kelp*, a sea plant that forms an underwater forest. Hundreds of species that depend on the kelp forest were adversely affected.

29) Based on Paragraph 1, what can be inferred about Theodore Roosevelt?
  (A) He was not generally supportive of hunting as a sport.
  (B) He was motivated to prevent extinction of all animals.
  (C) He allowed a social goal to override research-supported conclusions.
  (D) His attempts to replenish a species were misguided.

30) Which of the following can be inferred from Paragraph 1 about ecology?
  (A) Plants are the only living things that an ecological system cannot do without.
  (B) An ecological system that includes deer is likely to be problematic.
  (C) A habitat's top predators are crucial to maintaining ecological balance.
  (D) Efforts to manage species cannot be counterproductive.

31) Which of the following statements about a food chain can be inferred from Paragraph 2?
  (A) The orca is one of the top predatory animal of the North Pacific food chain.
  (B) Ocean environments are uniquely vulnerable to ecological imbalance.
  (C) Overfishing primarily affects large predators in an aquatic ecosystem.
  (D) Seals, sea lions, and otters occupy identical places in the Pacific food chain.

32) From Paragraph 2, it is LIKELY that
  (A) the fishing industry has diminished in size
  (B) technology has enabled the fishing industry to overfish the North Pacific
  (C) fishing vessels will be forced to move to the Atlantic Ocean to be successful
  (D) the consumers will find lower fish prices in markets

Read the passage and choose the best answer to each question.

A *Free Trade Agreement*, or FTA, is a pact between two or more countries to slash *tariffs*, or taxes that countries levy on imported goods. The benefit of free trade between nations was articulated by David Ricardo in 1817. He argued that if two countries participate in the free flow of goods, both of them will gain because each will gravitate toward its *comparative* advantage. As an illustration, even if "X" can produce wool AND cotton, and "Y" can produce only cotton, "X" has a comparative advantage specializing in wool, which creates a comparative advantage for "Y" in cotton. Wool *and* cotton will be less expensive to consumers in both countries, and everyone will have more cloth.

Generally speaking, manufacturers tend to support free trade because it lowers the price of their products in other countries, and they can sell more. Other supporters of free trade say that the practice strengthens ties between countries and allows for more *transparency*, or public access to information about businesses and trade. In contrast, opposition to free trade pacts often focuses on the effects on agriculture. For example, small corn farmers in Mexico could fail permanently if Mexican markets were flooded with cheaper corn from the United States. Representatives of labor unions also argue that the gains from free trade are not fairly distributed within countries. They say that with FTAs, factory jobs usually shift to poorer countries, where companies may exploit nonunion workers.

33) Based on Paragraph 1, which of the following is PROBABLY true about tariffs?
   (A) They started to taper off after 1817.
   (B) Less affluent countries have them more often.
   (C) Imposing tariffs discourages imports.
   (D) They create important tax revenue.

34) What can be inferred from the example of wool and cotton in Paragraph 1?
   (A) Wool will always produce better returns on investment than cotton.
   (B) The quality of a product will determine its comparative advantage.
   (C) A diverse economy is better than a singularly focused one.
   (D) Free trade will increase consumers' standard of living.

35) Based on Paragraph 2, what benefits do FTA supporters PROBABLY ascribe to *transparency*?
   (A) Disclosure of technological secrets
   (B) Increasing adherence to laws regarding production and trade
   (C) More government involvement in corporate transactions
   (D) Investors making better investments

36) From Paragraph 2, what can be inferred about opponents of FTAs?
   (A) They tend to be focused on manufacturing.
   (B) They are often farmers and labor unions.
   (C) They believe that financial transactions should be regulated.
   (D) They do not support trade with other countries.

Practice #10

Read the passage and choose the best answer to each question.

Many individuals in history have faced conflict between societal law and their personal understanding of divine law. The Greek playwright Sophocles explored the issue in 441 BCE with the play *Antigone*. In the play, the character Antigone is the niece of the King, Creon. He has forbidden anyone to bury Antigone's dead brother, who was considered a rebel and a traitor after trying to take kingship during an earlier civil war. Antigone defies her uncle because she believes that the laws of the Greek gods demand proper burial and that it would be more serious to defy the gods than her uncle. Creon tells her that she is not above his law, and that there is nothing worse than disobeying the king's authority. As a result of Antigone's transgression, Creon sentences her to be sealed in a cave. Antigone commits suicide instead of accepting her death sentence. Because Creon's son was in love with and engaged to Antigone, he commits suicide out of grief, which in turn causes Creon's wife to kill herself, filling Creon with remorse for his actions.

A real-life example of invoking a higher law is that of Oscar Romero, the Catholic archbishop of El Salvador from 1977 to 1980. Romero became distressed at the Salvadoran government's violent repression during the era, and in spite of death threats against him, he used his position to speak out. In one radio broadcast, Romero famously addressed government soldiers, telling them to stop following orders to kill: "No one has to fulfill an immoral law.... I beg you, I beseech you, I order you in the name of God: Stop the repression!" The next day, Romero was assassinated. Although years of civil war followed, Romero is now celebrated as a national hero in El Salvador.

37) Based on Paragraph 1, it can be inferred that the character Antigone believes that
   (A) her brother was blameless
   (B) she should be the ruler in place of Creon
   (C) gods do not care about the actions of humans
   (D) gods can be dangerous if angered

38) Based on Paragraph 1, what can be inferred about Creon's character?
   (A) He is skeptical about the existence of the gods.
   (B) He is envious of Antigone's loyalty to her brother.
   (C) He is conscientious of the needs of others.
   (D) He is resolute in his beliefs and decisions.

39) Based on Paragraph 2, which of the following is the PROBABLE belief of the author about death threats against Romero?
   (A) The threats did not frighten him.
   (B) Those in power wished to silence him.
   (C) Many people wanted to destroy the church.
   (D) The threats were inevitable for a public figure.

40) Which of the following can be inferred about El Salvador, based on Paragraph 2?
   (A) It has experienced much political change since Romero's era.
   (B) The impact of Romero's broadcast was negligible.
   (C) Leaders in the country are often murdered.
   (D) Salvadorans found Romero to be morally ambiguous.

POP QUIZ

Select the vocabulary word or phrase that has the closest meaning.

6. **divert**
   A. redirect
   B. injure
   C. concentrate
   D. assign

7. **subtle**
   A. novel
   B. affecting
   C. faint
   D. skilled

8. **elusive**
   A. massive
   B. evasive
   C. amiable
   D. pious

9. **incompatible**
   A. austere
   B. indistinct
   C. incompossible
   D. rudimentary

10. **garner**
    A. accentuate
    B. disclose
    C. lure
    D. gather

16. **reject**
    A. cherish
    B. assent
    C. discover
    D. refuse

17. **concentrate**
    A. speculate
    B. alloy
    C. focus
    D. deny

18. **perspective**
    A. outlook
    B. initiative
    C. aptitude
    D. diversity

19. **derive from**
    A. escape from
    B. stem from
    C. suffer from
    D. graduate from

20. **lucrative**
    A. profitable
    B. consumable
    C. predictive
    D. expansive

26. **unchecked**
    A. unrestrained
    B. nonessential
    C. unabashed
    D. nonoperative

27. **adversely**
    A. immediately
    B. additionally
    C. unfavorably
    D. apathetically

28. **override**
    A. damage
    B. overrule
    C. ascertain
    D. incorporate

29. **replenish**
    A. restore
    B. respect
    C. renovate
    D. recognize

30. **diminish**
    A. administer
    B. decrease
    C. embrace
    D. observe

1. **skeptical**
   A. fearless
   B. meager
   C. durable
   D. dubious

2. **dissipate**
   A. disappear
   B. augment
   C. deter
   D. accentuate

3. **hoax**
   A. specimen
   B. delusion
   C. fake
   D. misconception

4. **validate**
   A. authenticate
   B. reproduce
   C. imitate
   D. conceal

5. **sensory**
   A. accidental
   B. flexible
   C. noisy
   D. neurological

11. **satirize**
    A. tickle
    B. startle
    C. cause
    D. lampoon

12. **figurative**
    A. breakable
    B. generous
    C. metaphorical
    D. indigenous

13. **premiere**
    A. devotion
    B. debut
    C. drawback
    D. tendency

14. **spawn**
    A. produce
    B. underscore
    C. banish
    D. quarry

15. **backlash**
    A. chain reaction
    B. adverse reaction
    C. sudden response
    D. calm response

21. **encounter**
    A. restore
    B. meet
    C. include
    D. displace

22. **pillage**
    A. establish
    B. flourish
    C. correct
    D. plunder

23. **conquer**
    A. overthrow
    B. thrive
    C. mar
    D. moderate

24. **virtually**
    A. nearly
    B. morally
    C. actually
    D. allegedly

25. **fluctuation**
    A. stabilization
    B. integration
    C. finalization
    D. variation

31. **levy**
    A. combine
    B. command
    C. charge
    D. comprise

32. **disclosure**
    A. description
    B. revival
    C. assortment
    D. announcement

33. **remorse**
    A. reward
    B. victoryr
    C. confusion
    D. regret

34. **negligible**
    A. forsaken
    B. huge
    C. minor
    D. noticeable

35. **ambiguous**
    A. naïve
    B. cryptic
    C. supplementary
    D. eloquent

1D 2A 3C 4A 5D 6A 7C 8B 9C 10D 11D 12C 13B 14A 15B 16D 17C 18A 19B
20A 21B 22D 23A 24A 25D 26A 27C 28B 29A 30B 31C 32D 33D 34C 35B

I. What Is a Purpose Question?

Purpose

The purpose question asks you to identify how certain pieces of information help you understand either a detail or the main idea of the passage. A *purpose* is a reason why the author included particular information in a passage. For example, the purpose of a passage can be to inform you about a topic or to persuade the reader.

A. PURPOSE QUESTION MODEL

Leonardo da Vinci, who lived from 1452 to 1519, is best known as the Renaissance artist who painted *Mona Lisa*, but he was also an imaginative inventor, architect, and scientist. He kept daily records of ideas and observations. On many of his pages of sketches and notes, **Leonardo wrote his letters and sentences in reverse** in such a way that the notes could best be read by holding them up to a mirror. He also abbreviated many words in a kind of personal code. Scholars speculate about whether Leonardo wrote in such a way because he found it easier, or because he wanted to keep his budding ideas secret.

7. Why does the author mention the highlighted phrase in the passage?

(A) To praise Leonardo for a clever ability

(B) To prove that Leonardo was worried about plagiarism

(C) To point out a mysterious habit of a famous thinker

(D) To summarize characteristics of the pages

B. PURPOSE QUESTION FORMATS

The author discusses _____ in order to _____.

The author mentions _____ in order to _____.

Why does the author discuss _____?

Why does the author compare _____ to _____?

Why does the author mention _____?

Why does the author order the information by _____?

Why does the author use the word/the punctuation mark when discussing _____?

C. TIPS

1. Generally, purpose questions ask you to create logical connections between sentences or paragraphs.

2. The overall purpose sometimes can be found in the topic sentence, which is normally the first sentence.

3. Incorrect answers are too vague, are false according to the passage, or are unrelated to the passage.

II. Hacking Strategy

Purpose
Question

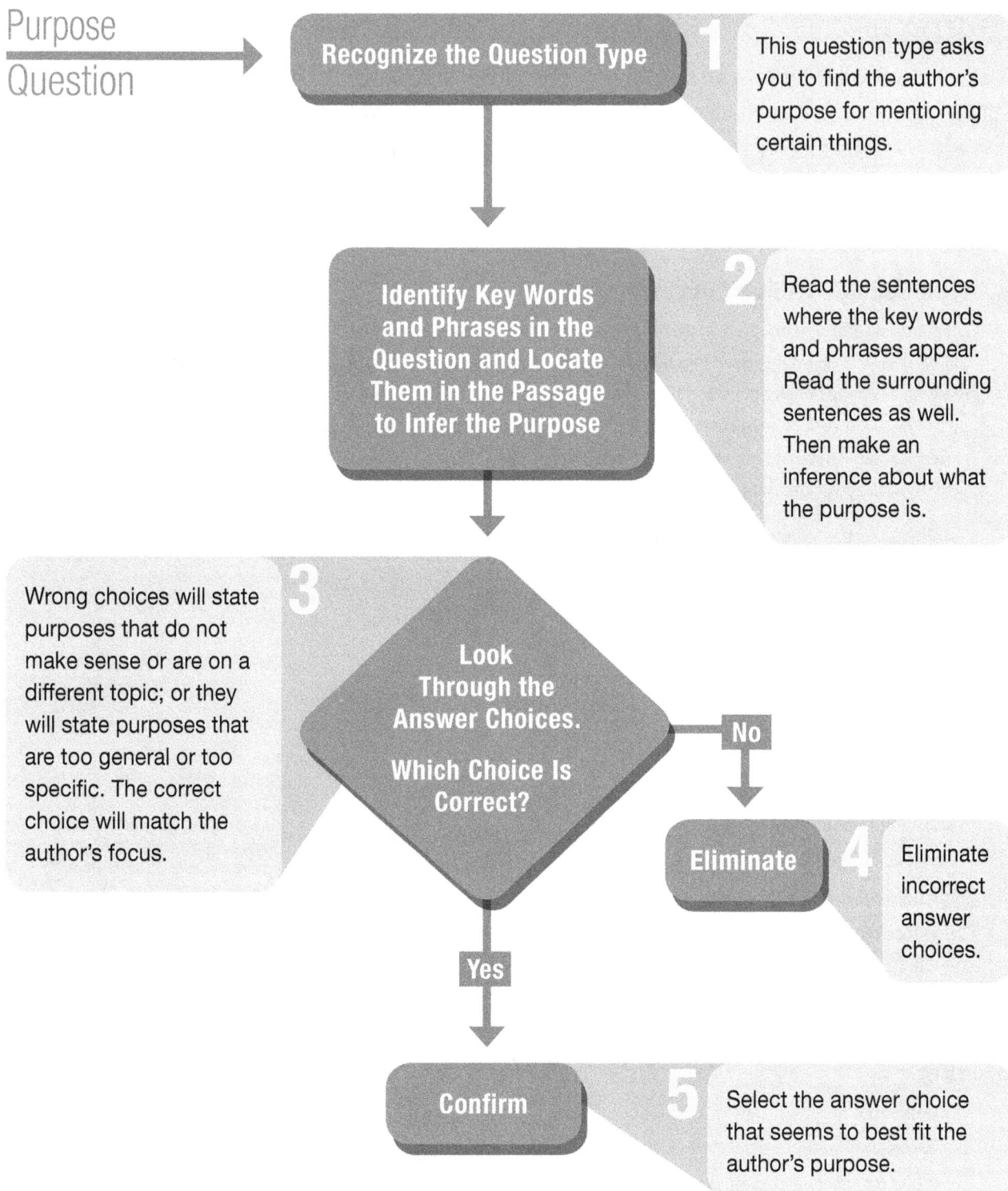

Recognize the Question Type

1 This question type asks you to find the author's purpose for mentioning certain things.

Identify Key Words and Phrases in the Question and Locate Them in the Passage to Infer the Purpose

2 Read the sentences where the key words and phrases appear. Read the surrounding sentences as well. Then make an inference about what the purpose is.

Wrong choices will state purposes that do not make sense or are on a different topic; or they will state purposes that are too general or too specific. The correct choice will match the author's focus.

3 **Look Through the Answer Choices.**

Which Choice Is Correct?

No

Yes

Eliminate

4 Eliminate incorrect answer choices.

Confirm

5 Select the answer choice that seems to best fit the author's purpose.

EXAMPLE

1

Leonardo da Vinci, who lived from 1452 to 1519, is best known as the Renaissance artist who painted *Mona Lisa*, but he was also a brilliant inventor, architect, and scientist. He kept daily records of ideas and observations. On many of his pages of sketches and notes, **Leonardo wrote his letters and sentences in reverse** in such a way that the notes could best be read by holding them up to a mirror. He also abbreviated many words in a kind of personal code. Scholars speculate about whether Leonardo wrote in such a way because he found it easier, or because he wanted to keep his budding ideas secret.

Why does the author mention the highlighted phrase in the passage?

(A) To praise Leonardo for a clever ability
(B) To prove that Leonardo was worried about plagiarism
(C) To point out a mysterious habit of a famous thinker
(D) To summarize characteristics of the pages

2

Why does the author mention the highlighted phrase in the passage?

Leonardo da Vinci, who lived from 1452 to 1519, is best known as the Renaissance artist who painted *Mona Lisa*, but he was also a brilliant inventor, architect, and scientist. He kept <u>daily records</u> of <u>ideas and observations</u>. On many of his pages of sketches and notes, **Leonardo wrote his letters and sentences in reverse** in such a way that the notes could best be read by holding them up to a mirror. He also abbreviated many words in a kind of <u>personal code</u>. <u>Scholars speculate</u> about whether Leonardo wrote in such a way because he found it easier, or because he wanted to keep his budding ideas secret.

The key words give us clues to the journal-like nature of the records. We can also infer from the key words "Scholars speculate" that Leonardo's motivation for writing his personal notes backward is unknown.

3

Look for the choice that focuses on the purpose and message of the passage.

Why does the author mention the highlighted phrase in the passage?

(A) To praise Leonardo for a clever ability
(B) To prove that Leonardo was worried about plagiarism
(C) To point out a mysterious habit of a famous thinker
(D) To summarize characteristics of the pages

• Select **Choice C** because the author brings the habit to the attention of the reader and explains that Leonardo's motivation is unknown, or *mysterious*.

4

• Eliminate **Choice A** because the author does not discuss the skill required to produce mirror-image writing.
• Eliminate **Choice B** because the author refers to speculation but not proof, making this choice inaccurate.
• Eliminate **Choice D** because the author mentions only two characteristics of the pages and not all of them, making this choice too general.

5

Select the correct answer — **Choice C**.

III. Quick Look

Words Used in Purpose Answer Choices

Word	Definition
Argue	to try to prove a point
Caution	to warn against
Classify	to put in a category
Compare	to examine two or more things in relation to each other
Contrast	to show that one thing is different from the other
Criticize	to show something's faults
Define	to tell what something is
Describe	to provide details about what something is like
Emphasize	to highlight important information
Explain	to tell why something is
Give Examples	to provide instances in order to further explain something
Identify	to tell what something is (similar to **Define**)
Illustrate	to give further information (similar to **Describe**)
Introduce	to bring forward a new idea or information
Persuade	to try to convince the reader to agree
Point Out	to bring something to attention
Praise	to admire or compliment something
Predict	to foretell something
Prove	to show that something is true
Show	to state something
Summarize	to state something in a shorter way, giving only the main ideas
Support	to show that something is true; to provide evidence for it
Trace	to follow the course of something's development
Warn	to give caution about something

IV. Warm Up

Read each topic and each detail below. Then choose whether the purpose of each detail is to:

*Persuade = PER	*Describe = DES	*Criticize = CR

1. **Topic:** College degree in philosophy   _____
   Detail: Some people may feel that earning a college degree in philosophy is impractical in terms of preparing for a job. However, studying philosophy can be worthwhile because it develops critical thinking and clear reasoning abilities. Many potential employers and graduate schools, especially law schools, may value such skills

2. **Topic:** The movie *Fantasia*, a 1940 motion picture produced by Walt Disney   _____
   Detail: The 1940s Walt Disney film *Fantasia* attempts to blend classical music and live action with cartoons. Today's audiences are likely to find the animated dinosaurs, dancing ostriches, and hippos wearing tutus to be slightly ludicrous and otherwise a bit dull.

3. **Topic:** Dietary Approaches to Stop Hypertension (DASH) diet plan   _____
   Detail: Medical research supports preventing or controlling high blood pressure with the U.S. government-backed Dietary Approach to Stop Hypertension, or DASH. The approach calls for consuming about 10 small servings of fruits and vegetables per day, as well as whole grains and low-fat proteins, and very little salt.

4. **Topic:** Bats of Carlsbad Caverns National Park in New Mexico   _____
   Detail: Carlsbad Caverns National Park in New Mexico is home to thousands of Mexican free-tailed bats. By day, the bats hang from the natural ceilings of vast caves, and at dusk they emerge, flying upwards in massive spirals. The bats spend the night eating mosquitoes, moths, and other insects.

5. **Topic:** Monty Python   _____
   Detail: Monty Python was a group of British comics who wrote and acted in the British television series *Monty Python's Flying Circus* from 1969 to 1974. The group later went on to create feature films that brought them international fame, including *Monty Python's Life of Brian*. The group forged a signature brand of surreal, unconventional humor that revolutionized comedy and should be considered classic.

6. **Topic**: American Revolutionary War spies _____

   Detail: During the American Revolutionary War, the American (or Continental) army and the British army both employed tricks, propaganda, bribery, and spying. Many of the spies were females who posed as cooks and maids. The most infamous spy, Benedict Arnold, was a general in the Continental Army but passed information to the British in exchange for money.

7. **Topic**: Video games _____

   Detail: Many popular video games are modeled on war, adventure, or space travel. Extended playing of violent games may have adverse psychological effects on those who may already be prone to violence. But even those who choose less violent games may be at risk of cramps and damage in the muscles, tendons, and ligaments of the hands and wrists.

8. **Topic**: Fashion industry _____

   Detail: Fashion consumers can mitigate their impact on the environment by purchasing clothing made of fabric that is sustainably produced. They can also donate used apparel to charities rather than throwing it away. However, neither of these actions will change the underlying environmental hazard: global markets produce clothing at prices that are too low so that people think of it as a disposable good.

9. **Topic**: Round houses _____

   Detail: A round or polygonal home can have a cone-shaped roof with beams supported by a center post, a design resembling spokes of a wheel. Traditional Mongolian yurts demonstrate the benefits of round homes. They can be simple and easy to build, and they are less vulnerable to wind than square homes. Because they have no corners and have fewer exterior walls, round homes may be easier to heat as well.

10. **Topic**: Soccer _____

    Detail: In soccer, if the ball goes over the goal lines out of bounds after a defending player has touched it, referees can award an attacking team a corner kick, or a chance to restart play with a kick from the corner of the field next to the goal. The attacking team may be able to score with the corner kick alone, but usually the corner kick provides a pass to another attacking player.

V. Quick Practice

Practice #1

Read the passage and choose the best answer to each question.

Sending convicted criminals to prison is a fairly recent development in human history. Until modern times, societies typically punished wrongdoers with execution, public beating, or exile. In Europe, jails were only for debtors or people who were awaiting trial or punishment. However, in 18th century England and France, ideals associated with **the Enlightenment** held that depriving people of liberty was punishment enough and more humane than execution, so communities began to imprison convicted criminals. **Ever since then, Western societies have been debating how best to build and manage prisons, including the ongoing question of whether they should keep prisoners together or apart.**

In the American colonies in 1773, the state of Pennsylvania launched a project to try to rehabilitate criminals: the Walnut Street Jail. The founders may have envisioned an enlightened form of correction, but in reality the jail was **horrendous**. No matter what their crime or mental state was, men, women, and children prisoners were kept together in large halls. Besides being dangerous, conditions were unsanitary and led to disease.

Eventually, reformers from the community convinced the state to improve conditions, and then to build small cells at the jail for individual isolation. Reformers believed that prisoners in total solitary confinement would utilize the time for self-reflection, prayer, and rehabilitation. However, it was discovered that total isolation from other humans caused the prisoners to develop mental health problems, and the program was abandoned, though the practice continued elsewhere.

1) Why does the author mention "**the Enlightenment**" in Paragraph 1?
   (A) To explain the scientific basis for community jails and prisons
   (B) To identify the background for new attitudes toward punishment
   (C) To argue that England and France have a history of humane philosophy
   (D) To contrast older and newer methods of criminal justice

2) Why does the author include the highlighted sentence in Paragraph 1?
   (A) To praise Western societies for seeking the best solutions
   (B) To caution readers not to draw conclusions about prisons
   (C) To describe the history of prisons in Western societies
   (D) To introduce a societal issue that is still unresolved

3) Why does the author use the word "**horrendous**" in Paragraph 2?
   (A) To contrast an ideal plan with its actual consequences
   (B) To persuade the reader that the jail was uncomfortable
   (C) To point out the cruelty of the jail's founders and operators
   (D) To classify the Walnut Street Jail as a failed experiment

4) The author probably mentions isolating prisoners in Paragraph 3 in order to
   (A) give an example of gradual changes in the Walnut Street Jail
   (B) praise the reformers who wanted to instill peace at the jail
   (C) trace the history of solitary confinement as a punishment
   (D) describe an extreme attempt to improve prisoners

Practice #2

Read the passage and choose the best answer to each question.

Benjamin Banneker was a free 18th-century African-American man who became well known for his math-related achievements, including helping to survey the boundaries for the new capital, **Washington, D.C.** He was born on his parents' farm in 1731 in Maryland. During his lifetime, enslavement of African Americans in the colonies was growing, and by the end of his life, slaves made up more than half the population in his state. Even free African Americans were treated as second-class citizens, and their children were not permitted to attend school with white children.

However, Banneker, learned to read from his grandmother, and then went to a school run by **Quakers**, a religious sect that opposed slavery. A Quaker friend later lent him books about mathematics and astronomy. An early sign of his cleverness was that, at the age of 22, Banneker made a carved wooden clock using only a pocket watch as a model. The **clock kept time accurately** for decades.

While running his parents' farm, Banneker created and published almanacs for the region based on his own calculations. An *almanac* provides information for the next calendar year, listing weather predictions, times for sunrises and sunsets, and tide charts. Banneker's almanac included astronomical and medical information, essays, and poetry. People working to abolish slavery, or *abolitionists*, used Banneker's almanacs as an example of what African Americans could accomplish if they had education and opportunity.

Banneker, too, was not afraid to make his abolitionist views public. At one point, he wrote to Thomas Jefferson, who had written passionately about freedom in the Declaration of Independence, to protest Jefferson's hypocritical ownership of slaves. Jefferson wrote back praising Banneker but not answering his protest. Banneker published the correspondence.

5) Why does the author mention "**Washington, D.C.**" in Paragraph 1?
   (A) To give an example of one of Banneker's many jobs
   (B) To identify the main reason for Banneker's fame
   (C) To point out an example of Banneker's math-related achievements
   (D) To emphasize how undeveloped the landscape was during Banneker's era

6) Why does the author mention "**Quakers**" in Paragraph 2?
   (A) To explain how Banneker had the opportunity to go to school
   (B) To identify an important influence on Banneker's anti-slavery views
   (C) To emphasize the role played by religion in Banneker's life
   (D) To summarize the social context of Banneker's achievements

7) Why does the author mention that the "**clock kept time accurately**" in Paragraph 2?
   (A) To praise the clock for working perfectly
   (B) To illustrate an important reason for Banneker's fame
   (C) To support the stated idea that Banneker was ingenious
   (D) To trace the history of Banneker's technical skill

8) What is the primary purpose of Paragraph 4?
   (A) To identify Thomas Jefferson as the author of an important document
   (B) To praise Banneker for writing to an important political figure
   (C) To describe Banneker's courage in publicly protesting slavery
   (D) To point out that Thomas Jefferson believed in freedom

Practice #3

Read the passage and choose the best answer to each question.

Sound is vibration that reaches the sensors in a listener's inner ear. For example, if someone plucks a guitar string, it starts a back-and-forth vibration in the matter surrounding it, usually air. Each vibration pressures the air in all directions around the guitar. The vibration's force pushes air molecules that then push other air molecules, propagating a wave of force through the air. Because air molecules are *elastic*, they are attracted back to their original position once the force has passed, so they are ready to propagate the next force or sound wave.

When the sound waves pass far enough through the air to reach an ear, they stimulate nerves that communicate sound to the brain. If there were no molecules of any substance around the plucked guitar string, for example if the moving string were in the vacuum of outer space with no air, there would be no sound.

Interestingly, water is a good conductor of sound because its molecules are denser and more elastic than air. In fact, sound waves pass through water five times faster than through air. Underwater environments are not as quiet for their inhabitants as people may imagine. Fish have internal "ears" that can sense sound vibrations, and because water in the ocean can effectively conduct sounds for long distances, ocean fish might be able to hear faraway earthquakes, whale songs, and colliding icebergs. Hearing allows fish to be more aware of predators and prey and to swim together in schools. In addition, more than 500 species of fish are known to make sounds in order to communicate with each other. By moving different parts of their bodies, some fish make sounds such as grunts, clicks, croaks, and rhythmic beats.

9) Why does the author order the information by starting with a definition in Paragraph 1?
   (A) To suggest important details that may be unknown to the reader
   (B) To persuade the reader that the information is accurate
   (C) To introduce the more extended explanation that follows
   (D) To define technical terms that will be used in the passage

10) The author mentions the "vacuum of outer space" in Paragraph 2 in order to
   (A) classify substances as either elastic or inelastic
   (B) describe something about space outside Earth's atmosphere
   (C) emphasize the importance of the air on Earth's surface
   (D) contrast the paragraph's main example with an opposite case

11) Why does the author include the highlighted sentence in Paragraph 3?
   (A) To compare different conceptual viewpoints about water
   (B) To support a hypothesis about marine sensory organs
   (C) To introduce details about an unpredictable environment
   (D) To point out technical information about sound in different mediums

12) Why does the author mention "grunts, clicks, croaks, and rhythmic beats" in Paragraph 3?
   (A) To argue that fish are not very different from people
   (B) To illustrate specific features of a particular habitat
   (C) To highlight the variety of fish in the oceans
   (D) To support the statement that fish make sounds

Practice #4

Read the passage and choose the best answer to each question.

Empirical research in the field of psychology has found that the more grateful a person feels, the better he or she feels. A number of studies have shown that people who develop a sense of gratitude tend to be happier, calmer, and more satisfied with their lives. They tend not to dwell on past problems and mistakes that they have made, but on how much their experiences have taught them. **Thus, grateful people tend to have more positive feelings about themselves and others**. When people are thankful for what they have learned and gained, they are also more inclined to be generous to others.

While the benefits of gratitude may provide a new focus for social science researchers, many of the world's religions have long histories of encouraging people to give thanks for what they have. Clear examples are the many ancient traditions of giving thanks to a deity or deities during harvest season when there is ample food. In many Asian cultures, autumn festivals of thanksgiving after the rice harvest center on the Moon. In China, people light lanterns, give each other "moon cakes," and gather with friends and family to view and appreciate the Moon. People set out offerings of thanks to the rejuvenating goddess who, according to tradition, lives on the Moon. Chinese culture associates roundness with unity and fulfillment, so the roundness of the Moon contributes to the festival's theme of gratitude.

In **Vietnam**, the autumn harvest festival focuses on the Moon but has evolved into a day to appreciate and give thanks for children. Under a full Moon, children in costumes participate in street parades by carrying colorful lanterns in the shapes of moons, stars, and animals. Parents give their children small cakes with round "moons" of sweet filling inside.

13) Why does the author mention "**Empirical research**" in Paragraph 1?
(A) To argue that the passage's statements are always true
(B) To identify the sources of the research referred to in the passage
(C) To give examples of the research that has been done
(D) To point out that the following statements are based on evidence

14) Why does the author include the second highlighted sentence in Paragraph 1?
(A) To explain why ungrateful people have more problems than others
(B) To praise people who manage to be optimistic in all situations
(C) To show a cause-and-effect relationship between gratitude and other feelings
(D) To warn readers about the consequences of a lack of self-esteem

15) Which of the following describes the relationship between Paragraphs 1 and 2?
(A) Paragraph 1 explains the psychological mysteries that Paragraph 2 summarizes.
(B) Paragraph 1 points out the basis of generosity, and Paragraph 2 explains it with further details.
(C) Paragraph 1 introduces a theory, and Paragraph 2 provides support based on ancient cultural practices.
(D) Paragraph 1 introduces valid points, and Paragraph 2 describes where they were discovered.

16) The author mentions "**Vietnam**" in Paragraph 3 in order to
(A) contrast the country's holiday customs with others
(B) illustrate the sights, sounds, and tastes of a unique place
(C) introduce one culture's unique focus at harvest time
(D) argue that Vietnamese people feel more gratitude than other people

Practice #5

Read the passage and choose the best answer to each question.

European and American social norms regarding hats have varied greatly across time and circumstances. During the Medieval period, knights removed coverings of their face and head when greeting a superior. **Removing outerwear** signaled vulnerability and deference in the same way that **bowing or kneeling** did. Moreover, an uncovered head and face allowed the other person to confirm a knight's identity and his **peaceful intentions**. Today, Western men are still expected to remove hats as a way of demonstrating humble respect for others. Taking off one's hat for funeral processions and patriotic displays is considered especially important. A man also is expected to remove his hat in many indoor situations.

Western women's hat-wearing norms developed differently, partly out of the idea that one signals respect of others by dressing in one's best outfit to see them. **In the 19th and early 20th century, Victorian etiquette rules dictated that upper-class ladies should wear highly decorated hats when engaged in the ritual of visiting other ladies' homes.** Because these lavish hats were often secured to the hair with pins, women were not expected to remove their hats inside others' homes. Though women do not usually wear such hats today, it is still normally acceptable for them to leave their hats in place.

Some religious settings call for covering the head to show respect. For example, some branches of Judaism, Christianity, and Islam have encouraged both men and women to cover their heads at times. In these traditions, head-covering may symbolize *humbleness, or spiritual humility*, among other virtues.

17) Why does the author compare "**removing outerwear**" to "**bowing or kneeling**" in Paragraph 1?
   (A) To illustrate similar means of demonstrating submission or yielding
   (B) To support and verify reasons for bowing or kneeling
   (C) To introduce theories about ancient military cultural norms
   (D) To persuade readers about the importance of good manners

18) In Paragraph 1, the author mentions "**peaceful intentions**" in order to
   (A) explain something about how knights greeted superiors
   (B) identify an underlying message that also showed respect
   (C) praise the moral character of people who remove their hats
   (D) describe a minor detail about etiquette for men during the Medieval period

19) Why does the author include the highlighted sentence in Paragraph 2?
   (A) To introduce a new topic regarding European history
   (B) To support the previous statement with a pertinent example
   (C) To trace the origin of hat ornamentation for ladies
   (D) To criticize a particular time period for its excessive fashions

20) Why does the author discuss "*humbleness, or spiritual humility*" in Paragraph 3?
   (A) To explore a different facet of the importance of head covering
   (B) To emphasize the belief that one is not more powerful than others
   (C) To summarize all the religious symbolism regarding covering the head
   (D) To classify head covering as a certain type of social norm

Practice #6

Read the passage and choose the best answer to each question.

Coffee "beans" are actually the seeds of red berries that grow on the *coffea* shrub. The plant originally grew wild in mountain rainforests of southwestern Ethiopia. Coffea probably evolved with the chemical *caffeine* as a **defense** in its leaves, berries, and seeds; caffeine paralyzes and kills some insects that eat it. For humans, caffeine is usually nontoxic, and in fact, it acts as a mild stimulant.

No one knows exactly how people learned to make coffee from the seeds of coffea. Legend tells of an Ethiopian goatherd named Kaldi who "discovered" the plant because he noticed that when his goats ate the red berries, they became energized. Yet another story attributes the discovery to a healer named Omar, who was **exiled** to the wilderness from the city of Mocha in what is now Yemen. Starving, he tried different ways of making the berries near his cave edible, including boiling the roasted beans. The drink gave Omar the energy he needed, and soon he was invited to return to Mocha, where he was declared a saint for discovering a "miracle" drug.

What is certain is that different ethnic groups made drinks and snacks using the ground-up berries and leaves of the coffea plant, which they later cultivated. The plant was cultivated by the 14th century in eastern Ethiopia and Yemen, where Islamic Sufi monks brewed coffee from the roasted beans, reportedly to boost their energy during prayer. By the mid-1500s, coffee drinking had spread throughout the Islamic world, including Northern Africa, Saudi Arabia, the Eastern Mediterranean, Persia, and Turkey. **Coffee houses** became popular places for men to gather for casual conversation and board games, as well as for political, business, or artistic exchanges.

21) Why does the author use the word "**defense**" in Paragraph 1?
   (A) To emphasize the threat that insects pose to a rainforest environment
   (B) To define the chemical processes within the coffea plant
   (C) To identify the evolutionary advantage of producing caffeine
   (D) To describe the environmental impact of the coffea plant

22) Why does the author mention "**exiled**" in Paragraph 2?
   (A) To describe a story's characters
   (B) To support a story's validity
   (C) To point out a story's theme
   (D) To set up a story's plot

23) Why does the author include the highlighted sentence in Paragraph 3?
   (A) To give examples of some uses of coffea that may be unfamiliar to readers
   (B) To support statements in the passage about the coffea plant
   (C) To describe early agricultural and culinary practices of some ethnic groups
   (D) To explain that some facts about the history of coffee are not based only on legend

24) In Paragraph 3, the author mentions "**coffee houses**" in order to
   (A) introduce a widespread cultural phenomenon that was spurred by coffee
   (B) contrast secular coffee drinking with earlier spiritual uses
   (C) describe a religious institution of the Islamic world in the 16th century
   (D) argue that coffee brings about political, business, and artistic development

Practice #7

Read the passage and choose the best answer to each question.

Glucose is a type of sugar that provides fuel for living organisms to "burn" in a chemical process that creates energy. The bodies of animals and humans break down food to get glucose, and then make the glucose available to cells. Most animal cells can burn glucose because they contain tiny but mighty *mitochondria*.

The mitochondrial process is not unlike a campfire. A campfire requires oxygen and burns wood for fuel, extracting the fuel's energy in the form of light and heat for the enjoyment of campers. The campfire releases carbon dioxide as a waste product. Mitochondria also use oxygen to burn glucose in a process called *aerobic respiration*, and they then release carbon dioxide as a waste product. The end product of the process is energy-rich molecules of adenosine triphosphate, or ATP. The cell can "spend" ATP as "currency," by breaking down ATP molecules and releasing charged electrons, which supply heat energy.

Mitochondria are quite different from other *organelles*, or parts within cells. Most organelles are pockets surrounded by one membrane, but each mitochondrion has two membranes. A mitochondrion is protected by its outer membrane, and has a **creased inner membrane** holding the water and proteins that it uses. **Most importantly, unlike other organelles, each mitochondrion contains its own genes, separate from the cell's.** Thus, scientists have hypothesized that mitochondria first formed 2 billion years ago when a type of bacteria began to live in organisms' cells in a *symbiotic relationship*. In other words, both the host organism and the guest bacteria gained an advantage. The bacteria helped the cells by providing energy, while the cells nurtured the bacteria. According to this hypothesis, the bacteria eventually evolved into mitochondria, but continued to maintain their own genetic material.

25) Which of the following describes the relationship between Paragraphs 1 and 2?
(A) Paragraph 2 corrects the common misunderstandings stated in Paragraph 1.
(B) Paragraph 2 elaborates on Paragraph 1's description of how organisms use mitochondria.
(C) Paragraph 2 contrasts the creation of glucose in Paragraph 1 with its consumption.
(D) Paragraph 2 points out and highlights the most important concepts from Paragraph 1.

26) In Paragraph 2, what is the author's primary purpose?
(A) To describe biological structures by using an example
(B) To improve comprehension of a process by using imagery
(C) To disprove abstract concepts by using metaphor
(D) To build a case for a hypothesis by using multiple details

27) In Paragraph 3, the author mentions mitochondria's "**creased inner membrane**" in order to
(A) show unique characteristics of mitochondria by providing details
(B) prove that mitochondria are more sophisticated than other organelles
(C) summarize all the unique characteristics of mitochondria
(D) classify the area surrounded by the inner membrane as a different type of organelle

28) Why does the author mention the highlighted sentence in Paragraph 3?
(A) To introduce the science of genetics to the discussion
(B) To predict that mitochondria could evolve independently from cells in the future
(C) To emphasize the previous point made in the paragraph
(D) To identify the basis of the scientific hypothesis that follows

Practice #8

Read the passage and choose the best answer to each question.

The 19th century was an era of industrialization in the United States. During this time, many people were working in factories and mines, often in miserable conditions at extremely low wages. Furthermore, to help their families earn a living, many **children had to work long hours underground or around perilous machinery**. Organizing worker protests against bad working conditions and inadequate wages had long been illegal, and workers seemed to have no *recourse*, or no way to seek change. Yet labor unions did manage to organize. One of the most famous early organizers was an unlikely leader: a 152-centimeters tall grandmotherly Irish woman, invariably wearing an antique black dress and a black hat. Mary Harris Jones, also known as "Mother Jones," gained national prominence as a feisty and fearless union organizer. One opponent called her "the most dangerous woman in America."

Jones had **arduous experiences** in her personal life, starting with her childhood in Ireland during the Great Potato Famine of 1845 to 1849. To escape the famine, she and her family immigrated to Canada. As an adult, Jones worked as a dressmaker and as a teacher, and married and settled in Tennessee, where she and her husband survived the Civil War. Shortly thereafter, however, her husband and their four young children all died in a yellow fever epidemic in 1867. Jones moved to Chicago and opened a dressmaking shop, but it burned down in the Great Chicago Fire of 1871, along with her home and possessions.

From that point on, Jones seldom had an established home, dedicating herself to labor activism for more than 50 years. Even when she was quite elderly, she traveled widely to lead or support workers' boycotts, strikes, and protests, which were still considered illegal at the time. A fiery, tough, humorous speaker, she was jailed many times for her defiant actions. Jones worked officially over many years for the United Mine Workers, **whose members she called "my boys."** She also worked to publicize and abolish child labor, and she lived to see many states outlaw it.

29) Why does the author include the highlighted information in Paragraph 1?
   (A) To describe the early experiences of Jones and her children
   (B) To contrast the work done by adults with that done by children
   (C) To criticize a practice that exploited vulnerable people
   (D) To persuade readers that industrialization was harmful overall

30) In Paragraph 1, how does the introduction of "Mother Jones" relate to the earlier discussion of workers?
   (A) It points out the natural consequences of low wages.
   (B) It introduces the only person who solved workers' problems.
   (C) It proves and supports earlier points about worker protests.
   (D) It sets a small person against a giant problem.

31) Why does the author detail Jones' arduous experiences in Paragraph 2?
   (A) To persuade readers to feel sympathy for Jones
   (B) To explain the events that shaped an unusual personality
   (C) To emphasize the most important point of the passage
   (D) To show the general effects of famine, war, disease, and fire

32) The author includes the highlighted information in Paragraph 3 in order to
   (A) criticize Jones for feeling a sense of ownership
   (B) give an example of Jones' charismatic public speaking
   (C) describe Jones' strong emotional commitment to miners
   (D) point out a historical fact that eventually caused change

Practice #9

Read the passage and choose the best answer to each question.

Many writers have imagined societies that they think would be ideal, or **_utopian_**, in terms of political and social structures. In the fourth century BCE, Plato outlined societal ideals in *The Republic*, and in 1516 CE, Thomas More described a fair and equal island community in his fictional book *Utopia*. It is more common, however, for writers to set their stories in dystopian societies. *Dystopias* are imagined worlds where life is degraded and unbearable, often because of political or corporate oppression. **Frequently, readers are able to recognize elements of contemporary society that the writer has extrapolated in an extreme form as a warning.** For example, the 2008 young adult series *The Hunger Games*, by Suzanne Collins, imagines a dehumanized post-apocalyptic world where privileged people enjoy watching children commit deadly violence on television.

Ray Bradbury's novel *Fahrenheit 451* was published in 1953, when American society feared the spread of communism so much that libraries and schools were **censoring books**. At the time, screenwriters, film directors, and actors were *blacklisted*, or denied employment, if they were suspected of having communist sympathies. In response to the censorship and blacklisting, Bradbury imagined a society of the future where individual thought seldom occurs. In his novel, the public has allowed itself to be nearly hypnotized by mass media, with television screens covering entire walls of houses. Even conversation is considered suspicious, and **"firemen" purposely set fire to the homes of book owners**. In the novel, the government enforces censorship mainly because it does not want people to notice that it is about to launch a nuclear war. This underscores Bradbury's warning that it is suicidal not to read and think for oneself.

33) The author mentions "***utopian***" societies in Paragraph 1 in order to
   (A) contrast one genre of literature with its opposite genre
   (B) praise works of literature that were unique in their time
   (C) classify the works of Plato and Thomas More together
   (D) argue that ideal political and social structures could exist

34) Why does the author include the highlighted sentence in Paragraph 1?
   (A) To warn readers that dystopian fiction is extrapolated
   (B) To point out that dystopian fiction is frighteningly real
   (C) To define a central component of most dystopian fiction
   (D) To trace the origin of the genre of dystopian fiction

35) Why does the author mention "**censoring books**" in Paragraph 2?
   (A) To explain Bradbury's concern that his books would be censored
   (B) To give an example of a phenomenon that the author extrapolated
   (C) To describe a surprising detail about the 1950s in the U.S.
   (D) To caution against supporting censorship of any kind

36) In Paragraph 2, the author includes the highlighted information in order to
   (A) summarize the setting in *Fahrenheit 451*
   (B) describe a drastic form of censorship
   (C) predict that most governments will find ways to censor
   (D) illustrate an important theme in Bradbury's novels

Practice #10

Read the passage and choose the best answer to each question.

José Guadalupe Posada has been called "the printmaker to the Mexican people." Born in 1852 in Northern Mexico, Posada eventually created an estimated 15,000 images in his work at lithography shops and small newspapers. Part of his job was to illustrate sensational news items of the day, such as murders, and print the illustrations on newspaper to be sold via street vendors. But his main legacy today is his political cartooning, which satirized Mexico's dictatorial ruler, Porfirio Díaz, and other powerful people. Posada's **visual statements** about injustices and abuse of power were easy for the largely illiterate public to understand. Thus Posada is credited with helping to instigate the Mexican Revolution of 1910, which overthrew Porfirio Díaz.

One way that Posada kept his satire humorous was to draw all the characters as skeletons, known as *calaveras*, adapted from the Spanish word for "skulls." The *calaveras* generally wore outlandish clothing and big grins. Although his message was usually serious, Posada's audience found his deathly clowns amusing because *pre-Columbian*, **or pre-Spanish, cultures in Mexico had long embraced a sense of familiarity with death and dead spirits**.

Posada died in 1913 in obscurity, but in the 1920s, after the revolution, his work was rediscovered and celebrated. Posada's cheerful skeletons became iconic symbols in Mexico, and they are now frequently incorporated into the work of contemporary artisans and artists. **Diego Rivera**, the internationally renowned 20th-century Mexican muralist, included a *calavera* at the center of a painting as a tribute to Posada. Rivera lived near Posada's lithography shop as a child and stopped in regularly. He later said that Posada had a major influence on his artistic development.

37) What is the author's primary purpose in Paragraph 1?
   (A) To explain the importance of newspaper illustrations in history
   (B) To criticize a dictatorial ruler of the early 20th century
   (C) To describe how a cartoonist gained historical prominence
   (D) To trace the roots of the Mexican Revolution

38) The author describes Posada's work as "**visual statements**" in Paragraph 1 in order to
   (A) emphasize the artist's conveying of information without words
   (B) point out the appealing look of the artist's graphic designs
   (C) prove the power of imagery in politics
   (D) criticize the artist for assuming his audience was illiterate

39) Why does the author include the highlighted phrase in Paragraph 2?
   (A) To caution the reader about threats to safety
   (B) To explain a peculiarity about the region
   (C) To entertain the reader with the paradox of jovial horror
   (D) To describe many aspects of early cultures in Mexico

40) Why does the author mention "**Diego Rivera**" in Paragraph 3?
   (A) To identify the reason that Posada is remembered in Mexico today
   (B) To compare Posada with one of the greatest artists of the 20th century
   (C) To explain the reason that Diego Rivera used a *calavera* in one of his paintings
   (D) To describe one aspect of Posada's impact on art and culture

Select the vocabulary word or phrase that has the closest meaning.

1. convicted
A. sentenced
B. allowed
C. disappointed
D. dispersed

2. deprive
A. inform
B. restrain
C. rob
D. dispel

3. enlightened
A. informed
B. activated
C. recognized
D. disciplined

4. horrendous
A. worthless
B. honorable
C. absurd
D. terrible

5. confinement
A. expiration
B. precursor
C. internment
D. faction

6. rehabilitation
A. extension
B. restoration
C. hazard
D. feasibility

7. abolish
A. eliminate
B. rebuke
C. forecast
D. praise

8. passionate
A. various
B. obsolete
C. promoted
D. ardent

9. hypocritical
A. dishonest
B. critical
C. durable
D. reclusive

10. correspondence
A. withdrawal
B. velocity
C. letter
D. demise

11. pluck
A. pick
B. prevent
C. involve
D. retreat

12. propagate
A. plant
B. spread
C. impair
D. notify

13. conceptual
A. innovative
B. overall
C. mature
D. theoretical

14. gratitude
A. seriousness
B. reaction
C. condemnation
D. thankfulness

15. rejuvenating
A. vitalizing
B. cultivating
C. blocking
D. monitoring

16. vulnerability
A. plausibility
B. irascibility
C. exposure
D. nomenclature

17. deference
A. praise
B. smugness
C. indifference
D. submission

18. humble
A. modest
B. plain
C. delightful
D. respectful

19. norms
A. standards
B. laws
C. anomalies
D. regulations

20. lavish
A. expensive
B. irrelevant
C. luxurious
D. ponderous

21. pertinent
A. grateful
B. vigorous
C. tantalizing
D. relevant

22. paralyze
A. degenerate
B. designate
C. fulfill
D. incapacitate

23. energize
A. compress
B. invigorate
C. extrapolate
D. initiate

24. attribute
A. refer
B. recommend
C. render
D. ascribe

25. extract
A. opportune
B. release
C. pilfer
D. express

26. respiration
A. restoration
B. breathing
C. greed
D. modification

27. perilous
A. submissive
B. improvised
C. audacious
D. hazardous

28. prominence
A. association
B. fame
C. designation
D. proponent

29. epidemic
A. outbreak
B. outdated
C. worthless
D. aesthetic

30. degrade
A. prevent
B. advance
C. debase
D. frustrate

31. unbearable
A. super
B. pivotal
C. generable
D. intolerable

32. oppression
A. suppression
B. construction
C. destruction
D. compassion

33. sensational
A. sensitive
B. shocking
C. operative
D. awkward

34. embrace
A. fulfill
B. acquiesce
C. allow
D. accept

35. obscurity
A. indecisiveness
B. anonymity
C. assurance
D. abruption

1A 2C 3A 4D 5C 6B 7A 8D 9A 10C 11A 12B 13D 14D 15A 16C 17D 18A 19A
20C 21D 22D 23B 24D 25B 26B 27D 28B 29A 30C 31D 32A 33B 34D 35B

I. What Is a Paraphrase Question?

Paraphrase

The paraphrase question asks you to identify the answer choice that best restates the meaning of the sentence(s) in a given passage. The restatement may summarize the main ideas in a simpler way and omit the less important details. The paraphrase may use *synonyms*, or different words that have similar meanings, to convey the same points. Furthermore, sentences may change when paraphrased: the sentence length and/or the sentence structure – the order of the words and the clauses within the sentence – may vary from the original.

A. PARAPHRASE QUESTION MODEL

Kangaroo Island off the southwestern coast of Australia retains some natural Australian "bush" habitat. The island has a population of around 4,600 people, but unlike the mainland, non-native rabbits and foxes were never introduced there, and the island was never completely grazed by sheep. **Native birds and other animals have continued to thrive in the island's pristine vegetation.** The Western grey kangaroo, which gives the island its name, shares protected coastal parks on the island with koalas, echidnas, and seals. Up to 140,000 tourists visit the island each year hoping to catch sight of some of the wildlife.

8. Which of the following best paraphrases the highlighted section?
    (A) Animals that evolved in the island's natural areas still survive there.
    (B) The bandicoot, the platypus, and many other animals live successfully on native plants there.
    (C) Animals such as native birds can live well on the island's lush greenery.
    (D) The island's unspoiled plant communities still nurture native fauna.

B. PARAPHRASE QUESTION FORMATS

Which of the following best expresses the highlighted section?
Which of the following best expresses the highlighted section of Paragraph _____?
Which of the following best paraphrases _____?

C. TIPS

1. Look for paraphrases that contain the necessary information.
2. Incorrect answers may:
    • include unnecessary information
    • omit essential information
    • add information not in the passage
    • be inaccurate according to the passage
    • have a different meaning than the original passage

II. Hacking Strategy

Paraphrase
Question

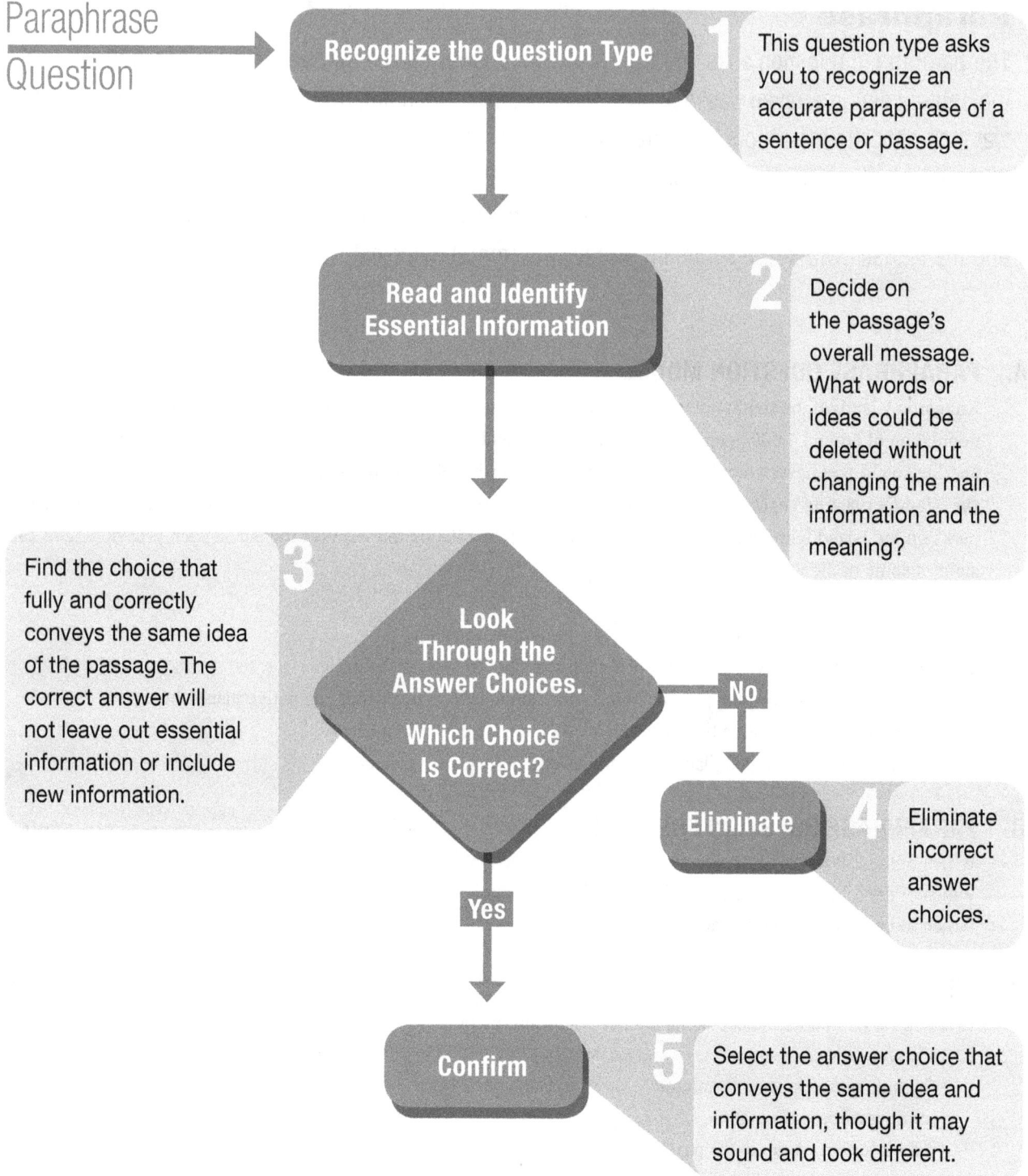

1 Recognize the Question Type

This question type asks you to recognize an accurate paraphrase of a sentence or passage.

2 Read and Identify Essential Information

Decide on the passage's overall message. What words or ideas could be deleted without changing the main information and the meaning?

3 Find the choice that fully and correctly conveys the same idea of the passage. The correct answer will not leave out essential information or include new information.

Look Through the Answer Choices.

Which Choice Is Correct?

No

4 Eliminate

Eliminate incorrect answer choices.

Yes

5 Confirm

Select the answer choice that conveys the same idea and information, though it may sound and look different.

1 Kangaroo Island off the southwestern coast of Australia retains some natural Australian "bush" habitat. The island has a population of around 4,600 people, but unlike the mainland, non-native rabbits and foxes were never introduced there, and the island was never completely grazed by sheep. **Native birds and other animals have continued to thrive in the island's pristine vegetation.** The Western grey kangaroo, which gives the island its name, shares protected coastal parks on the island with koalas, echidnas, and seals. Up to 140,000 tourists visit the island each year hoping to catch sight of some of the wildlife.

Which of the following best paraphrases the highlighted section?
(A) Animals that evolved in the island's natural areas still survive there.
(B) The bandicoot, the platypus, and many other animals live successfully on native plants there.
(C) Animals such as native birds can live well on the island's lush greenery.
(D) The island's unspoiled plant communities still nurture native fauna.

2 Native birds and other animals have continued to thrive in the island's pristine vegetation.

The passage emphasizes that native creatures flourish in the unspoiled vegetation. The correct answer will convey these key ideas.

3 **Which choice conveys the main idea in a different way, without introducing new conclusions or details?**

• Select **Choice D** because it uses synonyms to express the same information as the highlighted sentence and is therefore the best choice.

4
• Eliminate **Choice A** because it omits essential details about vegetation.
• Eliminate **Choice B** because it introduces the bandicoot and the platypus, which are not mentioned in the original sentence.
• Eliminate **Choice C** because it is inaccurate, as the passage does not describe the vegetation as "lush."

5 Select the correct answer — **Choice D**.

III. Quick Look

Paraphrase Structure Types

Type 1	Type 2	Type 3
Type 1 changes the wording and uses different sentence structure or different ordered clauses.	Type 2 uses synonyms and other expressions to convey the same idea.	Type 3 uses the referent instead of the pronoun to convey the same idea.
Original Sentence	**Original Sentence**	**Original Sentence**
If people are feeling adventurous, 1 they can join a river-rafting trip led 2 by a qualified rafter. 2 Clause 2 Clause 1 destination (resulting sentence)	Flying **through** the canyons **via** zip-line is an **excellent** outdoor activity for **thrill-seeking individuals**. excellent perfect	**The lodge** helps visitors to warm up and enjoy the scenery because **it** features a grand fireplace and a view of the waterfall. The lodge it referent pronoun
Paraphrase	**Paraphrase**	**Paraphrase**
Guided river-rafting expeditions 2 are available for those seeking a 2 1 thrilling experience. 1 Clause 1 Clause 2 destination (resulting sentence)	Flying **along** a zip-line course is a **perfect** outdoor activity for **thrill-seekers**. perfect excellent	**The lodge** helps warm up visitors with a blazing fire and offers windows overlooking the waterfall. The lodge referent

IV. Warm Up

Read each sentence below. Then choose the answer that provides the more accurate paraphrase.

1. Bread dough rises when microbes called *yeast* are activated by warm water; the yeast exhales carbon dioxide bubbles, which form the sponge-like holes in bread.
   - (A) The air pockets in bread come from carbon dioxide that is released in the form of bubbles by living yeast microbes.
   - (B) The first step in bread-making is to add dormant, dry yeast to tepid water, which activates it, and then add starches and sugars to feed the yeast.

2. Walt Whitman's poetry helped develop *free verse*, which relies on imagery and word choice rather than formal structure; as Whitman writes in a poem, "My words itch at your ears till you understand them."
   - (A) Walt Whitman was the first poet to use free verse, which is informal and should be read aloud to emphasize the sounds of the words.
   - (B) Walt Whitman broke away from conventional rules of poetry and wrote in *free verse*, or poetry that often creates images in the reader's mind.

3. The ancient Chinese, Assyrians, and Persians associated umbrellas with emperors and nobles of high social rank.
   - (A) People in some of the world's early civilizations considered the umbrella to be a symbol of elevated social status.
   - (B) Emperors throughout the ages have enjoyed the special privilege of going outside without discomfort from rain or hot sunshine due to umbrellas.

4. Rock climbing sometimes requires ascending vertical walls using only small indentations or protrusions in the rock face for finger-holds and toe-holds.
   - (A) Rock climbers who are attempting to go up a sheer wall may have to cling to tiny holes or bumps in the rock.
   - (B) The sport of rock climbing is psychologically and physically challenging because people may have to go up walls even if there are only slight cracks in them.

5. In 1929, British novelist Virginia Woolf wrote about an imaginary sister of William Shakespeare, who could not write brilliant literature despite her genius because she was busy with household chores.
   - (A) Virginia Woolf tried to analyze the work of William Shakespeare's sister, but she was not able to because of gender discrimination.
   - (B) Virginia Woolf argued that household demands would have prevented even the most potentially talented women from writing.

6. Through a telescope, Jupiter appears to have dark and light stripes parallel to its equator, but the "stripes" are actually powerful winds that never stop blowing in alternating directions.
   - (A) Jupiter's apparent bands of matter are caused by swift currents of air moving in opposite directions.
   - (B) Jupiter's gaseous surface features strong winds that cause relentless storms.

7. The first major Western work published in the field of *ichthyology*, or the study of fish, was the *Histoire Naturelle des Poissons*, which provided illustrations and descriptions of the 5,000 fish species known in 1848; it filled 22 volumes and took 20 years to write.

   (A) The *Histoire Naturelle des Poissons*, or the *Natural History of Fish*, was published in 1848 to elucidate everything known in the field of ichthyology at the time.

   (B) In 1848, it took 22 volumes to consolidate information about all 5,000 fish species known to Western ichthyologists, and it required 20 years to complete.

8. Music composers can determine a composition's mood by emphasizing bright higher-pitched instruments such as the piccolo and violin, or poignant lower-pitched instruments such as the bassoon and cello.

   (A) Composers of music must decide on a piece's *instrumentation*, or the instruments that will play certain parts, including when to emphasize wind sections or string sections of the orchestra.

   (B) Composers of music must be aware of how an instrument's pitch will affect the piece's mood; higher pitches may lend a happier note, and lower pitches may be more moving.

9. *Phonological awareness*, or the ability to recognize distinct sounds within a spoken word, is considered an important pre-reading skill in young children, and may be developed through rhymes.

   (A) Young children must learn rhymes or they cannot develop *phonological awareness*, or the awareness of the sounds of words, without which they may not be able to learn to read.

   (B) Rhyming helps children learn to distinguish different sounds within words, or gain *phonological awareness*, which is a fundamental aspect of literacy.

10. Magnets can generate electricity because fluctuating magnetic charges force movement of the free electrons in a conductor.

    (A) Magnets cause electrical currents when alternating positive and negative charges induce electrons to move within a conductor.

    (B) Magnetic and electrical forces are linked, as they can pass electrons back and forth between them.

V. Quick Practice

Practice
#1

Read the passage. Then answer the question that follows.

Within philosophy, ontology focuses on metaphysical questions involving existence. Questions such as "What is reality?" or "Is reality knowable?" are ontological questions. Ontological viewpoints can be broken into the two broad categories of materialism and idealism.

Greek materialists Democritus and Epicurus proposed in the fourth century BCE that reality consists of matter and processes caused by the collision of indivisible units of matter, which they called *atoms*. **For materialists, matter and energy are the ultimate reality, and even life itself and people's own thoughts are simply the end result of interacting matter.** Materialists tend to believe that since people's thoughts are not separate from their bodies, thoughts end at death. To discern what is real, materialists believe in observing nature and explaining it in terms of the laws of nature. The implication is that reality is objective – real objects and phenomena exist whether an individual perceives them or not.

Idealists, on the other hand, believe that the ultimate reality is immaterial. For some, reality is an all-inclusive consciousness, such as a god or gods. Moreover, reality for idealists involves mind and spirit, and therefore may only be experienced subjectively, as each person experiences it. For example, Wang Yangming, a Chinese philosopher who lived from 1472 to 1529, believed that the human mind constructed reality. He said that the world did not shape the mind, but rather that the mind made sense of the world.

1) Which of the following best expresses the information in the highlighted section of Paragraph 1?
   (A) Ontology seeks to uphold ideas proving a given individual's existence on Earth.
   (B) Whether any entity can be said to exist is an important consideration for any philosopher.
   (C) The branch of philosophy that examines fundamental questions about being is ontology.
   (D) When philosophical theories attempt to explain why and how life exists, they are involved in ontology.

2) Which of the following best expresses the information in the highlighted section of Paragraph 2?
   (A) Materialists tend to believe that mind and spirit exist, but they are not the most fundamental reality.
   (B) For materialists, life and other "real" things come to be through the interplay of substantive elements.
   (C) Materialists emphasize the importance of the natural processes of the universe.
   (D) Living, reasoning, and imagining are the ultimate reality, according to materialist philosophy.

3) Which of the following best expresses the information in the highlighted section of Paragraph 3?
   (A) Idealists visualize reality as having substance.
   (B) In idealism, reality does not exist.
   (C) The belief that reality is intangible is a feature of idealistic thought.
   (D) Idealist principles of reality directly oppose those of materialism.

Practice #2

Read the passage. Then answer the question that follows.

By the time he died in 1972, British archaeologist and paleoanthropologist Louis Leakey had influenced the future in many profound ways. **He and his wife, Mary, became world famous when they unearthed fossils and footprints of early hominids, early humans and their closely related species, in Africa's Olduvai Gorge in the 1950s and 1960s, illuminating important aspects of human evolution.** The Leakeys' children and one of their grandchildren also contributed to the field of archaeology.

Beyond his own work and that of his offspring, Louis Leakey's legacy includes his influence on primate research. **His interest in human evolution led to a curiosity about apes in the wild because apes and humans developed from a common ancestor.** As a result, he sought out people who would be willing to live in the wilderness observing apes. To fund the researchers' studies, he founded a nonprofit institute.

Three of the long-term field researchers Leakey recruited have been called *Leakey's Angels*, a reference to a television series in the 1970s called *Charlie's Angels*, in which an unseen man gave assignments to three female detectives. **One of Leakey's "angels" is Jane Goodall, who was a secretary when Leakey first hired her to observe chimpanzees in Tanzania in 1960.** Another is the late Dian Fossey, an occupational therapist whom he hired in 1967 to study mountain gorillas in Rwanda. The third is Birute Galdikas, a graduate student whom he sent to observe orangutans in Borneo starting in 1971. Each of the "angels" eventually published significant findings and launched ongoing efforts to save apes from extinction.

4) Which of the following best expresses the information in the highlighted section of Paragraph 1?
   (A) Louis and Mary Leakey spent many years making discoveries in an African riverbed known as the Olduvai Gorge.
   (B) Louis and Mary Leakey became celebrities in the 1950s and 1960s when they discovered and described the origins of humanity.
   (C) Louis and Mary Leakey were internationally known for finding fossils and other clues that helped explain how humans developed.
   (D) Louis and Mary Leakey were famous for finding footprints and remains of human-like individuals.

5) Which of the following best expresses the information in the highlighted section of Paragraph 2?
   (A) He wanted to study apes to see whether any of their behavior patterns were similar to those of humans.
   (B) He wanted to learn more about ape behavior because apes have shared ancestry with humans.
   (C) He was intrigued by the uncontrolled behavior of the human species' closest living relatives.
   (D) He was already knowledgeable about human evolution and wanted to learn about the evolution of apes.

6) Which of the following best expresses the information in the highlighted section of Paragraph 3?
   (A) In 1960, Leakey hired an amateur field researcher by the name of Jane Goodall.
   (B) Jane Goodall was an office worker in Africa when she contacted Leakey and ended up getting hired to watch chimpanzees.
   (C) Before Leakey hired her to study chimpanzees in 1960, Jane Goodall was a secretary.
   (D) Leakey called his secretary, Jane Goodall, one of his "angels" and arranged for her to observe chimpanzees.

Practice #3

Read the passage. Then answer the question that follows.

In physics, the term *work* does not translate to *labor for money* but rather has the particular meaning of *the transfer of energy by a force through a distance*. In other words, work is the redistribution of energy from one object to another that results in movement. **French mathematician and mechanical engineer Gaspard-Gustave Coriolis introduced the term "work" in 1826 while contemplating the effects of force within machinery.**

Coriolis' understanding of work came from the realization that causing an object to move is essentially a process of transferring energy to it. In regards to work, energy is either potential or kinetic. *Potential energy* can be thought of as stored energy. **When a ball rests at the top of a slope, it has gravitational potential energy since gravity will cause it to roll down the hill as soon as someone applies force – which is a component of work – to get the ball rolling.** When the ball begins to roll, the potential energy converts to *kinetic energy*, which is the energy that is expended while it is moving.

In order to demonstrate his ideas about force, rotation, and energy, Coriolis wrote a book about the game of *billiards*, or pool. **When a player strikes a cue ball in billiards, the ball receives kinetic energy from the player and accelerates toward other balls on the table to transfer that energy in the form of a collision.** Thus, billiards is fundamentally a game of force and energy transfer, as the player provides the initial work to transfer energy from one ball to another. Today, Coriolis' fundamental principles are applied to many areas of physics, from predicting the motions of the planets to the interactions of the smallest particles.

7) Which of the following best paraphrases the information in the highlighted section of Paragraph 1?
 (A) Gaspard-Gustave Coriolis' definition of "work" caused him to invent a new type of machine in 1826.
 (B) In the early 19th century, Gaspard-Gustave Coriolis developed the principle of "work" based on his examinations of machinery.
 (C) Gaspard-Gustave Coriolis defined "work" as the effects of machinery based on observations of French industry.
 (D) Gaspard-Gustave Coriolis invented "work" to help contemporaries understand how machines operated in the early 19th century.

8) Which of the following best expresses the information in the highlighted section of Paragraph 2?
 (A) A ball contains stored, or potential, energy as it sits atop a slope until an external influence causes the ball to begin rolling downwards.
 (B) Gravitational potential energy creates force, which provides a catalyst for a ball resting on a hill to begin rolling downwards.
 (C) Potential energy is converted to force when a ball resting atop a slope is pushed down a hill.
 (D) When a person pushes a ball down a hill, the ball converts gravity and force into gravitational potential energy.

9) Which of the following best paraphrases the information in the highlighted section of Paragraph 3?
 (A) A collision in billiards is a result of the cue ball receiving energy from the other balls on the table.
 (B) When struck, the kinetic energy within the cue ball is redistributed to give energy to both the other balls and the player of billiards.
 (C) A collision in billiards results from the other balls exerting a force on the cue ball, which transfers kinetic energy to the player.
 (D) In billiards, a player transfers energy to the cue ball, which then collides with other balls and redistributes the original energy.

Practice #4

Read the passage. Then answer the question that follows.

Author Mary Shelley was only 21 when she published the classic novel *Frankenstein* in 1818. She got the idea after sitting through a rainy vacation reading ghost stories aloud with some writer friends, including her future husband, Percy Shelley, and the poet Lord Byron. Byron challenged each member of the group to create a tale of the supernatural. **Mary Shelley spun a tale of a scientist named Victor Frankenstein, who discovers a procedure to animate body parts from human corpses for the creation of a hideous 244-centimeter tall man.**

Shelley later turned her tale into a novel called *Frankenstein*, which describes Victor's obsession with creating life and his horror of the finished creation. Victor is so appalled by his unnamed creation that he abandons the "creature," who wanders alone in the wilderness. **Unable to find acceptance anywhere and feeling desperate and wronged, the created man repeatedly tracks down Victor Frankenstein and his friends and family.** Although he seeks education and wishes to be accepted by society, the created man slowly realizes that his appearance makes him a monster, so he begins to adopt the role of a monster, starting with the murder of Victor's brother. When Victor confronts the created man, the "creature" begs for forgiveness. Receiving none, the created man continues to seek murderous revenge against his neglectful creator, killing Victor's wife. At this point, the enraged Victor stops fleeing from his creation and instead pursues him.

With its gloomy, suspenseful atmosphere, *Frankenstein* has thrilled generations of people and has never been *out of print*, or in other words, publishers have never stopped printing and selling it. **Perhaps readers still find relevance in the topics that the novel explores: the ethical dilemmas inherent in pursuing science and technology.**

10) Which of the following best expresses the information in the highlighted section of Paragraph 1?
   (A) Mary Shelley was spinning while she made up a story about a terrible-looking monster named "Frankenstein."
   (B) The monster that Mary Shelley imagined was an ugly giant discovered and energized by a scientist.
   (C) Victor Frankenstein creates life in a horrific being sewn together from the bodies of different dead people.
   (D) The protagonist of Mary Shelley's story manages to spark life in a collection of parts from cadavers.

11) Which of the following best expresses the information in the highlighted section of Paragraph 2?
   (A) The "monster" does not want to be seen as a monster, and tries to find companionship with Victor Frankenstein.
   (B) Seeking revenge, the created man hunts down the monster and those closest to him.
   (C) The man to whom Frankenstein gave life chases Frankenstein and his associates due to his anger at being an outcast.
   (D) Longing for love and companionship motivates both of the two main characters, Victor Frankenstein and the monster.

12) Which of the following best expresses the information in the highlighted section of Paragraph 3?
   (A) It may be that the classic novel is read by fewer modern readers although society continues to fear tragic consequences of discoveries.
   (B) Even today, readers no doubt find comfort in the novel's theme of working out problems in science and technology.
   (C) People probably remain interested in pondering the role of responsibility in scientific and technological innovations.
   (D) Readers may disagree with the novel's theme of immorality among scientists and inventors.

Practice #5

Read the passage. Then answer the question that follows.

Investigative journalism involves finding and publishing facts about corruption, scandal, or the misuse of power in government or business. Strategies for investigative reporting include scrutinizing lawsuits, corporate financial filings, government reports, and other public records, as well as interviewing people who are sources of information. **Frequently, investigative journalists hope to bring about change by exposing neglectful or exploitative behavior.**

One of the most famous examples of investigative journalism in the United States is *The Jungle*, a novel by Upton Sinclair published in 1906. While working for a socialist newspaper, **Sinclair took a job in the meatpacking industry in Chicago for seven months, concealing his identity as a journalist, and gathered information that he later included in his novel.** Sinclair intended to expose the plight of the workers. However, the American public focused on the outrageously unsanitary and careless butchering and processing that he described, and Congress launched investigative hearings into the meatpacking industry. Lawmakers then created the forerunner of today's Food and Drug Administration to monitor food sanitation and safety.

Another famous example of investigative journalism is the 1963 book *The American Way of Death*, by Jessica Mitford. **The humorously acerbic book presented well-documented facts to expose ways that many businesses in the funeral industry at the time took advantage of grieving customers by steeply overcharging for funeral and burial services.** Mitford also quoted an embalming textbook to explain the procedures to prepare bodies for viewing. Readers were so shocked at the revelations that the book led to more government regulations for the funeral industry as well as a consumer trend toward cremation rather than burial in caskets.

13) Which of the following best expresses the information in the highlighted section of Paragraph 1?
   (A) Reporters usually aim to make wrongdoing public so that it can be stopped.
   (B) Often journalists use investigative work to bring up issues that people have not cared about.
   (C) In many cases, ambitious young journalists become famous with their published investigations.
   (D) Transforming society is the main idea behind many investigative media reports.

14) Which of the following best expresses the information in the highlighted section of Paragraph 2?
   (A) Sinclair wanted to become acquainted with the type of people he was writing about to make legitimate points.
   (B) Sinclair worked in the meat-processing industry in order to secretly gather material for news and fiction writing.
   (C) Sinclair worked in low-wage butchering jobs so he could write a first-person account of them.
   (D) Pretending to be someone else, Sinclair processed unsanitary meat in Chicago for more than half a year.

15) Which of the following best expresses the information in the highlighted section of Paragraph 3?
   (A) Although the book is witty, it is blunt and thorough when documenting exploitative business practices in mortuaries and cemeteries.
   (B) The book uses sarcasm to shed light on abuse of the grief-stricken in American business.
   (C) *The American Way of Death* aims to present laughable evidence of how American society is allowing cheating and dishonesty.
   (D) Mitford's entertaining writing style undermines the serious intent of the book, which is to change what she calls the "American way of death."

Practice #6

Read the passage. Then answer the question that follows.

In the 1200s, Mongols conquered China and a vast section of the Eurasian continent, including much of the Middle East. Mongolian leaders established the *Yuan* dynasty in China from 1271 until 1368. China thus became part of a huge Mongol empire, a change that encouraged travel and trade between China and the Islamic world for nearly 100 years. **During this time, Chinese cartographers obtained Islamic maps and learned about the existence and the boundaries of far-away lands.**

The maps enabled Chinese cartographer Li Zemin to make a world map that must have seemed amazing to his contemporaries because it depicted lands beyond China, including the unfamiliar lands of the rest of Asia, the Middle East, Africa, and Europe. **While Li Zemin's map no longer exists, scholars know about it because other mapmakers wrote that they used it as a resource.** These included the cartographers of Korea's *Kangnido* map, created around 1402 at the beginning of the Korean *Joseon* dynasty, a government that strongly supported intellectual activity.

There are several extant copies of the original *Kangnido*. The copy in the best condition was painted on silk around 1470 and measures 158 centimeters by 163 centimeters. It includes obvious inaccuracies, such as the lack of the Bay of Bengal next to India, and Japan being turned on its side. Yet, it is quite revealing. At the center of the map is China, and just below it and to the east is an oversized Korea. **Some scholars have speculated that the Korean mapmakers demonstrated a pride and confidence about their new dynasty by their prominent placement of Korea.**

16) Which of the following best expresses the information in the highlighted section of Paragraph 1?
   (A) Mapmakers in China were especially lucky to get maps from distant Islamic locations.
   (B) The Chinese received maps from the Middle East and gained a greater awareness of lands that they had not yet explored.
   (C) Before sharing an empire with the Arab world, Chinese mapmakers were only familiar with Chinese borders and features.
   (D) The existence and shape of distant lands were well known by Islamic scholars at this time in history because of their maps.

17) Which of the following best expresses the information in the highlighted section of Paragraph 2?
   (A) Li Zemin's original work cannot be found, but there are extant copies of it.
   (B) The map made by Li Zemin has become a legendary artifact.
   (C) Li Zemin's map was the basis for many other mapmakers who followed.
   (D) Textual references to Li Zemin's map are the only present-day evidence of it.

18) Which of the following best expresses the information in the highlighted section of Paragraph 3?
   (A) According to scholars, the layout and design of the *Kangnido* may indicate the mapmakers' optimism regarding Korea's importance at the time.
   (B) Some historians suggest that mapmakers in the early 15th century configured Korea on the world map in terms of dynastic politics.
   (C) Historians can prove that at one point Korean cartographers drew Korea as a major entity on the world map.
   (D) Researchers conclude that Korean mapmakers likely felt anxious as they positioned their country near a rapidly growing world power.

Read the passage. Then answer the question that follows.

Many people fail to appreciate that registered nurses, or RNs, occupy a unique niche in the medical field. **RNs administer medication and other treatments prescribed by doctors, but they also have some autonomy, or the ability to use their own professional judgment, to make "care plans" for each patient.** RNs monitor patients' conditions and analyze and assess at what point a symptom needs medical intervention. They teach patients how to manage their own care at home, either between medical appointments or when they are discharged from a hospital. Nurses also are trained in active listening, providing emotional support, and taking measures to help patients feel comfortable, such as giving them ice packs, brushing their hair, or ordering late meals.

Nurses document and chart information about a patient's condition and treatment, making it possible to coordinate medical care with other nurses and members of the medical team. Nurses are the locus of medical care, protecting and promoting health and alleviating suffering. **Further generalizations about the scope of the job are unfeasible because nurses work in such diverse settings.** They support the public in birth, childhood, injury, sickness, surgery, crisis, old age, and sometimes even in death.

In the United States, education requirements vary by state, but in general RNs have more responsibilities – and thus must have more education and training – than Licensed Vocational Nurses, or LVNs. There are many types of specialized credentials and advanced degrees that RNs can pursue in the nursing field. **Most people picture nurses as women and think of nursing as a "feminine" occupation, but men make up a small but growing percentage of nurses.**

19) Which of the following best expresses the information in the highlighted section of Paragraph 1?
   (A) Nurses oversee doctors' decisions about various treatments by making plans for patient care.
   (B) Nurses follow doctors' orders but also follow their own protocols about many details of patient care.
   (C) Nurses may not prescribe medicine, but they are responsible for the patient receiving the right dosage at the right interval.
   (D) Nurses have the power to mandate medical plans for patients, as long as they follow directions from doctors about treatment and medicines.

20) Which of the following best expresses the information in the highlighted section of Paragraph 2?
   (A) Nurses have to meet so many different job requirements that their job cannot be described easily.
   (B) Beyond what has just been said, it is impossible to describe nurses because each nurse is unique and has a different field of specialization.
   (C) Additional conclusions would have to be hypothetical because of possible future developments in the nursing profession.
   (D) More overall statements about nursing jobs cannot be made with certainty because of the wide variety of jobs that nurses perform.

21) Which of the following best expresses the information in the highlighted section of Paragraph 3?
   (A) Imbalanced gender ratios in the nursing profession are beginning to change slightly in spite of the job's stereotypical image.
   (B) Men have gradually challenged gender-based prejudice and now dominate the nursing profession.
   (C) Nursing draws upon traits, such as nurturing, that once were considered to be in the domain of women.
   (D) Underestimating the professional responsibilities of nursing has discouraged men from entering the profession until recently.

Practice #8

Read the passage. Then answer the question that follows.

Animal researchers have made astounding findings about the large capacity for thought in birds of the crow family, which also includes ravens, jays, and rooks. The birds, with a brain-to-body mass ratio equal to that of apes and dolphins, have demonstrated a number of higher cognitive skills. Many skills involve clever strategies for attaining food, such as memorizing where other birds store food and then coming back later to steal it. One crow was known to wait for a red light to go into an intersection and safely retrieve nuts cracked by car tires. Crows also can fashion tools or use "found" tools. For example, rooks studied in a laboratory quickly figured out how to raise the water level in a vase by dropping pebbles into it. Thus, they were able to reach a worm floating in the water.

Crows live in groups that tend to be socially complex. Young crows play social games, such as "follow the leader," with other crows. **Crows also seem to vocalize quite specific ideas to each other, sometimes in large "meetings" in a tree where there may be a cacophony of *caws*, or crow calls, followed by sudden quiet.**

In one study, volunteers wearing masks adorned with identical images of a human's face captured a few crows to place bands around their legs and then released them. Over the following months, when volunteers wore the same masks to walk around the area, crows noticed them and seemed to "scold" and even dive at them, while they did not scold people in a control group wearing different masks. The crows that were scolding were largely those that had not been captured, indicating that crows learn about danger from each other and recognize and remember faces over time.

22) Which of the following best expresses the information in the highlighted section of Paragraph 1?
(A) Research shows that the avian family that includes crows and ravens is surprisingly intelligent.
(B) Zoological studies have found unprecedented abilities in species of the crow family.
(C) Scientists say that crows and their closest relatives, such as jays, are the smartest birds in the world.
(D) People have been stunned to learn what field researchers have documented about crows and species associated with them.

23) Which of the following best expresses the information in the highlighted section of Paragraph 2?
(A) Occasionally, crows seem to talk to each other using a complex language and attend community meetings to make decisions.
(B) Crow species somehow communicate about when to come together and when to go separate ways.
(C) When gathered for sessions marked with noisy caws and distinct endings, crows may be sharing specific information.
(D) Crows often converse in large groups, using calls with complex and mysterious meanings.

24) Which of the following best expresses the information in the highlighted section of Paragraph 3?
(A) Crows made harsh caws and attempted to harass people who walked under them wearing matching masks, unless the group was controlled.
(B) Compared to their behavior when exposed to ordinary masks, the crows seemed to be agitated when exposed to target masks.
(C) Crows demonstrated that they are capable of berating and bombarding people who threaten them as long as they are marked in some way.
(D) Crows appeared to become hostile when they saw the mask worn by people who had captured crows, but not when they saw other masks.

Practice #9

Read the passage. Then answer the question that follows.

United States President Andrew Jackson, whose face appears on the U.S. $20 bill, still garners both passionate admiration and blistering criticism nearly two centuries after his presidency. The dichotomy exists because Jackson was a fierce supporter of extending political power to some poor Americans, yet he also owned more than 100 slaves and built his military career partly by battling Native American tribes.

Some of his contemporaries considered Jackson to be the first "common man" to serve as president. He was born in 1767 to poor immigrant parents, but he gradually built his reputation as a country lawyer, politician, and military general. When Jackson was elected as the seventh president in 1828, he opposed the *Second Bank of the United States*, which functioned as a federally authorized central bank for the U.S. government and individuals while largely being owned by private shareholders. Jackson viewed the bank as emblematic of the rich exploiting the poor through unscrupulous lending practices; he wanted the nation's economy to be based on small farms, not on corporations built on credit. **Thus, in 1833 Jackson redirected all federal deposits into smaller state-chartered banks, causing the central bank to collapse.**

Supporters still hail Jackson as a defender of the "everyman," but opponents point out that his presidency did not result in the defense of every man; he had many racist views. For example, **while earlier presidents had favored acculturating the southeastern Native American tribes, Jackson pushed for their forced removal to make the land available for American settlers.** In 1830, President Jackson signed the *Indian Removal Act*, a move that likely helped him win reelection two years later. However, the act also sparked a decade of tragic military conflict and resulted in the "Trail of Tears," as U.S. troops forced thousands of Native Americans to move hundreds of miles from their homelands.

25) Which of the following best expresses the information in the highlighted sentence of Paragraph 1?
   (A) Though Andrew Jackson had many admirers during his presidency, most modern politicians criticize his policies.
   (B) Andrew Jackson's appearance on the U.S. $20 bill is a controversial topic.
   (C) The extent to which Andrew Jackson's political career was successful is still debated.
   (D) Some contemporaries debate whether to call Andrew Jackson's presidency a legacy.

26) Which of the following best expresses the information in the highlighted sentence of Paragraph 2?
   (A) The central bank collapsed because Jackson broke it into smaller private banks.
   (B) Because the central bank relied on government money, Jackson's withdrawal of funds ruined the institution.
   (C) Jackson shut down the central bank by removing and reinvesting wealthy investors' accounts.
   (D) Jackson created smaller banks and began placing new federal deposits in them in order to compete with the central bank.

27) Which of the following best expresses the information in the highlighted section of Paragraph 3?
   (A) Jackson wanted to relocate Native American tribes even though his predecessors had sought to integrate them into American culture.
   (B) Jackson continued the trend of previous presidents by forcing Native Americans from their homelands to southeastern territories.
   (C) Jackson wanted more land for American settlers, so he tried to move Native Americans from cities into southeastern lands.
   (D) Following in the footsteps of his predecessors, Jackson forced settlers and Native Americans to subdivide southeastern land.

Practice #10

Read the passage. Then answer the question that follows.

Archaeological evidence indicates that in the prehistoric and ancient world, people in widely varying cultures valued mirrors. People had no doubt seen their reflections only in water before they learned to polish *obsidian*, a volcanic glass-like stone. Archaeologists have found hand-crafted mirrors from 6200 BCE at Catalhoyuk in what is now Turkey. In South and Central America, people in some prehistoric cultures also made mirrors from shiny stones such as anthracite and obsidian.

Archaeologists point out that once people had perfected the art of grinding and polishing stone tools in the Stone Age, they would have found it simple to make obsidian mirrors. People may have made mirrors not only to monitor their appearance but also to reflect light into a dark room or mine, to signal someone far away, or to start a fire. Mirrors also might have been used for religious rites. For example, a mirror may have simulated the Sun in worship.

Once bronze was discovered, it was widely used for mirrors in many cultures. During China's Xia Dynasty, around 2000 BCE, Chinese crafters began making small circular bronze mirrors, often with a knob in the middle. The mirrors were usually reflective on one side and decorated with auspicious figures on the other. They were attached to clothing or held in the hand because mirrors were thought to accomplish what evil spirits despised the most: make the spirits visible. Thus, people believed that spirits fled from mirrors.

28) Which of the following best expresses the information in the highlighted section of Paragraph 1?
   (A) Archaeological excavations have uncovered numerous examples of highly valuable mirrors from international sites.
   (B) It is likely that people have enjoyed using mirrors in cultures all around the world from the time that they were first discovered.
   (C) Based on the evidence from the extensive archaeological research, it seems that the use of mirrors spread among many different groups.
   (D) Reflective objects from many ruins show that mirrors were a popular discovery in diverse places where human cultures developed.

29) Which of the following best expresses the information in the highlighted section of Paragraph 2?
   (A) People probably found few ways to use mirrors after they first utilized them to see their own reflections.
   (B) Modern humans can speculate that prehistoric and ancient people had many problems that were solved by mirrors, including gloomy, cold indoor space.
   (C) People likely used mirrors for their ability to deflect light, focus light, or reflect images.
   (D) Mirrors may have been tools for flashing messages to those far away, sparking flames, or illuminating interiors, as well as for grooming oneself.

30) Which of the following best expresses the information in the highlighted sentence in Paragraph 3?
   (A) Mirrors were placed in strategic locations around an individual's household to repel evil spirits, who hated seeing themselves reflected.
   (B) The Chinese believed that the evil spirits would be distracted by seeing themselves in mirrors carried by the Chinese.
   (C) People believed that evil spirits were so averse to being seen that they would avoid objects that could reflect their images.
   (D) According to ancient beliefs, mirrors make the ghostly seem corporeal and therefore should be carried at all times in daily life.

Select the vocabulary word or phrase that has the closest meaning.

6. **aspects**
   A. features
   B. epiphanies
   C. negatives
   D. discoveries

7. **ongoing**
   A. liberal
   B. contemporary
   C. continuing
   D. intentional

8. **arrange**
   A. plan
   B. perform
   C. control
   D. hypothesize

9. **contemplate**
   A. clog
   B. identify
   C. consider
   D. evaluate

10. **principle**
    A. agreement
    B. motivation
    C. augment
    D. rule

11. **redistribute**
    A. enlarge
    B. impress
    C. relocate
    D. demonstrate

12. **spin**
    A. create
    B. unite
    C. notice
    D. withdraw

13. **animate**
    A. motivate action
    B. create motion
    C. instill behavior
    D. rise up

14. **pursue**
    A. recede
    B. cause
    C. refuse
    D. seek

15. **ponder**
    A. throw
    B. contemplate
    C. depart
    D. weaken

16. **neglectful**
    A. inconsiderate
    B. negligent
    C. negligible
    D. derogatory

17. **plight**
    A. hardship
    B. growth
    C. treatment
    D. resolution

18. **outrageously**
    A. offensively
    B. apparently
    C. assuredly
    D. mysteriously

19. **exploitative**
    A. complicated
    B. explorative
    C. manipulative
    D. profitable

20. **extant**
    A. excellent
    B. reasonable
    C. significant
    D. existing

21. **revealing**
    A. documenting
    B. divulging
    C. elaborating
    D. pinpointing

22. **speculate**
    A. implant
    B. apply
    C. ascribe
    D. conclude

23. **locus**
    A. core
    B. expansion
    C. cost
    D. job

24. **alleviate**
    A. lessen
    B. announce
    C. incite
    D. designate

25. **unfeasible**
    A. inconceivable
    B. unsustainable
    C. impracticable
    D. unconditional

26. **astounding**
    A. reciprocal
    B. fertile
    C. obvious
    D. amazing

27. **complex**
    A. abundant
    B. inherent
    C. complicated
    D. primitive

28. **scold**
    A. berate
    B. enjoin
    C. interrogate
    D. scrutinize

29. **agitate**
    A. annoy
    B. soothe
    C. dismiss
    D. arouse

30. **blistering**
    A. gleaming
    B. severe
    C. sunny
    D. reliable

31. **emblematic**
    A. stigmatic
    B. thematic
    C. imagistic
    D. symbolic

32. **acculturate**
    A. accumulate
    B. overstate
    C. insulate
    D. assimilate

33. **polish**
    A. burnish
    B. vanish
    C. accomplish
    D. thrive

34. **auspicious**
    A. disturbing
    B. innovative
    C. pertinent
    D. promising

35. **corporeal**
    A. tangible
    B. intimate
    C. magnificent
    D. sensible

1. **implication**
   A. consideration
   B. conclusion
   C. objection
   D. distortion

2. **all-inclusive**
   A. all-knowing
   B. dominating
   C. precipitous
   D. comprehensive

3. **substantive**
   A. formal
   B. meaningful
   C. prevailing
   D. valid

4. **intangible**
   A. abstract
   B. ingenious
   C. essential
   D. notable

5. **profound**
   A. stingy
   B. great
   C. innocent
   D. irrelevant

I. What Is a Summary Question?

Summary

The summary question asks you to select the sentences that best explain the main idea of a given passage. A summary states the most important and major ideas in a shorter form.

A. SUMMARY QUESTION MODEL

Salamanders are amphibians closely related to frogs but with a lizard-like body shape. Salamanders are of interest to biologists and medical researchers for several reasons. The most dramatic is that salamanders are unique among *vertebrates* – animals with backbones – in that they have the ability to actually regenerate missing limbs and damaged vital organs. If salamander's healing processes could be replicated in humans, health care would be revolutionized.

A species of salamander that is frequently used in scientific education and research is the *axolotl*, an Aztec word meaning "water monster." The axolotl is a salamander indigenous to lakes in central Mexico. While nearly extinct in the wild, axolotls have been bred in captivity in large numbers. They are relatively easy to breed and keep in aquariums because they never leave the water.

Axolotls' aquatic lifestyle is the result of *neoteny*; that is, axolotls retain much of their juvenile "tadpole" form throughout their lives. Scientists have several theories about this adaptation and whether it is related to their quick regeneration of tissue. Because axolotls remain in their larval stage, they look somewhat like fish, except that they have flat, "smiling" faces; fern-like gills that protrude; and thin limbs with outstretched fingers and toes.

9. **Directions**: An introductory sentence for a brief summary of the passage is provided below. Complete the summary by selecting the THREE answer choices that express the most important ideas in the passage. Some sentences do not belong in the summary because they express ideas that are not presented in the passage or are minor ideas in the passage. **This question is worth 2 points.**

The axolotl is a species of salamander that is popular for scientific study.
-
-
-

Answer Choices
1. The axolotl is related to and looks like a frog.
2. Most axolotls are brown or black, but mutant strains can be pink.
3. Axolotls have a developmental process that is unusual for amphibians.
4. Axolotls are interesting because they rebuild their missing body tissue.
5. Most salamanders hatch from eggs in water in an adult form.
6. It is not difficult to raise axolotls in a laboratory aquarium.

B. TIPS
1. Make sure that you choose an answer that includes the most important ideas in the passage.
2. You can choose a paraphrase that omits minor ideas as long as the passage's meaning remains the same.
3. Incorrect answers are inaccurate or irrelevant, or contain minor ideas and details.
4. Because these questions ask you to select multiple correct answers, they are worth up to two points rather than one point.
5. You must select two correct answers to receive 1 point and three correct answers for 2 points.

II. Hacking Strategy

Summary
Question

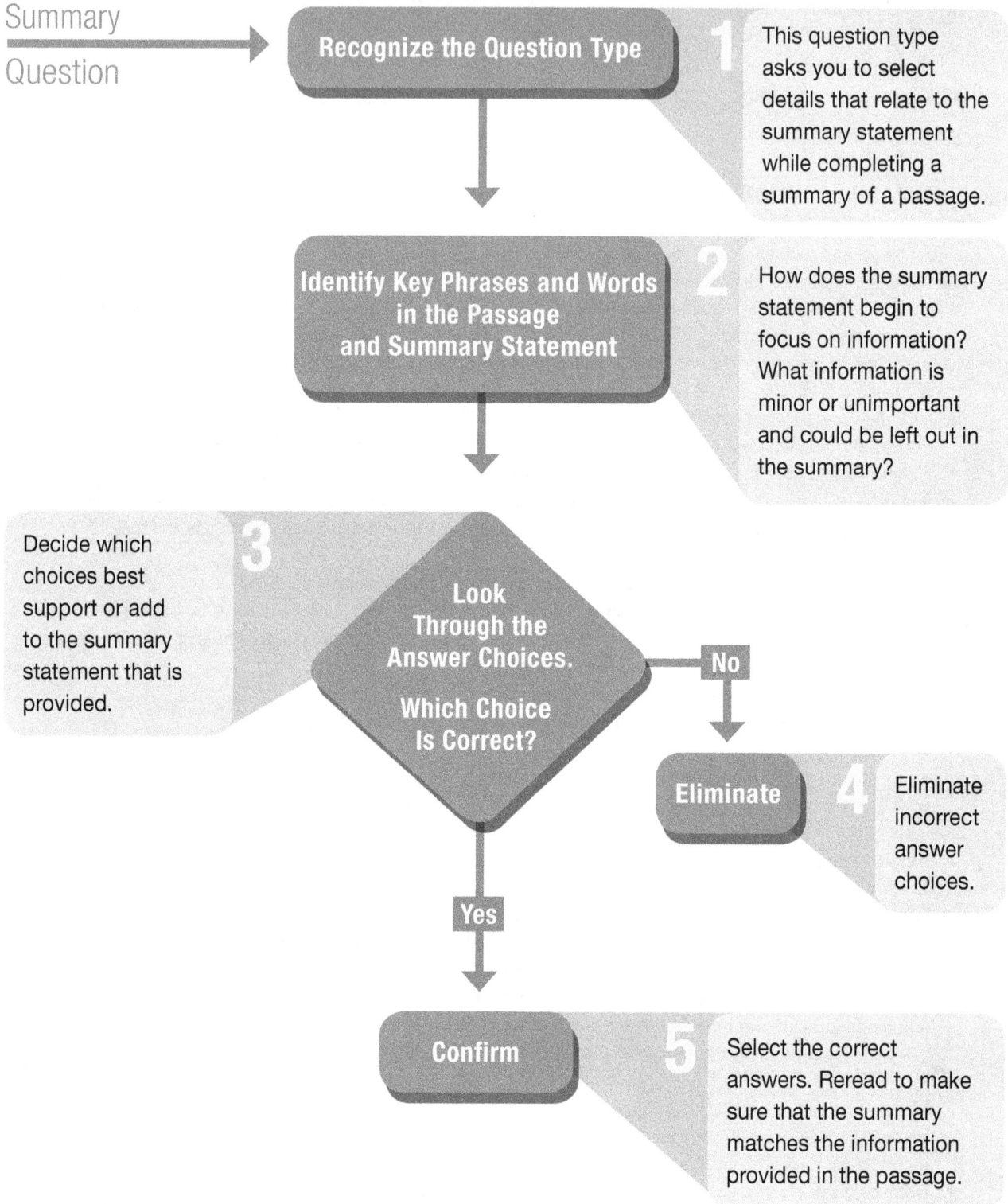

Recognize the Question Type

1 This question type asks you to select details that relate to the summary statement while completing a summary of a passage.

Identify Key Phrases and Words in the Passage and Summary Statement

2 How does the summary statement begin to focus on information? What information is minor or unimportant and could be left out in the summary?

Decide which choices best support or add to the summary statement that is provided.

3 **Look Through the Answer Choices.**

Which Choice Is Correct?

No

Eliminate

4 Eliminate incorrect answer choices.

Yes

Confirm

5 Select the correct answers. Reread to make sure that the summary matches the information provided in the passage.

EXAMPLE

1

Salamanders are amphibians closely related to frogs but with a lizard-like body shape. Salamanders are of interest to biologists and medical researchers for several reasons. The most dramatic is that salamanders are unique among vertebrates – animals with backbones – in that they have the ability to actually regenerate missing limbs and damaged vital organs, even parts of the brain. If salamander's healing processes could be replicated in humans, health care would be revolutionized.

A species of salamander that is frequently used in scientific education and research is the *axolotl*, an Aztec word meaning "water monster." The axolotl is a salamander indigenous to lakes in central Mexico. While nearly extinct in the wild, axolotls have been bred in captivity in large numbers. They are relatively easy to breed and keep in aquariums because they never leave the water.

Axolotls' aquatic lifestyle is the result of *neoteny*; that is, axolotls retain their juvenile "tadpole" form throughout their lives. Scientists have several theories about this adaptation and whether it is related to their quick regeneration of tissue. Because axolotls remain in their larval stage, they look somewhat like fish, except that they have flat, "smiling" faces; fern-like gills that protrude; and thin limbs with outstretched fingers and toes.

The axolotl is a species of salamander that is popular for scientific study.
-
-
-

Answer Choices

1. The axolotl is related to and looks like a frog.
2. Most axolotls are brown or black, but mutant strains can be pink.
3. Axolotls have a developmental process that is unusual for amphibians.
4. Axolotls are interesting because they rebuild their missing body tissue.
5. Most salamanders hatch from eggs in water in an adult form.
6. It is not difficult to raise axolotls in a laboratory aquarium.

2

The <u>axolotl</u> is a species of salamander that is <u>popular for scientific study</u>.
Salamanders are amphibians closely related to frogs but with a lizard-like body shape. Salamanders are of interest to biologists and medical researchers for several reasons. The most dramatic is that salamanders are unique among vertebrates – animals with backbones – in that they have the ability to actually <u>regenerate missing limbs and damaged vital organs</u>, even parts of the brain. If salamander's healing processes could be <u>replicated in humans</u>, health care would be revolutionized.

A species of salamander that is frequently used in scientific education and research is the <u>*axolotl*</u>, an Aztec word meaning "water monster." The axolotl is a salamander indigenous to lakes in central Mexico. While nearly extinct in the wild, axolotls have been <u>bred in captivity in large numbers</u>. They are relatively easy to keep in aquariums because they never leave the water.

Axolotls' aquatic lifestyle is the result of *neoteny*; that is, <u>axolotls retain their juvenile "tadpole" form throughout their lives</u>. Scientists have several theories about this adaptation and whether it is related to their quick regeneration of tissue. Because axolotls remain in their larval stage, they look somewhat like fish, except that they have flat, "smiling" faces; fern-like gills that protrude; and thin limbs with outstretched fingers and toes.

3

Find choices that are discussed in the passage AND logically connect to the summary statement:
"The axolotl is a species of salamander that is popular for scientific study."
- Select **Choice 3** because it is a major point of the passage AND supports the summary sentence.
- Select **Choice 4** because the passage states that axolotls interest scientists due to the fact that they *regenerate missing limbs*, which is relevant to the answer choice.
- Select **Choice 6** because the passage states that they are easy to *keep in aquariums*, which supports this choice.

4

- Eliminate **Choice 1** because it is a minor detail and it does not match the topic sentence concerning *scientific study*.
- Eliminate **Choice 2** because it is not mentioned in the passage and does not have to do with *scientific study*.
- Eliminate **Choice 5** because it is inaccurate and not mentioned in the passage.

5

Select the correct answers — **Choices 3**, **4**, and **6**.

III. Quick Look

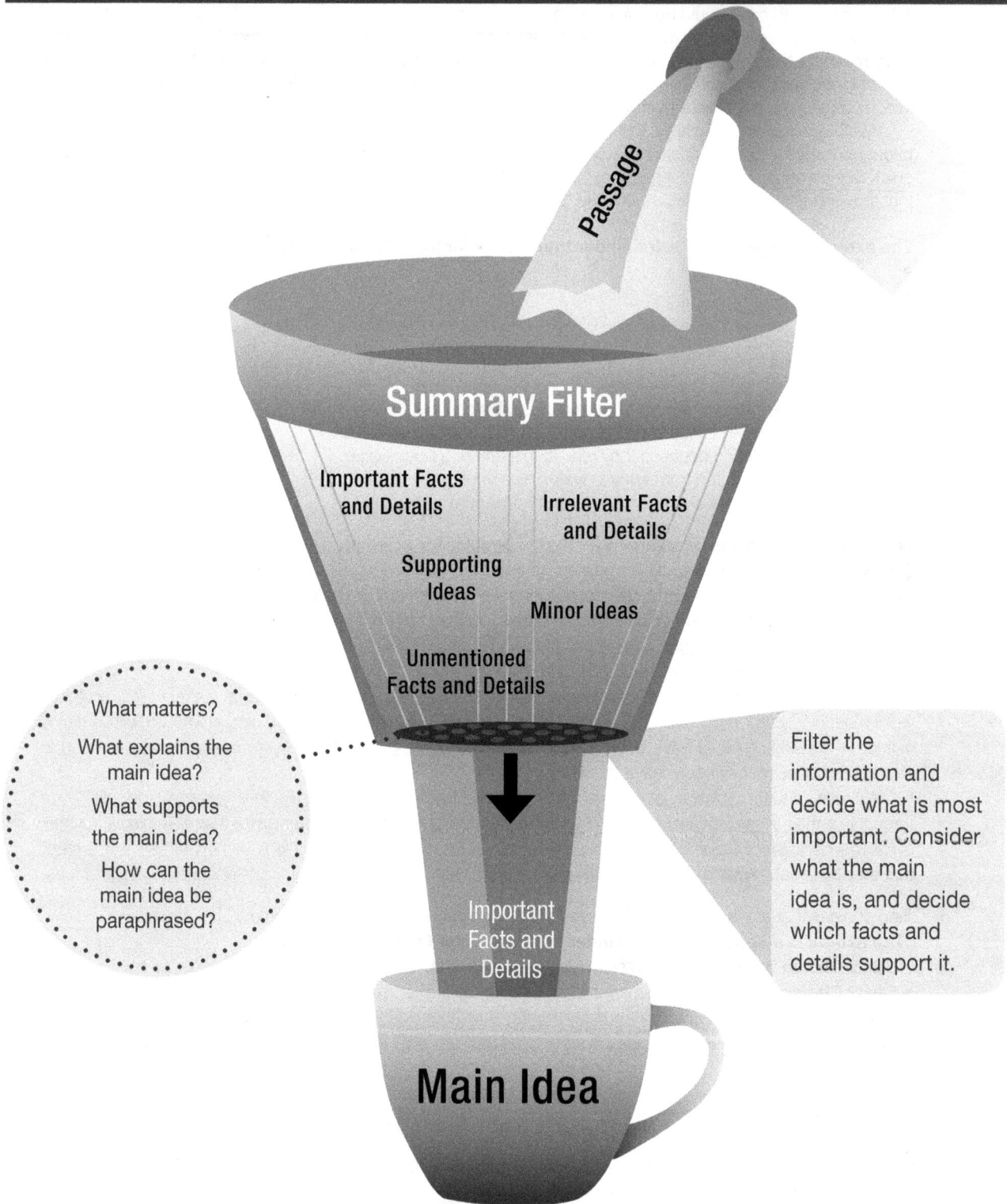

Passage

Summary Filter

Important Facts and Details

Irrelevant Facts and Details

Supporting Ideas

Minor Ideas

Unmentioned Facts and Details

What matters?
What explains the main idea?
What supports the main idea?
How can the main idea be paraphrased?

Filter the information and decide what is most important. Consider what the main idea is, and decide which facts and details support it.

Important Facts and Details

Main Idea

IV. Warm Up

Below is a topic sentence and three supporting details. Put a check mark next to the one detail that does NOT support the main idea.

1. Topic Sentence: **The ancient Egyptian Hypatia, who came to a tragic end, is the first female mathematician known in history.**

   _____ Support #1: Hypatia and her father coauthored commentaries on the works of classical philosophers, astronomers, and mathematicians.

   _____ Support #2: Hypatia was head of a school in Alexandria, Egypt, where she taught the works of Plato and Aristotle, including mathematics and logic.

   _____ Support #3: *Hypatia*, a novel by 19th-century writer Charles Kingsley, imagines reasons to explain why the scholarly Hypatia was murdered.

2. Topic Sentence: **The *Puritans*, or Protestants who came from England to North America, published children's literature to help children learn the austere Puritan lifestyle.**

   _____ Support #1: John Cotton, a Puritan minister, wrote the 15-page *Spiritual Milk for Boston Babes* in 1646.

   _____ Support #2: Educating, instructing, and entertaining children were the purposes of many traditional tales that were verbally passed down from generation to generation.

   _____ Support #3: *The New England Primer*, published at the end of the 17th century, taught reading essentials along with Puritan morals and religion.

3. Topic Sentence: **Scientists and theorists have come up with many differing theories to explain the meaning of dreams.**

   _____ Support #1: Electroencephalographs measure brain waves and can indicate when a sleeping person is entering a dream state.

   _____ Support #2: Sigmund Freud believed that dreams express worries or desires that people have "buried" or repressed.

   _____ Support #3: One theory in neurobiology is that the brain needs at least a minimum amount of stimulation at all times; during sleep, the stimulation must be supplied by random memories, which make up the content of dreams.

4. Topic Sentence: **Some species of butterflies are equipped for long-distance flying.**

   _____ Support #1: Twice a year, the Monarch butterfly migrates 4,000 kilometers over the course of three or four generations.

   _____ Support #2: Butterflies' lift-off into flight relies upon several aerodynamic structures and processes, including the Weis-Fogh *clap-and-fling* mechanism.

   _____ Support #3: Compared to butterflies, bees carry more pollen from flower to flower, but most species of butterfly carry pollen for a greater distance than do bees.

5. Topic Sentence: **Many artists have tried to capture the wide expanse of nature in landscape painting.**

_____ Support #1: The American artist Fitz Hugh Lane was known in New England as "the marine painter" for his nautical themes: sailing ships, the sea, and vast skies.

_____ Support #2: Pop artist Andy Warhol is known for utilizing common objects in his works, including cans of soup.

_____ Support #3: For centuries, Chinese artists used black ink on silk or paper to portray the enormity of mountains compared to humans.

6. Topic Sentence: **The modern free market provides many means to try to prevent or hide the effects of aging.**

_____ Support #1: One theory is that organisms age when unstable molecules called _free radicals_ damage cells.

_____ Support #2: Consumers in many cultures attempt to mask aging through the use of dyes, lotions, and cosmetics.

_____ Support #3: Many people claim that vitamin supplements play a role in anti-aging functions.

7. Topic Sentence: **_Galaxies_, or stars and other space objects held together by gravity, form several different shapes.**

_____ Support #1: Some galaxies resemble coils or spirals, and others have an elliptical shape.

_____ Support #2: Galaxies interact with each other, and sometimes the gravity from one galaxy will pull another into an irregular form.

_____ Support #3: Galaxies are separated by intergalactic space, where there may be as little as one atom of a gas per cubic meter.

8. Topic Sentence: **Many languages, including English, form some words by combining several different words together.**

_____ Support #1: When _smoke_ and _fog_ blend together, the mixture is called _smog_.

_____ Support #2: The word _radar_ is actually an acronym of the first letters in the words _RAdio Detection And Ranging_.

_____ Support #3: The words _health_ and _whole_ both can be traced to the Old English word _hal_, which meant _uninjured_.

9. Topic Sentence: **The _stage combat_, or choreographed fights in theater and film, are rehearsed carefully to avoid actual harm to the actors.**

_____ Support #1: Sound effects such as knives clashing and glass breaking can enhance fight scenes in theater and film.

_____ Support #2: Actors engaging in theatrical fights must practice techniques for striking beyond the other combatant's body or stopping just short of contact.

_____ Support #3: Fight choreography must be practiced at slow speeds first and then gradually speeded up in order to appear real yet still be safe.

10. Topic Sentence: **Ultraviolet (UV) radiation from the Sun can be both helpful and harmful to humans, so human skin contains the brown pigment melanin, which controls the amount of UV radiation absorbed by the body.**

_____ Support #1: Populations that live in areas with strong sun rays have historically adapted with more melanin to protect the skin from sun damage.

_____ Support #2: Older segments of the population experience fading skin color as individuals lose melanin-producing cells at a steady rate past the age of 30.

_____ Support #3: In areas farther from the equator, populations needed to maximize exposure to sunlight to absorb Vitamin D, and therefore adapted with less melanin.

V. Quick Practice

Practice #1

Read the passage. Then answer the question that follows.

In the tropical rainforests of central Africa, a number of indigenous hunter-gatherer groups are collectively known as *Pygmies*. The people in Pygmy groups tend to be small in stature, averaging 137 centimeters tall. Currently, many Pygmies struggle to maintain their communities and traditions in diminishing forests and war-torn regions. Although they have suffered a great deal of violence and discrimination, some Pygmy groups known as BaMbuti still live in the dense Ituri Forest in what is now the Democratic Republic of Congo. An important part of BaMbuti culture is a unique musical tradition, which is said to both echo and talk to the rainforest.

The complexity of BaMbuti music comes partly from *polyphony*, commonly known as singing "in the round." It occurs when different performers sing two or more repeating melodies in an overlapping pattern. In BaMbuti music, individuals add layers of variations in melody or rhythm to create a highly textured sound. Although there are specific lyrics, each individual singer seems to be making a descending, undulating vowel sound, with one or two callers eliciting choral responses from other singers in unison. The call-and-response pattern is accompanied by fast-paced percussive clapping or drumming.

Many BaMbuti memorize a vast repertoire of melodies by hearing and singing them from earliest childhood. Western visitors have described BaMbuti lives as seeming to have a movie soundtrack because someone is always singing, humming, or playing an instrument. As the BaMbuti people consider the forest to be like a parent to them, they have a musical ceremony to "wake up" the forest when times are difficult. They also have songs for gathering or hunting in the forest, as well as singing ceremonies to welcome forest spirits.

---

1) **Directions**: *An introductory sentence for a brief summary of the passage is provided below. Complete the summary by selecting the THREE answer choices that express the most important ideas in the passage. Some sentences do not belong in the summary because they express ideas that are not presented or are minor ideas in the passage.* **This question is worth 2 points.**

> **The BaMbuti peoples of the Central African rainforest have a distinctive musical tradition.**
> *
> *
> *

Answer Choices

1. A typical BaMbuti song features both solo and whole-group singing.
2. Many Pygmy groups, including those that are BaMbuti, have been victims of regional warfare.
3. Melodic and rhythmic complexity gives BaMbuti music a rich texture.
4. BaMbuti music is referential to life in the forest and the forest itself.
5. The BaMbuti include children in singing events once they reach a certain age.
6. The BaMbuti call-and-response format may have influenced other traditions.

Read the passage. Then answer the question that follows.

Theodor Geisel, an American children's book author who used the pen name Dr. Seuss, transformed the experience of reading for countless children around the world. Geisel wrote and illustrated more than 40 rhyming, comical children's books between 1937 and 1990. The books were a departure from the "reading primers" that had been available for reading instruction before his time. Geisel's cartoonish line drawings often put characters with furry or feathery bodies in settings with pom-pom trees, tilting platforms, free-standing improbable staircases, or machines with curving pipes. Main characters are often independent thinkers, if not downright stubborn.

Prior to writing books, Geisel worked in advertising and political cartooning, and during World War II, he animated Army training films; all of these professions helped him learn to convey abstract themes in simple language. In *How the Grinch Stole Christmas!*, a spiteful greenish creature called "the Grinch" steals all the Christmas gifts and food from the town of "Whoville" late on Christmas Eve. As the Grinch is making his getaway near morning, the townspeople whom he has robbed begin singing happily, even though they are now bereft of holiday goods. In disbelief, the Grinch goes back to join the people. Thus, the book translates a message about anger, materialism, and redemption into a form that young children can understand.

Geisel did not overtly moralize in his books, but he did use outlandish situations to address familiar, real concerns for children. This can be clearly seen in his "Beginner Books" that use a limited supply of simple words to assist brand-new readers. In these, Geisel used his humorous illustrations to make sense of rhymes such as a *pup in cup*, a *thing sing*, or a *fox in socks*. However, he integrates a wide range of emotion into the silliness, from a *sad dad*, to a *fish who is bad*, to a frustrating *song that goes on much too long*. Geisel's classic *Green Eggs and Ham*, which uses only 50 different words, follows the saga of a character who feels anxious about trying a new dish that inexplicably features green fried eggs.

2) **Directions**: *An introductory sentence for a brief summary of the passage is provided below. Complete the summary by selecting the THREE answer choices that express the most important ideas in the passage. Some sentences do not belong in the summary because they express ideas that are not presented or are minor ideas in the passage.* **This question is worth 2 points.**

> **Theodor Geisel, also known as Dr. Seuss, made learning to read engaging and fun for generations of people.**

-
-
-

Answer Choices

1. The books' pictures featured simple lines and depicted amusing settings.
2. The books' illustrations provided an intricately detailed realistic setting.
3. The books help parents teach their children moral lessons.
4. Some of the books use a small number of basic words to build literacy.
5. Using humor, the books address subjects that children care about.
6. The books shelter readers from any topics that may cause anxiety.

Practice #3

Read the passage. Then answer the question that follows.

A *turbine* is a mechanical device that can be caused to rotate by water, steam, or wind pressure on extruding parts. The pressure transfers usable energy to the turbine and then to other devices. One example of a turbine is the *waterwheel*, which is turned by flowing water. A *wind turbine* is not dissimilar in construction; when the wind pushes sails or blades attached to a central shaft, the blades spin in circles and rotate the shaft. The rotating shaft can move other mechanical parts.

The *windmill* is an early form of wind turbine, with origins dating back to the Roman Empire. In the first century CE, Hero, a Greek engineer living in the Egyptian city of Alexandria, is believed to have been the first to use a windmill. Hero wanted to build an improved musical pipe organ, as the pipe organs at the time relied on falling water for power, which was likely untenable in a theater. Hero constructed a small windmill with branching blades that attached to a simple piston, which in turn pushed air into the pipes of the organ.

In about the ninth century, farmers in Sistan, a windy region of what is now Iran and Afghanistan, discovered how to use windmills to grind grain and pump water. The discovery eventually spread throughout Asia and Europe. Windmills were critical in the establishment of the Netherlands, as they enabled 14th century farmers to pump water out of the "lowlands" in order to cultivate the land. Modern wind turbines apply many of the same mechanical principles as ancient windmills did, but today they mostly use generators to convert the rotational energy into electricity. Some current wind-powered generators have blade lengths exceeding 50 meters and can provide electricity to thousands of homes.

3) **Directions**: *An introductory sentence for a brief summary of the passage is provided below. Complete the summary by selecting the THREE answer choices that express the most important ideas in the passage. Some sentences do not belong in the summary because they express ideas that are not presented or are minor ideas in the passage.* **This question is worth 2 points.**

> **Wind turbines have long harnessed wind energy to meet many human needs.**
> -
> -
> -

Answer Choices

1. Wind turbines resemble water-propelled turbines in basic design.
2. The original windmill was a substitute for a more cumbersome turbine.
3. Agricultural innovations using wind occurred sometime around the year 800.
4. Windmills in Holland, or the Netherlands, were built at lower elevations.
5. Energy supply is the primary purpose of contemporary wind turbines.
6. These days, generators provide the force to turn wind turbines.

Practice #4

Read the passage. Then answer the question that follows.

The physiology of *pole vaulting*, a track and field event in which an athlete launches as much as 6 meters up in the air, is highly complex, as pole vaulters must use nearly every muscle in the body. First, pole vaulters must be able to sprint for 40 meters carrying a flexible 3- to 5-meter pole; then, relying on skill and timing, they plant the pole in the ground and hold on, using its rebound energy to gain altitude. They must be able to swing their legs above their heads and straighten their bodies, and for a split second they are almost completely inverted, with feet up and head down. Next, pole vaulters must be able to twist around and push off the top of the still-planted pole with their hands so that they are horizontal and face down, at the same time letting go of the pole and launching themselves over a horizontal bar with their feet first. As they clear the bar, they must be able to raise their upper bodies so that their chests do not touch the bar. Finally, they give in to gravity, leaning away from the bar so that they land on their backs upon soft padding.

All track and field events require lower-body strength in the hips, thighs, calves, and ankles. Pole vaulting also demands arm and wrist strength. Moreover, for successful swinging up of the body during the jump, pole vaulters need a strong "core." In other words, they must have strong abdominal and back muscles, especially the *rectus abdominus*, the main muscle that runs the length of the stomach. For twisting into a facedown position in the air, pole vaulters must have strong *external abdominal oblique* muscles, which run along the sides of the stomach. For extending their back, they must rely on their *erector spinae*, muscle groups on either side of the spine.

---

4) **Directions**: *An introductory sentence for a brief summary of the passage is provided below. Complete the summary by selecting the THREE answer choices that express the most important ideas in the passage. Some sentences do not belong in the summary because they express ideas that are not presented or are minor ideas in the passage.* **This question is worth 2 points.**

> **Pole vaulting requires speed, technique, and a great deal of strength.**

-
-
-

Answer Choices

1. Soft pads below the bar cushion a pole vaulter's landing.
2. Pole vaulters must know exactly how to plant a pole to maximize their liftoff.
3. The obliques and the spinal muscles are easily injured by over-twisting.
4. Strong leg muscles propel pole vaulters as they build up speed to power their leaps.
5. Abdominal muscles help pole vaulters lift their lower bodies up and over the bar.
6. Pole vaulters try to get over the bar head first, facing upward.

Practice #5

Read the passage. Then answer the question that follows.

Phytoplankton can be thought of as microscopic plants that float in the sunlit upper levels of fresh water or salt water, where photosynthesis is possible. There are many thousands of different kinds of phytoplankton; they produce much of the world's oxygen and serve as the base of aquatic food chains. The phytoplankton population is adversely affected by changes to the environment, such as the disappearance of a particular nutrient. Yet if a nutrient suddenly becomes unusually plentiful, phytoplankton can overtake a watery habitat.

For example, if farms allow agricultural fertilizers to drain into the ocean, the chemicals can provide an unusual excess of phosphate, leading to an overgrowth of phytoplankton, known as *algae*, off the coast. Such an overgrowth, also called an *algal bloom*, can seriously disrupt a marine ecosystem.

Algal blooms caused by some types of algae can turn water a reddish or brownish color, a phenomenon sometimes referred to as a *red tide*. Some red tides consist of algae cells that release toxins into the water. The water affected by red tides is not usually directly harmful to humans, but small marine animals such as shellfish may filter so much toxic material out of the water that it accumulates in lethal concentrations in their bodies. As a result, eating the shellfish may prove dangerous to marine mammals and humans.

One exceptional type of red tide is composed of the algae *Lingulodinium polyedrum*; when jostled, they emit a brief flash of blue light in a chemical process called *bioluminescence*. The organism may have developed the ability to produce light at night as a defense mechanism, possibly to make would-be night-prowling predators think that it is inedible. Though each tiny phytoplankton emits only a miniscule amount of light, a wave full of the organisms crashing into the shore causes billions of flashes. The remarkable outcome creates a long stripe of gleaming light along the beach as the wave hits.

---

5) **Directions**: *An introductory sentence for a brief summary of the passage is provided below. Complete the summary by selecting the THREE answer choices that express the most important ideas in the passage. Some sentences do not belong in the summary because they express ideas that are not presented or are minor ideas in the passage.* **This question is worth 2 points.**

> **Red tides are phenomena that have varying impacts on the environment and on humans.**
> *
> *
> *

Answer Choices

1. Some types of phytoplankton are microscopic animals that can be predators or prey.
2. When subjected to normal environmental constraints, algae benefit sea life.
3. All agricultural activity by humans eventually leads to toxic algal blooms.
4. Swimming through a red tide would likely be harmful to humans.
5. Poisons from them can condense within the bodies of water-filtering marine organisms.
6. The phytoplankton in some red tides shine briefly when they bump into something.

Practice #6

Read the passage. Then answer the question that follows.

The *Carnival of Venice* is a two-week festival held annually in the northern Italian city of Venice. The roots of this celebration may reach back to ancient Roman festivals. During the carnival, elaborately costumed spectators fill the narrow Venetian streets, and acrobats, jugglers, and other street entertainers perform on makeshift stages. Food vendors and costume parades crowd the squares, and boat parades float down the city's many canals. At night, giant halls house large banquets and dances. One of the most notable features of the Carnival of Venice is the use of masks, which are central to the celebration.

Although the use of Venetian carnival masks is inseparable from the carnival itself, the masks' origins remain shrouded in mystery. During the medieval period and Renaissance, Venice was a major trade center for Mediterranean merchants. Wealthy Venetian merchants sometimes wore masks to conceal their identities from competitors during business transactions. Since wearing a mask also gave commoners the opportunity to appear as prosperous merchants, some scholars suggest that Venetians adopted these masks to use during festivals to undermine the strict social hierarchy of medieval and Renaissance-era Venice. Regardless of their origins, the masks allow revelers to cross social boundaries and pursue romances and mischief at the festival while retaining their anonymity.

Most Venetian carnival masks are made from *papier mâché*, porcelain, or leather, and many masks are primarily white but lightly decorated with paint and beads. There are many different styles of masks; some reflect the joy of the carnival and are molded with huge smiles while others are associated with mystery and feature frowns or long, grotesque beaks. The combination of revelry and mystery at the Carnival of Venice has inspired the development of many other street festivals, such as the celebration of Mardi Gras in the American city of New Orleans.

6) **Directions**: *An introductory sentence for a brief summary of the passage is provided below. Complete the summary by selecting the THREE answer choices that express the most important ideas in the passage. Some sentences do not belong in the summary because they express ideas that are not presented or are minor ideas in the passage.* **This question is worth 2 points.**

> The Carnival of Venice has a rich cultural history that incorporates special masks.

-
-
-

Answer Choices

1. The carnival is based upon ancient religious rituals in the Venetian region.
2. Carnival masks come in a variety of jovial and enigmatic styles.
3. The carnival's use of masks may derive from the practices of Venetian tradesmen.
4. All street performers wear masks and perform for donations.
5. Only the wealthiest Venetians tend to wear masks at the carnival.
6. The masks can be made of varying material but are usually uniform in color.

Practice #7

Read the passage. Then answer the question that follows.

Western classical dance evolved in the 19th century in the form of opera and ballet, which used costumed characters and settings to relate specific narratives. Its emphasis was on graceful foot work and combinations of standard steps, largely performed facing the audience. The overall effect that ballet dancers aimed for was an illusion of floating, through lifts, leaps, and steps *en pointe*, or on the tips of toes. However, during the early and mid-20th century, some dancers and choreographers began to reject formal restrictions. Among them was the American Martha Graham, who became renowned for her contributions to modern dance.

Graham often used austere sets and costumes in order to focus the audience's attention on the visual effects and abstract emotions that were created by the dance movements. Dancers were often barefoot, and the staging was less classical, with dancers sometimes facing away from the audience. In her first works, Graham was interested in incorporating movements led more by the torso than by the feet. She developed a method of "contraction and release," a form of breath control that emphasized certain emotional states. During *contraction*, or exhalation, the chest becomes concave, giving the impression of grief and fear. *Release*, or inhalation, expands the chest, communicating joy and gregariousness. Another contrast was expressed by embracing gravity using choreographed *falls*, or controlled collapses, and *recoveries*, or standing up again. For Graham, a fall expressed mortality, and rising represented renewal.

Graham's 1948 production, *Diversion of Angles*, expressed facets of a woman's love through use of movement and color. The performance contains three primary dancers. First, a woman wearing a simple white costume performs a serene dance to represent "mature love." The next dancer wears yellow and uses darting, erratic movements; she represents "young love." The final dancer wears red and uses slow, seductive movements to convey "sensual love." Graham imbued her work with symbolism that members of the audience may interpret for themselves.

---

7) **Directions**: *An introductory sentence for a brief summary of the passage is provided below. Complete the summary by selecting the THREE answer choices that express the most important ideas in the passage. Some sentences do not belong in the summary because they express ideas that are not presented or are minor ideas in the passage.* ***This question is worth 2 points.***

Martha Graham asserted that one could communicate in dance through movement alone.

-
-
-

Answer Choices

1. She thought that dance performances should always follow a story line.
2. Her uses of falling and getting up within a dance often had great significance.
3. She believed that dance was the most fundamental form of communication.
4. A minimalist approach to apparel and set designs was a way to concentrate attention on movement.
5. Her use of breath control provided a simple method to express emotion.
6. Her performances would include collaborative audience participation on the stage.

Practice #8

Read the passage. Then answer the question that follows.

When one wants to understand how a toaster works, he or she may take the toaster apart piece by piece to comprehend how everything fits together. Similarly, physicists disassemble the building blocks of the universe piece by piece to see where they fit and how they interact with one another. However, subatomic particles are much too small to take apart by hand, so physicists break down the smallest known scales using high-energy collisions. A *particle collider* accelerates a cluster of particles, such as protons or electrons, to extremely high speeds and then guides it toward a solid surface or another speeding cluster of particles. The resulting collisions cause the particles to break into smaller pieces, which may reveal new information.

The Large Hadron Collider (LHC), located on the border of France and Switzerland, is the largest particle collider ever constructed. It sends proton beams through a 27-kilometer underground circuit that accelerates the particle clusters to 99.9 percent of the speed of light – just under 299,792,458 meters per second – before using enormous magnets to guide them into small but powerful collisions. Seven huge computer detectors within the LHC capture data from the process and search for evidence that may be detectable only for a brief instant after a collision.

In 2013, after many successful LHC collisions, scientists experimentally confirmed the discovery of the mysterious *Higgs boson*, a component of a field* that provides resistance to certain particles, explaining why some particles have mass while others, such as the photons that carry energy in the form of light, do not. Essentially, the *Higgs field* provides resistance to the particles that make up matter in the same way that people feel resistance when swimming through water. This pivotal discovery has elucidated why some particles, which are unaffected by the Higgs field, travel at the speed of light while other particles meet resistance and cannot reach such high speeds.

*Field: a region of space capable of applying a force

---

8) **Directions**: *An introductory sentence for a brief summary of the passage is provided below. Complete the summary by selecting the THREE answer choices that express the most important ideas in the passage. Some sentences do not belong in the summary because they express ideas that are not presented or are minor ideas in the passage. **This question is worth 2 points.***

> **The Large Hadron Collider (LHC) uses an enormous underground circuit to search for the fundamental materials that compose the universe.**
>
> •
> •
> •

Answer Choices

1. Scientists used the LHC to discover a field that provides as much resistance as water to certain particles.
2. The LHC uses large detectors to record and examine the data that results from crashing particles.
3. The LHC uses massive magnets to steer groups of protons moving at incredibly high velocities.
4. Scientists use the LHC to determine how fast certain particles can travel in response to magnetic fields.
5. Using the LHC, scientists hope to confirm the theories of forces such as gravity.
6. The LHC has provided evidence of a field that provides resistance to certain particles, giving them mass.

Practice #9

Read the passage. Then answer the question that follows.

During post-World War II war-crime trials, defendants accused of Nazi atrocities claimed that they were "just following orders." Social psychologists began to question whether most people would have followed such orders, even if the orders ran counter to personal ethics. In a 1960s Yale University study, volunteers were placed in a room and told that they had no choice but to administer electric shocks of escalating intensity to unseen people whom they could hear screaming. They were told the shocks would not cause permanent damage. The screams were supplied by actors, though the volunteers did not know that. More than half of the volunteers obediently administered what they thought were maximum shocks. Researchers concluded that circumstances play a larger role than personal ethics in whether people obey authority.

The *Stanford Prison Experiment*, conducted at Stanford University in 1971 by psychology professor Philip Zimbardo, attempted to further examine how easily people conform to expected roles. Zimbardo randomly assigned 24 volunteers to fill the role of either a guard or a prisoner in a mock-prison setting. Zimbardo instructed the guards to make the prisoners feel powerless and depersonalized without causing physical harm. Almost immediately, the guards became authoritarian and cruel, including expressing outrage over prisoners' trivial "mistakes," putting volunteers in solitary confinement, and taking away their bedding or clothes. The prisoners began to show signs of emotional trauma, and the two-week study had to be halted after just six days. The "guards" had surprised everyone with their willingness to subvert feelings of sympathy in order to comply with their roles.

Both the Yale and Stanford studies have been criticized by the science community for being unethical and unreliable. Some critics have claimed that neither study simulates real life situations, as the volunteer participants in both studies knew that they were part of a research experiment.

---

9) **Directions**: *An introductory sentence for a brief summary of the passage is provided below. Complete the summary by selecting the THREE answer choices that express the most important ideas in the passage. Some sentences do not belong in the summary because they express ideas that are not presented or are minor ideas in the passage.* **This question is worth 2 points.**

> **Social psychologists have conducted laboratory studies to determine whether most people would obey orders to harm others.**
>
> -
> -
> -

Answer Choices

1. Believing that they had no alternative, many participants in one study were persuaded to apply electric shocks to someone.
2. In the prison experiment, "guards" worked in shifts and were allowed to go home daily.
3. The Stanford experiment ended prematurely because volunteers were causing others to suffer.
4. The studies have been challenged on the basis that volunteers knew that they were not operating in "real" situations.
5. The experiments indicate that people with certain personalities always do the right thing.
6. The studies show that role-playing experiments can cause lasting psychological damage in participants.

Read the passage. Then answer the question that follows.

Fossil records show that about 4 million years ago, a species of tree-dwelling apes in Africa began to walk upright. By doing so, humanity's distant ancestors very gradually began using *bipedal motion*, or movement using two legs, replacing a body well adapted to life in the forest canopy. Using comprehensive fossil records, archaeologists have determined what changes occurred to allow for sustained bipedal locomotion.

Adaptations for two-footed walking included developing longer legs to allow for bigger, more efficient strides. Bipeds' spines curved outwards to help keep the center of gravity over the feet and support an upright posture. But arguably the largest change in physiology occurred in the foot. Whereas apes use their feet primarily as a tool for grabbing branches, hominid bipedal ancestors needed their feet to support body weight and provide smooth, enduring locomotion. Bipedal apes developed smaller toes because they needed solid launching power from the ball of the foot more than they needed to grasp branches. They also developed an arch in the foot to provide better propulsion and weight distribution while running or walking.

Even though researchers know *how* some apes slowly evolved to walk on two feet, there is still the question of *why* they gave up life in the trees. Naturalist Charles Darwin believed that bipedalism developed to free the hands for using tools. However, there is no evidence for the use of tools until 1.4 million years after the development of bipedalism. Other theories claim that bipedalism developed so that hominids could stand taller and see predators in tall grasses, or that they could more easily transport food over long distances. Regardless of its original benefits, bipedalism did allow for adroit hand-motor skills to develop as hominids used their freed hands more. Many researchers believe that dexterous hands eventually contributed to bigger brains.

---

10) **Directions**: *An introductory sentence for a brief summary of the passage is provided below. Complete the summary by selecting the THREE answer choices that express the most important ideas in the passage. Some sentences do not belong in the summary because they express ideas that are not presented or are minor ideas in the passage.* **This question is worth 2 points.**

> **Hominid development of bipedalism incorporated many beneficial physiological changes.**
> -
> -
> -

Answer Choices

1. The foot became much larger to better support body weight.
2. Hands were no longer used for locomotion, so they became more agile.
3. Bipedalism helped to cross natural barriers such as canyons and lakes.
4. Bipedalism may have developed to spot danger from further away.
5. The foot arch developed to allow for better forward momentum when moving.
6. Most ape species developed bipedalism at some point during their evolution.

Select the vocabulary word or phrase that has the closest meaning.

6. bereft
A. gigantic
B. persistent
C. required
D. lacking

7. redemption
A. reparation
B. declination
C. acclamation
D. culmination

8. inexplicably
A. firmly
B. vibrantly
C. oddly
D. irregularly

9. extrude
A. eject
B. revive
C. allure
D. examine

10. untenable
A. paramount
B. impossible
C. unsuitable
D. appreciate

1. indigenous
A. ingenious
B. flawless
C. strenous
D. native

2. collectively
A. contributory
B. integral
C. combined
D. participatory

3. overlapping
A. coinciding
B. diminishing
C. alternating
D. cascading

4. elicit
A. elucidate
B. outline
C. evoke
D. require

5. improbable
A. compulsory
B. liable
C. implausible
D. incompatible

11. convert
A. transcend
B. transfer
C. convolute
D. change

12. invert
A. inhibit
B. reverse
C. barter
D. suppose

13. launch
A. consume
B. locate
C. discover
D. propel

14. give in
A. cherish
B. present
C. hinder
D. yield

15. extend
A. lurch
B. twist
C. stretch
D. swing

16. particular
A. specific
B. frank
C. hypothetical
D. unfavorable

17. plentiful
A. prosperous
B. luxuriant
C. abundant
D. extravagant

18. accumulate
A. accomplish
B. devastate
C. disperse
D. amass

19. inedible
A. uneatable
B. indelible
C. misleading
D. prevalent

20. miniscule
A. muscular
B. harmful
C. tiny
D. irregular

21. inseparable
A. decisive
B. connected
C. reliable
D. nominal

22. shrouded
A. irrelevant
B. insignificant
C. hidden
D. engraved

23. jovial
A. jaded
B. enduring
C. lenient
D. joyful

24. enigmatic
A. abstruse
B. bellicose
C. dispersed
D. expandable

25. relate
A. connect
B. recount
C. depend
D. embellish

26. gregarious
A. talkative
B. ambiguous
C. anxious
D. sociable

27. imbue
A. infuse
B. expect
C. perceive
D. thrive

28. tentatively
A. extraordinarily
B. initially
C. consequently
D. provisionally

29. pivotal
A. vital
B. attractive
C. inconsistent
D. extreme

30. steer
A. heighten
B. deceive
C. compel
D. guide

31. velocity
A. custody
B. speed
C. operation
D. feasibility

32. obediently
A. accidently
B. obviously
C. dutifully
D. financially

33. subvert
A. agitate
B. acquire
C. undermine
D. release

34. comprehensive
A. all-around
B. all-inclusive
C. almighty
D. all-powerful

35. dexterous
A. adept
B. constant
C. essential
D. flourishing

I. What Is an Organization Question?

Organization

The organization question asks you to identify the facts and details that best fit the two to three subtopics of the passage. A passage has one main topic. To support the main topic, a passage can have multiple subtopics. Subtopics are supported by their facts and details.

A. ORGANIZATION QUESTION MODEL

In most states, local government or public agencies, such as county child welfare departments, fill the role of finding homes for infants and children who need them. Some children have been removed from their homes due to abuse or neglect, and some have lost parents through death or illness. Public agencies place children in foster homes, or licensed family homes, where they live while social workers try to reunite the children with parents or relatives. If reuniting the family becomes impossible, qualified couples may be able to adopt the child or children. Local governments provide financial support to foster families and charge few – if any – fees for adoptions.

As an alternative to working through a public agency, adoptive parents can instead pay licensed private agencies or lawyers to help them locate a child in need of adoption, either in the United States or abroad. Biological or birth parents in the U.S. also have choices and may be able to select potential adoptive parents for their child from a list containing an agency's approved applicants. Once an agreement has been reached, adoptive parents may pay maternity costs for the birth mother, and they usually take the child home from the hospital as a newborn.

10. **Directions**: Select the phrases that most appropriately match the descriptions of each type of adoption agency. TWO of the answer choices will NOT be used.

Answer Choices	Types of Adoption Agencies
1. This agency may allow birth parents to choose adoptive parents.	**Public agency**
2. This agency requires few, if any, payments from adoptive families.	●
3. This agency may require adoptive families to fill out innumerable forms.	●
4. This agency always requires adoptions of older children or sibling groups.	**Private agency**
5. This agency may first attempt to bring the birth family together again.	●
6. This agency might ensure that the adoptive parents can take care of a baby from birth.	●

All other organization questions have either five or seven correct answer choices. Above is a simplified example.

B. TIPS

1. Note any facts in the paragraph that refer to a subtopic.
2. Correct answers should be easily found in the passage.
3. An incorrect answer will be inaccurate, unrelated, or illogical according to the passage.
4. Because these questions ask you to select multiple correct answers, they are worth either 3 or 4 points.
5. If you are asked to select five correct choices, you must answer three out of five correctly for 1 point, four out of five for 2 points, and five out of five for 3 points. If you are asked to select seven correct choices, you must answer four out of seven correctly for 1 point, five out of seven for 2 points, six out of seven for 3 points, and seven out of seven for 4 points.

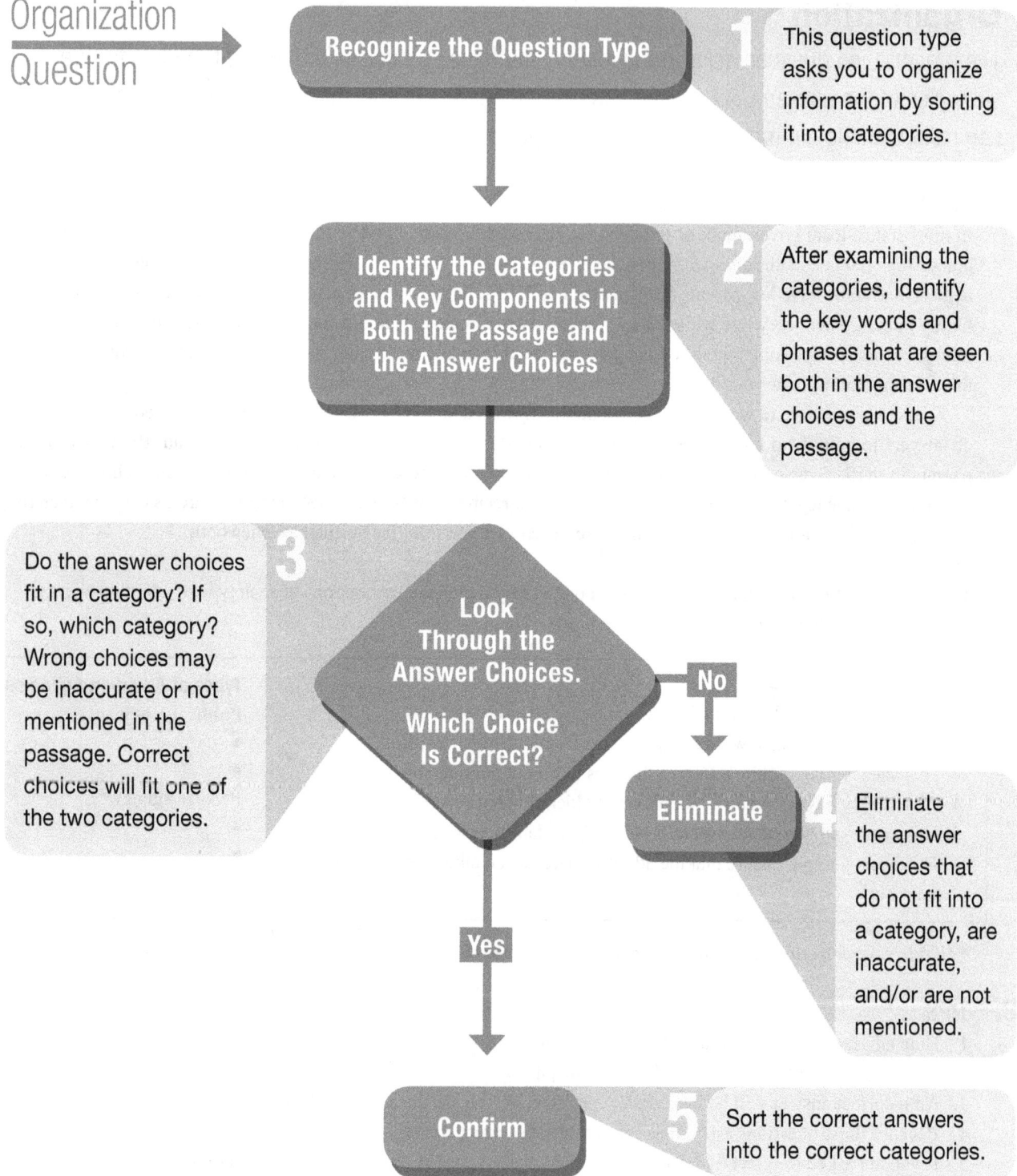

II. Hacking Strategy

Organization
Question →

Recognize the Question Type **1** This question type asks you to organize information by sorting it into categories.

Identify the Categories and Key Components in Both the Passage and the Answer Choices **2** After examining the categories, identify the key words and phrases that are seen both in the answer choices and the passage.

Do the answer choices fit in a category? If so, which category? Wrong choices may be inaccurate or not mentioned in the passage. Correct choices will fit one of the two categories. **3**

Look Through the Answer Choices. Which Choice Is Correct?

No → **Eliminate** **4** Eliminate the answer choices that do not fit into a category, are inaccurate, and/or are not mentioned.

Yes ↓

Confirm **5** Sort the correct answers into the correct categories.

EXAMPLE

1

In most states, local government or public agencies, such as county child welfare departments, fill the role of finding homes for infants and children who need them. Some children have been removed from their homes due to abuse or neglect, and some have lost parents through death or illness. Public agencies place children in foster homes, or licensed family homes, where they live while social workers try to reunite the children with parents or relatives. If reuniting the family becomes impossible, qualified couples may be able to adopt the child or children. Local governments provide financial support to foster families and charge few — if any — fees for adoptions.

As an alternative to working through a public agency, adoptive parents can instead pay licensed private agencies or lawyers to help them locate a child in need of adoption, either in the United States or abroad. Biological or birth parents in the U.S. also have choices and may be able to select potential adoptive parents for their child from a list containing an agency's approved applicants. Once an agreement has been reached, adoptive parents may pay maternity costs for the birth mother, and they usually take the child home from the hospital as a newborn.

Answer Choices

1. This agency may allow birth parents to choose adoptive parents.
2. This agency requires few, if any, payments from adoptive families.
3. This agency may require adoptive families to fill out innumerable forms.
4. This agency always requires adoptions of older children or sibling groups.
5. This agency may first attempt to bring the birth family together again.
6. This agency might ensure that the adoptive parents can take care of a baby from birth.

Types of Adoption Agencies

Public agency
●
●

Private agency
●
●

2

The category types are "public agency" and "private agency."

In most states, local government or public agencies, such as county child welfare departments, fill the role of finding homes for infants and children who need them. Some children have been removed from their homes due to abuse or neglect, and some have lost parents through death or illness. Public agencies place children in foster homes, or licensed family homes, where they live while <u>social workers try to reunite the children with parents or relatives</u>. If reuniting the family becomes impossible, qualified couples may be able to adopt the child or children. Local governments provide <u>financial support to foster families and charge few — if any fees — for adoptions</u>.

As an alternative to working through a public agency, adoptive parents can instead pay licensed private agencies or lawyers to help them locate a child in need of adoption, either in the United States or abroad. Biological or birth parents in the U.S. also have choices and may be able to <u>select potential adoptive parents</u> for their child from a list containing an agency's approved applicants. Once an agreement has been reached, adoptive parents may pay maternity costs for the birth mother, and they usually take the child <u>home from the hospital as a newborn</u>.

3

Compare key words in the choices to key words in the passage. Do they have the same information? Does the choice fit into one of the categories?

Public agency
• Select **Choice 2** because the passage states, "Local governments…charge few if any fees for adoption."
• Select **Choice 5** because the passage states, "social workers try to reunite the children with parents or relatives," which is consistent with this choice.

Private agency
• Select **Choice 1** because the passage claims that birth parents "may be able to select potential adoptive parents," which matches this choice.
• Select **Choice 6** because the passage states that adopting parents can "take the child home…as a newborn," a quote that supports this choice.

4

• Eliminate **Choices 3** and **4** because they are not mentioned in the passage.

5

Select the correct answers and put them into the correct category.
Public agency — Choices 2 and **5** / **Private agency — Choices 1** and **6**

III. Quick Look

Organization Diagram

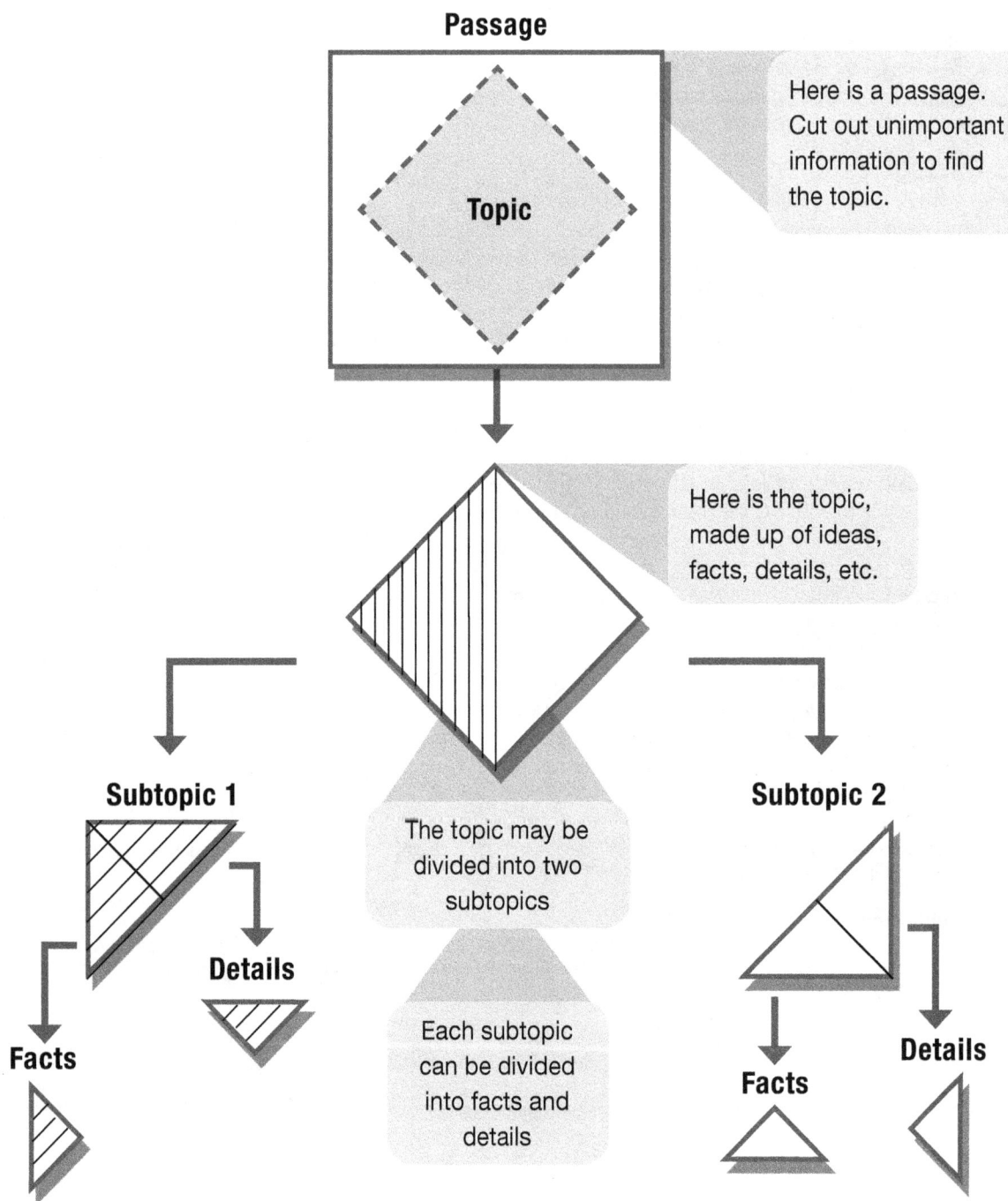

Passage

Topic

Here is a passage. Cut out unimportant information to find the topic.

Here is the topic, made up of ideas, facts, details, etc.

Subtopic 1

The topic may be divided into two subtopics

Subtopic 2

Details

Facts

Each subtopic can be divided into facts and details

Facts

Details

IV. Warm Up

Below are two categories and eight answer choices. Six of the answers belong in the categories. Two of the answers do not. Put the six appropriate answer choices into their corresponding categories.

1. **Choices**	Research skills	Writing skills
1. People use these when revising a draft.	——	——
2. People use these when conducting a study.	——	——
3. People use these when explaining a concept.	——	——
4. People use these when memorizing a speech.		
5. People use these when looking for information in online journals.		
6. People use these when printing out word-processing documents.		
7. People use these when employing a sophisticated vocabulary.		
8. People use these when seeking explanations for a phenomenon.		

2. **Choices**	Canada	Siberia
1. A railroad through this region connects to cities in China.	——	——
2. This region has land bridges connecting it to Iceland.	——	——
3. Antarctica is a short distance from this region.	——	——
4. This region was once colonized by the British but is now an independent nation.		
5. This region makes up 77 percent of Russia.		
6. The predominant language heard in this region is English.		
7. This region borders Mongolia to the south.		
8. The maple leaf has served as the symbol of this country since the 18th century.		

3. **Choices**	Muscle	Bone
1. This rigid organic material provides a structure for a body.	——	——
2. This soft material builds up when people eat too much.	——	——
3. This material can be temporarily injured when pulled or torn.	——	——
4. This material flows through the body to provide sustenance.		
5. This material expands and contracts as the body moves.		
6. This material does not usually decompose quickly after death.		
7. Exercise can increase the strength and size of this material.		
8. Cavities within this material contain a tissue called *marrow.*		

4. **Choices**   Synonym   Antonym

   1. *Plausible* and *believable* fall under this category.   ____   ____
   2. *Paper* and *pen* fit under this type.   ____   ____
   3. *Television* and *radio* are examples.   ____   ____
   4. Under this category, *humorous* and *funny* might be found.
   5. This category might include *inside* and *outside*.
   6. *Lengthy* and *short* are examples of this.
   7. *Creation* and *destruction* are included in this category.
   8. *Flee* and the phrase *make a getaway* fit under this type.

5. **Choices**   Coffee   Tea

   1. The juice of this substance is extracted from tropical fruit.   ____   ____
   2. More than half of these crops are grown in Latin America.   ____   ____
   3. The green type of this drink is quite popular in China, where it likely   ____   ____
      originated.
   4. This drink is prepared by first collecting the beans of the plant.
   5. This drink is made by pouring boiling water over dry, processed leaves.
   6. This drink is made by mixing the ground roots of a particular tree with
      water.
   7. This drink is often prepared through a process called *steeping*.
   8. This drink receives much of its flavor through a process called *roasting*.

6. **Choices**   Vaccine   Medication

   1. Doctors recommend that all children receive this substance.   ____   ____
   2. Pharmacies prohibit some people from obtaining this substance. ____   ____
   3. Doctors may prescribe this substance to ease symptoms.   ____   ____
   4. This substance may contain a few cells of a virus.
   5. This substance primarily serves as a placebo.
   6. This substance may be used to try to cure a disease.
   7. The polio virus was largely eliminated by this substance during the
      1950s.
   8. This substance is used to diagnose cognitive disorders.

7. **Choices**   Hurricane Snowstorm

   1. This is characterized by high winds and relentless rain.   ____   ____
   2. This forms deep underground before permeating Earth's surface. ____   ____
   3. This is characterized by copious amounts of snow and wind.   ____   ____
   4. This usually forms over large bodies of warm water.
   5. Plows are usually used to clear the roads after this passes.
   6. This is characterized by sunny yet very cold conditions.
   7. This also can be called a tropical cyclone.
   8. When this occurs in a mountainous region, it may result in an avalanche.

8. **Choices**   Mice   Elephants

    1. This type of mammal enjoys spraying water out of its nose.   _____   _____
    2. Many snakes can swallow these animals whole.   _____   _____
    3. This type of animal is known to be an effective predator.   _____   _____
    4. This type of mammal can overpopulate a home or barn.
    5. These animals typically eat more than 150 kg of plant material a day.
    6. This type of mammal is frequently kept in science laboratories.
    7. These animals are popular as pets in a yard or garden.
    8. Adult animals of this type can often defend themselves from lions.

9. **Choices**   New York City   Beijing

    1. The Statue of Liberty is located off the coast of this city.   _____   _____
    2. Within this city exists the ancient Forbidden City.   _____   _____
    3. Much of the population of this city lives on the island of Manhattan.   _____   _____
    4. This city hosted the 2008 Summer Olympic games.
    5. Many Hollywood celebrities live, shop, and socialize in and around this city.
    6. This city is located at the base of the Himalaya mountain range.
    7. This city is the capital of its respective country.
    8. This city contains a huge intersection known as *Times Square*, which leads to the "Broadway" district.

10. **Choices**   Nonprofit   Corporation

    1. This type of organization tries to earn money for investors.   _____   _____
    2. This entity enlists and trains people for military service.   _____   _____
    3. This type of organization is likely to recruit volunteer workers.   _____   _____
    4. This organization oversees the administration of public schools.
    5. This entity relies on grant funding for some or all of its support.
    6. *Shares*, or parts of a business, might be available for sale in this one.
    7. The oil and gas supplier British Petroleum is an example of this type of organization.
    8. The United Nations Children's Fund (UNICEF) is an example of this type of organization.

V. Quick Practice

Practice #1

Read the passage. Then answer the question that follows.

Thousands of English words derive from either Greek or Latin, and many such words are created by combinations of meaningful parts. A combined word conveys basic meaning by a *root* word, which can be altered in some way by an *affix*, such as a prefix or suffix. While this adds great flexibility in vocabulary, it also means that sometimes identical affixes may cause confusion. For example, two words with different meanings but identical prefixes are *paradigm* and *paradox*.

The word *paradigm* comes from the Greek prefix *para-*, which can mean "besides" or "beyond," and the Greek word *deiknynai*, or "to show." For the Greeks, a paradigm "showed beyond" what was obvious about daily life. It referred to the pattern underlying reality, specifically, the model used by the god who created the universe. Similarly, in modern English, *paradigm* refers to a viewpoint, a way of seeing and thinking about reality. Thus, a person's paradigm can shift or suddenly change. For example, Nicolaus Copernicus introduced a significant paradigm shift in the 16th century when he developed the *heliocentric model* of the solar system, which states that the Earth orbits the Sun as opposed to the Sun orbiting the Earth. Suddenly, people had to discard the concept of the world that included the Sun "rising" in the morning and had to envision the new paradigm of Earth moving through space.

A *paradox* also uses the Greek prefix *para-*, in the sense of "beyond" or "contrary to," combined with the Greek word *doxa*, which is "an opinion." A paradox, then, is a statement that is contrary to its own opinion, or *self-contradictory*, but not necessarily illogical. It is a paradox to have a "bittersweet" experience or to lead a "shockingly normal" life. Philosophy and literature often use paradox to provide insight. For example, in George Orwell's *Animal Farm*, the pigs declare that every animal is equal, but some are *more equal* than others.

1) **Directions**: *Select the sentences that most appropriately match the descriptions of each word using "para-." TWO of the answer choices will NOT be used.* **This question is worth 3 points.**

Answer Choices	Words Using "Para-"
1. This word refers to something that undergoes inevitable change.	**Paradigm**
2. This term means part of something is used to refer to the whole of something.	•
3. This word would aptly describe the phrase "fighting for peace."	•
4. This term encompasses all of that which seems obvious to a person.	•
5. This word describes a belief system that is most noticeable when it must change.	**Paradox**
6. This term describes a set of assumptions about what is true.	•
7. This term describes a combination of words that may be confusing at first glance.	•

Practice #2

Read the passage. Then answer the question that follows.

Mythologies from cultures around the world use stories as allegories for natural phenomena, explanations for traditional practices, or accounts of past events. A common theme in the mythology of many cultures is the quest for immortality.

The ancient Mesopotamian poem *The Epic of Gilgamesh* dates back to the 18th century BCE, making it one of the oldest surviving works of literature. The poem centers on Gilgamesh, a demigod and king who searches for a plant at the bottom of the sea that will grant him immortality. Though he recovers the plant, a snake almost immediately steals it. Ultimately, the poem implies that Gilgamesh must accept that he will one day die, but his deeds are immortal because they will live on in literature.

Nearly 3,000 years later, the 13th-century Icelandic historian Snorri Sturluson compiled the mythology of Scandinavians, also known as Norsemen, providing a written record of their beliefs. These texts depict gods who maintain their youth by eating golden apples picked from the "tree of life," *Yggdrasil*. One myth tells of a treacherous god, Loki, who gives the apples to giants in exchange for his freedom, but the other gods force him to recover the apples because without them the gods begin to grow old and feeble. However, immortality is ultimately unattainable even for the mighty Norse gods because they are fated to die in an apocalyptic event called *Ragnarök*.

Chinese mythology also tells of a fruit linked to immortality. Several stories describe a peach tree that produces one fruit every 1,000 years. Every 6,000 years the Jade Emperor, ruler of the cosmos, holds a banquet for the Eight Immortals, the saints that protect humanity, and serves peaches to ensure their continued immortality. However, the Jade Emperor does not grant these peaches to humans.

The prospect of cheating death through immortality provides appealing plots in stories, but human immortality remains unattainable even in mythology.

2) **Directions**: *Select the sentences that most appropriately match the descriptions of each cultural origin of mythologies. TWO of the answer choices will NOT be used.* **This question is worth 4 points.**

Answer Choices	Cultural Origins of Mythologies
1. This myth proposes that a person can achieve a kind of immortality by the written word.	**Mesopotamian** • • •
2. The character in this work must seek in the seas for the promise of eternal life.	
3. This mythology has a unique viewpoint in that even gods cannot live forever.	**Norse** • •
4. In this mythology, only deities can attend a feast where a special fruit is served.	
5. In this mythology, giants fight the gods for the right to immortality.	**Chinese** • •
6. Dating to a time of the earliest written documents, this work points out the inevitability of death.	
7. The Immortals in this work continue their never-ending lives at the whim of a princess.	
8. These myths were saved by being recorded during the 1200s.	
9. In this mythology, a tree bearing fruit every millennium is the source of continued life.	

Practice #3

Read the passage. Then answer the question that follows.

The *common chimpanzee* (*Pan troglodytes*) and the *bonobo* (*Pan paniscus*) are the two species of great ape that comprise the genus *Pan*. They diverged from a common ancestor about 1 million years ago when the Congo River began flowing through the ancestor's habitat. The river separated groups that later developed into bonobos south of the river and into chimpanzees north of the river. Though the bonobo and chimpanzee are similar in their omnivorous diets, appearance, and lifespan, this geographic divide has resulted in some basic differences between the two species.

Because the region south of the Congo River contains abundant food sources, bonobos rarely have to compete over resources or territory. As a result, bonobo social groups of up to 200 members frequently interact with one another in a gentle manner. Moreover, the region of the brain associated with empathy is exceptionally developed in bonobos, likely because of their social behavior. Though female bonobos are often smaller, their social groups are matriarchal, and a male bonobo's status is determined by his mother's social standing. Tool-using behavior is exceedingly rare amongst wild bonobos.

As compared to the bonobo habitat, the common chimpanzee's habitat is characterized by less edible vegetation and more competition for territory. Thus, interactions between chimpanzee social groups are often confrontational. Within their communities of between 40 to 60 individuals, there are subgroups of 10 or fewer chimpanzees. They form rigid intergroup hierarchies that are male-dominated, and dominant chimpanzees aggressively suppress challenges to this social order. Moreover, because of food scarcity, chimpanzees have learned to use tools to acquire sustenance. They may, for example, use rocks to break nuts, or sticks to gather honey from beehives.

3) **Directions**: *Select the sentences that most appropriately match the descriptions of each species of ape. TWO of the answer choices will NOT be used.* **This question is worth 3 points.**

Answer Choices	Species of Ape
1. These matriarchal groups attack other females who attempt to take over.	**Bonobos** • • •
2. These animals' friendly, social behavior may stem from a long history of ample nutrients.	
3. The dominant animals in this group have learned how to wield sticks to scare others away from food sources.	**Chimpanzees** • •
4. The area of the brain governing compassion is highly evolved in this great ape.	
5. Limitations in resources have led to these apes devising skillful ways to access food.	
6. The ranking order in this group is inflexible, and insubordination can result in threats and violence.	
7. A male offspring of this species relies on his mother's position in a social group for his ranking.	

Practice #4

Read the passage. Then answer the question that follows.

Physics describes the behavior of the universe by analyzing interactions between matter and energy. Ultimately, physicists hope to discover a theory that can explain and predict the interactions of all components in the universe; classical mechanics and quantum mechanics are two branches of physics that attempt to find such a unifying theory.

Physicist Isaac Newton is probably best known for the legend that he "discovered" gravity in the 17th century when he was sitting under an apple tree and an apple fell on his head. Whether or not an apple really gave Newton his first insights, he is credited with realizing that the Moon orbited the Earth based on the pull of gravity and developing formulas for gravity and other forces working on objects. These descriptions provided the foundation for *classical mechanics*. Newton's theories have proven so useful because they are *deterministic*. In other words, if one knows the variables and the forces acting upon an object such as a rocket, one can *determine* how fast and in what way it will move.

By the turn of the 20th century, experiments with atomic and subatomic particles were revealing that, when determining the behavior of miniscule objects with little or no mass, the laws of gravity and other aspects of classical mechanics are inapplicable. New formulas were needed to take into account the ways that energy and matter interact. These realizations led to the development of a new field of physics called *quantum mechanics*. Unlike classical mechanics, quantum mechanics is *probabilistic*; measurements are expressed as probabilities rather than definitive answers. Equations include an *uncertainty principle*, a group of mathematical inequalities that express the limits on knowing every physical property of a particle at any one moment.

4) **Directions**: *Select the sentences that most appropriately match the descriptions of each branch of physics. TWO of the answer choices will NOT be used.* **This question is worth 3 points.**

Answer Choices	Branches of Physics
1. This branch of physics can predict the course of a large flying or orbiting object.	**Classical mechanics** • • •
2. Research results in this branch of physics become unreliable at the atomic level.	
3. Researchers must accept findings as likelihoods rather than certainty in this field.	**Quantum mechanics** • •
4. The basis for this branch of physics was derived primarily from investigations in the 1600s.	
5. Researchers in this field look at the impact of strong force on proteins and cells.	
6. The behavior of an object is gauged by the object's particle interactions in this field of study.	
7. The force of gravity is not necessarily an essential factor in the research for this field.	

Practice #5

Read the passage. Then answer the question that follows.

The United States *civil rights movement* occurred in the 1950s and 1960s and was marked by a plethora of protests against racial and ethnic discrimination. However, not everyone involved in the struggle agreed about strategies and goals. A major philosophical divide was between two hugely influential African-American leaders – both of whom were assassinated at a young age – Martin Luther King, Jr., and Malcolm X.

Martin Luther King, Jr., was a Baptist minister who famously declared "I have a dream" – a dream of an integrated, just society where people of diverse ethnicity live side by side. He took inspiration from the powerful and peaceful protests of Mahatma Gandhi that ended British colonialism in India. From the early 1950s, King helped organize and inspire marches and boycotts. He encouraged protests that involved civil disobedience, such as sitting down at a lunch counter reserved for white people and refusing orders to move. Protestors were trained to nonviolently resist arrest and police brutality. The strategy was to focus public attention on unequal treatment and on the physical force that maintained it. King himself was arrested or detained 29 times.

Meanwhile, in northeastern cities, many African Americans were drawn to the defiant speeches of Malcolm X, a deputy of the radical Nation of Islam group. Malcolm X said that the "X" in his name was a substitute for his lost African name. His viewpoint was that through slavery and oppression, the U.S. government had exploited and degraded generations of Africans; therefore, it was naïve to think that any political action would bring justice. The Nation of Islam viewed "white" people as devils and supported a separate nation for "black" people. The group also urged African Americans to defend themselves "by any means necessary." In 1964, Malcolm X broke away from the Nation of Islam. He went on a Muslim pilgrimage to Mecca, where he described his astonishment at observing racial integration within Islam. Just before his death, he became more optimistic about implementing change through politics and, for the first time, began urging his American followers to vote.

5) **Directions**: *Select the sentences that most appropriately match the descriptions of each civil rights leader. TWO of the answer choices will NOT be used.* **This question is worth 3 points.**

Answer Choices	Civil Rights Leaders
1. This leader consistently encouraged followers to believe that the U.S. could become more fair.	**Martin Luther King, Jr.** • •
2. This leader said that longtime victims of oppression should be cynical about change rather than naïve.	
3. This leader's experiences led him to modify his own extremist viewpoints toward the end of his life.	**Malcolm X** • • •
4. This leader led a "Salt March" to protest the colonial government's taxes and control.	
5. This leader worked to organize armed attacks on centers of government power.	
6. This leader felt that peaceful protests could sway public opinion.	
7. This leader said that African Americans should defend themselves with force if attacked.	

Practice #6

Read the passage. Then answer the question that follows.

In medical terminology, a *syndrome* is a group of symptoms or recognizable signs that point to a specific mental or physical disorder, disease, or condition. Asperger's syndrome and Savant syndrome are two examples; people who have either of these syndromes may have different combinations of symptoms with varying severities. Researchers do not know exactly what causes either condition.

Asperger's syndrome is thought to be on the same spectrum of symptoms as autism*, but Asperger's syndrome is a milder condition. People with *Asperger's syndrome* have normal cognitive and speaking abilities but have difficulty engaging in social interactions. For instance, they may not easily understand other people's social cues or the back and forth of conversational exchanges. Their own facial expressions and gestures may be limited, and they may also avoid eye contact with others. Probably the most recognizable characteristic of Asperger's syndrome is the inclination toward restricted interests; for example, a person with Asperger's syndrome may memorize sports statistics and talk about them but not be interested in sports. People with Asperger's syndrome may focus on small details in the environment, with heightened sensitivity to lights, textures, and noises.

Savant Syndrome is a rare condition in which a person with serious mental disabilities has an "island of genius," a remarkable, even astounding talent that is incongruous with an overall disability. For example, a person with the syndrome may be able to instantaneously calculate complex math problems. Despite a strong connection with autism, not all savants are autistic. Rather, some savants have developmental disabilities or central nervous system injuries. The 1988 movie *Rain Man* was inspired by a real person who had memorized more than 12,000 books and could simultaneously read one page of a book with his left eye and the other page with his right, yet he had trouble buttoning his shirt and fared poorly on IQ tests.

Autism: a developmental disorder that may include difficulties with socializing

6) **Directions**: *Select the sentences that most appropriately match the descriptions of each type of syndrome. TWO of the answer choices will NOT be used.* **This question is worth 3 points.**

Answer Choices	Types of Syndrome
1. A new theory for this syndrome is finding acceptance throughout the medical community.	**Asperger's** • •
2. Individuals with this syndrome may have an exceptional ability in one cognitive task.	**Savant** • • •
3. People with this syndrome might not understand when someone has said something in a joking manner.	
4. A person with this syndrome may have experienced trauma to the central nervous system.	
5. Focusing on a narrow interest is one common characteristic of this syndrome.	
6. This syndrome may cause a person to be unable to speak or communicate with others.	
7. Someone with this syndrome may demonstrate extreme poles of brilliance and disability.	

Read the passage. Then answer the question that follows.

Dense vegetation, high rainfall, and biodiversity characterize rainforests, which are home to 50 percent of the planet's plants and animals. Rainforests are the *biome*, or major habitat, most essential for climate regulation, carbon dioxide absorption, and prevention of soil erosion. Called "the world's largest pharmacy," rainforests also contain vital sources of medicines, including 70 percent of the plants used to treat cancer. Among the many types of rainforests, the two most prevalent are tropical and temperate.

Tropical rainforests cover territory near the equator and between the Tropic of Cancer and Tropic of Capricorn; *subtropical rainforests* are located within this zone or bordering it. A tropical rainforest has the largest *biodiversity*, or variety of plants and animals, of any biome. Estimates conclude that millions of new species of insects, plants, and microorganisms have yet to be discovered in both of these warm, humid ecosystems. Typical plants in these rainforests include palms, bamboo, vines, and ferns; many plants produce flowers and fruit. Because it normally rains every day in a tropical rainforest, trees tend to have thin bark; thick, waxy leaves; and "buttress" supports around the trunk bases to cope with so much precipitation. Dense tropical vegetation supports animals such as jaguars, monkeys, parrots, and poisonous snakes.

Located in the middle latitudes, usually near an ocean, *temperate rainforests* support coniferous or broadleaf groves and are known for massive trees, including redwoods and Douglas firs, that dominate the habitat. Mosses, mushrooms, lichens, ferns, and blackberry brambles also grow in this ecosystem known for cool temperatures and long, wet winter and spring seasons. Of any biome, temperate rainforests have the largest *biomass*, the total mass of living matter within a habitat. Animals here include bears, cougars, raccoons, deer, elk, owls, and woodpeckers; poisonous snakes are not indigenous. In North America, temperate rainforests exist in the Pacific Northwest, the British Columbia coast, and other regions.

7) **Directions**: *Select the sentences that most appropriately match the descriptions of each type of rainforest. TWO of the answer choices will NOT be used.* **This question is worth 3 points.**

Answer Choices	Types of Rainforest
1. This type of rainforest has brisk winters and is devoid of venomous snakes.	**Tropical** ● ●
2. This type of rainforest may be found in regions where the northern and southern hemispheres meet.	**Temperate** ●
3. Giant cone-bearing trees tower over ferns and moss in this type of rainforest.	● ●
4. This type of rainforest has richer soil and less erosion than other types.	
5. This rainforest supports the greatest weight of organisms as a whole.	
6. This rainforest supports the greatest number of different plant and animal species.	
7. Only a few equatorial regions have this type of forest, as it evolved relatively recently.	

Practice #8

Read the passage. Then answer the question that follows.

In 1858, United States Senator Stephen A. Douglas was running for re-election in the state of Illinois. During his campaign, he found himself *dogged*, or followed around, by his challenger, a little-known lawyer named Abraham Lincoln. Douglas finally agreed to a series of seven public debates with Lincoln. The main topic was slavery, focusing on the question of slaveholders expanding into new U.S. territories and states. People flocked to the debates, as the issue of slavery had split the country into two contentious camps. Though no one knew it, the U.S. was about two years away from disunion and civil war.

Douglas did not discuss the morality of slavery, and his actual feelings about it were obscure. He believed that changes in the economy would end slavery gradually. In the meantime, Douglas insisted, the matter should be decided at the state or local level. He advocated giving voters more power over their own lives, a principle known as *popular sovereignty*. In fact, Douglas felt that the very idea of self-rule was at stake if people were not granted such a right. However, prior to the U.S. Civil War, only white men were allowed to vote, so only they would gain more of a voice under Douglas' plan.

Abraham Lincoln called slavery a "monstrous injustice" and believed that it was a question to be settled at the national level. He said that people of African descent were equally entitled to the rights called for in the Declaration of Independence: the right to "life, liberty and the pursuit of happiness." Lincoln disagreed with Douglas that slavery would fizzle out; rather he warned that if slavery expanded into America's new territories, it would thrive and spread to the whole nation. During the debates, Lincoln famously predicted, "A house divided against itself cannot stand. I believe this government cannot endure, permanently, half slave and half free.... It will become all one thing, or all the other." Lincoln lost the race for the senatorial seat but went on to win the presidency in 1860.

8) **Directions**: *Select the sentences that most appropriately match the descriptions of each Illinois senatorial candidate of 1858. TWO of the answer choices will NOT be used.* **This question is worth 3 points.**

Answer Choices	Illinois Senatorial Candidates of 1858
1. This candidate believed that each region should be self-determining on slavery.	**Stephen A. Douglas**
2. This candidate had already served in the U.S. Senate and was seeking to win another term in office.	•
3. This candidate supported the rights of people to declare independence from the Union.	•
4. This candidate was concerned about conflicting moral policies.	•
5. This candidate believed that slavery would become economically unfeasible.	**Abraham Lincoln**
6. This candidate was generally thought to be more charismatic than the other.	•
7. This candidate condemned slave-owning in the strongest possible terms.	•

Practice #9

Read the passage. Then answer the question that follows.

Works of literature in which magic supersedes reality and the laws of nature are commonly categorized as either *magical realism* or *fantasy*. Some literary critics argue that the two terms really refer to the same genre and that magical realism is simply a narrative strategy. In any case, there are certain characteristics associated with each term.

Many literary critics associate magical realism primarily with Latin American novels that depict absurdities in politics or society. Often, magical realism aims to prod the reader to question what is real. Mysterious or supernatural elements seem a natural part of an otherwise mundane, real-world setting. For example, Gabriel Garcia Marquez's classic novel *One Hundred Years of Solitude* draws on real political misdeeds, some of which Marquez witnessed in his native Colombia. The historical events are intertwined with the fictional yet realistic personal stories of a century of life in a jungle village. Throughout the novel, the narrator nonchalantly mentions impossible occurrences: a rainstorm lasts "four years, eleven months, and two days"; a priest levitates when he eats chocolate; a woman can see the future; a trail of blood travels and turns corners; and butterflies always follow one character.

In fantasy narratives, the settings tend to be imagined worlds inhabited by fictional creatures. Supernatural phenomena are logical within the settings and tend to be important parts of the plots. Many ancient myths and legends as well as some of the earliest written works in history fall into the fantasy genre. Fantastical elements include resourceful heroes and heroines, wise guides, lovely or terrifying locations in magical realms, and savage monsters. J.R.R. Tolkien's *The Hobbit* and *The Lord of the Rings* trilogy are modern examples of fantasy. The novels are replete with fictional beings, including humanoid hobbits, elves, goblins, and trolls, living in an idyllic place called "Middle-earth," which is nevertheless fraught with danger.

9) **Directions**: *Select the sentences that most appropriately match the descriptions of each literary genre incorporating magic. TWO of the answer choices will NOT be used.* **This question is worth 3 points.**

Answer Choices	Literary Genres Incorporating Magic
1. In this genre, protagonists usually confront or use magic as part of the plot.	**Magical realism**
2. This genre fuses the real world and the inexplicable in one seamless narrative.	•
3. Settings in this genre are always real Latin American locations.	•
4. This genre is often based on some aspect of science or technology.	**Fantasy**
5. *Alice in Wonderland* fits into this genre because it takes place in a magical realm.	•
6. Characters in this genre may include strange beasts or human-like species.	•
7. This genre often overtly or indirectly comments on political leadership.	•

Read the passage. Then answer the question that follows.

Two men have become American cultural icons based on their love of the wilderness and legendary ability to survive in it, their extensive travels on foot, and their ascetic lifestyles. John Chapman, born in 1774, is mythologized in American culture as "Johnny Appleseed," a barefoot traveler who carried only a bag of apple seeds and wore a cooking pot for a hat. Similarly, naturalist and writer John Muir, born in 1838, frequently took only bread, tea, and two blankets on his treks into wilderness areas. Yet the two men had divergent goals that were unique to their time and place.

According to the Johnny Appleseed legend, John Chapman's goal was to plant apple seeds on the frontier so that pioneers would have food. It is true that Chapman introduced apple trees to a frontier region, but he was actually a businessman who bought land, planted nurseries, and then sold the trees to settlers as they arrived. It is also true that he was known to generously give away saplings, and his trees helped those who were required by law to plant orchards so they could maintain their land claims. Nevertheless, he did profit from his unique strategy of planting ahead of homesteaders. Chapman's notoriety as a roaming seed planter stems from a romantic account about him that was published in a popular magazine.

John Muir was so passionate about nature that he once described climbing to the top of a 30-meter spruce tree during a windstorm simply for the experience. He became America's most influential conservationist, advocating for protection of natural resources at a time when logging companies were rapidly deforesting the country. Muir regularly wrote and spoke about the beauty that he encountered while traveling in the wilds of North America. He addressed the public, Congress, and even presidents with the plea to protect national forests for future generations. He is largely responsible for protecting California's Yosemite Valley as a national park. Muir also founded the *Sierra Club*, the first national environmental organization, which is still active today.

10) **Directions**: *Select the sentences that most appropriately match the descriptions of each iconic figure of the American wilderness. TWO of the answer choices will NOT be used.* **This question is worth 3 points.**

Answer Choices	Iconic Figures of the American Wilderness
1. This man planted fruit trees in the West because he wanted to encourage good nutrition.	**John Chapman**
2. Some people said that this man walked about shoeless, with few goods.	•
3. This man had a unique profit-making scheme to share property with farmers.	•
4. Through written accounts and lectures, this man described his backcountry experiences.	**John Muir**
5. This man's life story became exaggerated and idealized by others.	•
6. This man was an early American environmentalist, advocating on behalf of future generations.	•
7. This man was motivated by a desire to preserve America's woodlands.	•

Select the vocabulary word or phrase that has the closest meaning.

6. **depict**
   A. dig
   B. lodge
   C. portray
   D. launch

7. **treacherous**
   A. instructive
   B. noteworthy
   C. deceitful
   D. majestic

8. **confrontational**
   A. instantaneous
   B. adversarial
   C. extraordinary
   D. monumental

9. **scarcity**
   A. terror
   B. shortage
   C. interaction
   D. feature

10. **sustenance**
    A. food
    B. habitat
    C. impression
    D. magnification

1. **convey**
   A. concede
   B. impart
   C. expand
   D. extrapolate

2. **contradictory**
   A. scrupulous
   B. spectacular
   C. compulsory
   D. conflicting

3. **aptly**
   A. appropriately
   B. actively
   C. willingly
   D. reluctantly

4. **allegory**
   A. free verse
   B. dramatic monologue
   C. extended metaphor
   D. personal essay

5. **compile**
   A. misplace
   B. overlook
   C. preclude
   D. collect

11. **unify**
    A. clarify
    B. integrate
    C. collect
    D. superimpose

12. **orbit**
    A. rotate between
    B. spin on
    C. revolve around
    D. navigate through

13. **property**
    A. accommodation
    B. assessment
    C. process
    D. trait

14. **assassinate**
    A. adaptation
    B. emphasis
    C. indifference
    D. slay

15. **brutality**
    A. cruelty
    B. essence
    C. tragedy
    D. combat

16. **astonishment**
    A. crisis
    B. insight
    C. amazement
    D. flaw

17. **incongruous**
    A. inconsistent
    B. differential
    C. diverse
    D. elegant

18. **fare**
    A. perform
    B. encourage
    C. protect
    D. pay

19. **buttress**
    A. dismantle
    B. brace
    C. dwindle
    D. encounter

20. **brambles**
    A. leaves
    B. stems
    C. vines
    D. pods

21. **devoid of**
    A. plenty of
    B. ahead of
    C. appreciative of
    D. empty of

22. **contentious**
    A. continuous
    B. contented
    C. endowing
    D. disputatious

23. **disunion**
    A. disablement
    B. disarrangement
    C. devolution
    D. division

24. **fizzle**
    A. shout out
    B. comply reluctantly
    C. gradually end
    D. reject immediately

25. **absurdity**
    A. conversion
    B. responsibility
    C. stupidity
    D. exception

26. **prod**
    A. remind
    B. hide
    C. gather
    D. combine

27. **draw on**
    A. hide from
    B. try on
    C. extract from
    D. focus on

28. **intertwine**
    A. conceal
    B. join
    C. face
    D. intervene

29. **levitate**
    A. support
    B. rise
    C. mediate
    D. correspond

30. **replete**
    A. supplied
    B. chronic
    C. cognitive
    D. emptied

31. **idyllic**
    A. ironic
    B. catastrophic
    C. pleasant
    D. cautious

32. **seamless**
    A. smooth
    B. harmless
    C. aimless
    D. persistent

33. **divergent**
    A. burgeoning
    B. differing
    C. expanding
    D. various

34. **notoriety**
    A. disrepute
    B. complaint
    C. coincidence
    D. mixture

35. **roam**
    A. call
    B. sprint
    C. wonder
    D. wander

1B 2D 3A 4C 5D 6C 7C 8B 9B 10A 11B 12C 13D 14D 15A 16C 17A 18A 19B
20C 21D 22D 23D 24C 25C 26A 27C 28B 29B 30A 31C 32A 33B 34A 35D

Actual Practice

Our **Actual Practice** section provides 15 academic passages with a variety of associated questions to give students an opportunity to apply skills acquired throughout the first ten chapters before proceeding onto a simulation of a full-length TOEFL iBT Reading Test.

In Search of Troy

According to the *Iliad*, composed sometime around the eighth century BCE by the Greek poet Homer, the legendary city of Troy was the setting for a 10-year war between Troy's inhabitants, the Trojans, and the greatest warriors, such as Achilles and Ajax, from among the Greek city-states. Homer portrayed Troy as a city of splendor, containing temples filled with treasure and massive, impregnable walls guarded by the finest archers. Although the *Iliad* depicts only a series of events toward the end of the war, Greek mythology describes how the war begins when Paris, a prince of Troy, kidnaps the beautiful Queen Helen from her husband Menelaus, King of Sparta. Menelaus rallies sworn confederates from all Greek nations to besiege Troy, reclaim his wife, and plunder the treasures within the city. The Trojans lose the war after a Greek leader named Odysseus devises a shrewd plan to **infiltrate** Troy at night and open the gates to let the Greek troops past its imposing walls.

Because of Homer's powerful descriptions of the lives lost and glory won from war, the *Iliad* has proven to be one of the most enduring epics of Western literature. The mythical grandeur of Troy has inspired countless reinterpretations of the war and **its** outcome. In fact, some civilizations regarded Trojan culture so highly that they claimed their cultural roots stem from Troy. In his epic, the *Aeneid*, the Roman poet Virgil **attempted** to trace the origins of Roman civilization to a legendary Trojan hero named Aeneas, whom Homer also mentions in the *Iliad*. Over a millennium later, an Icelandic poet and historian composed the *Prose Edda*, which claims that the Norse gods were actually Trojan warriors who traveled to Northern Europe after the fall of Troy. According to the myth, the Norsemen perceived Trojan culture as superior to their own, and they deified the Trojan warriors.

Although the events of Homer's *Iliad* were widely accepted as historical fact during the period of Greco-Roman cultural dominance, by the 18th century CE, lack of tangible evidence caused most scholars to dismiss Troy as only a city of legend. However, a small group of archaeologists believed that the places mentioned in Homer's epics and other Greek myths were based upon actual locations. Thus, in the 19th century, some American and European archaeologists began searching for evidence of Troy.

During the 1860s, archaeologist Frank Calvert attempted minor excavations of a man-made hill located near the southern tip of the Dardanelles in what is now Turkey. This mound, known as *Hisarlik*, fit the description of Homer's legendary Troy, and in 1871, German archaeologist Heinrich Schliemann began a **two-decade-long** excavation of the site. **A** He quickly determined that Hisarlik was an archaeological site known as a *tell*, which occurs when new cities are built atop the remnants of their predecessors. **B Almost inconceivably**, he used dynamite to excavate the ruins on top, which may have destroyed much of the archaeological evidence for a historical Troy. **C** Schliemann's investigations led to neither the Troy of legend nor the oldest city in the tell. **D** Schliemann halted work upon unearthing evidence of a large, walled city and a cache of gold and jewels, which he believed to be the treasure of the Priam, the king of Troy during the legendary Trojan War. Modern archaeologists have determined that what Schliemann located was Troy II, the second city to be built upon that site.

Although Schliemann's search for the legendary Troy was only partially successful, his search at Hisarlik inspired a century of archaeologists to continue where he left off. **In 1932, American archaeologist Carl Blegen began a seven-year dig at Hisarlik. The dig reconfirmed that the ruins of nine cities were stacked atop each other to form the tell, but he was also unsuccessful in locating the Troy depicted in the *Iliad*.**

In 1988, German archaeologist Manfred Korfmann began excavating Hisarlik. He discovered bronze arrowheads and signs of conflict within Troy VIIa, a version of the city that existed during the 13th century BCE, which is when Homer's Trojan War may have occurred. Since then, archaeologists have continued to search for further evidence to substantiate **this claim**, yet the debate continues amongst scholars trying to separate the mythical from the historical.

1) The word "**infiltrate**" in Paragraph 1 probably means
    (A) surround
    (B) aggregate
    (C) intimidate
    (D) penetrate

2) According to Paragraph 1, why did the Trojan War begin?
    (A) Odysseus tried to sneak into the city during a siege.
    (B) A Trojan prince kidnapped the Queen of Sparta.
    (C) Homer's description of Troy made the Greeks jealous.
    (D) Queen Helen wanted to escape from King Menelaus.

3) The word "**its**" in Paragraph 2 refers to
    (A) western literature
    (B) mythical grandeur
    (C) the war
    (D) Troy

4) Why is "**attempted**" MOST LIKELY mentioned in Paragraph 2?
    (A) To show that Virgil's account is not necessarily historically accurate
    (B) To criticize Virgil for using the same setting as Homer
    (C) To emphasize the Trojan influences on Roman society
    (D) To point out Virgil's failures when depicting Trojan culture

5) According to Paragraphs 1 and 2, all of the following are myths told about Troy EXCEPT:
    (A) Only cunning and deception could lead to its downfall.
    (B) King Menelaus tried to capture Troy's beautiful queen.
    (C) Some of its defeated warriors became gods elsewhere.
    (D) One of its heroes established the roots of Roman civilization.

6) Why does the author mention "**two-decade-long**" in Paragraph 4?
    (A) To criticize Schliemann's search for locations that might be mythical
    (B) To give an example of a normal timeframe for an archaeological dig
    (C) To trace the origins of the archaeological search for the city of Troy
    (D) To emphasize Schliemann's dedication to ancient Greek culture

7) Look at the squares [■] that indicate where the following sentence could be added to Paragraph 4.

    Schliemann assumed that the Troy of the *Iliad* was the first of these cities and therefore would be located at the bottom of the tell.

    Where would the sentence best fit?
    Circle the square [■] to add the sentence.

8) The phrase "**Almost inconceivably**" in Paragraph 4 is closest in meaning to
    (A) Almost reasonably
    (B) Almost regrettably
    (C) Almost unthinkably
    (D) Almost certainly

In Search of Troy

Time
00:10:00

According to the *Iliad*, composed sometime around the eighth century BCE by the Greek poet Homer, the legendary city of Troy was the setting for a 10-year war between Troy's inhabitants, the Trojans, and the greatest warriors, such as Achilles and Ajax, from among the Greek city-states. Homer portrayed Troy as a city of splendor, containing temples filled with treasure and massive, impregnable walls guarded by the finest archers. Although the *Iliad* depicts only a series of events toward the end of the war, Greek mythology describes how the war begins when Paris, a prince of Troy, kidnaps the beautiful Queen Helen from her husband Menelaus, King of Sparta. Menelaus rallies sworn confederates from all Greek nations to besiege Troy, reclaim his wife, and plunder the treasures within the city. The Trojans lose the war after a Greek leader named Odysseus devises a shrewd plan to **infiltrate** Troy at night and open the gates to let the Greek troops past its imposing walls.

Because of Homer's powerful descriptions of the lives lost and glory won from war, the *Iliad* has proven to be one of the most enduring epics of Western literature. The mythical grandeur of Troy has inspired countless reinterpretations of the war and **its** outcome. In fact, some civilizations regarded Trojan culture so highly that they claimed their cultural roots stem from Troy. In his epic, the *Aeneid*, the Roman poet Virgil **attempted** to trace the origins of Roman civilization to a legendary Trojan hero named Aeneas, whom Homer also mentions in the *Iliad*. Over a millennium later, an Icelandic poet and historian composed the *Prose Edda*, which claims that the Norse gods were actually Trojan warriors who traveled to Northern Europe after the fall of Troy. According to the myth, the Norsemen perceived Trojan culture as superior to their own, and they deified the Trojan warriors.

Although the events of Homer's *Iliad* were widely accepted as historical fact during the period of Greco-Roman cultural dominance, by the 18th century CE, lack of tangible evidence caused most scholars to dismiss Troy as only a city of legend. However, a small group of archaeologists believed that the places mentioned in Homer's epics and other Greek myths were based upon actual locations. Thus, in the 19th century, some American and European archaeologists began searching for evidence of Troy.

During the 1860s, archaeologist Frank Calvert attempted minor excavations of a man-made hill located near the southern tip of the Dardanelles in what is now Turkey. This mound, known as *Hisarlik*, fit the description of Homer's legendary Troy, and in 1871, German archaeologist Heinrich Schliemann began a **two-decade-long** excavation of the site. **A** He quickly determined that Hisarlik was an archaeological site known as a *tell*, which occurs when new cities are built atop the remnants of their predecessors. **B** **Almost inconceivably**, he used dynamite to excavate the ruins on top, which may have destroyed much of the archaeological evidence for a historical Troy. **C** Schliemann's investigations led to neither the Troy of legend nor the oldest city in the tell. **D** Schliemann halted work upon unearthing evidence of a large, walled city and a cache of gold and jewels, which he believed to be the treasure of the Priam, the king of Troy during the legendary Trojan War. Modern archaeologists have determined that what Schliemann located was Troy II, the second city to be built upon that site.

Although Schliemann's search for the legendary Troy was only partially successful, his search at Hisarlik inspired a century of archaeologists to continue where he left off. **In 1932, American archaeologist Carl Blegen began a seven-year dig at Hisarlik. The dig reconfirmed that the ruins of nine cities were stacked atop each other to form the tell, but he was also unsuccessful in locating the Troy depicted in the *Iliad*.**

In 1988, German archaeologist Manfred Korfmann began excavating Hisarlik. He discovered bronze arrowheads and signs of conflict within Troy VIIa, a version of the city that existed during the 13th century BCE, which is when Homer's Trojan War may have occurred. Since then, archaeologists have continued to search for further evidence to substantiate **this claim**, yet the debate continues amongst scholars trying to separate the mythical from the historical.

9) What can be inferred about Hisarlik's location based on Paragraph 4?

   (A) The presence of a tell indicates that Troy once occupied an advantageous geographic position.

   (B) Troy would have been difficult to attack because it was strategically located atop a man-made mound.

   (C) Its location at the southern tip of the Dardanelles likely makes it a popular tourist attraction.

   (D) Schliemann believed that more treasure was located in the lower ruins of Hisarlik.

10) Which of the following best paraphrases the highlighted information in Paragraph 5?

   (A) Blegen discovered nine new cities while excavating Hisarlik, but he did not locate the mythological Troy.

   (B) Even after seven years of research at Hisarlik, Blegen discovered very little of value about Troy.

   (C) Blegen was not able to locate the Troy of legend, but his finding did reaffirm previous research.

   (D) Blegen's research confirmed that the Troy represented in the *Iliad* is likely fantasy rather than historical.

11) The phrase "**this claim**" in Paragraph 6 refers to the idea that

   (A) Korfmann discovered signs of conflict within Troy VIIa

   (B) Troy VIIa was present in the 13th century BCE

   (C) the Trojan War actually occurred at Troy VIIa

   (D) Troy VIIa is not the site of the Trojan War

12) According to the passage, who was the first archaeologist known to excavate Hisarlik?

   (A) Frank Calvert

   (B) Heinrich Schliemann

   (C) Carl Blegen

   (D) Manfred Kormann

13) **Directions**: Select the sentences that most appropriately match the descriptions of each unearthed city of Troy. TWO of the answer choices will not be used. **This question is worth 3 points.**

Troy II

-
-

Troy VIIa

-
-
-

Answer Choices

1. This city likely existed in the 1200s BCE.
2. Carl Blegen was the first to excavate this site.
3. Arrowheads were discovered at this site.
4. Researchers found the fossilized remains of King Priam at this site.
5. This site was excavated primarily by Manfred Korfmann.
6. A collection of treasure was found at this site.
7. Heinrich Schliemann was the first to excavate this site.

Frank Lloyd Wright

Time
00:20:00

Born in 1867, Frank Lloyd Wright was an American architect whose seven-decade career permanently altered the trajectory of American architecture. Wright fused philosophy and architecture to construct works that are an extension of their environment; his buildings emphasize rather than dominate nearby geographical features. Because no two landscapes are identical, each of Wright's projects is unique.

After establishing himself as a successful architect and drafter in the American Midwest, Wright helped pioneer *Prairie School architecture*, which grew from a late 19th-century artistic movement that rebelled against the dominant Greco-Roman architecture styles and the creation of cheap, identical products using industrial assembly lines. Thus, Prairie School architecture emphasized artisanship and durability and attempted to establish a uniquely "American" style of architecture. One of the fundamental features of Wright's Prairie-style structures is the use of long, horizontal lines, which accentuate the abundant open space of the American Midwest and integrate the buildings with the flat, **pastoral** terrain. To further integrate these early works into their surroundings, Wright often used minimal **ornamentation** and rustic colors. Many examples of Wright's Prairie-style structures are located in Illinois, the Midwestern state where Wright began his career.

During the 1920s, Wright constructed a number of buildings, primarily in Los Angeles, that he considered *textile block houses*. **Wright wanted to challenge himself by using what many considered one of the most unappealing objects as his primary building material: concrete blocks.** Drawing from the architecture and patterns used by the indigenous peoples of Mexico and Central America, Wright had geometric symbols carved into each concrete block, and when he assembled the blocks, the exterior of the house displayed complex geometrical patterns. Using this building method, Wright completed the "Hollyhock House" in 1920 and followed this success with a number of other textile block houses until he moved back to Wisconsin in 1924.

The style of architecture that earned Wright the most recognition developed shortly after his textile style. Wright's *organic style* architecture developed in the late 1920s and 1930s as a **culmination** of his previous architectural philosophies and styling. **A** Large balconies and terraces provide panoramic views, and spacious interiors provided by open floor plans help flood the living spaces with sunlight. **B** In 1935, Wright undertook the construction of "Fallingwater," a residence in rural Pennsylvania that many claim is the pinnacle of his organic style. **C** Wright built the house partly over a waterfall; the foundation mounts a stream and balconies brazenly extend over the edge of the falls. **D** The structure's sharp, cubist angles contrast with the fluidity of nature, but the colors and location allow **it** to blend harmoniously with the landscape.

Also during the mid-1930s, Wright began constructing a number of middle-income houses that represented his vision of how architecture could improve life for ordinary Americans. Wright called this final style of architecture **Usonian** because he felt that the word "American" could refer to all North American people, and he wanted to create a term that referred specifically to the people and cultures of the United States. Wright hoped that the few Usonian structures that he built would cater to a different audience than his past projects did, and provide a blueprint for a new, affordable, and accessible American architecture. These residences are relatively small and sparsely decorated, and contain **diminutive** kitchens and bedrooms that transition smoothly into large living rooms, encouraging social interaction within the house. Wright's Usonian houses helped pave the way for American *ranch-style houses*, which are usually single-story residences with simple ornamentation, large windows, and open floor plans. Ranch-style homes were the most commonly built new home into the 1960s, and they remain a popular style today.

Many examples of Wright's architecture still exist throughout America. During the 1960s, "Fallingwater" became a museum that has attracted millions of visitors. In 1959, Wright completed his last major work, New York City's Solomon R. Guggenheim Museum for modern art. The interior of the museum is an expansion of his organic style and is comprised of a massive, white spiral ramp that serves as the museum's main gallery. Wright's use of open spaces, from the spiral of the Guggenheim Museum to the large living rooms of the residences, continues to influence contemporary American architecture by pulling away from classical European styles, which tend to feature enclosed, segmented living spaces and more decorative embellishments.

1) What can be inferred about American architecture from Paragraph 2?
   (A) Styles of architecture that differed from Prairie School's style were not durable.
   (B) Prairie School architecture was unpopular outside of the United States.
   (C) America in the late 1800s lacked a strongly established architectural style of its own.
   (D) Prairie School architecture was the inspiration for all American architecture.

2) The word "**pastoral**" in Paragraph 2 means
   (A) crowded
   (B) arid
   (C) humid
   (D) rural

3) The word "**ornamentation**" in Paragraph 2 is closest in meaning to
   (A) rule
   (B) potential
   (C) imagination
   (D) embellishment

4) According to Paragraph 2, what is one reason Prairie School architecture was established?
   (A) To replicate the elegance of Greek and Roman buildings
   (B) To create structures that reflected the American landscape
   (C) To embrace the homogenization of manufactured products
   (D) To fill the abundant open space present in much of America

5) Which of the following best paraphrases the highlighted sentence in Paragraph 3?
   (A) Wright was the first architect to successfully create beautiful structures from concrete blocks.
   (B) Wright confronted the notion that concrete blocks are unattractive by using them in his building projects.
   (C) His architecture uses many concrete blocks to form unpleasant-looking yet sturdy structures.
   (D) Wright faced many construction obstacles when he decided to use concrete blocks for his prospective projects.

6) Why does the author MOST LIKELY use the word "**culmination**" in Paragraph 4?
   (A) To persuade the reader that Wright's organic style is his most accomplished
   (B) To trace the origins of Wright's organic style to earlier architects
   (C) To criticize Wright for not using entirely new techniques for each of his styles
   (D) To point out that each of Wright's styles builds upon the previous ones

7) Look at the squares [■] that indicate where the following sentence could be added in Paragraph 4.

   Structures of this style contain a living space that integrates itself as much as possible into nature.

   Where would the sentence best fit?
   Circle the square [■] to add the sentence.

8) The word "**it**" in Paragraph 4 refers to
   (A) nature
   (B) the cliff
   (C) the structure
   (D) the location

Frank Lloyd Wright

Born in 1867, Frank Lloyd Wright was an American architect whose seven-decade career permanently altered the trajectory of American architecture. Wright fused philosophy and architecture to construct works that are an extension of their environment; his buildings emphasize rather than dominate nearby geographical features. Because no two landscapes are identical, each of Wright's projects is unique.

After establishing himself as a successful architect and drafter in the American Midwest, Wright helped pioneer *Prairie School architecture*, which grew from a late 19th-century artistic movement that rebelled against the dominant Greco-Roman architecture styles and the creation of cheap, identical products using industrial assembly lines. Thus, Prairie School architecture emphasized artisanship and durability and attempted to establish a uniquely "American" style of architecture. One of the fundamental features of Wright's Prairie-style structures is the use of long, horizontal lines, which accentuate the abundant open space of the American Midwest and integrate the buildings with the flat, **pastoral** terrain. To further integrate these early works into their surroundings, Wright often used minimal **ornamentation** and rustic colors. Many examples of Wright's Prairie-style structures are located in Illinois, the Midwestern state where Wright began his career.

During the 1920s, Wright constructed a number of buildings, primarily in Los Angeles, that he considered *textile block houses*. **Wright wanted to challenge himself by using what many considered one of the most unappealing objects as his primary building material: concrete blocks.** Drawing from the architecture and patterns used by the indigenous peoples of Mexico and Central America, Wright had geometric symbols carved into each concrete block, and when he assembled the blocks, the exterior of the house displayed complex geometrical patterns. Using this building method, Wright completed the "Hollyhock House" in 1920 and followed this success with a number of other textile block houses until he moved back to Wisconsin in 1924.

The style of architecture that earned Wright the most recognition developed shortly after his textile style. Wright's *organic style* architecture developed in the late 1920s and 1930s as a **culmination** of his previous architectural philosophies and styling. **A** Large balconies and terraces provide panoramic views, and spacious interiors provided by open floor plans help flood the living spaces with sunlight. **B** In 1935, Wright undertook the construction of "Fallingwater," a residence in rural Pennsylvania that many claim is the pinnacle of his organic style. **C** Wright built the house partly over a waterfall; the foundation mounts a stream and balconies brazenly extend over the edge of the falls. **D** The structure's sharp, cubist angles contrast with the fluidity of nature, but the colors and location allow **it** to blend harmoniously with the landscape.

Also during the mid-1930s, Wright began constructing a number of middle-income houses that represented his vision of how architecture could improve life for ordinary Americans. Wright called this final style of architecture **Usonian** because he felt that the word "American" could refer to all North American people, and he wanted to create a term that referred specifically to the people and cultures of the United States. Wright hoped that the few Usonian structures that he built would cater to a different audience than his past projects did, and provide a blueprint for a new, affordable, and accessible American architecture. These residences are relatively small and sparsely decorated, and contain **diminutive** kitchens and bedrooms that transition smoothly into large living rooms, encouraging social interaction within the house. Wright's Usonian houses helped pave the way for American *ranch-style houses*, which are usually single-story residences with simple ornamentation, large windows, and open floor plans. Ranch-style homes were the most commonly built new home into the 1960s, and they remain a popular style today.

Many examples of Wright's architecture still exist throughout America. During the 1960s, "Fallingwater" became a museum that has attracted millions of visitors. In 1959, Wright completed his last major work, New York City's Solomon R. Guggenheim Museum for modern art. The interior of the museum is an expansion of his organic style and is comprised of a massive, white spiral ramp that serves as the museum's main gallery. Wright's use of open spaces, from the spiral of the Guggenheim Museum to the large living rooms of the residences, continues to influence contemporary American architecture by pulling away from classical European styles, which tend to feature enclosed, segmented living spaces and more decorative embellishments.

9) What can be inferred about Wright's architecture in Paragraph 5?

(A) The houses that preceded his Usonian style were built mostly for wealthy clients.

(B) Wright wanted to profit as much as possible from middle-class Americans.

(C) Wright's Usonian style was considered too cheap to be profitable.

(D) Most Americans rejected the small size of Wright's Usonian houses.

10) The word "**diminutive**" in Paragraph 5 means

(A) central

(B) partial

(C) small

(D) distinct

11) The author mentions "*Usonian*" in Paragraph 5 to describe

(A) the architecture found throughout North America

(B) the growing American middle class during the 1930s

(C) the traditions and artistic styles unique to the United States

(D) a type of house built especially for the wealthy

12) According to the passage, which of the following is NOT a characteristic of Wright's architecture?

(A) Structures with large spaces for socialization

(B) Structures that emphasize the neighboring landscape

(C) Structures with arches and columns that give an impression of grandeur

(D) Structures that use earthy colors and little embellishment

13) **Directions**: Select the sentences that most appropriately match the descriptions of each style of architecture. TWO of the answer choices will not be used. **This question is worth 4 points.**

Prairie School architecture

•

•

Textile architecture

•

•

•

Usonian architecture

•

•

Answer Choices

1. The exteriors of these structures contain intricate patterns.

2. The residence called "Fallingwater" is an example of this style.

3. This style uses horizontal lines to blend with a flat landscape.

4. Examples of this style can be found primarily in Los Angeles.

5. This style was developed primarily for a particular economic demographic.

6. Examples of this style are mostly in the American Midwest.

7. This style makes creative use of an unsightly construction material.

8. This style earned Wright the most public and critical acclaim.

9. A house of this style is designed to be conducive to socializing.

Six Degrees of Separation

Time
00:20:00

A The concept of "six degrees of separation" states that a chain of only six acquaintances or fewer separates every person in the world. **B** A 1990 play titled *Six Degrees of Separation* popularized the term, which became even more widespread after the play was made into a film three years later. **C** Moreover, several academic studies have attempted to prove the validity of an interconnected world. **D**

In 1929, Hungarian author Frigyes Karinthy published a short story, "Chains," about characters devising a game in which they try to connect themselves to any person on the planet through a sequence of no more than five individuals, with the first being a personal acquaintance. Karinthy's prediction that "five degrees of separation" exist between any two people on Earth was the first recorded proposal that one could **quantify** human interconnectivity.

Since Karinthy's time, many social scientists and mathematicians have attempted to use social network theory, which organizes data to reflect one's relationship to another to measure the level of global connectivity. The principles of social network theory can be applied to many fields of study. For example, in criminology, a network of a victim and suspect's recently dialed phone numbers, their addresses, and their recent financial transactions may reveal otherwise **indiscernible** relationships. When applied to human communication, network theory uses graphs to connect one person to all his or her acquaintances and all those acquaintances to everyone they know until a thick web of human contact forms.

However, even with these tools, verifying the "six degrees of separation" theory has proven problematic. Mathematical models, which test for interconnectivity among large populations, cannot take into account factors such as social class, as a wealthy person may be less likely to have many acquaintances among poorer people, and vice versa. Moreover, people may have difficulty calculating how many individuals they have been acquainted with throughout their lives. Because creating a web of acquaintances on an individual level is hindered by many personal circumstances, creating one for the entire world becomes seemingly impossible. Nevertheless, in 1967, American psychologist Stanley Milgram conducted *small-world experiments* to test the validity of Karinthy's claim. Milgram designed a procedure in which nearly 300 individuals in an American East Coast city attempted to relay a letter to one of two specific strangers in the American Midwest by sending the letter to an acquaintance who would then send **it** to another acquaintance and so on until the letter reached the target stranger. Of the nearly 300 letters originally distributed, only 64 reached one of the two targets. Yet the few letters that reached their destination had an *average path length*, or number of people between the original sender and final recipient, of six individuals. Hence, Milgram concluded that about six degrees of separation connect all individuals in the United States.

Since the time of their publication, Milgram's experiments have received much criticism. Some critics point out that not all individuals can connect to one another because isolated populations, such as reclusive indigenous peoples, have from little to no contact with the rest of the world. **Others** point out that only a fraction of the original letters reached their destination, which resulted in many unknown path lengths.

Many network theorists and psychologists suggest that the development of the Internet has greatly increased interconnectivity amongst people who are separated by geographical and social factors. Communication technologies such as cellular phones and email have made it easy to contact someone on the other side of the planet. In 2003, **Columbia University** recruited about 24,000 volunteers and instructed them to try to send an email to one of 18 people in 13 different countries by passing the message to an acquaintance and asking that acquaintance to do the same, and so on. Only a fraction of the emails made it to one of the 18 target individuals, but the nearly 400 emails that were successful arrived in approximately four steps. Ultimately, the Columbia email experiment possessed many of the same flaws as Milgram's experiment, but the experiment revealed that the communication made possible by the Internet has increased the "small-world phenomenon."

Although the rise of the World Wide Web has improved communication potential around the world, human interconnectivity remains constrained by social, political, and geographical barriers. Thus, the theory that "six degrees of separation" exist between all individuals is still subject to speculation.

1) Look at the squares [■] that indicate where the following sentence could be added to Paragraph 1.

   Both works focus on the idea that unseen ties connect all people, often in unexpected ways.

   Where would the sentence best fit?
   Circle the square [■] to add the sentence.

2) In Paragraph 2, what does the author say about Frigyes Karinthy?
   (A) He invented a game in which participants try to contact distant acquaintances.
   (B) He wrote a story proposing that all people on Earth are closely connected.
   (C) He was inspired to write a short story based on the play *Six Degrees of Separation*.
   (D) He proved that five links separate every individual on the planet in his story "Chains."

3) The word "**quantify**" in Paragraph 2 probably means
   (A) circumvent
   (B) publicize
   (C) measure
   (D) neglect

4) The word "**indiscernible**" in Paragraph 3 means
   (A) imperceptible
   (B) insignificant
   (C) impressive
   (D) infallible

5) In Paragraph 4, what does the author say about mathematical models that are used in network theory?
   (A) They are the most reliable method for calculating interconnectivity.
   (B) Stanley Milgram used them in his 1967 social network experiment.
   (C) Societal factors limit their accuracy when calculating human connections.
   (D) They are no longer used in social networking experiments.

6) The word "**it**" in Paragraph 4 refers to
   (A) procedure
   (B) the letter
   (C) an acquaintance
   (D) target stranger

7) What can be inferred from the information in Paragraphs 3 and 4?
   (A) In criminology, network theory has replaced field-detective work because it is more reliable.
   (B) Models of human interconnectivity likely vary because of subjective factors, such as the definition of "acquaintance."
   (C) Social network theory only generates accurate results when everyone in a network knows one another.
   (D) Mathematical models have provided the most effective methods for calculating human interconnectivity.

8) The word "**Others**" in Paragraph 5 refers to
   (A) Individuals
   (B) Populations
   (C) Critics
   (D) Peoples

9) What can be inferred about the information in Paragraph 5?
   (A) The average path length of the letters may have increased if every letter had reached its destination.
   (B) Reclusive indigenous peoples made up a small portion of Milgram's 300 letter-senders, generating criticism.
   (C) Most criticisms of Milgram's experiment came from supporters of Karinthy's "five degrees of separation."
   (D) Critics believe that so few letters made it to the recipients because Milgram removed letters with a path length greater than six degrees.

Six Degrees of Separation

Time
00:10:00

A The concept of "six degrees of separation" states that a chain of only six acquaintances or fewer separates every person in the world. **B** A 1990 play titled *Six Degrees of Separation* popularized the term, which became even more widespread after the play was made into a film three years later. **C** Moreover, several academic studies have attempted to prove the validity of an interconnected world. **D**

In 1929, Hungarian author Frigyes Karinthy published a short story, "Chains," about characters devising a game in which they try to connect themselves to any person on the planet through a sequence of no more than five individuals, with the first being a personal acquaintance. Karinthy's prediction that "five degrees of separation" exist between any two people on Earth was the first recorded proposal that one could **quantify** human interconnectivity.

Since Karinthy's time, many social scientists and mathematicians have attempted to use social network theory, which organizes data to reflect one's relationship to another to measure the level of global connectivity. The principles of social network theory can be applied to many fields of study. For example, in criminology, a network of a victim and suspect's recently dialed phone numbers, their addresses, and their recent financial transactions may reveal otherwise **indiscernible** relationships. When applied to human communication, network theory uses graphs to connect one person to all his or her acquaintances and all those acquaintances to everyone they know until a thick web of human contact forms.

However, even with these tools, verifying the "six degrees of separation" theory has proven problematic. Mathematical models, which test for interconnectivity among large populations, cannot take into account factors such as social class, as a wealthy person may be less likely to have many acquaintances among poorer people, and vice versa. Moreover, people may have difficulty calculating how many individuals they have been acquainted with throughout their lives. Because creating a web of acquaintances on an individual level is hindered by many personal circumstances, creating one for the entire world becomes seemingly impossible. Nevertheless, in 1967, American psychologist Stanley Milgram conducted *small-world experiments* to test the validity of Karinthy's claim. Milgram designed a procedure in which nearly 300 individuals in an American East Coast city attempted to relay a letter to one of two specific strangers in the American Midwest by sending the letter to an acquaintance who would then send **it** to another acquaintance and so on until the letter reached the target stranger. Of the nearly 300 letters originally distributed, only 64 reached one of the two targets. Yet the few letters that reached their destination had an *average path length*, or number of people between the original sender and final recipient, of six individuals. Hence, Milgram concluded that about six degrees of separation connect all individuals in the United States.

Since the time of their publication, Milgram's experiments have received much criticism. Some critics point out that not all individuals can connect to one another because isolated populations, such as reclusive indigenous peoples, have from little to no contact with the rest of the world. **Others** point out that only a fraction of the original letters reached their destination, which resulted in many unknown path lengths.

Many network theorists and psychologists suggest that the development of the Internet has greatly increased interconnectivity amongst people who are separated by geographical and social factors. Communication technologies such as cellular phones and email have made it easy to contact someone on the other side of the planet. In 2003, **Columbia University** recruited about 24,000 volunteers and instructed them to try to send an email to one of 18 people in 13 different countries by passing the message to an acquaintance and asking that acquaintance to do the same, and so on. Only a fraction of the emails made it to one of the 18 target individuals, but the nearly 400 emails that were successful arrived in approximately four steps. Ultimately, the Columbia email experiment possessed many of the same flaws as Milgram's experiment, but the experiment revealed that the communication made possible by the Internet has increased the "small-world phenomenon."

Although the rise of the World Wide Web has improved communication potential around the world, human interconnectivity remains constrained by social, political, and geographical barriers. Thus, the theory that "six degrees of separation" exist between all individuals is still subject to speculation.

10) Why does the author mention "**Columbia University**" in Paragraph 6?
   (A) To criticize the establishment for copying Milgram's experimental procedure
   (B) To show that a reputable research institute also was interested in the theory
   (C) To explain why the experiment required so many volunteers
   (D) To justify the use of emails as opposed to letters in the 2003 experiment

11) According to Paragraph 6, each of the following statements about the Columbia University study is true EXCEPT:
   (A) Volunteers each tried to start a chain of emails to reach a particular set of strangers.
   (B) Despite its successes, the experiment faced the same criticisms as earlier procedures.
   (C) The experiment was designed to test the hypothesis across international borders.
   (D) In 400 cases, emails successfully came back to the original volunteers who first sent them.

12) Which of the following best paraphrases the highlighted section in Paragraph 7?
   (A) Issues such as political differences will always prevent complete human interconnectivity.
   (B) Technologies must overcome many obstacles to ensure that all humans are linked to one another.
   (C) The growth of the Internet has strengthened human affiliation worldwide, but physical and cultural obstacles still limit connectivity.
   (D) The Internet will soon overcome civic and topographical restrictions and connect all individuals to one another.

13) **Directions**: An introductory sentence relating to the passage is written below. Complete the exercise by choosing THREE answers to support the sentence. Some sentences do not belong because they do not support the sentence. **This question is worth 2 points.**

There have been many attempts to determine the level of human interconnectivity.
   ●
   ●
   ●

Answer Choices
1. One study tried to measure connectivity by asking people to contact every single person on their email list.
2. Study methods have included using the postal system to relay messages from person to person.
3. Social network theorists often point out similarities between human and electronic networks.
4. Though their usefulness is limited, theories about degrees of separation have been represented by mathematical models.
5. Common sense dictates that advanced forms of communication have reduced the degrees of separation of some isolated populations.
6. Letter- and email-based studies claim to have obtained quantifiable results although many recipients did not continue to relay messages until they reached the target.

Washington Monument

Beginning in 1783, the early United States Congress decided that a statue to honor national hero George Washington, known as the "Father of His Country," should be erected in the nation's capital. During the American Revolution, Washington had led the colonial troops to victory against overwhelming odds. When the U.S. secured independence from Britain, Washington resigned his command. However, Washington was called back to civic duty when he was elected to head the committee drafting the fledgling country's Constitution. His outstanding management in that role led to public pressure for him to become the country's first president. Washington wanted to return to his plantation to farm, but he finally agreed to run for office. In 1789, he was easily elected in the first presidential election and served two terms, declining to run for a third.

History had provided very few examples of the ideal leadership skills needed for a president of a new nation, but Washington's strength and integrity set a **precedent** for the office. He had no interest in seizing control of the government, always recognizing the bounds of his legal authority. In remembering Washington, Thomas Jefferson, the country's third president, noted Washington's **adherence** to the rule of law, stating that he earned "everlasting remembrance."

The process to build an enduring tribute to Washington took nearly 100 years. Although Congress' proposal for a monument began in 1783, nearly 50 years passed before the formation of the Washington National Monument Society, which oversaw the monument's development and construction. Then a decade passed before the monument committee raised money and decided on a design, selected through a competition process. The committee chose a plan by architect Robert Mills. The elaborate neoclassical design included a nearly 183-meter-tall Egyptian-style *obelisk* – a four-sided stone pillar – as well as statues and ornate features. The campaign to secure $1 million to build the memorial had raised less than a quarter of the funds needed when work started on July 4, 1848. At that time, a ceremony drew 20,000 people to view the 11-metric-ton block of white marble laid for the monument's cornerstone.

In 1854, the Washington National Monument Society went bankrupt after being taken over by a group connected with the controversial *Know-Nothing Party*, a short-lived political party that objected to immigration. **The society's bankruptcy coincided with the conflicts leading up to the Civil War and went unresolved throughout the war, all of which halted construction of the memorial at 47.55 meters in height.** Around the time of the war, Mark Twain described the appearance of the incomplete monument as a "hollow, oversized chimney" and many people considered the structure an eyesore.

A few years before the country's centennial in 1876, Congress made plans to complete the monument in time for the celebration, but **the project** stalled in spite of the patriotic intentions. Delays resulted from questions about the design and the strength of the foundation to bear the monument's weight. To save costs, ensure stability, and expedite construction, the original design plan was discarded for a smaller obelisk without the originally proposed design elements. Architect Mills believed that the suggested changes would make the monument look "**like a stalk of asparagus**."

A Finally, work began again in 1879. The first task was to strengthen the structure's foundation. **B** Because stone needed for the obelisk was no longer available from the original quarry near Baltimore, another quarry was used, although the stone did not match the color and quality of the original material. **C** A more suitable quarry was later located; however, the variations in material from three sites are evident in the layers of the monument. **D**

At about 169 meters in height, the monument stood as the tallest building in the world at that time, exceeding the height of Cologne Cathedral. The Washington Monument remains the tallest structure in Washington, D.C., due to a city law passed in 1910 that limits the height of new buildings so that the monument's grandeur is maintained. Nearly 900 steps, as well as an elevator, lead to the pinnacle of the structure, which allows visitors to view the city. The monument weighs approximately 73,591 metric tons. In the interior walls, **commemorative stones** from throughout the world honor George Washington.

1) What does the author say in Paragraph 1 about George Washington's actions?
   (A) Congress determined that a monument should be erected to recognize Washington's resignation.
   (B) Washington was known publicly as the "Father of His Country" because he erected the nation's capital.
   (C) Washington single-handedly drafted the country's Constitution.
   (D) Washington gave up his role as military leader following the war.

2) According to Paragraph 1, all of the following were reasons to build a tribute to George Washington EXCEPT:
   (A) He presided over the Constitutional Convention, guiding the drafting process.
   (B) After becoming the nation's first president, he was elected for a second term.
   (C) He did not seek power but was pressured to provide leadership in different capacities.
   (D) He wanted to be commemorated as the "Father of His Country."

3) The word "**precedent**" in Paragraph 2 is closest in meaning to
   (A) example
   (B) guideline
   (C) goal
   (D) mandate

4) The word "**adherence**" in Paragraph 2 is closest in meaning to
   (A) management
   (B) faithfulness
   (C) defiance
   (D) intention

5) In Paragraph 2, what can be inferred about history offering few models of ideal leadership skills?
   (A) Many leaders over the course of history have sought to gain total control and power.
   (B) Washington is remembered as an honest but hugely flawed individual.
   (C) Washington looked to past historical figures on which to base his role as leader.
   (D) Not enough historical records exist to provide a full picture of past world leaders.

6) In Paragraphs 1 and 2, the author's primary purpose is to
   (A) describe how unique it was that Washington refused to snatch power
   (B) establish reasons why the country wanted to honor Washington
   (C) note how often Washington was asked to serve his country
   (D) highlight Washington's adherence to the law, as Jefferson pointed out

7) Which of the following best paraphrases the highlighted sentence in Paragraph 4?
   (A) The Washington National Monument Society's lack of funding led to the Civil War and resulted in the project stopping at an incomplete height.
   (B) The Washington National Monument Society shifted from its original purpose and held fundraisers to support Civil War reconstruction activities despite the incomplete memorial.
   (C) The Washington National Monument Society's bankruptcy and the unfinished tribute led to the increase in conflicts, contributing to the Civil War and the memorial project's early completion.
   (D) Lack of funding by the Washington National Monument Society and the impending Civil War interrupted work on the structure that was less than 50 meters in height.

Washington Monument

Time
00:10:00

Beginning in 1783, the early United States Congress decided that a statue to honor national hero George Washington, known as the "Father of His Country," should be erected in the nation's capital. During the American Revolution, Washington had led the colonial troops to victory against overwhelming odds. When the U.S. secured independence from Britain, Washington resigned his command. However, Washington was called back to civic duty when he was elected to head the committee drafting the fledgling country's Constitution. His outstanding management in that role led to public pressure for him to become the country's first president. Washington wanted to return to his plantation to farm, but he finally agreed to run for office. In 1789, he was easily elected in the first presidential election and served two terms, declining to run for a third.

History had provided very few examples of the ideal leadership skills needed for a president of a new nation, but Washington's strength and integrity set a **precedent** for the office. He had no interest in seizing control of the government, always recognizing the bounds of his legal authority. In remembering Washington, Thomas Jefferson, the country's third president, noted Washington's **adherence** to the rule of law, stating that he earned "everlasting remembrance."

The process to build an enduring tribute to Washington took nearly 100 years. Although Congress' proposal for a monument began in 1783, nearly 50 years passed before the formation of the Washington National Monument Society, which oversaw the monument's development and construction. Then a decade passed before the monument committee raised money and decided on a design, selected through a competition process. The committee chose a plan by architect Robert Mills. The elaborate neoclassical design included a nearly 183-meter-tall Egyptian-style *obelisk* – a four-sided stone pillar – as well as statues and ornate features. The campaign to secure $1 million to build the memorial had raised less than a quarter of the funds needed when work started on July 4, 1848. At that time, a ceremony drew 20,000 people to view the 11-metric-ton block of white marble laid for the monument's cornerstone.

In 1854, the Washington National Monument Society went bankrupt after being taken over by a group connected with the controversial *Know-Nothing Party*, a short-lived political party that objected to immigration. **The society's bankruptcy coincided with the conflicts leading up to the Civil War and went unresolved throughout the war, all of which halted construction of the memorial at 47.55 meters in height.** Around the time of the war, Mark Twain described the appearance of the incomplete monument as a "hollow, oversized chimney" and many people considered the structure an eyesore.

A few years before the country's centennial in 1876, Congress made plans to complete the monument in time for the celebration, but **the project** stalled in spite of the patriotic intentions. Delays resulted from questions about the design and the strength of the foundation to bear the monument's weight. To save costs, ensure stability, and expedite construction, the original design plan was discarded for a smaller obelisk without the originally proposed design elements. Architect Mills believed that the suggested changes would make the monument look "**like a stalk of asparagus**."

A Finally, work began again in 1879. The first task was to strengthen the structure's foundation. **B** Because stone needed for the obelisk was no longer available from the original quarry near Baltimore, another quarry was used, although the stone did not match the color and quality of the original material. **C** A more suitable quarry was later located; however, the variations in material from three sites are evident in the layers of the monument. **D**

At about 169 meters in height, the monument stood as the tallest building in the world at that time, exceeding the height of Cologne Cathedral. The Washington Monument remains the tallest structure in Washington, D.C., due to a city law passed in 1910 that limits the height of new buildings so that the monument's grandeur is maintained. Nearly 900 steps, as well as an elevator, lead to the pinnacle of the structure, which allows visitors to view the city. The monument weighs approximately 73,591 metric tons. In the interior walls, **commemorative stones** from throughout the world honor George Washington.

8) The term "**the project**" in Paragraph 5 refers to
   (A) the country's centennial
   (B) completing the monument
   (C) questions about the design
   (D) patriotic intentions

9) Why does the author mention "**like a stalk of asparagus**" in Paragraph 5?
   (A) To relay the architect's disappointment in the final design
   (B) To describe the new design plans for the Washington Monument
   (C) To explain how the monument would now be supported by the foundation
   (D) To communicate a concrete visual description of the unfinished tribute

10) Look at the squares [■] that indicate where the following sentence could be added to Paragraph 7.

   On December 6, 1884, a 1.5-metric-ton capstone was lifted to complete the obelisk.

   Where would the sentence best fit?
   Circle the square [■] to add the sentence.

11) According to Paragraph 7, all of the following describe the monument EXCEPT:
   (A) Visitors can walk up 900 steps or take an elevator to the top of the statue.
   (B) The nation's capital can be seen from the apex of the structure.
   (C) The building's peak is built from engraved bricks to memorialize Washington.
   (D) If placed on a scale, the monument would weigh nearly 74,000 metric tons.

12) The author mentions that the monument features "**commemorative stones**" in Paragraph 7 to
   (A) give meaning to a legacy
   (B) honor or preserve the memory of a person
   (C) describe an era for future generations
   (D) attract donors to fund a project

13) **Directions**: An introductory sentence relating to the passage is written below. Complete the exercise by choosing the THREE answers that support the sentence. Some sentences do not belong because they do not support the sentence. **This question is worth 2 points.**

   The U.S. government took steps to ensure that George Washington's legacy would be honored.

   -
   -
   -

   Answer Choices
   1. A reduced-size obelisk was selected without the original neoclassical additions.
   2. The monument was originally designed to tower over its surroundings with special decorative features.
   3. A law regulates the maximum height of other buildings in Washington, D.C.
   4. Visitors can see variations in quarry stone in the different levels of the monument.
   5. Inscribed or carved stones from worldwide locations have been mounted inside the memorial.
   6. Washington faced incredible barriers to triumph during the Revolutionary War.

Tenzing Norgay

Tenzing Norgay was a Nepalese Sherpa who in 1953 became one of the first known climbers, along with New Zealander Edmund Hillary, to reach the summit of Mount Everest, the tallest mountain in the world. Besides the personal accomplishment, his feat helped bring Himalayan people and many living in South Asia renewed pride and optimism after a history of European control in Asian regions.

Sherpas are a Himalayan people, traditionally Buddhists, living mostly in mountainous regions of Nepal near the border with Tibet. Since the first British expedition attempt to reach Everest in 1921, Sherpas have been renowned for their mountaineering expertise and extraordinary physiological abilities including strength and adaptation to the cold and high-altitude climbing. For decades, they have acted as guides for Everest climbers.

In his early twenties, Tenzing Norgay – generally referred to in the West as "Tenzing" – was a high-altitude porter for a 1935 British expedition to Everest, and his performance led to work as a porter for two other British Everest attempts. In the 1940s, Tenzing joined other climbs and in 1947 became the *sirdar*, or leader, of a Swiss expedition that was turned back from the Everest summit by a storm. He made the first ascent of Kedarnath Peak in the western Garhwal Himalayas with other climbers that same year. **In 1952, Tenzing participated in two Swiss expeditions that attempted Everest from the Nepalese side, opening up a new route during the trek.** Tenzing was considered a full expedition member then, which he called "the greatest honour that had ever been paid me." During the first 1952 expedition, he and another climber reached a record height on Everest.

In 1953, Tenzing went on his seventh climb up Everest in an expedition with British leader John Hunt and a team of 400 people. During the passage, Tenzing saved one of the climbers, Edmund Hillary, from falling to the bottom of a glacial crevasse* by using an ice axe to secure a rope that stopped his slide. This incident led Hillary to regard Tenzing as the ideal climbing partner for subsequent summit attempts.

Two climbers from the Hunt expedition tried to reach the Everest summit on May 26, 1953, but turned back when an oxygen system, which is necessary for most people at that altitude, failed. **A** At Hunt's direction, Tenzing and Hillary attempted to reach the summit three days later, camping first at 8,500 meters on May 28 and then leaving at 6:30 a.m. the next day with 14-kilogram packs for the final ascent. **B** The most **treacherous** section of the summit was a 12-meter rock face that the climbers managed to maneuver by wedging themselves up a crack between the rock wall and ice, with Hillary leading the way over what would later be designated the Hillary Step. **C** Finally, the two reached the 8,848-meter summit by 11:30 a.m. **D** Hillary and Tenzing stayed there for 15 minutes, using **precious** oxygen to savor their triumph and take photos. At the summit, Hillary photographed Tenzing in what would become a famous shot of him hoisting up his ice axe, with his face obscured by his oxygen mask. Tenzing had dedicated his life to this achievement, once stating, "the pull of Everest was stronger for me than any force on Earth."

Upon descent, Tenzing received great acclaim in India and Nepal and was awarded honors by heads of state. Hillary and Hunt were knighted by Queen Elizabeth II, while Tenzing received the George Medal, an award for acts of bravery by civilians. Questions linger as to why Tenzing was not knighted, creating a controversy that continues today, but Hillary and Tenzing insisted on equally sharing the credit for their enormous achievement.

Thirteen years after Tenzing's death in 1986, *Time* magazine included him as one of the 100 most influential people of the 20th century. American writer and mountaineer James Ramsey Ullman characterized the honor that Asia felt in Tenzing's accomplishment at the time, beyond the summit of Everest: he was "the first humbly born Asian in all history to attain world stature and world renown. And for other Asians **his feat** was not the mere climbing of a mountain, but a bright portent for themselves and for the future of the world."

In 2002, Jamling Tenzing Norgay and Peter Hillary, two of the eminent climbers' sons, summited Everest together to celebrate the 50th anniversary of their fathers' accomplishment.

*Crevasse: a deep opening or gap in ice or rock

1) According to Paragraph 2, all of the following describes Sherpas EXCEPT:
   (A) They are famous for their climbing aptitude in high elevations.
   (B) They have the ability to endure extremes of cold.
   (C) They have been known as expert mountaineers since the 19th century.
   (D) They live in the border region where two countries meet.

2) In Paragraph 2, what can be inferred about the Sherpas' mountaineering capabilities?
   (A) Sherpas may be genetically better adapted than outsiders.
   (B) The Sherpas may have created special clothing to help them stay warm in such frigid conditions.
   (C) The British may have helped Sherpas develop the strength needed for high-altitude mountaineering.
   (D) Sherpas may have difficulty adapting to life at lower altitudes.

3) Which of the following best paraphrases the highlighted sentence in Paragraph 3?
   (A) In 1952, Tenzing was a part of an expedition of two Swiss groups that reached the highest elevation.
   (B) In 1952, Tenzing was successful in ascending the southern peak of Everest through a new passage discovered by Swiss climbers.
   (C) In 1952, Tenzing was part of two Swiss climbing teams that created a southern course to Everest from Nepal.
   (D) In 1952, Tenzing became a full British team member and ascended the highest point at that time in the southern Himalayas.

4) In Paragraph 4, the author's primary purpose is to
   (A) provide further description of the dangerous route to the summit of Everest
   (B) show why Hillary chose Tenzing as his mountaineering partner
   (C) explain how Tenzing's determination grew through his Everest experiences
   (D) describe the quick thinking and mountaineering skills needed for an Everest climb

5) Look at the squares [■] that indicate where the following sentence could be added to Paragraph 5.

   According to Edmund Hillary, "A few more whacks of the ice axe in the firm snow, and we stood on top."

   Where would the sentence best fit?
   Circle the square [■] to add the sentence.

6) The word "**treacherous**" in Paragraph 5 is closest in meaning to
   (A) perilous
   (B) infamous
   (C) laborious
   (D) rapturous

7) Why does the author mention "**precious**" in Paragraph 5?
   (A) To illustrate that the climbers were recognizing a very special moment of victory
   (B) To show that the climbers celebrated their extraordinary teamwork at the summit
   (C) To point out how important it was to document their feat through photographs
   (D) To indicate what a valuable resource oxygen was for survival at that altitude

Tenzing Norgay

Time
00:10:00

Tenzing Norgay was a Nepalese Sherpa who in 1953 became one of the first known climbers, along with New Zealander Edmund Hillary, to reach the summit of Mount Everest, the tallest mountain in the world. Besides the personal accomplishment, his feat helped bring Himalayan people and many living in South Asia renewed pride and optimism after a history of European control in Asian regions.

Sherpas are a Himalayan people, traditionally Buddhists, living mostly in mountainous regions of Nepal near the border with Tibet. Since the first British expedition attempt to reach Everest in 1921, Sherpas have been renowned for their mountaineering expertise and extraordinary physiological abilities including strength and adaptation to the cold and high-altitude climbing. For decades, they have acted as guides for Everest climbers.

In his early twenties, Tenzing Norgay – generally referred to in the West as "Tenzing" – was a high-altitude porter for a 1935 British expedition to Everest, and his performance led to work as a porter for two other British Everest attempts. In the 1940s, Tenzing joined other climbs and in 1947 became the *sirdar*, or leader, of a Swiss expedition that was turned back from the Everest summit by a storm. He made the first ascent of Kedarnath Peak in the western Garhwal Himalayas with other climbers that same year. **In 1952, Tenzing participated in two Swiss expeditions that attempted Everest from the Nepalese side, opening up a new route during the trek.** Tenzing was considered a full expedition member then, which he called "the greatest honour that had ever been paid me." During the first 1952 expedition, he and another climber reached a record height on Everest.

In 1953, Tenzing went on his seventh climb up Everest in an expedition with British leader John Hunt and a team of 400 people. During the passage, Tenzing saved one of the climbers, Edmund Hillary, from falling to the bottom of a glacial crevasse* by using an ice axe to secure a rope that stopped his slide. This incident led Hillary to regard Tenzing as the ideal climbing partner for subsequent summit attempts.

Two climbers from the Hunt expedition tried to reach the Everest summit on May 26, 1953, but turned back when an oxygen system, which is necessary for most people at that altitude, failed. **A** At Hunt's direction, Tenzing and Hillary attempted to reach the summit three days later, camping first at 8,500 meters on May 28 and then leaving at 6:30 a.m. the next day with 14-kilogram packs for the final ascent. **B** The most **treacherous** section of the summit was a 12-meter rock face that the climbers managed to maneuver by wedging themselves up a crack between the rock wall and ice, with Hillary leading the way over what would later be designated the Hillary Step. **C** Finally, the two reached the 8,848-meter summit by 11:30 a.m. **D** Hillary and Tenzing stayed there for 15 minutes, using **precious** oxygen to savor their triumph and take photos. At the summit, Hillary photographed Tenzing in what would become a famous shot of him hoisting up his ice axe, with his face obscured by his oxygen mask. Tenzing had dedicated his life to this achievement, once stating, "the pull of Everest was stronger for me than any force on Earth."

Upon descent, Tenzing received great acclaim in India and Nepal and was awarded honors by heads of state. Hillary and Hunt were knighted by Queen Elizabeth II, while Tenzing received the George Medal, an award for acts of bravery by civilians. Questions linger as to why Tenzing was not knighted, creating a controversy that continues today, but Hillary and Tenzing insisted on equally sharing the credit for their enormous achievement.

Thirteen years after Tenzing's death in 1986, *Time* magazine included him as one of the 100 most influential people of the 20th century. American writer and mountaineer James Ramsey Ullman characterized the honor that Asia felt in Tenzing's accomplishment at the time, beyond the summit of Everest: he was "the first humbly born Asian in all history to attain world stature and world renown. And for other Asians **his feat** was not the mere climbing of a mountain, but a bright portent for themselves and for the future of the world."

In 2002, Jamling Tenzing Norgay and Peter Hillary, two of the eminent climbers' sons, summited Everest together to celebrate the 50th anniversary of their fathers' accomplishment.

*Crevasse: a deep opening or gap in ice or rock

8) Which of the following best describes the relationship between Paragraphs 5 and 6?
(A) Paragraph 5 describes reaching the summit, while Paragraph 6 describes the honors presented.
(B) Paragraph 5 explains the climb, while Paragraph 6 introduces the competition that arose.
(C) Paragraph 5 summarizes Tenzing's climbs, while Paragraph 6 traces his later life.
(D) Paragraph 5 describes Tenzing and Hillary's friendship, the details of which are amplified in Paragraph 6.

9) In Paragraph 6, what can be inferred about the controversy surrounding recognition by Queen Elizabeth?
(A) John Hunt also reached the summit with Tenzing and Hillary and deserved knighting.
(B) Although the medal was a lesser award, Tenzing and Hillary saw themselves as a team.
(C) Hillary was first up the rock wall to the summit and deserved the honor more.
(D) Tenzing was not knighted because he was not as proficient at climbing as Hillary.

10) The word "**his feat**" in Paragraph 7 refers to
(A) Tenzing dedicating his life to achievement
(B) Tenzing insisting on equally sharing credit
(C) Tenzing attaining world stature
(D) Tenzing characterizing the honor

11) According to Paragraph 7, all of the following are true about why Tenzing was celebrated in Asia EXCEPT:
(A) He came from humble roots but was able to conquer Everest.
(B) His accomplishment in reaching the summit of Everest made him world famous.
(C) Tenzing opened the door to greater economic opportunities in many countries.
(D) Tenzing's actions gave hope to other Asians that they, too, could gain global recognition for their feats.

12) In Paragraph 8, the author's primary purpose is to
(A) show that Tenzing and Hillary must have taught mountaineering skills to their children
(B) suggest that the renowned climbers' fellowship extended to the next generation
(C) indicate that the physical traits needed for climbing are often inherited
(D) prove that Tenzing not being knighted did not create resentment in his family

13) **Directions**: An introductory sentence relating to the passage is written below. Complete the exercise by choosing the THREE answers that support the sentence. Some sentences do not belong because they do not support the sentence. **This question is worth 2 points.**

Determined to summit Mount Everest, Tenzing Norgay made numerous attempts until he reached his objective.

-
-
-

Answer Choices
1. Tenzing was the first to summit Kedarnath Peak in 1947 along with other mountaineers.
2. Tenzing was the sirdar of a Swiss expedition stopped from an ascent by a storm.
3. Tenzing prevented Hillary from slipping into a crack, which led to a climbing partnership.
4. Tenzing received recognition for his feat from leaders throughout the world.
5. Tenzing helped start a new path to the peak from a location originating in Nepal.
6. Tenzing started working for a British group as a high-elevation porter in 1935.

Roswell

A 1947 incident in Roswell, New Mexico, spurred claims by Unidentified Flying Object (UFO) believers that extraterrestrials had visited Earth and that the United States government was concealing the truth. Receiving the most media attention of any UFO accounts, the case has become an American popular-culture phenomenon.

After World War II ended in 1945, a number of people in the U.S. and in other countries claimed that they had witnessed mysterious objects in the sky that **they** believed were spacecraft flown by extraterrestrials. During this epidemic of "flying saucer" sightings, an object crashed on a ranch in New Mexico during the first week of July 1947 near the town of Roswell and a military airfield. On July 8, a young Roswell Army Air Field (RAAF) information officer issued an **unauthorized** *press release*, an announcement of public interest to the news media. The statement indicated that a "flying disk" had been retrieved. Based on the press release, the local paper promptly ran a story with the headline "RAAF Captures Flying Saucer on Ranch in Roswell Region." The story soon was reprinted in newspapers across the country.

Quickly following the first military press release, military officials corrected the story, reporting to the press that what actually had been recovered at the crash site was a weather balloon. At a press conference, military personnel displayed the wreckage debris, including some silvery, flexible material.

Although the military denied the existence of a flying saucer, interest in the Roswell incident continued to some degree. However, in the late 1970s, attention to the events gained momentum when one of the military men involved in the recovery of the debris in 1947 was interviewed and stated that he believed that the crash debris was "not of this world." Soon, new accounts and new witnesses emerged, providing stories of alien bodies found, some alive and some dead, and *autopsies* – examinations after death – that had been performed. The Roswell events became popular among those interested in UFOs and gained national and international attention through an article in the *National Enquirer*. Further media attention fueled ongoing interest in the case. The popular-culture phenomenon increased due to books and media such as *The Roswell Incident*; a 1990s **bogus** short film called *Alien Autopsy: Fact or Fiction*; television shows featuring "witness" testimonies; and magazine and newspaper articles.

In response to growing public pressure, the U.S. Air Force investigated the Roswell incident in 1994 and detailed its findings in a report. The Air Force admitted that the 1947 weather balloon story was not accurate; the wreckage had in fact been from an experimental high-altitude **surveillance** balloon designed to track Soviet nuclear tests, part of a top-secret program at that time.

The 1994 document did not address the question of the **alleged** aliens that were found in the crash, and a second Air Force investigation was performed, resulting in the 1997 report "Case Closed." The study concluded that the sensational stories regarding extraterrestrials and UFO sightings were the result of a number of factors, including the passage of decades and faulty memories surrounding actual Air Force training accidents and fatalities. The report also suggested that people were experiencing transformed memories; they were confusing the supposed aliens with the lifelike *dummies*, or life-size dolls, that the military began using in 1950 for test operations. Furthermore, the statement noted the purposeful misrepresentations of incidents, or *hoaxes* – falsehoods meant to mislead and trick people – by some individuals seeking economic gain from the distortions.

A Among its body of evidence regarding actual events that may have been confused, the report cited a 1959 parachute jump from 32 kilometers high that led to a test pilot sustaining injuries that caused his head to swell, leaving just slits for his eyes, similar in appearance to how popular culture often depicts alien features. **B** The document suggested that witnesses who saw the man at the military hospital stated decades later that they had seen an alien. **C** In addition, *experimental space probes* – robotic spacecraft used for research – resembled flying saucers when **they** were dropped from balloons for testing purposes. **D**

The Air Force reports have not ended the debate for some UFO enthusiasts who have dismissed the explanations as "implausible" and "incompetent."

1) The word "**they**" in Paragraph 2 refers to
   (A) countries around the world
   (B) some people in the U.S.
   (C) people who said they had seen UFOs
   (D) sightings of unidentified flying objects

2) Why does the author mention "**unauthorized**" in Paragraph 2?
   (A) To explain that the officer did not get approval to issue the press release
   (B) To show that the details in the press release were factually accurate
   (C) To emphasize that there actually had been a flying saucer crash
   (D) To trace how the information about the incident reached the newspapers

3) Which of the following best describes the relationship between Paragraphs 1 and 2?
   (A) Paragraph 2 shows that the U.S. government had clear evidence of UFOs but hid it.
   (B) The paragraphs build a case for the military's view of the incident.
   (C) Details in Paragraph 2 contradict the popular-culture idea in Paragraph 1.
   (D) Paragraph 1 introduces the phenomenon, and Paragraph 2 shows how the story started.

4) Why does the author mention "**bogus**" in Paragraph 4?
   (A) To show how there was wide public interest in the case
   (B) To indicate that the "alien autopsy" was not genuine
   (C) To prove that there was convincing evidence of space visitors
   (D) To describe details of the alien autopsy findings

5) The word "**surveillance**" in Paragraph 5 means
   (A) observation
   (B) justification
   (C) representation
   (D) protection

6) In Paragraph 5, what can be inferred about why the military later admitted that it had covered up the surveillance program in 1947?
   (A) To continue to mislead the public about the spacecraft crash
   (B) To reveal the facts after the outdated program was no longer top secret
   (C) To apologize to the Soviets about the surveillance program
   (D) To cover up other high-security activities undertaken in the 1940s

7) The word "**alleged**" in Paragraph 6 is closest in meaning to
   (A) flawed
   (B) assigned
   (C) contradicted
   (D) supposed

8) Paragraph 6 states all of the following about the military report findings EXCEPT:
   (A) Over the years, people began thinking that the test dummies had been aliens.
   (B) Memories about early military training injuries and deaths had become distorted.
   (C) Any secret information about extraterrestrials could not be released to the public.
   (D) Deliberate misinformation was perpetuated by some people seeking to gain from it.

Roswell

A 1947 incident in Roswell, New Mexico, spurred claims by Unidentified Flying Object (UFO) believers that extraterrestrials had visited Earth and that the United States government was concealing the truth. Receiving the most media attention of any UFO accounts, the case has become an American popular-culture phenomenon.

After World War II ended in 1945, a number of people in the U.S. and in other countries claimed that they had witnessed mysterious objects in the sky that **they** believed were spacecraft flown by extraterrestrials. During this epidemic of "flying saucer" sightings, an object crashed on a ranch in New Mexico during the first week of July 1947 near the town of Roswell and a military airfield. On July 8, a young Roswell Army Air Field (RAAF) information officer issued an **unauthorized** *press release*, an announcement of public interest to the news media. The statement indicated that a "flying disk" had been retrieved. Based on the press release, the local paper promptly ran a story with the headline "RAAF Captures Flying Saucer on Ranch in Roswell Region." The story soon was reprinted in newspapers across the country.

Quickly following the first military press release, military officials corrected the story, reporting to the press that what actually had been recovered at the crash site was a weather balloon. At a press conference, military personnel displayed the wreckage debris, including some silvery, flexible material.

Although the military denied the existence of a flying saucer, interest in the Roswell incident continued to some degree. However, in the late 1970s, attention to the events gained momentum when one of the military men involved in the recovery of the debris in 1947 was interviewed and stated that he believed that the crash debris was "not of this world." Soon, new accounts and new witnesses emerged, providing stories of alien bodies found, some alive and some dead, and *autopsies* – examinations after death – that had been performed. The Roswell events became popular among those interested in UFOs and gained national and international attention through an article in the *National Enquirer*. Further media attention fueled ongoing interest in the case. The popular-culture phenomenon increased due to books and media such as *The Roswell Incident*; a 1990s **bogus** short film called *Alien Autopsy: Fact or Fiction*; television shows featuring "witness" testimonies; and magazine and newspaper articles.

In response to growing public pressure, the U.S. Air Force investigated the Roswell incident in 1994 and detailed its findings in a report. The Air Force admitted that the 1947 weather balloon story was not accurate; the wreckage had in fact been from an experimental high-altitude **surveillance** balloon designed to track Soviet nuclear tests, part of a top-secret program at that time.

The 1994 document did not address the question of the **alleged** aliens that were found in the crash, and a second Air Force investigation was performed, resulting in the 1997 report "Case Closed." The study concluded that the sensational stories regarding extraterrestrials and UFO sightings were the result of a number of factors, including the passage of decades and faulty memories surrounding actual Air Force training accidents and fatalities. The report also suggested that people were experiencing transformed memories; they were confusing the supposed aliens with the lifelike *dummies*, or life-size dolls, that the military began using in 1950 for test operations. Furthermore, the statement noted the purposeful misrepresentations of incidents, or *hoaxes* – falsehoods meant to mislead and trick people – by some individuals seeking economic gain from the distortions.

A Among its body of evidence regarding actual events that may have been confused, the report cited a 1959 parachute jump from 32 kilometers high that led to a test pilot sustaining injuries that caused his head to swell, leaving just slits for his eyes, similar in appearance to how popular culture often depicts alien features. **B** The document suggested that witnesses who saw the man at the military hospital stated decades later that they had seen an alien. **C** In addition, *experimental space probes* – robotic spacecraft used for research – resembled flying saucers when **they** were dropped from balloons for testing purposes. **D**

The Air Force reports have not ended the debate for some UFO enthusiasts who have dismissed the explanations as "implausible" and "incompetent."

9) Look at the squares [■] that indicate where the following sentence could be added to Paragraph 7.

The report also indicated that the military had tested parachutes and spy gear by dropping human-like dummies from high altitudes, which may have been misconstrued as extraterrestrials.

Where would the sentence best fit?

Circle the square [■] to add the sentence.

10) In Paragraph 7, what can be inferred about how people interpreted the sight of the injured test pilot?

(A) People deliberately made up wild stories about seeing a space alien.

(B) Distorted recollections over many years may have impacted witnesses' perceptions.

(C) People who witnessed the shocking sight immediately contacted the media.

(D) Witnesses later determined that what they had seen was the result of an accident.

11) The word "**they**" in Paragraph 7 refers to

(A) unidentified flying saucers

(B) balloons used for experiments

(C) alien features

(D) space probes

12) Which of the following best paraphrases Paragraph 8?

(A) UFO proponents believed that the military reports were inaccurate and poorly prepared.

(B) The false reports have generated a greater number of Roswell UFO enthusiasts.

(C) The misleading Air Force findings provide even more evidence of government cover-ups.

(D) UFO researchers documented their evidence to counter the military's reports.

13) **Directions**: An introductory sentence relating to the passage is written below. Complete the exercise by choosing the THREE answers that support the sentence. Some sentences do not belong because they do not support the sentence. **This question is worth 2 points.**

Media attention increased decades after the 1947 Roswell event, sparking greater interest in the UFO legends.

-
-
-

Answer Choices

1. Additional purported eyewitnesses came forward in the news to describe the space creatures.

2. Some authorities debunked the myth by pointing out documented facts around the case.

3. A popular tabloid ran a story about the UFO, drawing worldwide attention.

4. Publications and TV programs provided sensationalistic versions of the events.

5. The military conducted two investigations to explain how the public misinterpreted incidents.

6. The Air Force said that the crash debris was really a surveillance balloon, not a weather balloon.

Genetic Drift

Time
00:20:00

Parents pass characteristics to their offspring in the form of *genes*, or sequences of DNA that determine the traits of an organism. Every person has two copies of genes, one from the father and one from the mother. Genes are not identical from individual to individual because alternative forms of genes called *alleles* carry different pieces of information for the same trait. **These variations** explain why siblings can inherit, for example, different eye color. If one sibling is born with brown eyes, but her brother is born with blue eyes, then the parents passed on different allele combinations for the genes that determine eye coloration.

Natural selection is the process by which, over many generations, certain alleles that help organisms survive in **their** environment become dominant and replace less successful variations on the same gene. Whereas **environmental factors** influence natural selection, a process called genetic drift introduces an element of randomness to evolution. *Genetic drift* describes the process by which certain alleles appear with more or less frequency in a species based on how many members of the species who possess those alleles happen to reproduce.

In small populations, genetic drift can cause a reduction of alleles, but it does not affect large populations to the same extent. Because every individual has a different set of alleles for any given trait, the genetic mixing that results from procreation ensures that a wide variety of alleles will exist in any large population. This genetic pool helps a species survive because one set of alleles may be better suited for a certain environment than another set. For example, the genes that control skin color in humans vary because humans have inhabited all climates and need to absorb or repel varying degrees of sunlight. The variety of alleles resulting from divergent allele combinations is called *genetic variance*.

Because humans are among the most populous mammals on Earth, one would expect humans to have one of the largest genetic variances. **Paradoxically**, humans have even less genetic variance than their closest living relatives, primates. This surprising discovery has led many scientists to conclude that all humans today come from a relatively small gene pool that may be due in part to a population bottleneck or the founder effect.

A A *population bottleneck* occurs when a **catastrophic** event, such as a flood, famine, or overhunting, causes a large decrease in the overall population of a species. **B** Because such an event causes random groups of a population to die, allele frequencies change, increasing the chance of a significant genetic drift. **C** Some researchers suggest that humans experienced a population bottleneck during the Toba catastrophe. **D** Approximately 70,000 years ago, at Lake Toba in Indonesia, a huge volcanic eruption may have plunged the Earth into a decade-long "volcanic winter," when volcanic ash blocked the Sun's light and killed much of Earth's vegetation and animal population. Estimates place the human population at 3,000 to 10,000 individuals shortly after the eruption. **Thus, humankind's current genetic diversity may be the result of small, isolated groups drawing from a limited genetic pool to repopulate the Earth after the eruption.**

However, some researchers claim that the Toba catastrophe did not significantly decrease the human population; they believe that human populations were consistently very low and isolated until recent millennia. In fact, genetic research suggests that the hominid* population was below 26,000 individuals approximately one million years ago, which explains the relative lack of genetic variance among humans. Migrations may also contribute to limited genetic variance. A *founder effect* occurs because a small population that splits from a main species group will have less genetic variance, providing an extreme example of genetic drift. The most widespread example of the founder effect amongst modern humans (*Homo sapiens*) is gradual migration from Africa by some groups, beginning about 200,000 years ago. As small bands of migrants moved further away, their genetic variance decreased compared to the main population that remained in Africa. **This millennia-long migration is known as a *serial founder effect* and, when combined with the hypothesis of a small original population, helps elucidate why people in various regions of the world have developed minor physical and genetic differences from people in distant regions.**

Hominid: the family of bipedal primates that includes modern humans and their extinct ancestors

1) The phrase "**These variations**" in Paragraph 1 refers to
   (A) traits of an organism
   (B) two copies of genes
   (C) alternative forms of genes
   (D) pieces of information

2) According to Paragraph 1, an individual's genes
   (A) are identical to the genes of any other individual of the same species
   (B) differ from the genes of other individuals because of allele diversity
   (C) usually develop once that individual begins to reproduce
   (D) only determine traits of physical appearance, such as eye color

3) The word "**their**" in Paragraph 2 refers to
   (A) generations
   (B) alleles
   (C) organisms
   (D) variations

4) Why does the author mention "**environmental factors**" in Paragraph 2?
   (A) To point out how natural selection differs from genetic drift
   (B) To emphasize the primary use of natural selection in biology
   (C) To contrast influential and insignificant evolutionary processes
   (D) To explain the process of genetic drift using a concrete example

5) Why does the author use "**Paradoxically**" in Paragraph 4?
   (A) To emphasize a surprising fact about human genetics
   (B) To argue that other primates are better adapted to their environment
   (C) To compare similar traits in humans and primates
   (D) To summarize the content in the previous sentence

6) According to Paragraph 4, modern primates
   (A) have less genetic variance than humans
   (B) have a larger population distribution than humans
   (C) have more genetic variance than humans
   (D) may be experiencing a population bottleneck

7) Look at the squares [■] that indicate where the following sentence could be added to Paragraph 5.

   For instance, overhunting drove the American bison population down to fewer than 1,000 individuals by the early 20th century.

   Where would the sentence best fit?
   Circle the square [■] to add the sentence.

8) The word "**catastrophic**" in Paragraph 5 is closest in meaning to
   (A) confined
   (B) ruinous
   (C) incredible
   (D) documented

Genetic Drift

Parents pass characteristics to their offspring in the form of *genes*, or sequences of DNA that determine the traits of an organism. Every person has two copies of genes, one from the father and one from the mother. Genes are not identical from individual to individual because alternative forms of genes called *alleles* carry different pieces of information for the same trait. **These variations** explain why siblings can inherit, for example, different eye color. If one sibling is born with brown eyes, but her brother is born with blue eyes, then the parents passed on different allele combinations for the genes that determine eye coloration.

Natural selection is the process by which, over many generations, certain alleles that help organisms survive in **their** environment become dominant and replace less successful variations on the same gene. Whereas **environmental factors** influence natural selection, a process called genetic drift introduces an element of randomness to evolution. *Genetic drift* describes the process by which certain alleles appear with more or less frequency in a species based on how many members of the species who possess those alleles happen to reproduce.

In small populations, genetic drift can cause a reduction of alleles, but it does not affect large populations to the same extent. Because every individual has a different set of alleles for any given trait, the genetic mixing that results from procreation ensures that a wide variety of alleles will exist in any large population. This genetic pool helps a species survive because one set of alleles may be better suited for a certain environment than another set. For example, the genes that control skin color in humans vary because humans have inhabited all climates and need to absorb or repel varying degrees of sunlight. The variety of alleles resulting from divergent allele combinations is called *genetic variance*.

Because humans are among the most populous mammals on Earth, one would expect humans to have one of the largest genetic variances. **Paradoxically**, humans have even less genetic variance than their closest living relatives, primates. This surprising discovery has led many scientists to conclude that all humans today come from a relatively small gene pool that may be due in part to a population bottleneck or the founder effect.

A A *population bottleneck* occurs when a **catastrophic** event, such as a flood, famine, or overhunting, causes a large decrease in the overall population of a species. **B** Because such an event causes random groups of a population to die, allele frequencies change, increasing the chance of a significant genetic drift. **C** Some researchers suggest that humans experienced a population bottleneck during the Toba catastrophe. **D** Approximately 70,000 years ago, at Lake Toba in Indonesia, a huge volcanic eruption may have plunged the Earth into a decade-long "volcanic winter," when volcanic ash blocked the Sun's light and killed much of Earth's vegetation and animal population. Estimates place the human population at 3,000 to 10,000 individuals shortly after the eruption. **Thus, humankind's current genetic diversity may be the result of small, isolated groups drawing from a limited genetic pool to repopulate the Earth after the eruption.**

However, some researchers claim that the Toba catastrophe did not significantly decrease the human population; they believe that human populations were consistently very low and isolated until recent millennia. In fact, genetic research suggests that the hominid* population was below 26,000 individuals approximately one million years ago, which explains the relative lack of genetic variance among humans. Migrations may also contribute to limited genetic variance. A *founder effect* occurs because a small population that splits from a main species group will have less genetic variance, providing an extreme example of genetic drift. The most widespread example of the founder effect amongst modern humans (*Homo sapiens*) is gradual migration from Africa by some groups, beginning about 200,000 years ago. As small bands of migrants moved further away, their genetic variance decreased compared to the main population that remained in Africa. **This millennia-long migration is known as a *serial founder effect* and, when combined with the hypothesis of a small original population, helps elucidate why people in various regions of the world have developed minor physical and genetic differences from people in distant regions.**

Hominid: the family of bipedal primates that includes modern humans and their extinct ancestors

9) Which of the following best paraphrases the highlighted sentence in Paragraph 5?

(A) Isolated groups of modern humans have a genetic variance similar to populations after the eruption.

(B) Remote human populations that survived the eruption may have procreated and provided modern humans' genetic variations.

(C) Small populations after the eruption had the same genetic diversity as modern humans.

(D) Genetic variance among living humans comes from groups of ancient humans that gathered together to diversify their gene pool.

10) What can be inferred about the outcome of the Toba catastrophe in Paragraph 5?

(A) Humans underwent physical changes to adapt to the long "volcanic winter."

(B) Human survivors constantly fought each other for resources.

(C) Most humans died out because of insufficient food supplies.

(D) Areas far from Indonesia were not greatly affected by the eruption.

11) What can be inferred from the highlighted sentence in Paragraph 6?

(A) Different alleles became dominant among disparate migrating populations.

(B) The serial founder effect has only been observed among human populations.

(C) Migration explains how the human population recovered after the Toba catastrophe.

(D) Migrations out of Africa explain why humans have a high genetic variance.

12) According to the passage, all of the following are true about genetic drift EXCEPT:

(A) It may affect populations with low genetic variance.

(B) It works with natural selection to ensure the survival of a species.

(C) The founder effect provides an example of it.

(D) It does not usually impact larger populations of a species.

13) **Directions**: Select the sentences that most appropriately match the descriptions of each cause of genetic drift. TWO of the answer choices will not be used. **This question is worth 3 points.**

Population bottleneck

-
-

Founder effect

-
-
-

Answer Choices

1. This often occurs because small populations separate from a main group.

2. This occurs among humans once every few millennia.

3. The Toba catastrophe may have caused this among humans.

4. This causes a very gradual decrease in genetic variance among migrating populations.

5. This generally causes a species to have a high genetic variance.

6. An example of this likely occurred about 200,000 years ago, beginning in Africa.

7. This occurs when a destructive event greatly reduces the population of a species.

Nongovernmental Organizations

There is a long history of people gathering private donations to help others or to further a cause. In fact, organized networks of people attempting to solve human problems outside of business or government can be traced to at least the 18th century, when efforts were made to halt the trans-Atlantic slave trade. Charities and advocacy groups grew in number and size into the 20th century, and in 1945, some even began to participate in the first United Nations (U.N.) activities. The U.N. sees them as "non-state actors" – in other words, not representing countries, but still valued advisors and partners in many U.N. programs. Because such **subsidiary** groups tend to work "on the ground" on issues surrounding poverty, their role is to voice the needs of people who would otherwise not be heard. Today the U.N. recognizes more than 30,000 such non-state actors, also known as *nongovernmental organizations*, or NGOs. In addition, there are hundreds of thousands, perhaps even millions, of NGOs that are not directly associated with the U.N. but seek to serve the public in some way. They have become virtually indispensable in the U.S. and other countries. Yet with such numbers and diversity, it is not surprising that NGOs frequently provoke both enormous admiration and considerable controversy.

One large survey found that people in many Western countries tend to trust NGOs such as Save the Children more than they do governments, media outlets, or businesses. Many NGOs earn stellar reputations by collecting donations from individuals and businesses in more affluent countries to provide services such as vaccinations, disaster relief, schools, and food to impoverished people. Other NGOs act as advocacy groups that promote democracy and human rights or seek to protect the environment.

While NGOs generally target crises that deserve attention, most NGOs, unlike democratic governments, are not elected by the people whom they serve. Rather, their financial survival may depend on meeting their donors' objectives. Thus, some critics say that there is a built-in bias toward donor-driven expectations and **cultural hegemony**, rather than toward change that is *grassroots*, or initiated by the affected community. For example, even with the best intentions, an NGO may upset a community by trying to change hierarchical structures; by distributing goods that usurp products of local industries; or by attempting to spread a particular religion or viewpoint. **Sometimes, assistance can seem overbearing and meddlesome to the recipients.** Russia, China, and India are among the nations that have monitored and regulated foreign-based NGOs out of concern for **such issues**.

A Critics of NGOs also charge that there is little control over how NGOs decide to spend money. **B** Many NGOs respond by becoming more *transparent*, or financially accountable. **C** However, a more general criticism is that some NGOs may spend charitable funds in ways that foster dependency. **D** For example, after an earthquake struck Haiti in 2010, many international aid organizations arrived overflowing with donations to help rebuild. Yet two years later, almost none of the reconstruction contracts had been awarded to Haitian firms, supporting critics' claims that the Haitian people were excluded from rebuilding their own country. Thus, an opportunity to more permanently fortify the Haitian economy was wasted.

Sensitive to all of the potential problems that "helpers" can cause, many NGOs now try to stimulate sustainable, market-based programs. For example, "fair trade" NGOs arrange for certification stamps on products such as coffee when they can guarantee that the farmers who produced it earned a fair price and had good working conditions. Certain consumers are willing to pay more when they see the stamp on the label, simply because they agree that farmers deserve fair compensation. NGOs are also offering assistance in establishing farmer cooperatives*, which give farmers power as a group to profit directly from trade rather than individually being vulnerable to trading companies' low prices. Cooperative members elect fellow members to administer the cooperative and set the group's priorities. For example, a cocoa farmers' cooperative in Ghana with about 60,000 members has chosen to **reinvest** some of its profits into water wells, skills training, loans, and supplemental crops.

Cooperative: an association of consumers or farmers who create or distribute services or goods

1) What is the author's primary purpose in Paragraph 1?
   (A) To persuade the reader that charities are basically worthwhile
   (B) To establish a brief background of private nonprofit organizations
   (C) To point out the United Nations' reliance on private efforts
   (D) To explain the difference between private and public organizations

2) The word "**subsidiary**" in Paragraph 1 is closest in meaning to
   (A) affiliate
   (B) benefactor
   (C) supervisor
   (D) employee

3) What can be inferred from Paragraph 2 about NGOs' reputations?
   (A) Many people in Western societies respect NGOs because they work with governments.
   (B) NGOs do not have to concern themselves with building their reputations.
   (C) NGOs deserve excellent reputations because they are based in affluent countries.
   (D) Good publicity in wealthy societies is important to NGOs.

4) According to Paragraph 2, all of the following are typical NGO activities EXCEPT
   (A) distributing food to the hungry
   (B) organizing health care activities
   (C) raising awareness about an environmental crisis
   (D) earning profits for investors

5) In Paragraph 3, "**cultural hegemony**" is closest in meaning to
   (A) the eradication of a regional heritage
   (B) the suppression of historical events
   (C) the domination of one culture over another
   (D) the modernization of traditions

6) Which of the following is a structural problem with NGOs described in Paragraph 3?
   (A) NGOs are not created or selected by the populations that they serve.
   (B) NGOs create "needs" where there are none.
   (C) No one knows how a given NGO is structured.
   (D) Relying on donations makes an NGO's continuity unpredictable.

7) Which of the following best paraphrases the highlighted sentence in Paragraph 3?
   (A) Some people do not like hand-outs and would rather have jobs.
   (B) A helping hand can be seen as controlling and interfering.
   (C) NGOs are motivated by vanity or self-promotion.
   (D) Recipients view NGOs as tyrannical and stubborn.

8) In Paragraph 3, "**such issues**" refers to
   (A) making well-intentioned efforts
   (B) upsetting communities
   (C) usurping local production
   (D) helping in a way that is overbearing

Nongovernmental Organizations

There is a long history of people gathering private donations to help others or to further a cause. In fact, organized networks of people attempting to solve human problems outside of business or government can be traced to at least the 18th century, when efforts were made to halt the trans-Atlantic slave trade. Charities and advocacy groups grew in number and size into the 20th century, and in 1945, some even began to participate in the first United Nations (U.N.) activities. The U.N. sees them as "non-state actors" – in other words, not representing countries, but still valued advisors and partners in many U.N. programs. Because such **subsidiary** groups tend to work "on the ground" on issues surrounding poverty, their role is to voice the needs of people who would otherwise not be heard. Today the U.N. recognizes more than 30,000 such non-state actors, also known as *nongovernmental organizations*, or NGOs. In addition, there are hundreds of thousands, perhaps even millions, of NGOs that are not directly associated with the U.N. but seek to serve the public in some way. They have become virtually indispensable in the U.S. and other countries. Yet with such numbers and diversity, it is not surprising that NGOs frequently provoke both enormous admiration and considerable controversy.

One large survey found that people in many Western countries tend to trust NGOs such as Save the Children more than they do governments, media outlets, or businesses. Many NGOs earn stellar reputations by collecting donations from individuals and businesses in more affluent countries to provide services such as vaccinations, disaster relief, schools, and food to impoverished people. Other NGOs act as advocacy groups that promote democracy and human rights or seek to protect the environment.

While NGOs generally target crises that deserve attention, most NGOs, unlike democratic governments, are not elected by the people whom they serve. Rather, their financial survival may depend on meeting their donors' objectives. Thus, some critics say that there is a built-in bias toward donor-driven expectations and **cultural hegemony**, rather than toward change that is *grassroots*, or initiated by the affected community. For example, even with the best intentions, an NGO may upset a community by trying to change hierarchical structures; by distributing goods that usurp products of local industries; or by attempting to spread a particular religion or viewpoint. **Sometimes, assistance can seem overbearing and meddlesome to the recipients.** Russia, China, and India are among the nations that have monitored and regulated foreign-based NGOs out of concern for **such issues**.

A Critics of NGOs also charge that there is little control over how NGOs decide to spend money. **B** Many NGOs respond by becoming more *transparent*, or financially accountable. **C** However, a more general criticism is that some NGOs may spend charitable funds in ways that foster dependency. **D** For example, after an earthquake struck Haiti in 2010, many international aid organizations arrived overflowing with donations to help rebuild. Yet two years later, almost none of the reconstruction contracts had been awarded to Haitian firms, supporting critics' claims that the Haitian people were excluded from rebuilding their own country. Thus, an opportunity to more permanently fortify the Haitian economy was wasted.

Sensitive to all of the potential problems that "helpers" can cause, many NGOs now try to stimulate sustainable, market-based programs. For example, "fair trade" NGOs arrange for certification stamps on products such as coffee when they can guarantee that the farmers who produced it earned a fair price and had good working conditions. Certain consumers are willing to pay more when they see the stamp on the label, simply because they agree that farmers deserve fair compensation. NGOs are also offering assistance in establishing farmer cooperatives*, which give farmers power as a group to profit directly from trade rather than individually being vulnerable to trading companies' low prices. Cooperative members elect fellow members to administer the cooperative and set the group's priorities. For example, a cocoa farmers' cooperative in Ghana with about 60,000 members has chosen to **reinvest** some of its profits into water wells, skills training, loans, and supplemental crops.

Cooperative: an association of consumers or farmers who create or distribute services or goods

9) Look at the squares [■] that indicate where the following sentence could be added to Paragraph 4.

There have probably been scandals involving charities misusing donations as long as there have been charities, and such scandals still occur today.

Where would the sentence best fit?

Circle the square [■] to add the sentence.

10) According to Paragraph 4, critics have complained about the process of post-earthquake rebuilding in Haiti because
   (A) foreign construction companies did the work
   (B) the money was spent too slowly
   (C) the rebuilding required Haitian citizens to make monetary donations
   (D) projects did not receive property owners' permission

11) The author mentions "**reinvest**" in Paragraph 5 to show that a cocoa farmers' cooperative
   (A) uses business earnings to improve the company and community
   (B) distributes money that investors have earned back to investors
   (C) sets aside an emergency fund
   (D) uses resources for personal bonuses

12) How does Paragraph 5 relate to the earlier discussion about fostering dependence?
   (A) It further develops examples of fostering dependence.
   (B) It tries to persuade the reader that the criticism is unsupported.
   (C) It describes and illustrates current attempts to avoid the problem.
   (D) It points out the importance of the topic in everyday life.

13) **Directions**: An introductory sentence relating to the passage is written below. Complete the exercise by choosing THREE answers to support the sentence. Some sentences do not belong because they do not support the sentence. **This question is worth 2 points.**

Though some NGOs' goals or methods draw criticism, many play crucial roles throughout the world.

-
-
-

Answer Choices

1. Almost all NGOs respond in the aftermath of disasters such as earthquakes and tsunamis.
2. The United Nations allows NGOs to vote on major issues in the international community.
3. NGOs can speak up for poorer people whose interests are not well represented by their governments.
4. NGOs sometimes make decisions on behalf of the communities that they serve.
5. NGOs can collect money from more affluent countries to serve worthy causes in developing countries.
6. Most critics of NGOs say that NGOs do not send enough donated food, water, fuel, and clothing to poorer communities.

Artificial Intelligence

The concept of creating *artificial intelligence* (AI), or designing structures that possess characteristics associated with human intelligence, has intrigued humankind for millennia. In ancient times, the Greeks imagined that the god of artisanship, Hephaestus, fashioned mechanical men to work in his fiery forge. Centuries later, author Mary Shelley wrote *Frankenstein*, which explores the moral implications of defying nature by creating conscious life using science. However, modern understanding for the potential of AI has transformed myth and speculation into real possibility.

The rise of computer technology at the end of the 20th century has made dreams and fears of replicating human intelligence a **contingency**. Because computers are able to store large amounts of information, scientists can use them to simulate areas of the brain. Yet computers still lack many of the abilities possessed by a human brain. For instance, humans can reflect upon actions and events, which allows people to learn from mistakes and synthesize seemingly unrelated information into new ideas. Moreover, the human brain is much more efficient than any extant computer. Because humans easily retrieve known information from memory and apply it to real-world problems, people can recognize and identify objects much faster than a computer and require significantly less energy for comparable computations.

In order to achieve human levels of intelligence in machines or computers, scientists must first fully understand how intelligence functions in humans by probing the deepest recesses of the human brain. In 2005, the Swiss Brain and Mind Institute began the *Blue Brain Project*, which is an attempt to reverse-engineer the human brain using computer models. About a year after the project formally began, scientists completed a computer simulation of a rat's *neocortical column*, a tiny piece of the mammalian brain usually associated with conscious thought. **This project** served as one of many precursor projects to the ultimate goal: to simulate a human brain containing 100 billion cells by the year 2023.

The possibility that computers may be able to replicate a human brain has provoked some to speculate about a future of "mind uploading," or the **hypothetical** process by which an active biological brain is relayed to a mechanical device. Essentially, this process would ensure the immortality of a human mind that is no longer constrained by biological aging. Those whose minds have been "uploaded" could then exist in a *virtual reality* – a computer simulation of the real world – or have their computerized brain connected to a humanoid robot to allow for interaction with the real world. However, many scientists dismiss "mind uploading," claiming that the human brain is too complex to be perfectly replicated.

Although the simulated reconstruction of a human brain is still unattainable, developments in computing technologies have allowed scientists to make enormous advancements in AI. **A** For instance, in 2000 Honda revealed ASIMO, a 130-centimeter humanoid robot. ASIMO, which is an acronym for Advanced Step in Innovative MObility, was designed to help individuals who have difficulty with mobility accomplish day-to-day tasks. **B** ASIMO is bipedal, and it can navigate uneven terrain such as stairs, attaining a maximum speed of 6 kilometers per hour. **C** Using two camera "eyes," the robot is programmed to respond to human gestures, determine distance and direction, and recognize and name up to ten individuals. **D**

However, the prospect of creating machines with human qualities has also **engendered** many fears and anxieties. Philip K. Dick's 1968 novel, *Do Androids Dream of Electric Sheep?*, takes place in a dystopian society where androids, which appear human and contain implanted human memories **but lack empathy**, are forced to do work that is too difficult or dangerous for humans. When six of these androids rebel, a bounty hunter has to track down and destroy them. The novel questions what differentiates humans from machines and explores the morality of destroying a machine that believes that it is human.

Nevertheless, humans have yet to completely fathom the workings of their own minds, and AI has not yet produced machines that compete with human intelligence. Certainly innovations like ASIMO and the Blue Brain Project have provided a foundation for robots with human mobility that may one day also possess human-like minds.

1) The word "**contingency**" in Paragraph 2 is closest in meaning to
   (A) reality
   (B) possibility
   (C) fantasy
   (D) solution

2) According to Paragraph 2, what is a difference between the human brain and a computer?
   (A) The human brain is currently better understood than any computer.
   (B) Computers retrieve information and make more calculations than a human brain.
   (C) Computers require less energy than the human brain to perform similar tasks.
   (D) The human brain can make connections through self-reflection while computers cannot.

3) Which of the following best paraphrases the highlighted sentence in Paragraph 3?
   (A) Because the human brain is so complicated, scientists must use computers to map it accurately.
   (B) In order to make computers as intelligent as humans, people must first determine the similarities between the two.
   (C) Scientists must fully understand the human mind before they can reproduce it using technology.
   (D) Scientists must test the maximum capabilities of the human mind before transplanting a human brain into a computer.

4) In Paragraph 3, the phrase "**This project**" refers to
   (A) The Swiss Brain and Mind Institute
   (B) The simulation of a rat's neocortical column
   (C) Blue Brain Project
   (D) Reverse-engineering the human brain

5) Why does the author probably mention the word "**hypothetical**" in Paragraph 4?
   (A) To criticize theoretical research in the field of AI
   (B) To contrast the Blue Brain Project with "mind uploading"
   (C) To caution readers against believing in "mind uploading"
   (D) To emphasize that "mind uploading" does not yet exist

6) According to Paragraph 4, what is one implication of "mind uploading?"
   (A) Only parts of the complex human brain can be uploaded.
   (B) Uploaded minds can be placed back into a biological human body.
   (C) The human consciousness can live forever in a computerized form.
   (D) It would allow the human brain to absorb much more information.

7) Look at the squares [■] that indicate where the following sentence could be added to Paragraph 5.

   To promote interest in the sciences, ASIMO often makes public appearances in which he performs choreographed dances and displays his understanding of voice commands.

   Where would the sentence best fit?
   Circle the square [■] to add the sentence.

8) What can be inferred from Paragraph 5?
   (A) ASIMO is not capable of autonomous thought.
   (B) ASIMO can accomplish many tasks that many humans cannot.
   (C) ASIMO's creation generated much controversy.
   (D) ASIMO is equipped with a human-like brain.

Artificial Intelligence

The concept of creating *artificial intelligence* (AI), or designing structures that possess characteristics associated with human intelligence, has intrigued humankind for millennia. In ancient times, the Greeks imagined that the god of artisanship, Hephaestus, fashioned mechanical men to work in his fiery forge. Centuries later, author Mary Shelley wrote *Frankenstein*, which explores the moral implications of defying nature by creating conscious life using science. However, modern understanding for the potential of AI has transformed myth and speculation into real possibility.

The rise of computer technology at the end of the 20th century has made dreams and fears of replicating human intelligence a **contingency**. Because computers are able to store large amounts of information, scientists can use them to simulate areas of the brain. Yet computers still lack many of the abilities possessed by a human brain. For instance, humans can reflect upon actions and events, which allows people to learn from mistakes and synthesize seemingly unrelated information into new ideas. Moreover, the human brain is much more efficient than any extant computer. Because humans easily retrieve known information from memory and apply it to real-world problems, people can recognize and identify objects much faster than a computer and require significantly less energy for comparable computations.

In order to achieve human levels of intelligence in machines or computers, scientists must first fully understand how intelligence functions in humans by probing the deepest recesses of the human brain. In 2005, the Swiss Brain and Mind Institute began the *Blue Brain Project*, which is an attempt to reverse-engineer the human brain using computer models. About a year after the project formally began, scientists completed a computer simulation of a rat's *neocortical column*, a tiny piece of the mammalian brain usually associated with conscious thought. **This project** served as one of many precursor projects to the ultimate goal: to simulate a human brain containing 100 billion cells by the year 2023.

The possibility that computers may be able to replicate a human brain has provoked some to speculate about a future of "mind uploading," or the **hypothetical** process by which an active biological brain is relayed to a mechanical device. Essentially, this process would ensure the immortality of a human mind that is no longer constrained by biological aging. Those whose minds have been "uploaded" could then exist in a *virtual reality* – a computer simulation of the real world – or have their computerized brain connected to a humanoid robot to allow for interaction with the real world. However, many scientists dismiss "mind uploading," claiming that the human brain is too complex to be perfectly replicated.

Although the simulated reconstruction of a human brain is still unattainable, developments in computing technologies have allowed scientists to make enormous advancements in AI. **A** For instance, in 2000 Honda revealed ASIMO, a 130-centimeter humanoid robot. ASIMO, which is an acronym for Advanced Step in Innovative MObility, was designed to help individuals who have difficulty with mobility accomplish day-to-day tasks. **B** ASIMO is bipedal, and it can navigate uneven terrain such as stairs, attaining a maximum speed of 6 kilometers per hour. **C** Using two camera "eyes," the robot is programmed to respond to human gestures, determine distance and direction, and recognize and name up to ten individuals. **D**

However, the prospect of creating machines with human qualities has also **engendered** many fears and anxieties. Philip K. Dick's 1968 novel, *Do Androids Dream of Electric Sheep?*, takes place in a dystopian society where androids, which appear human and contain implanted human memories **but lack empathy**, are forced to do work that is too difficult or dangerous for humans. When six of these androids rebel, a bounty hunter has to track down and destroy them. The novel questions what differentiates humans from machines and explores the morality of destroying a machine that believes that it is human.

Nevertheless, humans have yet to completely fathom the workings of their own minds, and AI has not yet produced machines that compete with human intelligence. Certainly innovations like ASIMO and the Blue Brain Project have provided a foundation for robots with human mobility that may one day also possess human-like minds.

9) The word "**engendered**" in Paragraph 6 is closest in meaning to
(A) prevented
(B) elucidated
(C) generated
(D) discovered

10) According to Paragraph 6, which of the following best describes the novel *Do Androids Dream of Electric Sheep?* by Philip K. Dick?
(A) It promotes further research into androids with human memories.
(B) It challenges the distinction between biological and synthetic beings.
(C) It depicts a future in which machines and humans are treated equally.
(D) It predicts that research into AI is certain to create a dystopian society.

11) Why does the author PROBABLY mention "**but lack empathy**" in Paragraph 6?
(A) To criticize Dick's depiction of non-human intelligence
(B) To persuade readers that androids possess morals
(C) To argue that empathy is the most important characteristic in androids
(D) To point out what differentiates androids and humans

12) What can be inferred from the information in Paragraphs 5 and 6?
(A) ASIMO's design is based on the design of the androids from Philip K. Dick's novel.
(B) Implanted human memories are the main factors separating robots like ASIMO from humans.
(C) People generally imagine that all machines with human-like characteristics also have a human-like appearance.
(D) Philip K. Dick's anxieties about AI technology have been brought into existence with the creation of ASIMO.

13) **Directions**: An introductory sentence relating to the passage is written below. Complete the exercise by choosing THREE answers to support the sentence. Some sentences do not belong because they do not support the sentence. **This question is worth 2 points**.

In spite of some societal misgivings, researchers continue to pursue replicating human intelligence due to the potential benefits.

-
-
-

Answer Choices
1. Computers can store vast amounts of knowledge, possibly even the memories and thought processes of an individual human.
2. AI research regards the human brain as a computer to understand the similarities between the two.
3. Scientists believe that a mammal's neocortical column is involved in conscious thought.
4. Philip K. Dick imagined a world where robots resemble humans in almost every way except empathy.
5. Research into replicating human intelligence may yield a greater understanding of how the human brain operates.
6. Robots who seem to see, talk, and walk can help people with disabilities.

The Tale of Genji

The Tale of Genji is an 11th-century work of Japanese historical fiction written by an author known only as "Lady Murakashi," which may be a pseudonym. Murakashi is believed to have been one of the attendants to Empress Shoshi during the peaceful Heian period. Many scholars consider her work the first notable "modern novel" because it **chronicles** the life of a main character through a series of episodic glimpses. Though the work is not the first to adopt this episodic format, it outshines all other **contemporaneous** works of similar structure because of its complex characters and their **believable interactions**. *The Tale of Genji* spans decades and includes more than 400 minor characters.

Murakashi likely wrote *The Tale of Genji* between 1000 and 1012, largely during her time at the imperial court, located in the modern-day city of Kyoto. During this era, Japan was beginning to break away from Chinese cultural and political influences and establish a strong cultural identity of its own. Though politicians and administrators communicated using Chinese writing symbols, this period saw the rise of *kana*, or abbreviated Chinese characters that represent Japanese sounds phonologically, more like an alphabet. **Women were not educated in Chinese to ensure that they could not interfere with political affairs, but aristocratic women were allowed to use kana and produced poetry and art to pass the time at the imperial court.**

Although many men and women of the Heian court wrote poetry, Murakashi's narrative stands out partly because she had an unusual education. Murakashi had become fluent in spoken and written Chinese, possibly by eavesdropping while her father read Chinese to her brother. **In *The Tale of Genji*, Murakashi makes use of the more natural kana because the novel was directed toward a female aristocratic audience, but she switches to Chinese writing when her characters discuss politics, contributing to the accuracy and realism of the work.** Thus, *The Tale of Genji* gives an unparalleled glimpse of the political atmosphere of the Heian period.

The Tale of Genji takes place several decades before Murakashi's time, but still during the Heian period. **A** The novel centers on the life of "Shining" Genji, the illegitimate son of Emperor Kiritsubo, as he grows up in the imperial court. **B** Though Genji is politically and romantically successful, he is exiled for conducting an illicit affair. **C** While in exile, he has a daughter who later becomes empress. **D** The next emperor, his son through another affair, ends Genji's banishment, but once again his life deteriorates in amorous and political realms upon his return to imperial court. Genji dies midway through the novel, and the later portion describes a power struggle between his son and nephew. Some scholars speculate that the book details his relatives' conflicts after his death to contrast Genji's virtues with the pettiness of his descendants. The novel ends mid-sentence, which some argue was intentional while others claim that the work remains incomplete.

The novel's personal and sometimes gossipy details provide an in-depth look at daily life in the Heian court unlike almost any other historical literary work. Japanese culture of the time called for strictly divided gender spheres, so women did not often interact with men outside their families. Although abundant poetry by female authors exists from this period, their work rarely overtly describes interactions between men and women. However, *The Tale of Genji* breaks this convention by making a man the center of the novel, and then recounting many relationships between Genji and his love interests. Genji's numerous romantic **endeavors** also reveal the centrality of poetry and metaphor in the daily life of both men and women of 11th-century Japan. Genji uses poetry to express his love, and dialogue in the novel often includes traditional Japanese poems that the speaker excerpts to fit a situation. Murakashi uses nearly 800 pre-existing, well-known Japanese poems throughout the novel to emphasize the emotional thematic contrasts of love and loss, contributing to **its** beauty and timelessness.

1) The word "**chronicles**" in Paragraph 1 is closest in meaning to
   (A) describes
   (B) conceals
   (C) interrogates
   (D) disperses

2) The word "**contemporaneous**" in Paragraph 1 is closest in meaning to
   (A) condemned
   (B) conclusive
   (C) concurrent
   (D) conservative

3) Why does the author mention "**believable interactions**" in Paragraph 1?
   (A) To praise Murakashi's unique use of symbolism and metaphor
   (B) To provide an example of why *The Tale of Genji* is an enduring work of literature
   (C) To compare Murakashi's intentions with those of other writers of the era
   (D) To point out what genre *The Tale of Genji* falls under

4) According to Paragraph 2, the development of kana
   (A) strengthened gender divisions within the Heian-era imperial court
   (B) provided a language with which aristocratic women could compose literature
   (C) led to many Japanese citizens rebelling against the dominant Chinese influences
   (D) gave women more political power outside of the imperial court

5) What can be inferred from the highlighted sentence in Paragraph 2?
   (A) China was the dominant political force in Japan at the time.
   (B) Poetry was too difficult to compose in Chinese.
   (C) Women strongly desired to be educated about Chinese culture.
   (D) Only wealthy women knew how to use kana.

6) Which of the following best paraphrases the highlighted sentence in Paragraph 3?
   (A) *The Tale of Genji* appealed to politicians and administrators because it used Chinese characters.
   (B) The use of multiple languages makes *The Tale of Genji* a confusing yet enduring work of literature.
   (C) Murakashi's situational use of different Japanese writing systems adds to *The Tale of Genji*'s believability.
   (D) Murakashi's knowledge of politics was considered unusual for a Heian-era aristocratic woman.

7) Look at the squares [■] that indicate where the following sentence could be added to Paragraph 4.

   Murakashi depicts Genji as an incredibly attractive and charismatic man, and much of the novel focuses on his many romantic relationships.

   Where would the sentence best fit?
   Circle the square [■] to add the sentence.

The Tale of Genji

Time
00:10:00

The Tale of Genji is an 11th-century work of Japanese historical fiction written by an author known only as "Lady Murakashi," which may be a pseudonym. Murakashi is believed to have been one of the attendants to Empress Shoshi during the peaceful Heian period. Many scholars consider her work the first notable "modern novel" because it **chronicles** the life of a main character through a series of episodic glimpses. Though the work is not the first to adopt this episodic format, it outshines all other **contemporaneous** works of similar structure because of its complex characters and their **believable interactions**. *The Tale of Genji* spans decades and includes more than 400 minor characters.

Murakashi likely wrote *The Tale of Genji* between 1000 and 1012, largely during her time at the imperial court, located in the modern-day city of Kyoto. During this era, Japan was beginning to break away from Chinese cultural and political influences and establish a strong cultural identity of its own. Though politicians and administrators communicated using Chinese writing symbols, this period saw the rise of *kana*, or abbreviated Chinese characters that represent Japanese sounds phonologically, more like an alphabet. **Women were not educated in Chinese to ensure that they could not interfere with political affairs, but aristocratic women were allowed to use kana and produced poetry and art to pass the time at the imperial court.**

Although many men and women of the Heian court wrote poetry, Murakashi's narrative stands out partly because she had an unusual education. Murakashi had become fluent in spoken and written Chinese, possibly by eavesdropping while her father read Chinese to her brother. **In *The Tale of Genji*, Murakashi makes use of the more natural kana because the novel was directed toward a female aristocratic audience, but she switches to Chinese writing when her characters discuss politics, contributing to the accuracy and realism of the work.** Thus, *The Tale of Genji* gives an unparalleled glimpse of the political atmosphere of the Heian period.

The Tale of Genji takes place several decades before Murakashi's time, but still during the Heian period. **A** The novel centers on the life of "Shining" Genji, the illegitimate son of Emperor Kiritsubo, as he grows up in the imperial court. **B** Though Genji is politically and romantically successful, he is exiled for conducting an illicit affair. **C** While in exile, he has a daughter who later becomes empress. **D** The next emperor, his son through another affair, ends Genji's banishment, but once again his life deteriorates in amorous and political realms upon his return to imperial court. Genji dies midway through the novel, and the later portion describes a power struggle between his son and nephew. Some scholars speculate that the book details his relatives' conflicts after his death to contrast Genji's virtues with the pettiness of his descendants. The novel ends mid-sentence, which some argue was intentional while others claim that the work remains incomplete.

The novel's personal and sometimes gossipy details provide an in-depth look at daily life in the Heian court unlike almost any other historical literary work. Japanese culture of the time called for strictly divided gender spheres, so women did not often interact with men outside their families. Although abundant poetry by female authors exists from this period, their work rarely overtly describes interactions between men and women. However, *The Tale of Genji* breaks this convention by making a man the center of the novel, and then recounting many relationships between Genji and his love interests. Genji's numerous romantic **endeavors** also reveal the centrality of poetry and metaphor in the daily life of both men and women of 11th-century Japan. Genji uses poetry to express his love, and dialogue in the novel often includes traditional Japanese poems that the speaker excerpts to fit a situation. Murakashi uses nearly 800 pre-existing, well-known Japanese poems throughout the novel to emphasize the emotional thematic contrasts of love and loss, contributing to **its** beauty and timelessness.

8) In Paragraph 4, all of the following are true about the novel's plot EXCEPT:
   (A) Genji must leave imperial life for a period of time.
   (B) Several romantic encounters have huge consequences.
   (C) Genji's biological relatives wield power throughout.
   (D) Genji's offspring fail to surpass Genji's status in the imperial court.

9) The word "**endeavors**" in Paragraph 5 is closest in meaning to
   (A) efforts
   (B) theories
   (C) exploitations
   (D) stipulations

10) The word "**its**" in Paragraph 5 refers to
    (A) love
    (B) novel
    (C) loss
    (D) situation

11) What does the author mention about poetry in Paragraph 5?
    (A) Few men wrote poetry during the Heian period.
    (B) Murakashi's characters incorporate poetry into conversations.
    (C) All the poems used in *The Tale of Genji* are love poems.
    (D) Murakashi created 800 poems specifically for *The Tale of Genji*.

12) According to the passage, *The Tale of Genji* contains all of the following EXCEPT
    (A) hundreds of characters
    (B) an ambiguous ending
    (C) the virtues of aristocratic life
    (D) Chinese and kana writing

13) **Directions**: An introductory sentence relating to the passage is written below. Complete the exercise by choosing the THREE answers that support the sentence. Some sentences do not belong because they do not support the sentence. **This question is worth 2 points.**

Though it is fiction, *The Tale of Genji* provides an authentic view of life 1,000 years ago in Japan.

   ●

   ●

   ●

Answer Choices

1. It includes many conversations between Japanese men and women of the period.
2. It includes one of the first literary instances of an anti-hero.
3. It reveals the ruthlessness and immorality of Heian-era Japanese politicians.
4. It alternates between kana and Chinese writing to accurately display male and female language restrictions.
5. It is primarily written in Chinese, the political language of Japan at the time.
6. It depicts everyday aristocratic life at the Japanese imperial court.

Whale Evolution

Because whales are among the largest creatures on Earth, they inspire awe and fear among many cultures, and their **unfathomable** aquatic life has often inspired humans to speculate about what they could not observe. The Vietnamese traditionally regarded whales as holy creatures associated with luck and protection. Ancient Chinese people believed that a giant whale with human limbs ruled the oceans and caused fearsome typhoons when angered. However, improved observation of whales in their natural habitat has allowed researchers to separate whales from their mythology. Today, whales are acknowledged as one of the most intelligent animals on Earth, **using complex forms of communication and developing long-lasting social connections**. Ultimately, the scientific explanation of how an air-breathing mammal has become one of the dominant species of the oceans is much stranger than fiction.

Approximately 55 million years ago, at the onset of the Eocene epoch, Earth was undergoing a 7-million-year heat wave. Under hot, humid conditions, a family of mammals called Ambulocetidae emerged. These 3-meter-long predators resembled crocodiles: they had long snouts and tails, as well as large feet attached to short, straight legs needed for paddling through rivers and coastal regions. Ambulocetids were *amphibious*; they were adept swimmers but could also hunt on land. To adapt to an increasingly aquatic lifestyle, ambulocetids developed a bone structure that allowed for acute underwater hearing and the ability to swallow prey while submerged. Some ambulocetids evolved into the earliest *cetaceans*, or today's whales, dolphins, and porpoises.

About 50 million years ago, ambulocetids gradually lost their dependency on terrestrial movement. A descendent of the ambulocetid family, Remingtonocetidae, possessed underdeveloped *semicircular canals* in their ears, which mammals use for terrestrial balance; researchers consider this trait as evidence that remingtonocetids rarely ventured onto land. Between 41 and 35 million years ago, a branch of semi-aquatic mammals, possibly the remingtonocetids, became the fully aquatic Basilosauridae family. These creatures utilized long tails and flipper-like forelimbs adapted to an aquatic environment and probably grew up to 16 meters in length. Although these early cetaceans developed very acute underwater hearing, they had not yet advanced to the degree of some extant whale species.

The final leap toward the evolution of modern whales occurred approximately 30 million years ago. During this time, whales in the genus *Aetiocetus* developed a loose jaw hinge and **primitive structures** for siphoning out small aquatic organisms. The structures later evolved into baleen, causing the split of toothed whales (*Odontoceti*) from baleen whales (*Mysticeti*) that form the two suborders of cetaceans present today.

The suborder of toothed whales, which contains about 77 species including dolphins and porpoises, hunt using *echolocation*, or the emission of sound waves that bounce off objects or animals to determine **their** location. **A** Unlike baleen whales, toothed whales mostly use echolocation rather than vision because many species hunt deep in the ocean where light is minimal and because sound travels about five times faster in water than through air. **B** The prey of toothed whales varies greatly, from fish and cephalopods to other marine mammals. **C** Moreover, toothed whales swallow their prey whole without chewing, so some species use their teeth for purposes other than hunting. **D** For instance, the narwhal only has one tooth, which looks like a 2-meter horn growing from the whale's snout and is used for defensive purposes and for breaking though thick ice in its Arctic habitat.

Baleen whales, of which there are only about 10 species, are usually larger than toothed whales, yet they dine on some of the smallest creatures in the ocean. Baleen whales likely split from toothed whales because of a **profusion** of small organisms that were inaccessible without some sort of filtration system, such as baleen. In order to feed, a baleen whale takes in a large amount of ocean water, pushes its tongue against the plates of baleen that extend from the roof of its mouth to filter out the water, and consumes only the small animals that are left behind in its mouth. The species of baleen whale called the blue whale, which is the largest creature to have ever lived, can weigh upward of 180 metric tons and consume up to four metric tons of food in a single day.

1) The word "**unfathomable**" in Paragraph 1 is closest in meaning to
   (A) unforgettable
   (B) unfortunate
   (C) unattractive
   (D) unknowable

2) Why does the author PROBABLY mention the highlighted phrase in Paragraph 1?
   (A) To praise whales' intricate yet largely peaceful lifestyle
   (B) To give examples demonstrating whales' intelligence
   (C) To compare whale behavior to human behavior
   (D) To persuade the reader of the value in studying whales

3) From Paragraph 1, what can be inferred about the human understanding of whales?
   (A) Enhanced submersible recording technology provides better surveillance of whale behavior.
   (B) Researchers can understand and communicate with many species of whales.
   (C) The Vietnamese and Chinese were the first to conduct scientific observations of whales.
   (D) Researchers suggest that the intelligence of some whales may rival human intelligence.

4) According to Paragraph 2, one adaptation of ambulocetids was that
   (A) they developed small flippers to navigate rivers
   (B) they possessed great underwater vision and smell
   (C) they were able to consume food while underwater
   (D) they lived in water to escape the hot climate of the Eocene epoch

5) Why does the author PROBABLY mention "**primitive structures**" in Paragraph 4?
   (A) To compare whales with their terrestrial ancestors
   (B) To explain why *Aetiocetus* eventually went extinct
   (C) To argue that modern whales are more intelligent than *Aetiocetus*
   (D) To emphasize that baleen in modern whales is more developed

6) According to Paragraphs 3 and 4, which of the following was the first completely aquatic mammal?
   (A) Ambulocetidae
   (B) Basilosauridae
   (C) Remingtonocetidae
   (D) *Aetiocetus*

7) The word "**their**" in Paragraph 5 refers to
   (A) 77 species
   (B) dolphins and porpoises
   (C) sound waves
   (D) objects or animals

8) Look at the squares [■] that indicate where the following sentence could be added to Paragraph 5.

   For example, the 18-meter-long sperm whale will regularly dive to depths exceeding 300 meters to hunt giant squid.

   Where would the sentence best fit?
   Circle the square [■] to add the sentence.

Whale Evolution

Time
00:10:00

Because whales are among the largest creatures on Earth, they inspire awe and fear among many cultures, and their **unfathomable** aquatic life has often inspired humans to speculate about what they could not observe. The Vietnamese traditionally regarded whales as holy creatures associated with luck and protection. Ancient Chinese people believed that a giant whale with human limbs ruled the oceans and caused fearsome typhoons when angered. However, improved observation of whales in their natural habitat has allowed researchers to separate whales from their mythology. Today, whales are acknowledged as one of the most intelligent animals on Earth, **using complex forms of communication and developing long-lasting social connections**. Ultimately, the scientific explanation of how an air-breathing mammal has become one of the dominant species of the oceans is much stranger than fiction.

Approximately 55 million years ago, at the onset of the Eocene epoch, Earth was undergoing a 7-million-year heat wave. Under hot, humid conditions, a family of mammals called Ambulocetidae emerged. These 3-meter-long predators resembled crocodiles: they had long snouts and tails, as well as large feet attached to short, straight legs needed for paddling through rivers and coastal regions. Ambulocetids were *amphibious*; they were adept swimmers but could also hunt on land. To adapt to an increasingly aquatic lifestyle, ambulocetids developed a bone structure that allowed for acute underwater hearing and the ability to swallow prey while submerged. Some ambulocetids evolved into the earliest *cetaceans*, or today's whales, dolphins, and porpoises.

About 50 million years ago, ambulocetids gradually lost their dependency on terrestrial movement. A descendent of the ambulocetid family, Remingtonocetidae, possessed underdeveloped *semicircular canals* in their ears, which mammals use for terrestrial balance; researchers consider this trait as evidence that remingtonocetids rarely ventured onto land. Between 41 and 35 million years ago, a branch of semi-aquatic mammals, possibly the remingtonocetids, became the fully aquatic Basilosauridae family. These creatures utilized long tails and flipper-like forelimbs adapted to an aquatic environment and probably grew up to 16 meters in length. Although these early cetaceans developed very acute underwater hearing, they had not yet advanced to the degree of some extant whale species.

The final leap toward the evolution of modern whales occurred approximately 30 million years ago. During this time, whales in the genus *Aetiocetus* developed a loose jaw hinge and **primitive structures** for siphoning out small aquatic organisms. The structures later evolved into baleen, causing the split of toothed whales (*Odontoceti*) from baleen whales (*Mysticeti*) that form the two suborders of cetaceans present today.

The suborder of toothed whales, which contains about 77 species including dolphins and porpoises, hunt using *echolocation*, or the emission of sound waves that bounce off objects or animals to determine **their** location. **A** Unlike baleen whales, toothed whales mostly use echolocation rather than vision because many species hunt deep in the ocean where light is minimal and because sound travels about five times faster in water than through air. **B** The prey of toothed whales varies greatly, from fish and cephalopods to other marine mammals. **C** Moreover, toothed whales swallow their prey whole without chewing, so some species use their teeth for purposes other than hunting. **D** For instance, the narwhal only has one tooth, which looks like a 2-meter horn growing from the whale's snout and is used for defensive purposes and for breaking though thick ice in its Arctic habitat.

Baleen whales, of which there are only about 10 species, are usually larger than toothed whales, yet they dine on some of the smallest creatures in the ocean. Baleen whales likely split from toothed whales because of a **profusion** of small organisms that were inaccessible without some sort of filtration system, such as baleen. In order to feed, a baleen whale takes in a large amount of ocean water, pushes its tongue against the plates of baleen that extend from the roof of its mouth to filter out the water, and consumes only the small animals that are left behind in its mouth. The species of baleen whale called the blue whale, which is the largest creature to have ever lived, can weigh upward of 180 metric tons and consume up to four metric tons of food in a single day.

9) The word "**profusion**" in Paragraph 6 is closest in meaning to
   (A) intricacy
   (B) abundance
   (C) progression
   (D) consumption

10) Based on Paragraph 6, baleen developed in order to
   (A) filter out toxic creatures that some whale species encounter when they feed
   (B) assist in the process of echolocation for communication and hunting
   (C) help some whale species access miniscule organisms for food supply
   (D) extract more nutrition from some whales' scarce food sources

11) According to Paragraph 6, what can be inferred about baleen whales?
   (A) They do not often face much competition for nourishment.
   (B) Their predatory habits make them dangerous to humans.
   (C) They are more numerous than toothed whales.
   (D) They travel in large groups to capture their prey.

12) According to the passage, all of the following animals are *Odontoceti* EXCEPT
   (A) porpoises
   (B) dolphins
   (C) blue whales
   (D) narwhals

13) **Directions**: Select the sentences that most appropriately match the descriptions of each suborder of whale. TWO of the answer choices will NOT be used. **This question is worth 3 points.**

Odontoceti

●

●

●

Mysticeti

●

●

Answer Choices

1. This type of whale includes the largest creature on Earth.
2. This type of whale is the oldest living mammal species.
3. This type of whale locates prey using reflected sound waves.
4. This type of whale filters its sustenance from water.
5. This type of whale usually resides in the deepest parts of the ocean.
6. This type of whale often seeks prey in parts of the ocean where little light permeates.
7. This type of whale has a diverse diet that includes other mammals.

The Pueblo People

For decades, the public has been fascinated by the sophisticated ancient Native Americans who built entire villages in nearly inaccessible cliff walls but suddenly moved away around 1280 CE. This culture, called Anasazi, first appeared as early as 1500 BCE in what is now the American Southwest. The members of the Anasazi community are called the Ancient Pueblo; their descendants comprise the current-day Pueblo tribes. ***Pueblo* is a Spanish word meaning "village," a term first used by the 16th-century Spanish explorers to name the distinctive communities of the area's inhabitants.**

Archaeological evidence from about 500 CE shows that the Ancient Pueblo started to construct partially sunken homes, which protected them from the weather and provided storage for harvested foods. Between 700 and 900 CE, they began building above-ground dwellings as the result of a greater reliance on agriculture and the necessity to store foods for longer periods. About 900 CE, the above-ground, single-story pueblos developed into larger complexes with different levels resembling modern apartment buildings. The Ancient Pueblo built the multifamily dwellings with stones shaped from sandstone and held together by mud and clay mortar, while the roofs were crafted from logs and sticks covered by shrubbery and clay.

About 1200 CE, not long before they left the area, many of the Ancient Pueblo began building their settlements on natural shelves within cliffs, in areas that were almost impossible to reach. The village sites, known as "cliff dwellings," point to a need for defensible architecture and protected locations. To reach their homes, the villagers built ladders made of felled tree trunks with notches for steps, although there are dwellings that seem nearly impossible to reach even with ropes and modern climbing gear. Some log ladders are still present on ledges hundreds of meters off the ground. **A** Visitors can see the well-preserved villages today. **B** Mesa Verde National Park has more than 600 cliff dwellings. **C** Chaco Culture National Historic Park and Canyon de Chelly National Monument also provide opportunities to see the preserved villages. **D**

Chaco Canyon, located in what is now western New Mexico, was the cultural center for the Anasazi civilization during the 10th and 11th centuries. At that time, about 30,000 people inhabited the homeland. Evidence suggests that Chaco Canyon was also the center for astronomy and *cosmology*, the study of the origin and development of the universe. *Petroglyphs*, or designs carved in rock, at a site on Fajada Butte in Chaco Canyon are considered evidence of a **celestial calendar**. There, the Sun passing over a crack in sandstone on the day of the summer solstice casts a sliver of light that strikes the very center of a spiral petroglyph on the otherwise shaded rock wall. On the day of the winter solstice, two daggers of sunlight exactly bracket the spiral petroglyph. Research shows that the spiral also was used to track a lunar cycle.

The Ancient Pueblo people had to be resourceful to farm corn, beans, onions, and squash in canyons and atop mesas. They captured rain runoff for their crops and made use of reservoirs and small dams. Although over time the people relied more on farming than hunting, they continued to hunt deer, antelope, and elk and gather wild plants, piñon nuts, and berries. They also took part in a widespread network of trade that brought items such as parrots and copper bells from regions that included the Gulf of Mexico, the Pacific Coast, and the Great Plains, although most trade was conducted among the Ancient Pueblo groups.

Researchers suspect that one contributing factor for the sudden migration of the Ancient Pueblo was a drought that most likely wiped out crops. Tree rings found in the trunks of living trees, as well as **those** found in beams used for dwellings, document the climate record. Abnormally narrow ring growth from that time indicates much less precipitation. Another factor for the exodus may have been the overuse of resources in the area; the Ancient Pueblo people may have **inadvertently** deforested the area as a result of collecting the wood for roof beams and firewood.

Some researchers believe that environmental stresses and crises such as food shortages led to political conflicts and infighting, and perhaps competition and warfare with non-Pueblo groups, all of which would explain the rise of the Pueblo's use of architecture designed for defense. In fact, using **forensic science**, archaeologists have found evidence pointing to violence, executions, and even cannibalism in the ancient communities.

1) Paragraph 1 states all of the following about the Ancient Pueblo people EXCEPT:
   (A) The advanced group of Native Americans suddenly abandoned their communities.
   (B) The Ancient Pueblo constructed their homes in almost unreachable bluffs.
   (C) The descendants of the Ancient Pueblo are the contemporary Pueblo people.
   (D) The Ancient Pueblo disappeared for many obvious reasons in the 13th century.

2) Which of the following best paraphrases the highlighted sentence in Paragraph 1?
   (A) The Spanish explorers in the 1500s used their word *Pueblo*, or "village," to refer to the unique sites of the area's native people.
   (B) *Pueblo* means "village" in Spanish, a term used by the early Spanish explorers in the 1500s for the native people's abandoned communities.
   (C) The Spanish explorers termed the Southwest region *Pueblo* in the 1500s for the impressive buildings that they found, a name that later was applied to the area's people.
   (D) A 16th-century Spanish expedition in the Southwest region traded with people they called *Pueblo*, a Spanish term for native villages.

3) Look at the squares [■] that indicate where the following sentence could be added to Paragraph 3.

   Chaco Canyon's 10th-century village, Pueblo Bonito, contains a five-story-tall complex with about 650 to 800 rooms.

   Where would the sentence best fit?
   Circle the square [■] to add the sentence.

4) In Paragraphs 2 and 3, the author's primary purpose is to
   (A) explain the introduction of farming to the Ancient Pueblo way of life
   (B) trace the early evidence pointing to the villagers' later migration from their sites
   (C) summarize how the Ancient Pueblo residents protected their homes
   (D) describe the evolution of the dwellings constructed by the Ancient Pueblo people

5) Why does the author mention "**celestial calendar**" in Paragraph 4?
   (A) To indicate that the Ancient Pueblo predicted astronomical events
   (B) To show that the tribe used methods to track its planting cycles
   (C) To point out that the Ancient Pueblo monitored cycles of rainfall
   (D) To illustrate that the Ancient Pueblo identified months of the year

6) In Paragraphs 4 and 5, the author's primary purpose is to
   (A) describe how advanced the Ancient Pueblo culture was
   (B) point out underlying reasons for the villager's failure to keep their homeland
   (C) illustrate how sophisticated the inhabitants' cultivation techniques were
   (D) emphasize how far-reaching Pueblo influence was through trade

7) What does the author say in Paragraph 5 about how the people obtained food?
   (A) The Ancient Pueblo relied on cultivation techniques but returned to hunting when precipitation levels declined.
   (B) The people eventually depended more on agriculture but continued to hunt and gather food.
   (C) Besides farming and hunting, the people also relied on a vast chain of trade exchanges to acquire items such as piñon nuts.
   (D) The Ancient Pueblo developed sophisticated methods to irrigate their crops in the arid region.

The Pueblo People

Time
00:10:00

For decades, the public has been fascinated by the sophisticated ancient Native Americans who built entire villages in nearly inaccessible cliff walls but suddenly moved away around 1280 CE. This culture, called Anasazi, first appeared as early as 1500 BCE in what is now the American Southwest. The members of the Anasazi community are called the Ancient Pueblo; their descendants comprise the current-day Pueblo tribes. **Pueblo is a Spanish word meaning "village," a term first used by the 16th-century Spanish explorers to name the distinctive communities of the area's inhabitants.**

Archaeological evidence from about 500 CE shows that the Ancient Pueblo started to construct partially sunken homes, which protected them from the weather and provided storage for harvested foods. Between 700 and 900 CE, they began building above-ground dwellings as the result of a greater reliance on agriculture and the necessity to store foods for longer periods. About 900 CE, the above-ground, single-story pueblos developed into larger complexes with different levels resembling modern apartment buildings. The Ancient Pueblo built the multifamily dwellings with stones shaped from sandstone and held together by mud and clay mortar, while the roofs were crafted from logs and sticks covered by shrubbery and clay.

About 1200 CE, not long before they left the area, many of the Ancient Pueblo began building their settlements on natural shelves within cliffs, in areas that were almost impossible to reach. The village sites, known as "cliff dwellings," point to a need for defensible architecture and protected locations. To reach their homes, the villagers built ladders made of felled tree trunks with notches for steps, although there are dwellings that seem nearly impossible to reach even with ropes and modern climbing gear. Some log ladders are still present on ledges hundreds of meters off the ground. **A** Visitors can see the well-preserved villages today. **B** Mesa Verde National Park has more than 600 cliff dwellings. **C** Chaco Culture National Historic Park and Canyon de Chelly National Monument also provide opportunities to see the preserved villages. **D**

Chaco Canyon, located in what is now western New Mexico, was the cultural center for the Anasazi civilization during the 10th and 11th centuries. At that time, about 30,000 people inhabited the homeland. Evidence suggests that Chaco Canyon was also the center for astronomy and *cosmology*, the study of the origin and development of the universe. *Petroglyphs*, or designs carved in rock, at a site on Fajada Butte in Chaco Canyon are considered evidence of a **celestial calendar**. There, the Sun passing over a crack in sandstone on the day of the summer solstice casts a sliver of light that strikes the very center of a spiral petroglyph on the otherwise shaded rock wall. On the day of the winter solstice, two daggers of sunlight exactly bracket the spiral petroglyph. Research shows that the spiral also was used to track a lunar cycle.

The Ancient Pueblo people had to be resourceful to farm corn, beans, onions, and squash in canyons and atop mesas. They captured rain runoff for their crops and made use of reservoirs and small dams. Although over time the people relied more on farming than hunting, they continued to hunt deer, antelope, and elk and gather wild plants, piñon nuts, and berries. They also took part in a widespread network of trade that brought items such as parrots and copper bells from regions that included the Gulf of Mexico, the Pacific Coast, and the Great Plains, although most trade was conducted among the Ancient Pueblo groups.

Researchers suspect that one contributing factor for the sudden migration of the Ancient Pueblo was a drought that most likely wiped out crops. Tree rings found in the trunks of living trees, as well as **those** found in beams used for dwellings, document the climate record. Abnormally narrow ring growth from that time indicates much less precipitation. Another factor for the exodus may have been the overuse of resources in the area; the Ancient Pueblo people may have **inadvertently** deforested the area as a result of collecting the wood for roof beams and firewood.

Some researchers believe that environmental stresses and crises such as food shortages led to political conflicts and infighting, and perhaps competition and warfare with non-Pueblo groups, all of which would explain the rise of the Pueblo's use of architecture designed for defense. In fact, using **forensic science**, archaeologists have found evidence pointing to violence, executions, and even cannibalism in the ancient communities.

8) The word "**those**" in Paragraph 6 refers to
 (A) tree rings
 (B) tree trunks
 (C) roof beams
 (D) cliff dwellings

9) What can be inferred about the use of tree ring studies mentioned in Paragraph 6?
 (A) A tree is able to add a thicker band to its trunk in a wetter year.
 (B) Researchers can determine deforestation patterns in a region.
 (C) Researchers can trace past rainfall totals for many regions using a tree trunk from the Ancient Pueblo sites.
 (D) Researchers can predict future precipitation totals in a region.

10) The word "**inadvertently**" in Paragraph 6 means
 (A) instantaneously
 (B) deliberately
 (C) unintentionally
 (D) abruptly

11) The author mentions "**forensic science**" in Paragraph 7 to reveal that archaeologists used
 (A) technology to uncover evidence and determine what occurred
 (B) tree-ring dating methods to identify time periods
 (C) written historical records to gather information
 (D) archaeological techniques to create a detailed map of a site

12) According to Paragraphs 6 and 7, what is NOT a suggested reason for the Ancient Pueblo people's departure?
 (A) Lack of rainfall could have destroyed agricultural food sources.
 (B) Conflicts with other tribes may have forced out the inhabitants.
 (C) The people may have exhausted their supply of timber.
 (D) The people may have fled when the Spanish explorers arrived.

13) What purpose does Paragraph 7 serve in the discussion of the defensible style of the cliff dwellings and the people's sudden departure from their homeland?
 (A) To introduce the main idea of warring factions as the reason for the style of architecture and withdrawal from the region
 (B) To tie the difficult environmental factors to conflicts, which would explain the protective architecture and the need to flee the area
 (C) To link possible conflicts with distant trading groups to the protection of their homes and eventual flight from their homeland
 (D) To imply that disease also may have been a factor that drove people to build protective homes and later evacuate the villages

14) **Directions**: An introductory sentence relating to the passage is written below. Complete the exercise by choosing the THREE answers that support the sentence. Some sentences do not belong because they do not support the sentence. **This question is worth 2 points.**

The Ancient Pueblo developed successful agricultural techniques.

 •
 •
 •

Answer Choices
1. The Ancient Pueblo used rock art to track lunar cycles.
2. The Ancient Pueblo devised methods to store rainfall.
3. Housing changes indicated a need to preserve harvested goods.
4. The people participated in a far-reaching trading system.
5. The Ancient Pueblo fled to other areas of the Southwest.
6. Eventually the people participated in fewer hunting activities.

13

Radiation

Time
00:20:00

Every second, the Sun releases 4 million tons of energy in the form of *electromagnetic radiation*, or waves of energy that spread outward from the Sun **in all directions**. The sunlight that passes through the atmosphere and reaches Earth's surface is composed of infrared, visible, and ultraviolet (UV) light, all three of which are types of radiation. Because visible and infrared radiation are entirely harmless to humans but exposure to UV radiation causes sunburn, one can conclude that not all radiation behaves in the same way.

The **ubiquitous** infrared, visible, and UV radiation that humans experience as "sunlight" make up only a sliver of the infinitely broad *electromagnetic spectrum* that encompasses the range of all possible wavelengths. Long wavelengths are *low frequency* because their waves **oscillate** less often than shorter wavelengths, which have a *high frequency*. All electromagnetic radiation travels at the speed of light and carries energy, which transfers to substances that the radiation interacts with. Thus, the wavelength's frequency determines the amount of energy that the wavelength carries, and high-frequency radiation carries more energy than low-frequency radiation.

Radiation can have one of two effects on an atom or molecule: excitation or ionization. *Excitation* occurs when radiation permeates a substance and transfers some of its energy to electrons attached to atoms in the substance. The affected electrons become "excited" because of the extra energy, and they release the excess energy in the form of heat to restore their original energy levels. However, radiation that carries sufficient energy completely removes a particle, such as a positively charged proton or negatively charged electron, from an otherwise balanced atom or molecule, altering its structure and causing **it** to assume a positive or negative charge in a process called *ionization*. Furthermore, altering living tissue's molecular structure can cause hazardous mutations. Thus, electromagnetic radiations with higher frequencies, such as gamma radiation and x-radiation, carry more energy and cause more damage to living structures.

Based on the effects of excitation and ionization, scientists divide radiation into *non-ionizing radiation*, which simply excites electrons and generally is not harmful, and *ionizing radiation*, which is harmful to all living things. Because different atoms and molecules have different *ionization energies*, or the amount of energy required to extract a particle from an atom, the difference between non-ionizing and ionizing radiation varies from one material to another.

A For humans, who are composed mostly of water molecules, high-energy UV radiation is at the threshold* for ionizing radiation, but exposure to any UV radiation can potentially cause skin damage in the form of sunburn or cancer. **B** Thus, even though UV radiation makes up about 10 percent of the energy that leaves the Sun, it only constitutes about 3 percent of the sunlight that reaches Earth's surface when the Sun is at its zenith. **C** Although it is not ionizing, low-frequency UV radiation damages skin by overly exciting chains of DNA, prompting the release of *melanin*, a skin pigment that can quickly absorb UV radiation and tan the skin to prevent further DNA damage. **D Sunburns often cause pain because overexposure to UV radiation provokes the body to release a protein called CXCL5 that stimulates nerves located in the skin, leading to swelling and itching to warn the person who has been exposed to the Sun for too long.**

Although high-frequency electromagnetic radiation is potentially harmful to all living things, it also has many uses, especially within the medical field. An x-radiation machine, or x-ray machine, allows doctors to see a patient's internal structures because an x-ray, which has a higher frequency than UV radiation, passes through human tissue. When the radiation reaches dense bone molecules, which have higher ionization energy than tissue, the radiation becomes absorbed. A technician captures the images of bone and tissue by using a camera that exposes the film to x-rays. The x-ray image produced by the camera shows the bones, which absorbed the radiation, as white structures whereas the tissue, which the x-ray passed through, appears black or gray. Thus, a broken bone is easily discernible because a gap will be visible in the bone structure. However, doctors now use x-rays sparingly due to the fact that high-frequency radiation poses health risks such as DNA mutation that can lead to cancer.

*Threshold: the point at which a stimulus begins to generate an effect

1) Paragraph 1 MOST LIKELY mentions "**in all directions**" in order to
   (A) give an example of how radiation travels through space
   (B) show how sunlight affects the rest of the solar system
   (C) point out that not all radiation from the Sun reaches Earth
   (D) illustrate a fundamental property of the energy in radiation

2) The word "**ubiquitous**" in Paragraph 2 is closest in meaning to
   (A) incredible
   (B) pervasive
   (C) enigmatic
   (D) harmful

3) In Paragraph 2, the word "**oscillate**" means
   (A) abate
   (B) overcompensate
   (C) fluctuate
   (D) accelerate

4) The word "**it**" in Paragraph 3 refers to
   (A) particle
   (B) atom or molecule
   (C) proton or electron
   (D) radiation

5) According to Paragraph 3, ionization
   (A) results when high-frequency radiation separates a particle from an atom or molecule
   (B) adds a proton or electron to a molecule, creating a new, heavier molecule
   (C) causes an electron to release energy in the form of heat
   (D) increases the frequency of radiation until it becomes harmful to living tissue

6) Look at the squares [■] that indicate where the following sentence could be added in Paragraph 5.

   Fortunately, Earth's atmosphere blocks all high-frequency UV radiation and other high-energy radiation from the Sun.

   Where would the sentence best fit?
   Circle the square [■] to add the sentence.

7) Which of the following best paraphrases the highlighted sentence in Paragraph 5?
   (A) UV radiation carries a protein into the body that causes sunburn pain such as the itching and swelling of the skin.
   (B) The body produces a protein that increases UV exposure, resulting in more radiation absorption and eventually sunburn.
   (C) Proteins that help absorb UV radiation also increase skin sensitivity that causes the pain associated with sunburn.
   (D) Sunburn discomfort results when UV exposure triggers the release of proteins that increase skin sensitivity.

8) According to Paragraph 5, all of the following are true about UV radiation EXCEPT:
   (A) It triggers the release of particular proteins in humans.
   (B) Approximately 3 percent of UV radiation is ionizing.
   (C) A certain pigment located in humans absorbs it.
   (D) It prompts possibly dangerous changes in human DNA.

Radiation

Every second, the Sun releases 4 million tons of energy in the form of *electromagnetic radiation*, or waves of energy that spread outward from the Sun **in all directions**. The sunlight that passes through the atmosphere and reaches Earth's surface is composed of infrared, visible, and ultraviolet (UV) light, all three of which are types of radiation. Because visible and infrared radiation are entirely harmless to humans but exposure to UV radiation causes sunburn, one can conclude that not all radiation behaves in the same way.

The **ubiquitous** infrared, visible, and UV radiation that humans experience as "sunlight" make up only a sliver of the infinitely broad *electromagnetic spectrum* that encompasses the range of all possible wavelengths. Long wavelengths are *low frequency* because their waves **oscillate** less often than shorter wavelengths, which have a *high frequency*. All electromagnetic radiation travels at the speed of light and carries energy, which transfers to substances that the radiation interacts with. Thus, the wavelength's frequency determines the amount of energy that the wavelength carries, and high-frequency radiation carries more energy than low-frequency radiation.

Radiation can have one of two effects on an atom or molecule: excitation or ionization. *Excitation* occurs when radiation permeates a substance and transfers some of its energy to electrons attached to atoms in the substance. The affected electrons become "excited" because of the extra energy, and they release the excess energy in the form of heat to restore their original energy levels. However, radiation that carries sufficient energy completely removes a particle, such as a positively charged proton or negatively charged electron, from an otherwise balanced atom or molecule, altering its structure and causing **it** to assume a positive or negative charge in a process called *ionization*. Furthermore, altering living tissue's molecular structure can cause hazardous mutations. Thus, electromagnetic radiations with higher frequencies, such as gamma radiation and x-radiation, carry more energy and cause more damage to living structures.

Based on the effects of excitation and ionization, scientists divide radiation into *non-ionizing radiation*, which simply excites electrons and generally is not harmful, and *ionizing radiation*, which is harmful to all living things. Because different atoms and molecules have different *ionization energies*, or the amount of energy required to extract a particle from an atom, the difference between non-ionizing and ionizing radiation varies from one material to another.

A For humans, who are composed mostly of water molecules, high-energy UV radiation is at the threshold* for ionizing radiation, but exposure to any UV radiation can potentially cause skin damage in the form of sunburn or cancer. **B** Thus, even though UV radiation makes up about 10 percent of the energy that leaves the Sun, it only constitutes about 3 percent of the sunlight that reaches Earth's surface when the Sun is at its zenith. **C** Although it is not ionizing, low-frequency UV radiation damages skin by overly exciting chains of DNA, prompting the release of *melanin*, a skin pigment that can quickly absorb UV radiation and tan the skin to prevent further DNA damage. **D** **Sunburns often cause pain because overexposure to UV radiation provokes the body to release a protein called CXCL5 that stimulates nerves located in the skin, leading to swelling and itching to warn the person who has been exposed to the Sun for too long.**

Although high-frequency electromagnetic radiation is potentially harmful to all living things, it also has many uses, especially within the medical field. An x-radiation machine, or x-ray machine, allows doctors to see a patient's internal structures because an x-ray, which has a higher frequency than UV radiation, passes through human tissue. When the radiation reaches dense bone molecules, which have higher ionization energy than tissue, the radiation becomes absorbed. A technician captures the images of bone and tissue by using a camera that exposes the film to x-rays. The x-ray image produced by the camera shows the bones, which absorbed the radiation, as white structures whereas the tissue, which the x-ray passed through, appears black or gray. Thus, a broken bone is easily discernible because a gap will be visible in the bone structure. However, doctors now use x-rays sparingly due to the fact that high-frequency radiation poses health risks such as DNA mutation that can lead to cancer.

*Threshold: the point at which a stimulus begins to generate an effect

9) According to Paragraphs 4 and 5, human tissue has an ionization energy that approximately equals
(A) high-frequency UV radiation
(B) an electron in an excited state
(C) a chain of DNA
(D) the amount of melanin in human skin

10) According to Paragraph 6, x-radiation passes through human tissue but is absorbed into bone because
(A) human tissue is made of larger molecules, which are more likely to contact an x-ray
(B) it takes more energy to ionize a bone molecule than other human tissue
(C) bones are located inside the body, further away from the x-radiation
(D) human tissue only contains individual atoms while bone contains molecules

11) Which of the following can be inferred about x-rays in Paragraph 6?
(A) Whereas x-rays pass harmlessly through skin, they can cause permanent bone damage.
(B) X-rays are absorbed into damaged or broken bones, which facilitates the healing process.
(C) Overexposure to x-radiation can potentially ionize human tissue.
(D) X-ray images can only be produced when x-radiation ionizes every cell in a human's bone.

12) According to the passage, which form of radiation PROBABLY has the highest frequency?
(A) Infrared radiation
(B) Visible radiation
(C) UV radiation
(D) X-radiation

13) **Directions**: Select the sentences that most appropriately match the descriptions of each type of radiation. TWO of the answer choices will NOT be used. **This question is worth 3 points.**

Non-ionizing radiation
-
-

Ionizing radiation
-
-
-

Answer Choices
1. This type of radiation does not interact with molecules or atoms.
2. Infrared radiation is an example of this type of radiation.
3. This type of radiation alters the composition of an atom or molecule.
4. This type of radiation temporarily transfers energy to an electron.
5. This type of radiation is harmful to living tissue.
6. This type of radiation does not have a wavelength or frequency.
7. An x-ray machine uses this type of radiation for medical purposes.

Edgar Allan Poe

Time
00:20:00

Edgar Allan Poe was one of America's most influential writers. His short stories remain popular with readers nearly 200 years after their publication. If Poe could know this, he would be surprised by his renown today, as he led a **turbulent** life frequently mired in poverty. Though it was unusual in the United States at the time, he decided to attempt to support himself with his writing. Thus, he was motivated to produce fiction that would sell, which may have been a factor in the dark sensationalism of his work. **After his death, Poe became even more of a literary icon due to his irresistibly horrifying tales and innovations in entertaining genres.**

Tragic death is a prevalent theme in Poe's writing, perhaps stemming from his personal experiences. Born in 1809 to traveling actors, Poe was an infant when his father abandoned the family and his mother died. He was reared by a wealthy foster family in Virginia, though his foster mother died as well. As a young man, Poe attended the University of Virginia, but he was forced to drop out when he could not pay for tuition because of mounting gambling debts. Afterward, he served in the U.S. Army, and then studied at the Military Academy at West Point but was expelled for not attending classes. Disputes over money and other tensions led to a break with his foster father. From then on, Poe struggled to earn a living, editing and writing at a number of publications in different cities. His young wife contracted tuberculosis in 1842, from which she died in 1847.

In spite of many challenges, Poe continued to write until his own early death. He achieved some success with his poetry and scathing reviews of other writers' work. In addition, most literary scholars agree that Poe virtually invented detective fiction. In 1841, he published "The Murders in the Rue Morgue," the first in a series of stories that featured C. Auguste Dupin, a bright but eccentric detective who solves crimes through analytical reasoning. **The plots provide multiple layers of clues that nevertheless lead to unexpected twists at the conclusions.** Poe's stories about Dupin reportedly inspired the Sherlock Holmes series by Scottish author Arthur Conan Doyle, ultimately prompting the detective or mystery genre to expand in the 20th century with vast numbers of stories, novels, and films.

Poe also took note of the newly developing science fiction genre, publishing several short stories about impossible adventures using new technology, scattered with scientific-sounding details, which were presented as factual accounts. These hoaxes probably fooled few readers at the time; Poe's "adventures" **predict** innovations that were hardly imaginable in his day, such as traveling by air and reaching outer space. For example, "The Unparalleled Adventures of One Hans Pfaall" is about a man who goes to the moon in a hot-air balloon. Poe's *The Narrative of A. Gordon Pym* was another "**factual account**." The novel involves a journey to a lost civilization in Antarctica.

A Poe's famous macabre tale "The Fall of the House of Usher" is considered a masterpiece of Gothic fiction. **B** The story is set in a mansion in a bleak landscape, where the narrator goes to help his friend, Roderick Usher, with physical and mental illness. **C** Usher's twin sister dies, and the narrator helps Usher place her body in the family vault. **D** Over the next few days, Usher begins to believe that there are sounds coming from the vault; he worries that his sister may have been buried alive. The tension builds on a stormy night as the sounds from the vault become louder and more frequent, and both men believe that they see the sister standing at the door. The shock kills Usher and sends the narrator running as the house collapses.

"The Cask of Amontillado," Poe's last and perhaps best short story, is a dark mood piece told from the first-person perspective of a murderer named Montresor. In the story, the narrator Montresor believes that his friend Fortunato has injured and insulted him, so Montresor vows revenge. He describes encountering Fortunato during a festival and luring him to a *catacomb*, an underground cemetery, with promises of a rare brandy called Amontillado. After Fortunato walks into a crypt, the narrator chains him to a wall and then slowly seals the cell with building stone and mortar to Fortunato's growing horror. **Montresor leaves Fortunato to die and then explains at the tale's end that the incident occurred 50 years earlier, with the tomb remaining undisturbed for the duration.**

1) In Paragraph 1, the word "**turbulent**" means
   (A) moderately sad
   (B) surprisingly calm
   (C) generally sensitive
   (D) relatively unstable

2) What can be inferred about Edgar Allan Poe based on Paragraph 1?
   (A) He suspected that he would be long remembered.
   (B) He believed that people would buy fiction that was shocking.
   (C) He created personal problems for himself with a gloomy outlook.
   (D) He predicted that he would always be poor as a writer.

3) Which of the following best paraphrases the highlighted sentence in Paragraph 1?
   (A) Poe's ability to attract and hold the public's attention, and his contributions to new formats in fiction, made him even more famous posthumously.
   (B) Poe's death prevented him from knowing that he would become America's most important serious literary artist.
   (C) Poe created fiction that frightened or confused people of his era, but long after his death, his work was rediscovered and became well loved by the public.
   (D) Poe's inspiring and amusing stories ensured that he would be remembered long after his death.

4) Based on Paragraph 2, a factual biography of Poe would NOT include
   (A) descriptions of him grieving for women who died young
   (B) explanations of his failure in college and the military
   (C) descriptions of him living in various mansions that seemed eerie
   (D) evidence that he argued irreparably with his foster father

5) Why does the author include the highlighted sentence in Paragraph 3?
   (A) To describe the details of the story that was mentioned
   (B) To persuade the reader that the story is worthwhile even today
   (C) To explain the paradox of rational thought and surprise in the story
   (D) To identify a pattern in Poe's detective fiction

6) In Paragraph 3, the author's primary purpose is to
   (A) show how the Sherlock Holmes series may have originated
   (B) compare Poe's mystery writing to the work of other writers that he influenced
   (C) describe Poe's work in the mystery genre and its impact on other writers
   (D) highlight the timeless fascination that readers have for detective novels

7) Why does the author mention "**predict**" in Paragraph 4?
   (A) To reference Poe's ominous Gothic-like prophecies for the future
   (B) To emphasize Poe's keen sense of timing in his science fiction work
   (C) To explain that Poe's science fiction foretold several modern developments
   (D) To illustrate how Poe's work was the manual for future advancements

8) In Paragraph 4, the phrase "**factual account**" refers to
   (A) hoax that fooled readers
   (B) imagined mechanical innovation
   (C) story of space travel
   (D) journey to a lost civilization

Edgar Allan Poe

Edgar Allan Poe was one of America's most influential writers. His short stories remain popular with readers nearly 200 years after their publication. If Poe could know this, he would be surprised by his renown today, as he led a **turbulent** life frequently mired in poverty. Though it was unusual in the United States at the time, he decided to attempt to support himself with his writing. Thus, he was motivated to produce fiction that would sell, which may have been a factor in the dark sensationalism of his work. **After his death, Poe became even more of a literary icon due to his irresistibly horrifying tales and innovations in entertaining genres.**

Tragic death is a prevalent theme in Poe's writing, perhaps stemming from his personal experiences. Born in 1809 to traveling actors, Poe was an infant when his father abandoned the family and his mother died. He was reared by a wealthy foster family in Virginia, though his foster mother died as well. As a young man, Poe attended the University of Virginia, but he was forced to drop out when he could not pay for tuition because of mounting gambling debts. Afterward, he served in the U.S. Army, and then studied at the Military Academy at West Point but was expelled for not attending classes. Disputes over money and other tensions led to a break with his foster father. From then on, Poe struggled to earn a living, editing and writing at a number of publications in different cities. His young wife contracted tuberculosis in 1842, from which she died in 1847.

In spite of many challenges, Poe continued to write until his own early death. He achieved some success with his poetry and scathing reviews of other writers' work. In addition, most literary scholars agree that Poe virtually invented detective fiction. In 1841, he published "The Murders in the Rue Morgue," the first in a series of stories that featured C. Auguste Dupin, a bright but eccentric detective who solves crimes through analytical reasoning. **The plots provide multiple layers of clues that nevertheless lead to unexpected twists at the conclusions.** Poe's stories about Dupin reportedly inspired the Sherlock Holmes series by Scottish author Arthur Conan Doyle, ultimately prompting the detective or mystery genre to expand in the 20th century with vast numbers of stories, novels, and films.

Poe also took note of the newly developing science fiction genre, publishing several short stories about impossible adventures using new technology, scattered with scientific-sounding details, which were presented as factual accounts. These hoaxes probably fooled few readers at the time; Poe's "adventures" **predict** innovations that were hardly imaginable in his day, such as traveling by air and reaching outer space. For example, "The Unparalleled Adventures of One Hans Pfaall" is about a man who goes to the moon in a hot-air balloon. Poe's *The Narrative of A. Gordon Pym* was another "**factual account**." The novel involves a journey to a lost civilization in Antarctica.

A Poe's famous macabre tale "The Fall of the House of Usher" is considered a masterpiece of Gothic fiction. **B** The story is set in a mansion in a bleak landscape, where the narrator goes to help his friend, Roderick Usher, with physical and mental illness. **C** Usher's twin sister dies, and the narrator helps Usher place her body in the family vault. **D** Over the next few days, Usher begins to believe that there are sounds coming from the vault; he worries that his sister may have been buried alive. The tension builds on a stormy night as the sounds from the vault become louder and more frequent, and both men believe that they see the sister standing at the door. The shock kills Usher and sends the narrator running as the house collapses.

"The Cask of Amontillado," Poe's last and perhaps best short story, is a dark mood piece told from the first-person perspective of a murderer named Montresor. In the story, the narrator Montresor believes that his friend Fortunato has injured and insulted him, so Montresor vows revenge. He describes encountering Fortunato during a festival and luring him to a *catacomb*, an underground cemetery, with promises of a rare brandy called Amontillado. After Fortunato walks into a crypt, the narrator chains him to a wall and then slowly seals the cell with building stone and mortar to Fortunato's growing horror. **Montresor leaves Fortunato to die and then explains at the tale's end that the incident occurred 50 years earlier, with the tomb remaining undisturbed for the duration.**

9) Look at the squares [■] that indicate where the sentence below could be added to Paragraph 5.

In spite of these important literary contributions, Poe's fame rests squarely on his dark *Gothic* fiction, or stories about some kind of torment or hair-raising experience set in gloomy places.

Where would the sentence best fit?
Circle the square [■] to add the sentence.

10) According to Paragraph 5, the plot in "The Fall of the House of Usher" has a disastrous ending caused by
(A) the frightening arrival of an unexpected figure
(B) many ghostly figures haunting the House of Usher
(C) a haunted mansion in a bleak landscape
(D) a stormy night in a rural, isolated mansion

11) What can be inferred from the highlighted sentence in Paragraph 6?
(A) Montresor is looking back with remorse at what he did.
(B) Fortunato did not escape, and Montresor was never suspected.
(C) Montresor is boasting about his act of revenge and would do it again.
(D) The narrator is musing about his own fears of mortality.

12) Which of the following best describes the relationship between Paragraphs 5 and 6?
(A) Paragraph 5 describes a story that is important in the Gothic genre, and Paragraph 6 supplies another prime example.
(B) Both paragraphs trace the way that Poe's personal tragedies affected his plots.
(C) Paragraph 6 provides proof that Poe's later work improved over his earlier efforts described in Paragraph 5.
(D) Paragraph 5 describes a narrator who claims that he is innocent, while Paragraph 6 describes a much more daring claim.

13) **Directions**: Select the sentences that most appropriately match the descriptions of each style of fiction writing. TWO of the answer choices will not be used. **This question is worth 4 points.**

Gothic fiction
-
-
-

Science fiction
-
-

Detective fiction
-
-

Answer Choices
1. Readers try to solve a crime as they read, identifying the perpetrator by the end.
2. Poe's only finished novel fell under this genre of fiction.
3. A dreary setting provides the backdrop for morbid events in this type of story.
4. Poe used this genre to explore a character's calm retelling of his own outrageous act.
5. This genre might include a series of travel tales narrated in the first person.
6. These stories involve speculating about technology that may be discovered.
7. Poe's ingenious character became a prototype for other characters in this genre.
8. Readers might feel drawn into fear of ghosts with this kind of tale.
9. This genre tends to emphasize moral or ethical lessons learned by characters.

Black Holes

Nearly 5 billion years ago, a massive cloud of dust and gas, which was composed mostly of hydrogen and helium atoms, gathered in a concentrated area in space because of the attractive force of gravity. Over millions of years, this force compressed a portion of the dust and gas into a progressively smaller area until the pressure and temperature at the center of the cloud became so great that four of the hydrogen atoms within the cloud fused together. By doing so, they formed the next heaviest element, helium, and pushed out some energy in the process. As the pressure within the cloud increased, more hydrogen atoms fused into helium, and the ever-increasing density at the center of the cloud caused gravity to pull more and more of the cloud into a ball. Thus, the Sun was born, and the process of compression and fusion caused the Sun to enlarge over the course of billions of years. Even today, the fusion pushing energy outward and gravity pulling mass inward maintain the Sun in a process called *hydrostatic equilibrium.*

Eventually, all stars burn out when **this balance** is interrupted. A small star, such as Earth's Sun, will run out of hydrogen and other light elements to fuse together, and gravity will compress the core of the Sun into a very dense, but relatively cool white dwarf star. **When a star much more massive than the Sun runs out of fuel, the outside of the star explodes in an immense expulsion of matter called a *supernova*;** however, the center of a star implodes because the massive elements there require too much energy to be fused together. Thus, the remains of the massive star may become a *black hole*, a region of space so dense that the inward force of gravity overpowers the outward force of atomic fusion. Within the boundaries of a black hole, the force of gravity is so strong that no particle of matter or energy that strays too close can escape. **A**

B However, astronomers and physicists know that black holes exist because they influence the movement of nearby stars. **C** For instance, if astronomers detect a star orbiting some unseen force, they conclude that the force must be a black hole drawing the star into orbit with its irresistible gravity. **D**

Additionally, physicists have used **sophisticated** mathematical equations to determine the **anatomy** of a black hole: the center of a black hole contains a singularity, which is surrounded by an event horizon. The gravitational force of a black hole on matter acts like a current pulling an unfortunate boat toward the top of a waterfall: the closer the boat gets to the waterfall, the faster it moves toward the falls. The boat may still be able to escape just before it reaches the falls, but suddenly it comes to a point of no return and plummets down. In a black hole, this point of no return is the *event horizon*, and not even light can escape once it hits this point. Once something passes beyond the event horizon, it plunges toward the black hole's *singularity*, or a point in the center of a black hole where the human understanding of space and time fails because an infinite density is contained in an infinitely small point. In other words, a singularity is a mathematical and physical mystery that cannot be observed because black holes are inherently unobservable.

Like most space objects, black holes come in different varieties. A *stellar black hole*, with a mass from about five to ten times the mass of the Sun, forms when a large star collapses. However, at the center of nearly every observable galaxy sits a supermassive black hole that, as its name implies, is much larger. For example, scientists estimate that the supermassive black hole at the center of Earth's galaxy, the Milky Way, is approximately 4.3 million times more massive than the Sun. Some scientists speculate that *supermassive black holes* are **primordial** stellar black holes that have consumed aeons*' worth of mass. Fortunately, the nearest detected black hole is 1,600 light years away, too far away to affect the Earth.

Aeon: a length of time equal to 1 billion years

1) According to Paragraph 1, all of the following are true about the Sun's life cycle EXCEPT:

(A) Intense pressure caused elements to fuse together.

(B) Hydrostatic equilibrium keeps the Sun stable.

(C) The Sun achieved an equal ratio of hydrogen to helium atoms.

(D) The Sun began as an enormous collection of dust and gas.

2) The phrase "**this balance**" in Paragraph 2 refers to

(A) the fusion of hydrogen and helium

(B) hydrostatic equilibrium

(C) gravity's pull on massive objects

(D) clouds of dust and gas forming stars

3) Which of the following best paraphrases the highlighted phrase in Paragraph 2?

(A) A supernova occurs when the exterior of a large star at the end of its life cycle bursts.

(B) When a large star has too much energy, the exterior of the star bursts outward in a supernova.

(C) Stars that become too large become supernovas because they consume too much fuel.

(D) The outside of an enormous star is called a *supernova*, which explodes when it becomes unstable.

4) According to Paragraph 2, why does a large star become a black hole?

(A) The gravitational force resulting from a supernova causes the center of a star to collapse.

(B) The center of the star collapses in on itself because gravity overcomes atomic fusion.

(C) When a star becomes incredibly dense, it reverses its gravitational field and becomes a black hole.

(D) The gravitational pull from nearby stars overpowers the atomic fusion at the center of a large star.

5) Which of the following can be inferred from the information in Paragraphs 1 and 2?

(A) The Sun is much larger than the cloud of gas and dust from which it formed.

(B) Stars that are larger than the Sun fuse heavier elements together.

(C) All clouds of gas and dust in space form into stars.

(D) Gravity is the strongest force that scientists have observed.

6) Look at the squares [■] that indicate where the sentence below could be added to Paragraph 2 or 3.

Black holes cannot be directly observed, as not even light can escape their confines.

Where would the sentence best fit?
Circle the square [■] to add the sentence.

7) In Paragraph 4, the word "**sophisticated**" most nearly means

(A) perfect

(B) hypothetical

(C) complex

(D) revealing

8) The author MOST LIKELY mentions "**anatomy**" in Paragraph 4 in order to

(A) classify each type of black hole according to its characteristics

(B) emphasize similarities between a black hole and a body

(C) introduce the different components of any given black hole

(D) persuade readers that a black hole is simpler than it seems

Black Holes

Nearly 5 billion years ago, a massive cloud of dust and gas, which was composed mostly of hydrogen and helium atoms, gathered in a concentrated area in space because of the attractive force of gravity. Over millions of years, this force compressed a portion of the dust and gas into a progressively smaller area until the pressure and temperature at the center of the cloud became so great that four of the hydrogen atoms within the cloud fused together. By doing so, they formed the next heaviest element, helium, and pushed out some energy in the process. As the pressure within the cloud increased, more hydrogen atoms fused into helium, and the ever-increasing density at the center of the cloud caused gravity to pull more and more of the cloud into a ball. Thus, the Sun was born, and the process of compression and fusion caused the Sun to enlarge over the course of billions of years. Even today, the fusion pushing energy outward and gravity pulling mass inward maintain the Sun in a process called *hydrostatic equilibrium.*

Eventually, all stars burn out when **this balance** is interrupted. A small star, such as Earth's Sun, will run out of hydrogen and other light elements to fuse together, and gravity will compress the core of the Sun into a very dense, but relatively cool white dwarf star. **When a star much more massive than the Sun runs out of fuel, the outside of the star explodes in an immense expulsion of matter called a *supernova*;** however, the center of a star implodes because the massive elements there require too much energy to be fused together. Thus, the remains of the massive star may become a *black hole*, a region of space so dense that the inward force of gravity overpowers the outward force of atomic fusion. Within the boundaries of a black hole, the force of gravity is so strong that no particle of matter or energy that strays too close can escape. **A**

B However, astronomers and physicists know that black holes exist because they influence the movement of nearby stars. **C** For instance, if astronomers detect a star orbiting some unseen force, they conclude that the force must be a black hole drawing the star into orbit with its irresistible gravity. **D**

Additionally, physicists have used **sophisticated** mathematical equations to determine the **anatomy** of a black hole: the center of a black hole contains a singularity, which is surrounded by an event horizon. The gravitational force of a black hole on matter acts like a current pulling an unfortunate boat toward the top of a waterfall: the closer the boat gets to the waterfall, the faster it moves toward the falls. The boat may still be able to escape just before it reaches the falls, but suddenly it comes to a point of no return and plummets down. In a black hole, this point of no return is the *event horizon*, and not even light can escape once it hits this point. Once something passes beyond the event horizon, it plunges toward the black hole's *singularity*, or a point in the center of a black hole where the human understanding of space and time fails because an infinite density is contained in an infinitely small point. In other words, a singularity is a mathematical and physical mystery that cannot be observed because black holes are inherently unobservable.

Like most space objects, black holes come in different varieties. A *stellar black hole*, with a mass from about five to ten times the mass of the Sun, forms when a large star collapses. However, at the center of nearly every observable galaxy sits a supermassive black hole that, as its name implies, is much larger. For example, scientists estimate that the supermassive black hole at the center of Earth's galaxy, the Milky Way, is approximately 4.3 million times more massive than the Sun. Some scientists speculate that *supermassive black holes* are **primordial** stellar black holes that have consumed aeons*' worth of mass. Fortunately, the nearest detected black hole is 1,600 light years away, too far away to affect the Earth.

*Aeon: a length of time equal to 1 billion years

9) Why does the author compare a black hole to a waterfall in Paragraph 4?
   (A) To emphasize the importance of gravity on a waterfall's current
   (B) To summarize how an event horizon forms
   (C) To illustrate an unobservable phenomenon in visual terms
   (D) To prove that black holes may potentially form on Earth

10) What can be inferred about the characteristics of black holes based on the information in Paragraph 4?
   (A) Black holes possess gravity, but they do not possess mass.
   (B) Only massive objects such as stars can cross an event horizon.
   (C) The size of a black hole is determined by measuring its event horizon.
   (D) Scientists are unsure of what happens to matter that enters a black hole.

11) The word "**primordial**" in Paragraph 5 is closest in meaning to
   (A) enormous
   (B) ancient
   (C) enigmatic
   (D) unstable

12) According to Paragraph 5, black holes are categorized by
   (A) how they form
   (B) their mass
   (C) where they form
   (D) their shape

13) **Directions**: An introductory sentence relating to the passage is written below. Complete the exercise by choosing THREE answers to support the sentence. Some sentences do not belong because they do not support the sentence. **This question is worth 2 points.**

Black holes are amazing yet mysterious cosmological phenomena.

-
-
-

Answer Choices
1. Any matter or energy that traverses an event horizon becomes trapped in the black hole.
2. The Sun will become a white dwarf star once it runs out of fuel to burn.
3. Black holes can only rarely be seen using modern telescopes.
4. Centers of galaxies contain ancient and enormous black holes.
5. Scientists must use complex calculations to determine properties of black holes.
6. When black holes absorb too much energy, they explode in a supernova.

Actual Test

Review Help Back Next

Reading Section Directions

In this section, you will read three passages and answer reading comprehension questions about each passage. Most questions are worth one point, but the last question in each set is worth more than one point. The directions indicate how many points you may receive.

You will have 60 minutes to read all of the passages and answer the questions. Some passages include a word or phrase that is underlined and printed in blue. Click on the word or phrase to see a definition or an explanation.

When you want to move on to the next question, click on **Next**. You can skip questions and go back to them later as long as there is time remaining. If you want to return to previous questions, click on **Back**. You can click on **Review** at any time and the review screen will show you which questions you have answered and which you have not. From this review screen, you may go directly to any question that you have already seen in the reading section.

Confirm later after calculating....

	Very Poor	Poor	Good	Very Good	Excellent
Points	1 - 21	22 - 29	30 - 34	35 - 38	39 - 43
Scale	1 - 14	15 - 19	20 - 23	24 - 26	27 - 30
Your Score					

Questions 1 - 4

More Available

1) The word "**covert**" in Paragraph 1 is closest in meaning to
(A) secret
(B) suspicious
(C) reconnaissance
(D) unavoidable

2) Which of the following best describes the relationship between Paragraph 1 and Paragraph 2?
(A) Paragraph 1 introduces the Underground Railroad, and Paragraph 2 details the harsh treatment that many slaves endured.
(B) Paragraph 1 explains Tubman's achievements and sets the historical background, while Paragraph 2 describes her life before her escape.
(C) Paragraph 1 provides background on the abolitionist movement and Tubman's role in it, illustrated further in Paragraph 2.
(D) Paragraph 1 summarizes the significance of Harriet Tubman; Paragraph 2 explains her preparations to escape.

3) What can be inferred about the Religious Society of Friends from Paragraph 4?
(A) They were fugitives assisting other slaves trying to reach freedom.
(B) They worked on the railway system and helped slaves sneak aboard trains.
(C) They were abolitionists, and some assisted fugitives.
(D) They were involved in the Philadelphia abolitionist movement.

4) The phrase "**this community**" in Paragraph 4 refers to
(A) the northern community
(B) the southern community
(C) the Quaker community
(D) the abolitionist community

Harriet Tubman

Harriet Tubman was a 19th-century African-American woman who became a famous figure in the struggle against slavery in the United States. She is mostly known for her **covert** trips to lead groups of escaping slaves to freedom in northern states where slavery was illegal. She participated in running the Underground Railroad, which was a secret network of safe houses, routes, and means of transportation for escaping slaves. While there are no exact records, Tubman made more than a dozen trips and may have helped hundreds of slaves escape.

Tubman's passion and courage came from her own experiences. She was born into slavery in the state of Maryland in 1820. Even as a child she did exhausting work in the fields. Like all slaves, she lived under the threat of brutal beatings and seeing family members sold to distant plantations. One day when Tubman was a teenager, an overseer threw a heavy weight at another slave, but hit her instead. She suffered a traumatic head injury and was unconscious for days. Upon recuperating, she was immediately sent back to work in the fields. The injury caused her to suffer from seizures, severe headaches, and sudden episodes of sleep called *narcolepsy*, for the rest of her life. Ironically, however, the injury also triggered visions and intense dream states from which she drew inspiration.

When she was around 29 years old, Tubman came to believe that she would soon be sold, which prompted her to run away from her current "owner." She and two of her brothers did manage to escape, but her brothers quickly reconsidered their actions and forced Tubman to return to the plantation with them. Tubman soon escaped alone, ending up in the northern city of Philadelphia, Pennsylvania.

Members of the Religious Society of Friends, also called *Quakers*, were active in the Maryland Underground Railroad at the time of Tubman's escape, and she probably stopped first in **this community**. She journeyed by foot, most likely using a common route for fugitive slaves that ran along a river in Delaware and into Pennsylvania, a 145-kilometer trip that could take between five days and three weeks. Along the route, Underground Railroad "conductors" used a number of deceptions to help slaves get away

Time

00:15:00

Review Help Back Next

Questions 5 - 8

5) According to Paragraph 5, all of the following describe Tubman's reaction to freedom EXCEPT:
   (A) She felt as if she had undergone physical transformation.
   (B) She saw magnificence in all of her surroundings.
   (C) She was in a blissful state, feeling that she had reached a holy place.
   (D) She was overjoyed, remembering how she had conquered adversity.

6) Look at the squares [■] that indicate where the following sentence could be added to Paragraph 6.

   Tubman's work helping slaves escape grew more perilous as a result.

   Where would the sentence best fit?
   Click on a square [■] to add the sentence.

7) What can be inferred about the Fugitive Slave Act in Paragraph 6?
   (A) Before 1850, slaves who had escaped to free states were protected.
   (B) It mandated that police officers help those seizing escaped slaves.
   (C) It emancipated those who were still enslaved in the South.
   (D) It called for lawyers to cease assisting fugitives.

8) In Paragraph 8, the author's primary purpose is to
   (A) describe Tubman's abolitionist work and her role as a spy and military leader during the Civil War
   (B) explain the work of leading abolitionists at that time and the events of the Civil War
   (C) summarize Tubman's accomplishments as a spy for the Union Army during the Civil War
   (D) provide details about a raid that Tubman led

safely. For example, at one of Tubman's early stops, a family hid her in a cart to transport her at night to the next safe house. She also walked at night, using the North Star to guide her, and most likely hid in the river marshes during the day when she was not at a safe house.

When Tubman crossed into Pennsylvania the first time after her arduous trip, she was ecstatic. She recalled later, "I looked at my hands to see if I was the same person. There was such glory over everything; the sun came like gold through trees...I felt like I was in Heaven."

A In 1850, the U.S. Congress passed the Fugitive Slave Act, which allowed slave owners and bounty hunters to capture escaped slaves in the North and return them to slavery. **B** The regulations also required law enforcement officials to aid in the apprehension, even in free states. **C** Undeterred, Tubman moved to Canada, which prohibited slavery, and continued to sneak into the South to help slaves, using the Underground Railroad network to successfully lead fugitives on the long trek north to Canada. **D**

Tubman was given the nickname "Moses" because, like the Moses in Hebrew scriptures, she led **those** who were enslaved to freedom. She was always able to evade detection, even though large rewards were offered for her capture. For a number of years, slaveholders in the region did not realize that a former slave woman was behind the ongoing escapes.

In the 1850s, Harriet Tubman took a step further and became involved in the abolitionist movement, speaking at meetings and working with many of the leading figures. When the Civil War commenced in 1861, she performed duties as a nurse and a cook for the Union Army and soon became an armed scout and a spy, utilizing the skills that she had gained before the war to infiltrate dangerous areas, maneuver surreptitiously, and conduct espionage. Tubman provided **intelligence** that assisted in several Union victories. She also became the first woman to lead an armed assault during the Civil War. **The raid resulted in the liberation of 700 slaves and brought about the recruitment of newly freed men for the Union Army.**

Although she still faced racial discrimination, Tubman lived to see the end of slavery. When she died many years later in 1913, Tubman was buried with military honors.

Questions 9 - 12

9) What does the author say in Paragraph 8 about Tubman's abolitionist work?
   (A) She gathered an impressive amount of critical data for the abolitionist movement.
   (B) She provided complex accounts during her presentations at abolitionist meetings.
   (C) She undertook activities with principal abolitionists and gave speeches at events.
   (D) She essentially became the leader of the abolitionist movement.

10) The word "**intelligence**" in Paragraph 8 is closest in meaning to
   (A) shrewd strategies
   (B) secret information
   (C) common knowledge
   (D) cached ammunition

11) Which of the following best paraphrases the highlighted sentence in Paragraph 8?
   (A) The invasion freed hundreds of slaves, some of whom enlisted to fight for the Union.
   (B) Union army troops were discharged from service after the battle that freed slaves.
   (C) Hundreds of slaves were emancipated during the war and headed north to settle in the Union.
   (D) Seven hundred slaves were captured during a battle and recruited for the Union Army.

12) According to Paragraph 8, all of the following describe Tubman's work in the Civil War EXCEPT:
   (A) She helped provide medical assistance to the wounded.
   (B) She used her undercover experience to gather strategic information.
   (C) She was the first female to head a military attack in the Civil War.
   (D) She trained former slaves to become soldiers for the Union Army.

More Available

Harriet Tubman

Harriet Tubman was a 19th-century African-American woman who became a famous figure in the struggle against slavery in the United States. She is mostly known for her **covert** trips to lead groups of escaping slaves to freedom in northern states where slavery was illegal. She participated in running the Underground Railroad, which was a secret network of safe houses, routes, and means of transportation for escaping slaves. While there are no exact records, Tubman made more than a dozen trips and may have helped hundreds of slaves escape.

Tubman's passion and courage came from her own experiences. She was born into slavery in the state of Maryland in 1820. Even as a child she did exhausting work in the fields. Like all slaves, she lived under the threat of brutal beatings and seeing family members sold to distant plantations. One day when Tubman was a teenager, an overseer threw a heavy weight at another slave, but hit her instead. She suffered a traumatic head injury and was unconscious for days. Upon recuperating, she was immediately sent back to work in the fields. The injury caused her to suffer from seizures, severe headaches, and sudden episodes of sleep called *narcolepsy*, for the rest of her life. Ironically, however, the injury also triggered visions and intense dream states from which she drew inspiration.

When she was around 29 years old, Tubman came to believe that she would soon be sold, which prompted her to run away from her current "owner." She and two of her brothers did manage to escape, but her brothers quickly reconsidered their actions and forced Tubman to return to the plantation with them. Tubman soon escaped alone, ending up in the northern city of Philadelphia, Pennsylvania.

Members of the Religious Society of Friends, also called *Quakers*, were active in the Maryland Underground Railroad at the time of Tubman's escape, and she probably stopped first in **this community**. She journeyed by foot, most likely using a common route for fugitive slaves that ran along a river in Delaware and into Pennsylvania, a 145-kilometer trip that could take between five days and three weeks. Along the route, Underground Railroad "conductors" used a number of deceptions to help slaves get away

Time

00:05:00

Question 13

Review   Help   Back   Next

13) **Directions**: An introductory sentence relating to the passage is written below. Complete the exercise by choosing the THREE answers that support the sentence. Some sentences do not belong because they do not support the sentence. **This question is worth 2 points.**

Harriet Tubman demonstrated her indomitable courage in the struggle against slavery.

- •
- •
- •

Answer Choices

1. She snuck back South to assist captives in surreptitious flights to safety.
2. She made furtive trips to gain inside information during the Civil War.
3. She once moved fugitives, hidden in a cart, along the Underground Railroad route.
4. She continued liberating those in bondage in spite of severe laws.
5. She stopped her brothers from turning back after they had escaped.
6. She conducted subversive activities that helped her avoid being captured.

safely. For example, at one of Tubman's early stops, a family hid her in a cart to transport her at night to the next safe house. She also walked at night, using the North Star to guide her, and most likely hid in the river marshes during the day when she was not at a safe house.

When Tubman crossed into Pennsylvania the first time after her arduous trip, she was ecstatic. She recalled later, "I looked at my hands to see if I was the same person. There was such glory over everything; the sun came like gold through trees…I felt like I was in Heaven."

A In 1850, the U.S. Congress passed the Fugitive Slave Act, which allowed slave owners and bounty hunters to capture escaped slaves in the North and return them to slavery. **B** The regulations also required law enforcement officials to aid in the apprehension, even in free states. **C** Undeterred, Tubman moved to Canada, which prohibited slavery, and continued to sneak into the South to help slaves, using the Underground Railroad network to successfully lead fugitives on the long trek north to Canada. **D**

Tubman was given the nickname "Moses" because, like the Moses in Hebrew scriptures, she led **those** who were enslaved to freedom. She was always able to evade detection, even though large rewards were offered for her capture. For a number of years, slaveholders in the region did not realize that a former slave woman was behind the ongoing escapes.

In the 1850s, Harriet Tubman took a step further and became involved in the abolitionist movement, speaking at meetings and working with many of the leading figures. When the Civil War commenced in 1861, she performed duties as a nurse and a cook for the Union Army and soon became an armed scout and a spy, utilizing the skills that she had gained before the war to infiltrate dangerous areas, maneuver surreptitiously, and conduct espionage. Tubman provided **intelligence** that assisted in several Union victories. She also became the first woman to lead an armed assault during the Civil War. **The raid resulted in the liberation of 700 slaves and brought about the recruitment of newly freed men for the Union Army.**

Although she still faced racial discrimination, Tubman lived to see the end of slavery. When she died many years later in 1913, Tubman was buried with military honors.

Actual Test

Reading 2

Time
00:20:00

Review Help Back Next

Questions 14 - 17

14) According to Paragraph 1, all of the following statments are true about neurons EXCEPT:
   (A) The brain is denser with neurons than other parts of the body.
   (B) Neurons help interpret sensory input from one's environment.
   (C) Neurons found in the brain are composed of a soft tissue.
   (D) Neurons transmit information through chemical signals.

15) The word "**synchronize**" in Paragraph 3 is closest in meaning to
   (A) reverse
   (B) sustain
   (C) imitate
   (D) coordinate

16) In Paragraph 3, what does the author say about one specific octopus species' imitation abilities?
   (A) Octopuses imitate an attacking predator in order to adopt its best defense mechanisms.
   (B) Octopuses impersonate predators to hunt for unsuspecting prey.
   (C) Octopuses mimic predatory animals to deter being attacked.
   (D) Octopuses replicate each other's behavior to relay warnings.

17) What can be inferred about octopuses based on the information in Paragraph 3?
   (A) Most species of octopuses have well-developed defense behaviors.
   (B) Octopuses have difficulties coordinating the movement of their tentacles.
   (C) It is unknown how octopuses camouflage themselves.
   (D) Octopuses have the best eyesight of any aquatic animal.

More Available

Animal and Human Brains

The brain of every animal is composed of clusters of cells called *neurons*, which are encased in soft tissue within the brain. Each neuron communicates with surrounding neurons by sending out chemical signals. Although neurons exist throughout the body, the brain contains exceptionally high concentrations. Thus, the brain is in charge of making connections; it is the main center to help the body make sense of and interact with the outside world, and it helps one part of the body communicate with another. In general, the more neurons in an animal's brain, the more connections that animal can make. The brain of every species develops differently to suit its particular needs and environment.

Because brain processes require a large amount of energy, a creature's brain will not become any bigger than necessary for survival. For instance, an invertebrate such as a clam feeds by filtering nutrients from the water. To fulfill this simple task, a clam requires a brain that only consists of a few *ganglia*, or bundles of nerves that regulate motor and vital functions. On the other end of the invertebrate intelligence spectrum, an octopus has an extremely complicated brain that is arranged in *lobes* and *tracts* that contain more neurons and are more specialized than ganglia. The *optical lobes*, located just behind the eyes, are the largest features of the brain and emphasize an octopus' reliance on sight.

Moreover, about 60 percent of an octopus' nearly 300 million neurons are not located in the brain at all. Each of an octopus' eight tentacles has its own *nervous system*, or collection of nerves that regulate voluntary and involuntary actions and send neural signals to the brain. Thus, scientists suspect that an octopus' brain will tell the limbs *what* to do, but the complex nervous system in each limb determines *how* to accomplish the action. In fact, the unique coordination between an octopus' brain and its eight limbs helps it quickly **synchronize** full-body color changes, which it uses to either avoid or ward off predators. An octopus camouflages itself using reflective pigment cells called *chromatophores*, which cover the exterior of its body and change size in order to alter the cells' ability to reflect light, allowing for color changes. Using their excellent eyesight, octopuses can adjust

18) According to Paragraphs 2 and 3, an octopus' brain
(A) is composed of a complex network of ganglia
(B) only contains about 40 percent of the animal's neurons
(C) uses chromatophores to communicate with its limbs
(D) only receives sensory input through its optical lobes

19) Why does the author mention "**manipulate**" in Paragraph 4?
(A) To compare octopuses' environment to other aquatic habitats
(B) To summarize octopuses' camouflage and mimicry abilities
(C) To warn the reader that octopuses' abilities make them untrustworthy
(D) To emphasize the extent to which octopuses interact with their environment

20) Look at the squares [■] that indicate where the following sentence could be added to Paragraph 5.

Although the human brain contains the same components as other mammalian brains, some lobes have grown larger to support complex processes.

Where would the sentence best fit?
Click on a square [■] to add the sentence.

21) The author PROBABLY mentions "**Like octopuses**" in Paragraph 5 in order to
(A) introduce a comparison between dissimilar organisms
(B) summarize the reason that brains are worth researching
(C) point out a main feature of octopus behavior
(D) argue that all creatures with large brains are similar

the size of chromatophores to match the color of the ocean floor. One species of octopus even uses its acute observational skills to imitate venomous fish or sea snakes by morphing its boneless body and changing color. It uses its highly developed memory centers to recall which imitation will best scare off a specific predator.

Because octopuses are solitary and have soft, exposed bodies, researchers believe that they needed to develop an incredible brain to **manipulate** their environment for survival. For example, researchers have observed octopuses using shells to form temporary homes, proving that their memory, problem-solving, and motor skills are developed enough to use tools, a skill usually associated mainly with primates.

A **Like octopuses**, humans (*Homo sapiens*) are a relatively vulnerable species. **B** Unable to run quickly, and lacking sizable defenses such as shells or sharp teeth, humans have compensated for **these frailties** by developing the most sophisticated brains in the animal kingdom, containing upwards of 85 billion neurons. **C** For instance, the *temporal lobe*, which regulates language comprehension and long-term memory storage, is much larger in humans than in any other primate. **D** The human temporal lobe may have developed as language became more complicated and abstract.

One of the most remarkable areas of the mammalian brain is the *frontal lobe*, a large structure at the front of the brain that takes sensory input from elsewhere in the cerebrum and determines an acceptable balance between basic needs, such as sleeping and finding food, and the possible personal and social consequences of these actions. Thus, the frontal lobe allows a person to visualize several outcomes of an action and determine which one will yield the best consequence. **The frontal lobe is most highly developed in humans, great apes, and dolphins because these species rely on group cooperation to survive and therefore must balance social relationships with survival needs.**

Actual Test

Reading 2

Time
00:10:00

Review Help Back Next

Questions 22 - 24

22) The phrase "**these frailties**" in Paragraph 5 refers to
- (A) humans' many natural predators
- (B) the 85 billion neurons in a human brain
- (C) humans' cognitive similarities to octopuses
- (D) humans' scarcity of natural defenses

23) According to Paragraph 5, what PROBABLY contributed to the growth of the temporal lobe in humans?
- (A) The difficulty of depicting abstract concepts in the form of art
- (B) The need to process an increasingly conceptual language
- (C) The desire to comprehend the languages of different cultures
- (D) The need to name unfamiliar plants and animals as humans migrated

24) Which of the following best paraphrases the highlighted phrase in Paragraph 6?
- (A) Humans, great apes, and dolphins are the only mammals to develop a frontal lobe because they rely on collaboration to make decisions.
- (B) Because of their dependence on social interactions, humans, great apes, and dolphins have evolved complex frontal lobes.
- (C) Frontal lobes form in animals such as humans, great apes, and dolphins because these species work the hardest at survival.
- (D) Social mammals such as humans, great apes, and dolphins survive because they always develop large frontal lobes.

More Available ▲

Animal and Human Brains

The brain of every animal is composed of clusters of cells called *neurons*, which are encased in soft tissue within the brain. Each neuron communicates with surrounding neurons by sending out chemical signals. Although neurons exist throughout the body, the brain contains exceptionally high concentrations. Thus, the brain is in charge of making connections; it is the main center to help the body make sense of and interact with the outside world, and it helps one part of the body communicate with another. In general, the more neurons in an animal's brain, the more connections that animal can make. The brain of every species develops differently to suit its particular needs and environment.

Because brain processes require a large amount of energy, a creature's brain will not become any bigger than necessary for survival. For instance, an invertebrate such as a clam feeds by filtering nutrients from the water. To fulfill this simple task, a clam requires a brain that only consists of a few *ganglia*, or bundles of nerves that regulate motor and vital functions. On the other end of the invertebrate intelligence spectrum, an octopus has an extremely complicated brain that is arranged in *lobes* and *tracts* that contain more neurons and are more specialized than ganglia. The *optical lobes*, located just behind the eyes, are the largest features of the brain and emphasize an octopus' reliance on sight.

Moreover, about 60 percent of an octopus' nearly 300 million neurons are not located in the brain at all. Each of an octopus' eight tentacles has its own *nervous system*, or collection of nerves that regulate voluntary and involuntary actions and send neural signals to the brain. Thus, scientists suspect that an octopus' brain will tell the limbs *what* to do, but the complex nervous system in each limb determines *how* to accomplish the action. In fact, the unique coordination between an octopus' brain and its eight limbs helps it quickly **synchronize** full-body color changes, which it uses to either avoid or ward off predators. An octopus camouflages itself using reflective pigment cells called *chromatophores*, which cover the exterior of its body and change size in order to alter the cells' ability to reflect light, allowing for color changes. Using their excellent eyesight, octopuses can adjust

Questions 25 - 26

25) What can be inferred about the frontal lobe from Paragraph 6?
- (A) The frontal lobe is the most important part of the brain.
- (B) Solitary animals rarely develop large frontal lobes.
- (C) The frontal lobe encourages selfish behavior.
- (D) The frontal lobe is the first part of the brain to develop after birth.

26) **Directions**: Select the sentences that most appropriately match the descriptions of each type of brain. TWO of the answer choices will NOT be used. **This question is worth 3 points.**

Octopus brain
-
-
-

Human brain
-
-

Answer Choices
1. This brain has the largest volume of any mammalian species.
2. This brain communicates with multiple autonomous nervous systems.
3. This brain has evolved to accommodate social interactions.
4. This brain receives sensory input primarily through its sensitive touch receptors.
5. This brain's largest features are the optical lobes.
6. This brain may have evolved to process complex communications.
7. This brain can regulate camouflage and tool usage.

the size of chromatophores to match the color of the ocean floor. One species of octopus even uses its acute observational skills to imitate venomous fish or sea snakes by morphing its boneless body and changing color. It uses its highly developed memory centers to recall which imitation will best scare off a specific predator.

Because octopuses are solitary and have soft, exposed bodies, researchers believe that they needed to develop an incredible brain to **manipulate** their environment for survival. For example, researchers have observed octopuses using shells to form temporary homes, proving that their memory, problem-solving, and motor skills are developed enough to use tools, a skill usually associated mainly with primates.

A **Like octopuses**, humans (*Homo sapiens*) are a relatively vulnerable species. **B** Unable to run quickly, and lacking sizable defenses such as shells or sharp teeth, humans have compensated for **these frailties** by developing the most sophisticated brains in the animal kingdom, containing upwards of 85 billion neurons. **C** For instance, the *temporal lobe*, which regulates language comprehension and long-term memory storage, is much larger in humans than in any other primate. **D** The human temporal lobe may have developed as language became more complicated and abstract.

One of the most remarkable areas of the mammalian brain is the *frontal lobe*, a large structure at the front of the brain that takes sensory input from elsewhere in the cerebrum and determines an acceptable balance between basic needs, such as sleeping and finding food, and the possible personal and social consequences of these actions. Thus, the frontal lobe allows a person to visualize several outcomes of an action and determine which one will yield the best consequence. **The frontal lobe is most highly developed in humans, great apes, and dolphins because these species rely on group cooperation to survive and therefore must balance social relationships with survival needs.**

Review Help Back Next

Questions 27 - 30

27) What can be inferred about the history of surfing based on Paragraph 1?
- (A) Only men were allowed to surf until the 20th century.
- (B) Polynesian and Hawaiian surfing techniques were not widely diffused until the 20th century.
- (C) Because surfing was an expensive practice, only the wealthiest Polynesians and Hawaiians were allowed to surf.
- (D) Ancient Polynesian people often surfed and competed with ancient Hawaiians.

28) The word "**quell**" in Paragraph 2 is closest in meaning to
- (A) support
- (B) examine
- (C) discover
- (D) repress

29) In Paragraph 2, the author's primary purpose is to
- (A) describe how surfing spread outside of secluded populations
- (B) praise Hawaiians for spreading surfing throughout the world
- (C) illustrate how surfing received worldwide recognition
- (D) emphasize that surfing became popular despite efforts by missionaries

30) The word "**perpetuated**" in Paragraph 3 means
- (A) petrified
- (B) dispersed
- (C) continued
- (D) altered

More Available

Surfing Ocean Waves

Although surfing is primarily recreational today, it began as a socioreligious practice central to Polynesian and Hawaiian cultures. In ancient Polynesia, the chief received the best surfboard and access to the beaches with the largest waves. Similarly, in Hawaii one's surfing skills helped determine his or her social standing, and surfing was woven into Hawaiian myths and religion. In one such myth, a beautiful and accomplished female surfer named Kelea managed to beat all nearby chiefs in a surfing contest, winning great fame and a prestigious social position as a result. Other Hawaiian myths use surfing as a means to find true love or communicate with spirits of nature. Despite these ancient origins and rich history, the outside world knew little about surfing before the 20th century.

Christian missionaries who discouraged traditional Hawaiian religious practices attempted to **quell** surfing, but some native Hawaiian surfers resumed the sport in the early 20th century. Surfing received recognition outside of small island communities in 1907 when Hawaiian surfer George Freeth traveled to California and surfed in front of spectators. Between 1912 and 1915, other island surfers traveled to the East Coast of the United States and Australia and put on similar displays, exposing a limited audience to the sport of riding waves.

However, it was the release of the film *Gidget* in 1959 that garnered surfing worldwide attention. The film depicts early California surf culture as comprised of young, attractive individuals who use surfing to bond with one another. The 1966 surf documentary *Endless Summer* **perpetuated** this romantic image by following young surfers to beautiful locations around the world as they searched for ideal surfing conditions.

The success of many 1960s surf films also spurred the rise of "surf music," pioneered by groups such as The Beach Boys, who emphasized the potential for romance and friendship through surfing, and electric guitar-driven instrumental music by artists such as Dick Dale and the Del-Tones. Surf music is usually mid- to up-tempo dance music in which the guitar is modified using reverberation or other techniques to simulate the sound of crashing

Time

00:15:00

Questions 31 - 34

31) What does the author say about the success of surf music in Paragraph 4?
 (A) It distracted people from the spiritual and philosophical aspects of surfing.
 (B) It caused many people to travel to California to participate in surfing.
 (C) It helped bring international attention to a surf culture.
 (D) It caused many listeners to link surfing with pressing social issues.

32) Which of the following best paraphrases the highlighted sentence in Paragraph 5?
 (A) By combining exhilaration and leisure, surfing appealed to younger people during the 1960s.
 (B) Surf culture developed in the 1960s because young people had ample leisure time to spend at the beach.
 (C) Because riding waves is challenging, surfers spent most of their time relaxing and socializing on the beach in the 1960s.
 (D) All young people in the 1960s went to the beach to make friends and improve their surfing skills.

33) The phrase "**These practices**" in Paragraph 5 refers to
 (A) accepting the wisdom of experienced Californian, Australian, and Hawaiian surfers
 (B) taking up Hawaiian philosophies in order to find more excitement in surfing
 (C) spending one's time relaxing at the beach and surfing with friends
 (D) accepting Hawaiian ideologies and embracing one's environment

34) In Paragraph 5, the word "**apprehension**" is closest in meaning to
 (A) chaos
 (B) confusion
 (C) anxiety
 (D) duty

waves. Most surf-music groups grew from the expanding surf culture of Southern California. The international success of some surf bands helped spread the perception of surfing as a carefree and youthful activity.

The surf culture of the 1960s appealed primarily to teens and young adults, and it emphasized romance and lack of obligations by combining the relaxation of socializing on sunny beaches with the excitement of launching toward the shore atop a wave. Many early Californian and Australian surfers also adopted Hawaiian surf philosophies and treated surfing as a way to connect to nature. **These practices**, when combined with the time-consuming demand of searching for desirable waves, led to the "soul surfer" lifestyle, in which dedicated surfers center their lives on finding spiritual balance through surfing. "Soul surfers" have even developed their own vocabulary to discuss surfing, using words such as "stoked," a verb that describes the mixture of excitement and **apprehension** at surfing a large wave. Often, "soul surfers" will forgo responsibilities to pursue ideal surfing conditions, leading some to view surfers as largely unmotivated in school or work.

With the advent of new technologies, manufacturers began to create shorter and lighter boards using **fiberglass and foam** rather than wood in the 1970s. The short boards gave surfers more maneuverability on waves and contributed to the rise of competitive surfing, which added an element of professionalism and sponsorship to a sport previously associated with relaxation and freedom. Professional surfers attained international stardom as competitive surfing became more popular, and many clothing lines developed *surf wear*, or swim suits, jackets, and other apparel associated with surf culture.

A However, many "soul surfers" reject the commercialization of surfing because they believe that surfing should be a spiritual and personal experience rather than one driven by popular image and profits. **B** Thus, within two decades of surfing's popularization, two camps had formed amongst surfers. **C** Even in contemporary surfing, some devoted surfers dream of professionalism while **others** maintain that surfing is primarily a way to connect to nature and oneself. **D**

Time

00:10:00

Review Help Back Next

Questions 35 - 38

35) Why does the author mention "**fiberglass and foam**" in Paragraph 6?
   (A) To illustrate the board-shaping process
   (B) To give examples of how surfboards became lighter
   (C) To explain why short boards are superior to long boards
   (D) To emphasize the significance of new surf technology

36) Look at the squares [■] that indicate where the following sentence could be added to Paragraph 7.

   Regardless of why people pursue the sport, in the span of a century, surfing has transformed from an ancient yet largely unknown practice to a worldwide phenomenon.

   Where would the sentence best fit?
   Click on a square [■] to add the sentence.

37) The word "**others**" in Paragraph 7 refers to
   (A) profits
   (B) decades
   (C) camps
   (D) surfers

38) According to Paragraphs 5 and 7, each of the following sentences describes "soul surfers" EXCEPT:
   (A) They often condemn the commercialization of surfing.
   (B) They use their own jargon to discuss surfing.
   (C) They are generally considered the best surfers.
   (D) They incorporate some Hawaiian values regarding surfing.

More Available

Surfing Ocean Waves

Although surfing is primarily recreational today, it began as a socioreligious practice central to Polynesian and Hawaiian cultures. In ancient Polynesia, the chief received the best surfboard and access to the beaches with the largest waves. Similarly, in Hawaii one's surfing skills helped determine his or her social standing, and surfing was woven into Hawaiian myths and religion. In one such myth, a beautiful and accomplished female surfer named Kelea managed to beat all nearby chiefs in a surfing contest, winning great fame and a prestigious social position as a result. Other Hawaiian myths use surfing as a means to find true love or communicate with spirits of nature. Despite these ancient origins and rich history, the outside world knew little about surfing before the 20th century.

Christian missionaries who discouraged traditional Hawaiian religious practices attempted to **quell** surfing, but some native Hawaiian surfers resumed the sport in the early 20th century. Surfing received recognition outside of small island communities in 1907 when Hawaiian surfer George Freeth traveled to California and surfed in front of spectators. Between 1912 and 1915, other island surfers traveled to the East Coast of the United States and Australia and put on similar displays, exposing a limited audience to the sport of riding waves.

However, it was the release of the film *Gidget* in 1959 that garnered surfing worldwide attention. The film depicts early California surf culture as comprised of young, attractive individuals who use surfing to bond with one another. The 1966 surf documentary *Endless Summer* **perpetuated** this romantic image by following young surfers to beautiful locations around the world as they searched for ideal surfing conditions.

The success of many 1960s surf films also spurred the rise of "surf music," pioneered by groups such as The Beach Boys, who emphasized the potential for romance and friendship through surfing, and electric guitar-driven instrumental music by artists such as Dick Dale and the Del-Tones. Surf music is usually mid- to up-tempo dance music in which the guitar is modified using reverberation or other techniques to simulate the sound of crashing

Time

00:05:00

Question 39

Review   Help   Back   Next

39) **Directions**: An introductory sentence relating to the passage is written below. Complete the exercise by choosing the THREE answers that support the sentence. Some sentences do not belong because they do not support the sentence. **This question is worth 2 points.**

Many factors led to the popularization of surf culture throughout the 20th century.

-
-
-

Answer Choices

1. Films such as *Endless Summer* focus on the dangers of big wave surfing.
2. Advertising and sponsorship provide worldwide exposure for professional surfers.
3. The success of musical groups such as The Beach Boys spread surf culture.
4. The "soul surfer" lifestyle contributed to the commercialization of surfing.
5. The United States and Australia held demonstrations to display the prowess of surfers from remote islands.
6. Instrumental surf bands performed for large audiences to support surfing professionals.

waves. Most surf-music groups grew from the expanding surf culture of Southern California. The international success of some surf bands helped spread the perception of surfing as a carefree and youthful activity.

The surf culture of the 1960s appealed primarily to teens and young adults, and it emphasized romance and lack of obligations by combining the relaxation of socializing on sunny beaches with the excitement of launching toward the shore atop a wave. Many early Californian and Australian surfers also adopted Hawaiian surf philosophies and treated surfing as a way to connect to nature. **These practices**, when combined with the time-consuming demand of searching for desirable waves, led to the "soul surfer" lifestyle, in which dedicated surfers center their lives on finding spiritual balance through surfing. "Soul surfers" have even developed their own vocabulary to discuss surfing, using words such as "stoked," a verb that describes the mixture of excitement and **apprehension** at surfing a large wave. Often, "soul surfers" will forgo responsibilities to pursue ideal surfing conditions, leading some to view surfers as largely unmotivated in school or work.

With the advent of new technologies, manufacturers began to create shorter and lighter boards using **fiberglass and foam** rather than wood in the 1970s. The short boards gave surfers more maneuverability on waves and contributed to the rise of competitive surfing, which added an element of professionalism and sponsorship to a sport previously associated with relaxation and freedom. Professional surfers attained international stardom as competitive surfing became more popular, and many clothing lines developed *surf wear*, or swim suits, jackets, and other apparel associated with surf culture.

A However, many "soul surfers" reject the commercialization of surfing because they believe that surfing should be a spiritual and personal experience rather than one driven by popular image and profits. **B** Thus, within two decades of surfing's popularization, two camps had formed amongst surfers. **C** Even in contemporary surfing, some devoted surfers dream of professionalism while **others** maintain that surfing is primarily a way to connect to nature and oneself. **D**

Actual TOEFL Vocabulary Test

1. **impediment**
   A. assistance
   B. exception
   C. obstruction
   D. inclusion

2. **impermeable**
   A. impenetrable
   B. informative
   C. infrequent
   D. inferential

3. **impulse**
   A. aversion
   B. desire
   C. distaste
   D. exercise

4. **in principle**
   A. uncertainly
   B. theoretically
   C. hesitantly
   D. genuinely

5. **in tandem**
   A. totally
   B. separately
   C. commonly
   D. together

6. **inaugurate**
   A. terminate
   B. presume
   C. initiate
   D. restrict

7. **incidentally**
   A. by chance
   B. in support of
   C. in particular
   D. as a result of

8. **inclement**
   A. agreeable
   B. unfavorable
   C. preventative
   D. increasing

9. **informally**
   A. unnaturally
   B. casually
   C. rarely
   D. hardly

10. **instructive**
    A. insignificant
    B. important
    C. informative
    D. influential

11. **intangible**
    A. immaterial
    B. factual
    C. materialistic
    D. uncommon

12. **interlocked**
    A. defused
    B. canceled
    C. interfered
    D. meshed

13. **intermediate**
    A. susceptible
    B. transitional
    C. expert
    D. proficient

14. **intricate**
    A. intelligible
    B. systematic
    C. directed
    D. complicated

15. **inviolable**
    A. sacred
    B. profane
    C. destructive
    D. productive

16. **irrevocable**
    A. permanent
    B. alterable
    C. canceled
    D. careless

17. **locate**
    A. fulfill
    B. forfeit
    C. find
    D. fail

18. **magnitude**
    A. amount
    B. omission
    C. moment
    D. repute

19. **match**
    A. conflict
    B. leave
    C. vary
    D. equal

20. **meager**
    A. scarce
    B. substantial
    C. scary
    D. sufficient

21. **meet**
    A. quit
    B. convene
    C. invite
    D. leave

22. **mundane**
    A. ordinary
    B. exceptional
    C. heavenly
    D. monetary

23. **myriad**
    A. countless
    B. acquisitive
    C. measurable
    D. abstract

24. **obstacle**
    A. assistance
    B. obscure
    C. barrier
    D. blessing

25. **occasional**
    A. steady
    B. constant
    C. irrelevant
    D. infrequent

26. **occasionally**
    A. after
    B. never
    C. sometimes
    D. always

27. **on the whole**
    A. entirely
    B. generally
    C. finally
    D. rarely

28. **ongoing**
    A. continued
    B. waited
    C. remained
    D. decreased

29. **opaque**
    A. unclear
    B. fatigued
    C. lucid
    D. abstruse

30. **orientation**
    A. insubordination
    B. intervention
    C. introduction
    D. instruction

31. **ornament**
    A. damage
    B. adjustment
    C. adornment
    D. order

32. **ornamental**
    A. manifest
    B. plain
    C. laborious
    D. decorative

33. **overly**
    A. genially
    B. excessively
    C. moderately
    D. carefully

34. **overwhelming**
    A. staggering
    B. outstretched
    C. impotent
    D. trifling

35. **paradox**
    A. contradiction
    B. concession
    C. confession
    D. confirmation

36. **paradoxical**
    A. supposed
    B. discernible
    C. undisguised
    D. incompatible

37. **paradoxically**
    A. prodigiously
    B. ordinarily
    C. peculiarly
    D. perplexingly

38. **paramount**
    A. subsidiary
    B. serving
    C. supreme
    D. secondary

39. **partake**
    A. assume
    B. abstain
    C. release
    D. participate

40. **persuade**
    A. repress
    B. convince
    C. participate
    D. hesitate

41. **persuasively**
   A. convincingly
   B. conclusively
   C. completely
   D. certainly

42. **pool**
   A. comprehend
   B. detach
   C. combine
   D. achieve

43. **pragmatic**
   A. fantastic
   B. realistic
   C. romantic
   D. idealistic

44. **precipitate**
   A. pull out
   B. touch off
   C. put in
   D. take in

45. **preoccupied with**
   A. launch into
   B. attend to
   C. indifferent to
   D. engrossed in

46. **prerequisite**
   A. requirement
   B. reputation
   C. restriction
   D. refreshment

47. **preserve**
   A. dispatch
   B. retain
   C. ruin
   D. transmit

48. **previously**
   A. constantly
   B. subsequently
   C. formerly
   D. currently

49. **primitive**
   A. postponed
   B. early
   C. stayed
   D. quick

50. **prior to**
   A. before
   B. afterward
   C. thereafter
   D. presently

51. **projection**
   A. inclusion
   B. exclusion
   C. doubt
   D. estimate

52. **proper**
   A. inadequate
   B. available
   C. affordable
   D. appropriate

53. **regulate**
   A. manage
   B. disturb
   C. upset
   D. ruffle

54. **renowned**
   A. obscure
   B. concealed
   C. famous
   D. superior

55. **replenish**
   A. refill
   B. fulfill
   C. empty
   D. neglect

56. **residue**
   A. reminder
   B. result
   C. restriction
   D. remainder

57. **resume**
   A. reuse
   B. continue
   C. begin
   D. generate

58. **routinely**
   A. consequently
   B. regularly
   C. constantly
   D. scarcely

59. **scrutiny**
   A. examination
   B. elimination
   C. election
   D. explanation

60. **seek**
   A. take
   B. ask
   C. search
   D. wait

61. **seemingly**
   A. vaguely
   B. apparently
   C. indefinitely
   D. considerably

62. **shift**
   A. charge
   B. choose
   C. chance
   D. change

63. **snaking**
   A. directing
   B. winding
   C. straightening
   D. guiding

64. **sought**
   A. desired
   B. disliked
   C. disgusted
   D. denied

65. **sovereign**
   A. apprentice
   B. master
   C. trainee
   D. applicant

66. **splendid**
   A. believable
   B. expected
   C. marvelous
   D. conventional

67. **splendor**
   A. simplicity
   B. modesty
   C. majesty
   D. insipidity

68. **spontaneous**
   A. automatic
   B. standard
   C. manual
   D. hand-operated

69. **standstill**
   A. inaction
   B. alteration
   C. affection
   D. modification

70. **static**
   A. irregular
   B. unsettled
   C. inconstant
   D. unchanging

71. **steadfast**
   A. enduring
   B. temporary
   C. changeable
   D. unfixed

72. **steadfastly**
   A. loosely
   B. firmly
   C. flexibly
   D. roughly

73. **stimulate**
   A. absolve
   B. condemn
   C. provoke
   D. discourage

74. **stimulus**
   A. control
   B. check
   C. impetus
   D. block

75. **sturdy**
   A. fluffy
   B. luminous
   C. famous
   D. durable

76. **subsist**
   A. renew
   B. decease
   C. expire
   D. exist

77. **subsistence**
   A. experience
   B. livelihood
   C. submission
   D. provision

78. **supersede**
   A. override
   B. persist
   C. resolve
   D. survive

79. **suppress**
   A. restrain
   B. maintain
   C. entertain
   D. sustain

80. **surmise**
   A. convince
   B. misconceive
   C. guess
   D. measure

81. tenacity
A. irresolution
B. stubbornness
C. indolence
D. flexibility

82. therefore
A. unsuitably
B. nevertheless
C. otherwise
D. consequently

83. thoroughly
A. nearly
B. partially
C. inadequately
D. completely

84. threshold
A. limit
B. beyond
C. infinity
D. continuum

85. timid
A. outstanding
B. assured
C. fearful
D. courageous

86. turbulence
A. agreement
B. gentleness
C. agitation
D. relaxation

87. turbulent
A. passive
B. violent
C. gentle
D. possible

88. typically
A. usually
B. exceptionally
C. rarely
D. finely

89. undermine
A. reinforce
B. empower
C. develop
D. weaken

90. underrate
A. undervalue
B. inflate
C. exaggerate
D. encourage

91. undoubtedly
A. entirely
B. dubiously
C. certainly
D. questionably

92. unleash
A. cultivate
B. maintain
C. release
D. unify

93. unresolved
A. assured
B. undecided
C. undisputed
D. rectified

94. unsophisticated
A. complicated
B. simple
C. various
D. ambiguous

95. unsuitable
A. felicitous
B. adapted
C. convenient
D. inappropriate

96. utilitarian
A. practical
B. futile
C. useless
D. unrealistic

97. utilize
A. scrap
B. discard
C. leave
D. use

98. vanish
A. disappear
B. attain
C. arrive
D. enter

99. versatile
A. inflexible
B. determined
C. adaptable
D. serious

100. vertical
A. decayed
B. lying
C. downright
D. upright

101. whereas
A. thus
B. although
C. hence
D. wherefore

102. witness
A. observe
B. overpass
C. overlook
D. obligate

103. worshipers
A. minsters
B. critics
C. devotees
D. judges

104. aberrant
A. habitual
B. average
C. archaic
D. abnormal

105. accessible
A. married
B. obtainable
C. artless
D. atypical

106. accommodate
A. combine
B. shelter
C. recoil
D. shatter

107. accompany
A. follow
B. avoid
C. misbehave
D. conform

108. accomplished
A. required
B. defected
C. allowed
D. achieved

109. accordingly
A. correspondingly
B. agreeably
C. unsuitably
D. faultily

110. acknowledge
A. repudiate
B. recognize
C. renounce
D. reuse

111. acquire
A. obtain
B. yield
C. object
D. refuse

112. adhere
A. cover
B. stick
C. attain
D. remove

113. adherent
A. instructor
B. attendee
C. secretary
D. supporter

114. adorn
A. deform
B. reinforce
C. spoil
D. decorate

115. affluent
A. satisfied
B. regretful
C. prosperous
D. scarce

116. aggravate
A. worsen
B. accord
C. satisfy
D. improve

117. aid
A. charge
B. release
C. require
D. assist

118. akin to
A. temp to
B. similar to
C. add to
D. resort to

119. allure
A. revoke
B. crash
C. repulse
D. entice

120. altogether
A. completely
B. solely
C. partially
D. finally

121. **ambivalent**
   A. secure
   B. inactive
   C. unsure
   D. undoubted

122. **ancient**
   A. overused
   B. immature
   C. crispy
   D. old

123. **annual**
   A. daily
   B. yearly
   C. early
   D. ordinary

124. **anomaly**
   A. conformity
   B. irregularity
   C. normality
   D. volatility

125. **antagonistic**
   A. hostile
   B. antecedent
   C. allowing
   D. charitable

126. **antique**
   A. common
   B. unique
   C. unripe
   D. aged

127. **apparatus**
   A. appointment
   B. attachment
   C. equipment
   D. environment

128. **approximately**
   A. nearly
   B. appropriately
   C. frequently
   D. timidly

129. **archaic**
   A. modern
   B. obsolete
   C. stodgy
   D. prospective

130. **artificial**
   A. crumbling
   B. routine
   C. fresh
   D. imitating

131. **artisans**
   A. crafters
   B. drafters
   C. trainers
   D. attendees

132. **as a rule of thumb**
   A. in the end
   B. in general
   C. in case of
   D. in writing

133. **ascend**
   A. rise
   B. decrease
   C. prompt
   D. slump

134. **attempting**
   A. hoping
   B. discriminating
   C. moderating
   D. trying

135. **authentic**
   A. prudent
   B. careless
   C. genuine
   D. counterfeit

136. **autonomous**
   A. coordinate
   B. subordinate
   C. independent
   D. subject

137. **awkward**
   A. skillful
   B. adroit
   C. clumsy
   D. credible

138. **back up**
   A. support
   B. increase
   C. diminish
   D. release

139. **belittle**
   A. esteem
   B. argue
   C. respect
   D. discredit

140. **beneficial**
   A. hurtful
   B. helpful
   C. harmful
   D. hopeful

141. **bizarre**
   A. rare
   B. strange
   C. bitter
   D. typical

142. **blur**
   A. twinkle
   B. obscure
   C. clear
   D. blind

143. **bold**
   A. timid
   B. firm
   C. daring
   D. small

144. **burgeoning**
   A. expanding
   B. shrinking
   C. lengthening
   D. shortening

145. **capacity**
   A. ability
   B. limitation
   C. function
   D. foundation

146. **capture**
   A. carry
   B. lose
   C. track
   D. trap

147. **catastrophic**
   A. baleful
   B. fearful
   C. useful
   D. harmful

148. **cautious**
   A. careful
   B. useless
   C. helpful
   D. heedless

149. **champion**
   A. deposit
   B. promote
   C. overdo
   D. hinder

150. **chief**
   A. last
   B. large
   C. major
   D. minor

151. **choosing**
   A. releasing
   B. opting
   C. waiting
   D. gathering

152. **chronic**
   A. persistent
   B. pregnable
   C. relenting
   D. reluctant

153. **chronicle**
   A. tragedy
   B. present
   C. evidence
   D. record

154. **classic**
   A. typical
   B. reserved
   C. abnormal
   D. careful

155. **clear**
   A. absolve
   B. reduce
   C. attain
   D. remote

156. **clue**
   A. analysis
   B. theory
   C. information
   D. investigation

157. **cognitive**
   A. spiritual
   B. unconscious
   C. physical
   D. mental

158. **coinage**
   A. choreography
   B. currency
   C. coexistence
   D. mining

159. **coincide**
   A. perceive
   B. correspond
   C. occur
   D. differ

160. **coincidence**
   A. event
   B. condition
   C. fluke
   D. intention

121C 122D 123B 124B 125A 126D 127C 128A 129B 130D 131A 132B 133A 134D 135C 136C 137C 138A 139D 140B
141B 142B 143C 144A 145A 146D 147D 148A 149B 150C 151B 152A 153D 154A 155A 156C 157D 158B 159B 160C

ACTUAL TOEFL VOCABULARY TEST | 257

161. collectively
A. altogether
B. conditionally
C. singly
D. sometimes

162. complicated
A. hasty
B. scarce
C. facile
D. complex

163. composite
A. fluid
B. classification
C. mixture
D. assortment

164. comprehensible
A. understandable
B. unbelievable
C. uncomfortable
D. unreasonable

165. compress
A. raise
B. compact
C. loose
D. release

166. compulsorily
A. finally
B. kindly
C. frequently
D. forcibly

167. compulsory
A. preferred
B. required
C. optional
D. selected

168. conceal
A. disclose
B. reveal
C. hide
D. enclose

169. conceive
A. imagine
B. remind
C. disregard
D. judge

170. concentrated
A. controlled
B. condensed
C. confirmed
D. conveyed

171. conclude
A. trust
B. hesitate
C. decide
D. persevere

172. confront
A. face
B. hide
C. rear
D. hinder

173. conjunction
A. attachment
B. condition
C. detachment
D. combination

174. constant
A. changeable
B. stable
C. definable
D. readable

175. constantly
A. rarely
B. always
C. often
D. completely

176. constellation
A. construction
B. strategy
C. assemblage
D. creation

177. constrain
A. refund
B. restrict
C. refuse
D. recognize

178. contemplate
A. neglect
B. dismiss
C. decide
D. consider

179. contour
A. outline
B. article
C. curriculum
D. trait

180. contribute
A. deprive
B. control
C. donate
D. collect

181. controversial
A. definite
B. determinant
C. debatable
D. detrimental

182. convert
A. refresh
B. change
C. remain
D. continue

183. conviction
A. religion
B. confidence
C. disbelief
D. prevention

184. cornerstone
A. completion
B. building
C. foundation
D. process

185. corroborate
A. confirm
B. deny
C. realize
D. discredit

186. creative
A. stolen
B. respective
C. classic
D. inventive

187. crisis
A. anticipation
B. astonishment
C. disaster
D. peace

188. criticize
A. complement
B. condemn
C. comment
D. concern

189. culminate in
A. repose
B. return
C. crash
D. climax

190. cushion
A. protect
B. attack
C. injure
D. heal

191. depict
A. carve
B. stimulate
C. portray
D. interpret

192. deplete
A. refresh
B. exhaust
C. reject
D. escape

193. derive
A. originate
B. terminate
C. establish
D. promote

194. designate
A. encourage
B. depress
C. confuse
D. appoint

195. deter
A. define
B. blend
C. stop
D. energize

196. determine
A. decide
B. point
C. start
D. bring

197. dictate
A. terminate
B. command
C. respond
D. mediate

198. differential
A. regulation
B. standardization
C. variance
D. definition

199. dim
A. ambiguous
B. clear
C. unique
D. faint

200. diminish
A. decrease
B. improve
C. leave
D. prohibit

161A 162D 163C 164A 165B 166D 167B 168C 169A 170B 171C 172A 173D 174B 175B 176C 177B 178D 179A 180C
181C 182B 183B 184C 185A 186D 187C 188B 189D 190A 191C 192B 193A 194D 195C 196A 197B 198C 199D 200A

258 | iBT TOEFL® PATTERN Reading III

201. **discard**
   A. readapt
   B. research
   C. reject
   D. regard

202. **disgust**
   A. desire
   B. distaste
   C. detection
   D. detachment

203. **dismantle**
   A. take away
   B. take apart
   C. take back
   D. take at word

204. **diverge**
   A. separate
   B. combine
   C. organize
   D. generate

205. **divergent**
   A. convergent
   B. different
   C. reminiscent
   D. independent

206. **diverse**
   A. cruel
   B. similar
   C. varied
   D. humane

207. **diversity**
   A. conviction
   B. conformity
   C. variety
   D. repudiation

208. **divest**
   A. confer
   B. scrape
   C. present
   D. deprive

209. **doctrine**
   A. principle
   B. president
   C. profile
   D. persuasion

210. **document**
   A. research
   B. rework
   C. record
   D. revise

211. **dormant**
   A. busy
   B. inactive
   C. detailed
   D. alternative

212. **drawback**
   A. disadvantage
   B. convenience
   C. feature
   D. inattention

213. **dryness**
   A. temperature
   B. climate
   C. condition
   D. aridity

214. **dual**
   A. double
   B. triple
   C. bilingual
   D. monolingual

215. **duration**
   A. strength
   B. stream
   C. span
   D. space

216. **dwindle**
   A. increase
   B. decrease
   C. restrict
   D. forward

217. **dynamic**
   A. laggard
   B. persistent
   C. inert
   D. active

218. **edible**
   A. eatable
   B. poisonous
   C. tasteless
   D. prepared

219. **elegant**
   A. crude
   B. exact
   C. graceful
   D. rough

220. **emerge**
   A. hide
   B. appear
   C. decline
   D. arise

221. **emergence**
   A. rotation
   B. stability
   C. appearance
   D. elaboration

222. **eminently**
   A. slightly
   B. inconsiderably
   C. moderately
   D. exceptionally

223. **enable**
   A. allow
   B. prohibit
   C. inspect
   D. overwhelm

224. **encounter**
   A. strike
   B. elude
   C. depart
   D. meet

225. **encourage**
   A. distress
   B. promote
   C. dishonor
   D. prostrate

226. **endow**
   A. grant
   B. contend
   C. deprive
   D. justify

227. **endowing**
   A. deterring
   B. serving
   C. providing
   D. disarming

228. **engender**
   A. cure
   B. issue
   C. create
   D. impress

229. **enlist**
   A. maintain
   B. terminate
   C. recruit
   D. remove

230. **ensuing**
   A. exterior
   B. interior
   C. previous
   D. subsequent

231. **envision**
   A. misunderstand
   B. challenge
   C. conform
   D. imagine

232. **estimate**
   A. approximate
   B. subtract
   C. eliminate
   D. express

233. **excrete**
   A. absorb
   B. expel
   C. adjust
   D. extort

234. **expend**
   A. climb
   B. resign
   C. spend
   D. export

235. **extent**
   A. extreme
   B. orbit
   C. height
   D. range

236. **extraordinary**
   A. unusual
   B. unable
   C. unified
   D. underneath

237. **faithful**
   A. accurate
   B. careless
   C. vague
   D. contingent

238. **far-reaching**
   A. restricted
   B. ambiguous
   C. extensive
   D. explicit

239. **feature**
   A. abnormality
   B. advantage
   C. detriment
   D. characteristic

240. **firmly**
   A. loosely
   B. securely
   C. lightly
   D. gently

201C 202B 203B 204A 205B 206C 207C 208D 209A 210C 211B 212A 213D 214A 215C 216B 217D 218A 219C 220B
221C 222D 223A 224D 225B 226A 227C 228C 229C 230D 231D 232A 233B 234C 235D 236A 237A 238C 239D 240B

ACTUAL TOEFL VOCABULARY TEST | 259

241. flaw
A. fault
B. perfection
C. scorn
D. approval

242. flawed
A. cramped
B. capacious
C. appropriate
D. incorrect

243. flexible
A. comprehensive
B. stubborn
C. adaptable
D. fluent

244. foremost
A. unimportant
B. primary
C. determined
D. irresolute

245. from time to time
A. occasionally
B. frequently
C. steadily
D. scantly

246. further
A. additional
B. necessary
C. diminished
D. spacious

247. gradually
A. slowly
B. intensely
C. radically
D. tolerably

248. gross
A. sufficient
B. capable
C. entire
D. adequate

249. habitat
A. background
B. foreground
C. environment
D. birthplace

250. hallmark
A. birthmark
B. trademark
C. cancellation
D. specification

251. highlight
A. prosecute
B. execute
C. depreciate
D. emphasize

252. hitherto
A. previously
B. currently
C. eventually
D. lastly

253. humble
A. brave
B. modest
C. courageous
D. insolent

254. illuminate
A. light
B. dim
C. obscure
D. discover

255. illuminated
A. disconsolate
B. cheerful
C. dreary
D. bright

256. imaginative
A. impotent
B. productive
C. creative
D. ungifted

257. immediate
A. eventual
B. instant
C. later
D. earlier

258. immoral
A. unethical
B. suitable
C. awkward
D. correct

259. impending
A. passing
B. understanding
C. receding
D. approaching

260. impressive
A. predictable
B. remarkable
C. measurable
D. imperceptible

261. in earnest
A. obviously
B. seriously
C. absolutely
D. lightly

262. in essence
A. definitely
B. patiently
C. basically
D. faintly

263. incentive
A. motivation
B. inspiration
C. signification
D. observation

264. incessantly
A. readily
B. constantly
C. finally
D. carelessly

265. incorporate
A. seclude
B. exclude
C. include
D. conclude

266. indeed
A. freely
B. moderately
C. completely
D. actually

267. indifferent
A. uninterested
B. impressed
C. annoyed
D. concerned

268. inflict
A. endure
B. fade
C. yield
D. cause

269. inhabit
A. present
B. interact
C. reside
D. receive

270. inhibit
A. hinder
B. assist
C. ease
D. cure

271. innate
A. acquired
B. inborn
C. trivial
D. inessential

272. insight into
A. planning about
B. studying for
C. awareness of
D. listening to

273. instantaneous
A. subsequent
B. ulterior
C. expressed
D. immediate

274. instigate
A. calculate
B. provoke
C. concern
D. construct

275. intermingle
A. isolate
B. detach
C. mix
D. sever

276. interplay
A. interact
B. intercept
C. interpret
D. interrogate

277. interval
A. finish
B. discovery
C. interim
D. indolence

278. invade
A. depart
B. trespass
C. withdraw
D. transit

279. involved
A. eliminated
B. uncomplicated
C. complicated
D. estimated

280. keen
A. sharp
B. dull
C. hidden
D. apparent

281. **keenly**
A. furiously
B. softly
C. roughly
D. shrewdly

282. **laborious**
A. plain
B. manageable
C. immense
D. difficult

283. **lag**
A. delay
B. depart
C. decline
D. deceive

284. **landscape**
A. scent
B. scenery
C. scarcity
D. suspense

285. **largely**
A. exceptionally
B. occasionally
C. mostly
D. readily

286. **launch**
A. complete
B. destine
C. start
D. resolve

287. **lavish**
A. rich
B. destitute
C. obligatory
D. right

288. **lax**
A. careless
B. helpless
C. regardless
D. hopeless

289. **lodge**
A. emerge
B. embed
C. elucidate
D. escape

290. **loose**
A. stayed
B. restricted
C. strict
D. free

291. **mainstay**
A. obstacle
B. substitution
C. anchor
D. supplementary

292. **majestic**
A. magnificent
B. offensive
C. evident
D. disputable

293. **manageable**
A. measurable
B. probable
C. understandable
D. controllable

294. **materialize**
A. authorize
B. restrain
C. appear
D. vanish

295. **merit**
A. obstruction
B. worth
C. aid
D. worthlessness

296. **meticulous**
A. reliable
B. inattentive
C. deceptive
D. careful

297. **migrate**
A. wander
B. glance
C. bypass
D. return

298. **milestone**
A. useless event
B. important event
C. cancelled event
D. urgent event

299. **mingle with**
A. work with
B. associate with
C. agree with
D. compete with

300. **misleading**
A. stimulating
B. delaying
C. confusing
D. obliging

301. **relatively**
A. accurately
B. comparatively
C. doubtfully
D. skeptically

302. **vibrant**
A. dim
B. vivid
C. serious
D. happy

303. **depend on**
A. rely on
B. settle on
C. focus on
D. take on

304. **assure**
A. contradict
B. guarantee
C. discourage
D. condemn

305. **afford**
A. conceal
B. refrain
C. oppose
D. provide

306. **mandate**
A. order
B. denial
C. refusal
D. answer

307. **repercussion**
A. cause
B. failure
C. effect
D. hatred

308. **feat**
A. achievement
B. failure
C. fatigue
D. excess

309. **figure out**
A. doubt
B. determine
C. allure
D. follow

310. **primary**
A. fundamental
B. additional
C. informal
D. secondary

311. **enhance**
A. impair
B. worsen
C. assure
D. improve

312. **brittle**
A. easily seen
B. easily fixed
C. easily learned
D. easily broken

313. **annihilate**
A. revive
B. animate
C. enjoy
D. destroy

314. **luminous**
A. obscure
B. gloomy
C. brilliant
D. famous

315. **presumably**
A. exactly
B. unlikely
C. supposedly
D. doubtfully

316. **appreciate**
A. assist
B. confuse
C. understand
D. enhance

317. **endorse**
A. advance
B. repel
C. support
D. compromise

318. **approach**
A. effect
B. section
C. influence
D. method

319. **at the urging of**
A. in opposition to
B. with the disapproval of
C. at the insistence of
D. in reference to

320. **emit**
A. consider
B. evolve
C. accomplish
D. discharge

321. **prevalent**
A. widespread
B. isolated
C. heartening
D. ranked

322. **handle**
A. ease
B. repose
C. rest
D. manage

323. **sole**
A. proud
B. only
C. safe
D. careful

324. **conserve**
A. convert
B. save
C. present
D. produce

325. **belch**
A. suddenly emit
B. suddenly absorb
C. suddenly withhold
D. suddenly depart

326. **boon**
A. great protest
B. great benefit
C. great harm
D. great increase

327. **allocate**
A. condemn
B. retract
C. keep
D. designate

328. **provided**
A. or
B. and
C. if
D. so

329. **flow**
A. obstruction
B. movement
C. countless
D. tributary

330. **devastation**
A. preservation
B. conservation
C. destruction
D. description

331. **mechanism for**
A. payment for
B. reason for
C. explanation for
D. method for

332. **allude**
A. suggest
B. allow
C. oppose
D. conceal

333. **restricted**
A. caused
B. limited
C. effected
D. altered

334. **enact**
A. establish
B. destroy
C. abolish
D. correct

335. **unaccounted for**
A. unavailable
B. unexplained
C. undecided
D. understood

336. **unique**
A. common
B. distinct
C. similar
D. unclear

337. **terrain**
A. scenery
B. land
C. ocean
D. atmosphere

338. **cluster**
A. clarity
B. claim
C. group
D. awe

339. **equilibrium**
A. imbalance
B. space
C. balance
D. heavy

340. **retain**
A. resume
B. release
C. bend
D. maintain

341. **retard**
A. delay
B. finish
C. lose
D. save

342. **ruthlessly**
A. mercifully
B. heartlessly
C. eventually
D. constantly

343. **invariably**
A. nearly
B. irregularly
C. constantly
D. briefly

344. **attribute A to B**
A. move A to B
B. ascribe A to B
C. bring A to B
D. recommend A to B

345. **coincidentally**
A. separately
B. simultaneously
C. subsequently
D. speedily

346. **abandon**
A. give as
B. give up
C. give in
D. give to

347. **arduous**
A. passionate
B. difficult
C. clever
D. unknown

348. **give rise to**
A. interfere
B. revise
C. cause
D. discover

349. **relic**
A. content
B. unity
C. whole
D. artifact

350. **miniature**
A. huge
B. small
C. important
D. worthless

351. **convey**
A. retain
B. communicate
C. construct
D. equivocate

352. **perpetually**
A. originally
B. continually
C. surprisingly
D. directly

353. **contiguous**
A. precious
B. complex
C. neighboring
D. replaced

354. **compel**
A. conduct
B. hinder
C. allow
D. force

355. **viable**
A. feasible
B. tangible
C. resistible
D. movable

356. **concede**
A. conceal
B. dismiss
C. admit
D. reject

357. **concentrate on**
A. done with
B. focus on
C. skim through
D. start on

358. **allegedly**
A. questionably
B. supposedly
C. doubtfully
D. accordingly

359. **expandable**
A. flexible
B. rigid
C. separate
D. unbending

360. **exceedingly**
A. roughly
B. mildly
C. highly
D. actually

361. allocation
A. alliance
B. rejection
C. assignment
D. collection

362. contraction
A. construction
B. expansion
C. prediction
D. reduction

363. comprehensive
A. through
B. slight
C. thorough
D. exclusive

364. emphasize
A. stress
B. distribute
C. mislead
D. dispersed

365. hint
A. specialty
B. clue
C. statement
D. recognition

366. evaluate
A. focus
B. assess
C. create
D. invent

367. vulnerable
A. probable
B. defenseless
C. viable
D. protected

368. innovation
A. old development
B. new development
C. shocking development
D. no development

369. countering
A. opposing
B. cooperative
C. accommodating
D. cautious

370. conquer
A. battle
B. construct
C. defeat
D. surrender

371. remarkable
A. notable
B. native
C. normal
D. natural

372. pertinent
A. inappropriate
B. relevant
C. mistaken
D. various

373. appreciable
A. unnoticed
B. necessary
C. significant
D. appropriate

374. cumbersome
A. graceful
B. wholesome
C. resourceful
D. burdensome

375. constitute
A. command
B. confirm
C. connect
D. comprise

376. colonize
A. destroy
B. inhabit
C. remodel
D. transfer

377. devour
A. invent
B. consume
C. engineer
D. develop

378. dense
A. abnormal
B. thick
C. pure
D. actual

379. deceiving
A. transparent
B. apparent
C. decaying
D. misleading

380. traumatic
A. pleasing
B. upsetting
C. tiring
D. calming

381. successive
A. interrupted
B. causal
C. in sequence
D. leading

382. embodiment
A. description
B. submission
C. manifestation
D. statement

383. decline
A. weaken
B. debate
C. strengthen
D. wander

384. demise
A. creation
B. birth
C. end
D. belief

385. deem
A. define
B. consider
C. assess
D. evolve

386. rudimentary
A. basic
B. rude
C. impressive
D. respectful

387. master
A. bind
B. release
C. unleash
D. learn

388. incompatible
A. constant
B. consistent
C. conflicting
D. conventional

389. barren
A. agile
B. fertile
C. busy
D. lifeless

390. embody
A. assure
B. characterize
C. trust
D. produce

391. impart
A. settle
B. observe
C. take
D. provide

392. fashion
A. behavior
B. conduct
C. performance
D. style

393. sophisticated
A. highly refined
B. highly trusted
C. highly interested
D. highly supported

394. commonly
A. generally
B. occasionally
C. rarely
D. specially

395. furnish
A. distinguish
B. impede
C. utilize
D. provide

396. absurd
A. reasonable
B. rational
C. ridiculous
D. reflective

397. palatial
A. practical
B. forbidden
C. frightening
D. magnificent

398. discrete
A. united
B. disturbing
C. distant
D. separate

399. anchor
A. remove
B. fasten
C. locate
D. discuss

400. dominate
A. surpass
B. control
C. follow
D. precede

401. intrinsic
A. interesting
B. learned
C. inherent
D. popular

402. fuse
A. banish
B. detach
C. combine
D. protect

403. disintegrate
A. break down
B. build up
C. blow up
D. give in

404. adopt
A. begin to amaze
B. begin to help
C. begin to realize
D. begin to use

405. concern
A. ignorance
B. interest
C. popularity
D. specialty

406. reluctant
A. reliable
B. distrust
C. mysterious
D. unwilling

407. generate
A. destroy
B. abandon
C. produce
D. guide

408. dramatically
A. unskillfully
B. easily
C. expertly
D. greatly

409. hazard
A. humor
B. respect
C. safety
D. danger

410. bustling
A. loud
B. lethargic
C. lively
D. languid

411. prosperous
A. unsuccessful
B. flourishing
C. relieving
D. proper

412. approximate
A. close to
B. native to
C. far from
D. different from

413. eclectic
A. various
B. simple
C. same
D. boring

414. erratic
A. consistent
B. unpredictable
C. natural
D. enthusiastic

415. resilient
A. slow to recover
B. quick to recover
C. do not recover
D. will recover

416. enactment
A. argument
B. establishment
C. destruction
D. correction

417. obvious
A. unclear
B. opposite
C. evident
D. optional

418. presume
A. assure
B. disbelieve
C. reserve
D. assume

419. justify
A. support
B. signify
C. oppose
D. judge

420. fabricate
A. destroy
B. connect
C. produce
D. pretend

421. imply
A. demonstrate
B. insinuate
C. illustrate
D. indicate

422. swift
A. quick
B. smart
C. slow
D. mute

423. subsequent
A. following
B. including
C. generating
D. preceding

424. durable
A. temporary
B. doable
C. short-lived
D. long-lasting

425. thus
A. consequently
B. clearly
C. commonly
D. obviously

426. ultimately
A. finally
B. previously
C. deadly
D. originally

427. confines
A. boundaries
B. locations
C. buildings
D. conditions

428. contemporary
A. attentive
B. current
C. old-fashioned
D. temporary

429. disperse
A. arrange
B. disturb
C. continue
D. spread

430. bulk
A. majority
B. priority
C. minority
D. loyalty

431. account for
A. complicate
B. explain
C. write
D. confuse

432. exert
A. drop
B. find
C. apply
D. lose

433. foster
A. encourage
B. discourage
C. accept
D. decline

434. vigor
A. variety
B. difference
C. attraction
D. energy

435. initial
A. original
B. final
C. literate
D. instructed

436. furthermore
A. initially
B. additionally
C. accordingly
D. finally

437. attainment
A. failure
B. attachment
C. achievement
D. rejection

438. substantial
A. unimportant
B. significant
C. independent
D. intelligent

439. initiate
A. increase
B. finish
C. free
D. begin

440. cope with
A. struggle with
B. compare with
C. deal with
D. cover with

441. prevailing
A. widespread
B. minor
C. unknown
D. familiar

442. abruptly
A. occasionally
B. suddenly
C. steadily
D. usually

443. attributable to
A. repulsed by
B. appealed by
C. affected by
D. caused by

444. intriguing
A. inspiring
B. encouraging
C. interesting
D. boring

445. contend
A. honor
B. retreat
C. argue
D. disrespect

446. confine
A. discredit
B. restrict
C. confuse
D. prove

447. inducement
A. introduction
B. hindrance
C. incentive
D. process

448. potent
A. fragile
B. breakable
C. powerful
D. unable

449. distinction
A. difference
B. obedience
C. similarity
D. rebellion

450. consequent
A. original
B. resultant
C. conditional
D. objective

451. impetus
A. challenge
B. stimulus
C. collapse
D. interim

452. impose
A. detach
B. exist
C. force
D. relax

453. alteration
A. loss
B. remain
C. modification
D. accident

454. phenomenal
A. normal
B. refused
C. extraordinary
D. approved

455. fragment
A. take up
B. break up
C. bring out
D. pull out

456. massive
A. enormous
B. sensitive
C. cruel
D. minute

457. essential
A. true
B. minor
C. vital
D. false

458. aggregated
A. dispersed
B. exported
C. imported
D. combined

459. consumption
A. completion
B. utilization
C. stability
D. scarcity

460. uniquely
A. commonly
B. exceptionally
C. hardly
D. occasionally

461. aggregate
A. collect
B. control
C. plan
D. forget

462. inevitable
A. inexpensive
B. unnecessary
C. unavoidable
D. countable

463. extended
A. reduced
B. experienced
C. affected
D. lengthened

464. refine
A. decline
B. improve
C. learn
D. suggest

465. persist
A. continue
B. leave
C. stop
D. accelerate

466. skeptical
A. believable
B. dishonest
C. dispirited
D. doubtful

467. abound in
A. be plentiful
B. be limited
C. be careful
D. be effective

468. persistent
A. short-lived
B. long-lasting
C. pleasing
D. annoying

469. consent
A. agree
B. disapprove
C. affect
D. contain

470. minute
A. tiny
B. huge
C. great
D. poor

471. inadvertently
A. unintentionally
B. deliberately
C. knowingly
D. identically

472. abundance
A. plenty
B. deficiency
C. absence
D. existence

473. fragmented
A. completed
B. divided
C. weakened
D. strengthened

474. distinct
A. careful
B. distant
C. capable
D. noticeable

475. disseminate
A. disagree
B. collect
C. spread
D. prove

476. modest
A. complex
B. minor
C. simple
D. proud

477. contentious
A. terrible
B. effective
C. argumentative
D. controversial

478. refinement
A. small improvement
B. small invention
C. small argument
D. small interest

479. adjacent
A. neighboring
B. considering
C. abstract
D. firm

480. embark on
A. discourage
B. start
C. finish
D. challenge

481. imposing
  A. impressive
  B. attentive
  C. unimportant
  D. repulsive

482. distinctive
  A. abnormal
  B. characteristic
  C. controversial
  D. unclear

483. evident
  A. apparent
  B. uncertain
  C. mistaken
  D. capable

484. encompass
  A. include
  B. join
  C. exclude
  D. direct

485. conspicuous
  A. unseen
  B. familiar
  C. mysterious
  D. obvious

486. detect
  A. destroy
  B. manage
  C. discover
  D. delete

487. sequentially
  A. consecutively
  B. secularly
  C. suddenly
  D. abruptly

488. astonishing
  A. boring
  B. amazing
  C. interesting
  D. annoying

489. exhausted
  A. taken off
  B. used up
  C. covered by
  D. brought in

490. deliberate
  A. harmful
  B. unwilling
  C. helpful
  D. intentional

491. exceptionally
  A. mildly
  B. flamboyantly
  C. excitingly
  D. distinctively

492. harness
  A. utilize
  B. produce
  C. complete
  D. harden

493. offset
  A. understand
  B. operate
  C. destroy
  D. balance

494. assume
  A. know
  B. consume
  C. release
  D. suppose

495. onset
  A. invention
  B. attraction
  C. interest
  D. beginning

496. prolonged
  A. reduced
  B. bonded
  C. lengthened
  D. provided

497. radically
  A. subsequently
  B. additionally
  C. apparently
  D. drastically

498. obscured
  A. exposed
  B. hidden
  C. offensive
  D. obvious

499. conjecture
  A. surprise
  B. prove
  C. close
  D. guess

500. conclusive
  A. adequate
  B. definitive
  C. unequal
  D. strange

501. comprise
  A. encompass
  B. confirm
  C. destroy
  D. exclude

502. virtually
  A. artificially
  B. violently
  C. differently
  D. importantly

503. eventually
  A. in fact
  B. at least
  C. in the end
  D. in the middle

504. optimize
  A. make the best use of
  B. make the worst use of
  C. make the least use of
  D. make no use of

505. subsequently
  A. unfamiliarly
  B. previously
  C. lower
  D. later

506. fragmentation
  A. creation
  B. conclusion
  C. deprivation
  D. disintegration

507. potential
  A. probable
  B. unavailable
  C. conceptual
  D. impossible

508. notable
  A. insignificant
  B. unable
  C. outstanding
  D. conclusive

509. prominence
  A. insignificance
  B. intelligence
  C. ignorance
  D. importance

510. deliberation
  A. discussion
  B. destruction
  C. unwillingness
  D. instruction

511. predominantly
  A. mainly
  B. certainly
  C. approximately
  D. questionably

512. integrate
  A. segregate
  B. switch
  C. divide
  D. combine

513. contention
  A. conflict
  B. effect
  C. challenge
  D. disrespect

514. forage
  A. search for food
  B. drop food
  C. grow food
  D. eat food

515. exclusively
  A. solely
  B. partially
  C. approximately
  D. hardly

516. ingenious
  A. very honest
  B. very deceitful
  C. very clever
  D. very awkward

517. assess
  A. evaluate
  B. begin
  C. finish
  D. access

518. intrigued
  A. bored
  B. warned
  C. rejected
  D. fascinated

519. obscure
  A. extreme
  B. perfect
  C. careless
  D. unclear

520. decimate
  A. rule
  B. destroy
  C. create
  D. yield

521. **entire**
A. whole
B. incomplete
C. halfway
D. clear

522. **analogous**
A. passionate
B. different
C. analyzed
D. similar

523. **prevail**
A. be mature
B. be dominant
C. be weak
D. be afraid

524. **precise**
A. vague
B. steep
C. exact
D. gradual

525. **intense**
A. silent
B. calm
C. noisy
D. extreme

526. **roughly**
A. approximately
B. greatly
C. precisely
D. specifically

527. **inherent**
A. unable
B. capable
C. additional
D. innate

528. **elaborate**
A. immense
B. creative
C. complicated
D. simple

529. **merely**
A. definitely
B. continually
C. completely
D. only

530. **prominent**
A. outstanding
B. alluring
C. different
D. imminent

531. **considerably**
A. calmly
B. greatly
C. lightly
D. unknowingly

532. **notably**
A. particularly
B. approximately
C. generally
D. rarely

533. **readily**
A. narrowly
B. willingly
C. widely
D. fairly

534. **justly**
A. wrongly
B. rightfully
C. unfairly
D. automatically

535. **lethal**
A. deadly
B. safe
C. harmless
D. reachable

536. **predominant**
A. historic
B. willing
C. principal
D. minor

537. **barely**
A. altogether
B. just
C. always
D. quite

538. **immensely**
A. certainly
B. extremely
C. doubtfully
D. moderately

539. **proliferation**
A. growth
B. reduction
C. excellence
D. production

540. **ample**
A. scarce
B. plentiful
C. incomplete
D. whole

541. **eventual**
A. first
B. final
C. early
D. proper

542. **configuration**
A. significance
B. arrangement
C. agreement
D. definition

543. **optimum**
A. most current
B. most promising
C. most acceptable
D. most favorable

544. **execute**
A. perform
B. explain
C. exercise
D. blame

545. **consequence**
A. cause
B. trouble
C. agreement
D. outcome

546. **profound**
A. possible
B. impossible
C. significant
D. trivial

547. **proliferate**
A. lessen
B. multiply
C. decrease
D. agree

548. **convention**
A. theory
B. invention
C. exclusive
D. conference

549. **vastly**
A. mildly
B. roughly
C. greatly
D. precisely

550. **ultimate**
A. additional
B. extra
C. eventual
D. unnecessary

551. **consume**
A. collect from
B. share with
C. use up
D. divide by

552. **vast**
A. narrow
B. enormous
C. insignificant
D. precise

553. **phenomenon**
A. regularity
B. tradition
C. refusal
D. occurrence

554. **modify**
A. change
B. remain
C. design
D. create

555. **accumulate**
A. order
B. correct
C. collect
D. consider

556. **compelling**
A. convincing
B. computing
C. increasing
D. producing

557. **advent**
A. improvement
B. advancement
C. certainty
D. beginning

558. **initially**
A. at last
B. in the end
C. at first
D. in time

559. **consequently**
A. almost
B. therefore
C. always
D. sometimes

560. **striking**
A. typical
B. remarkable
C. influential
D. enormous

561. **pose**
   A. present
   B. gather
   C. reject
   D. accept

562. **component**
   A. factor
   B. potential
   C. comfort
   D. collection

563. **immense**
   A. large
   B. little
   C. intense
   D. delicate

564. **abundant**
   A. scarce
   B. limited
   C. numerous
   D. unbounded

565. **prolong**
   A. extend
   B. shorten
   C. produce
   D. remove

566. **postulate**
   A. possess
   B. claim
   C. instruct
   D. pretend

567. **potentially**
   A. unlikely
   B. strongly
   C. possibly
   D. greatly

568. **principal**
   A. standard
   B. minor
   C. main
   D. different

569. **pronounced**
   A. indistinct
   B. notable
   C. ordinary
   D. upright

570. **extensive**
   A. widespread
   B. expensive
   C. restricted
   D. precious

571. **plausible**
   A. incredible
   B. believable
   C. unlikely
   D. worthy

572. **severe**
   A. various
   B. extreme
   C. moderate
   D. individual

573. **decimation**
   A. creation
   B. domination
   C. destruction
   D. submission

574. **unprecedented**
   A. new
   B. outdated
   C. common
   D. alternative

575. **amplify**
   A. increase
   B. complete
   C. decrease
   D. empty

576. **intact**
   A. separated
   B. unaffected
   C. combined
   D. damaged

577. **integration**
   A. union
   B. collection
   C. donation
   D. division

578. **marked**
   A. vague
   B. ambiguous
   C. obvious
   D. obscure

579. **considerable**
   A. insignificant
   B. dependent
   C. moderate
   D. significant

580. **conjecture**
   A. fact
   B. doubt
   C. assumption
   D. collection

581. **lucrative**
   A. vague
   B. clear
   C. profitable
   D. unprofessional

582. **significantly**
   A. unwillingly
   B. carefully
   C. considerably
   D. expensively

583. **attain**
   A. assure
   B. lose
   C. retain
   D. reach

584. **flourish**
   A. appear
   B. lose
   C. fail
   D. prosper

585. **remnant**
   A. remains
   B. remembrances
   C. alterations
   D. difficulties

586. **significant**
   A. simple
   B. serious
   C. important
   D. unnecessary

587. **crucial**
   A. effective
   B. insignificant
   C. efficient
   D. important

588. **sequence**
   A. disorder
   B. order
   C. confusion
   D. origin

589. **consensus**
   A. continuity
   B. argument
   C. suspension
   D. approval

590. **sustained**
   A. endured
   B. abounded
   C. substantiated
   D. eschewed

591. **exploitation**
   A. abuse
   B. rejection
   C. start
   D. exploration

592. **fragmentary**
   A. forgetful
   B. pleasant
   C. incomplete
   D. conclusive

593. **fluctuation**
   A. change
   B. uniformity
   C. relaxation
   D. easiness

594. **induce**
   A. bring about
   B. focus on
   C. take from
   D. introduce to

595. **critical**
   A. important
   B. unnecessary
   C. possible
   D. clinical

596. **conventional**
   A. traditional
   B. competitive
   C. inconsistent
   D. significant

597. **minutely**
   A. in order
   B. in detail
   C. in absence
   D. in danger

598. **crude**
   A. cruel
   B. primitive
   C. polished
   D. current

599. **exceptional**
   A. effortless
   B. widespread
   C. reasonable
   D. extraordinary

600. **sustain**
   A. take
   B. assume
   C. support
   D. bring

601. inherent in
A. characteristic of
B. knowledge of
C. critical of
D. inside of

602. particular
A. public
B. specific
C. general
D. familiar

603. exploit
A. take off
B. take care of
C. take advantage of
D. take away

604. substantially
A. correctly
B. insignificantly
C. inadequately
D. considerably

605. predominated
A. most controversial
B. most dangerous
C. most helpful
D. most noticeable

606. intermittently
A. intentionally
B. secretly
C. knowingly
D. periodically

607. simultaneously
A. at different times
B. at the same time
C. at the end
D. at the most

608. stipulate
A. acquire
B. excite
C. imply
D. require

609. account
A. amount
B. report
C. result
D. addition

610. indispensable
A. independent
B. unnecessary
C. essential
D. healthy

611. markedly
A. noticeably
B. slightly
C. extremely
D. mildly

612. mimic
A. control
B. imitate
C. differ
D. oppose

613. radical
A. extreme
B. advanced
C. superficial
D. analytical

614. vigorous
A. various
B. horrible
C. strong
D. weak

615. severity
A. standard
B. seriousness
C. movement
D. fairness

616. albeit
A. while
B. although
C. since
D. whether

617. ingenuity
A. honesty
B. denseness
C. ignorance
D. inventiveness

618. alter
A. change
B. manage
C. turn
D. repair

619. entirely
A. clearly
B. completely
C. separately
D. inadequately

620 optimal
A. flawed
B. absent
C. ideal
D. present

621. advocate
A. oppose
B. compete
C. support
D. clash

622. manipulate
A. generate
B. create
C. control
D. ruin

623. fundamental
A. different
B. efficient
C. difficult
D. basic

624. promote
A. behave
B. encourage
C. process
D. divide

625. enigma
A. knowledge
B. advancement
C. mystery
D. energy

626. expansion
A. reduction
B. concentration
C. growth
D. difficulty

627. frigid
A. cold
B. fresh
C. clean
D. particular

628. excavate
A. uncover
B. exist
C. conceal
D. influence

629. application
A. starvation
B. utilization
C. satisfaction
D. redemption

630. intrusive
A. inattentive
B. indifferent
C. intentional
D. interfering

631. prolific
A. fertile
B. barren
C. famous
D. unpopular

632. subject to
A. relevant to
B. unlikely to
C. susceptible to
D. forced to

633. compacted
A. compressed
B. flexible
C. inflated
D. revealed

634. abandoned
A. accepted
B. supported
C. deserted
D. provided

635. rigid
A. patient
B. flexible
C. kind
D. strict

636. deviation
A. reflection
B. conversation
C. departure
D. development

637. deposit
A. recall
B. delete
C. place
D. lower

638. broadly
A. locally
B. rarely
C. generally
D. exactly

639. probe
A. investigate
B. command
C. warrant
D. breach

640. assimilate
A. absorb
B. reject
C. mistake
D. differ

641. succession
A. decline
B. sequence
C. damage
D. mischief

642. facilitate
A. make hard
B. make easy
C. make known
D. make unknown

643. strategy
A. plan
B. account
C. rally
D. mystery

644. momentous
A. reliable
B. monotonous
C. significant
D. devious

645. hazardous
A. trivial
B. predictable
C. dangerous
D. undecided

646. concern
A. contain
B. deliver
C. accept
D. worry

647. erect
A. erase
B. delay
C. escape
D. raise

648. uniformly
A. consistently
B. unnaturally
C. roughly
D. unevenly

649. impede
A. facilitate
B. initiate
C. attract
D. inhibit

650. epitomize
A. rush
B. tangle
C. corrupt
D. exemplify

651. transitory
A. brief
B. lengthy
C. boring
D. exciting

652. consistently
A. slowly
B. rarely
C. early
D. regularly

653. be accustomed to
A. be saved from
B. be increased to
C. be known for
D. be used to

654. pinpoint
A. locate directly
B. locate inexactly
C. locate exactly
D. locate early

655. invariable
A. changeable
B. constant
C. convertible
D. careless

656. secrete
A. report
B. reveal
C. review
D. release

657. inflation
A. distinction
B. compression
C. connection
D. expansion

658. justified
A. exclusive
B. rationalized
C. extreme
D. contradicted

659. grasp
A. unleash
B. understand
C. grow
D. establish

660. successively
A. one coming later
B. two at a time
C. one before the other
D. one after another

661. found
A. organize
B. institute
C. establish
D. finish

662. rebound
A. collapse
B. merit
C. recover
D. create

663. diffuse
A. discuss
B. determine
C. distribute
D. discover

664. prosperity
A. economic well-being
B. economic disadvantage
C. economic struggle
D. economic battle

665. enigmatic
A. known
B. clear
C. energetic
D. puzzling

666. ambiguous
A. predictable
B. accurate
C. obvious
D. uncertain

667. enormous
A. quiet
B. loud
C. small
D. huge

668. embed
A. find
B. implant
C. emphasize
D. excite

669. extant
A. existing
B. misplaced
C. bemused
D. found

670. subtle
A. hard to recognize
B. hard to recommend
C. hard to resist
D. hard to react

671. broaden
A. widen
B. consume
C. compress
D. lower

672. precarious
A. pointed
B. fast
C. strong
D. unstable

673. celebrated
A. unknown
B. famous
C. typical
D. rare

674. now and then
A. occasionally
B. seemingly
C. presently
D. ultimately

675. feasible
A. achievable
B. available
C. agreeable
D. arguable

676. hinder
A. consider
B. explore
C. prevent
D. determine

677. correspondingly
A. unfairly
B. extremely
C. accordingly
D. unsuitably

678. cling to
A. stick to
B. remove from
C. add to
D. take with

679. staple
A. minor item
B. exciting item
C. basic item
D. extreme item

680. ritual
A. informal
B. uncustomary
C. ceremonial
D. bizarre

641B 642B 643A 644C 645D 646D 647D 648A 649D 650D 651A 652D 653D 654C 655B 656C 657D 658B 659B 660D
661C 662C 663C 664A 665D 666D 667D 668B 669A 670A 671A 672D 673B 674A 675A 676C 677C 678A 679C 680C

270 | iBT TOEFL® PATTERN Reading III

681. **rigorous**
   A. mild
   B. severe
   C. special
   D. kind

682. **transform**
   A. simplify
   B. preserve
   C. transfer
   D. change

683. **utterly**
   A. talkatively
   B. partially
   C. personally
   D. completely

684. **integral**
   A. supplemental
   B. useless
   C. essential
   D. voluntary

685. **exhibit**
   A. conceal
   B. veil
   C. show
   D. disguise

686. **breakthrough**
   A. sudden advance
   B. delayed advance
   C. no advance
   D. timely advance

687. **key**
   A. promising
   B. insignificant
   C. professional
   D. important

688. **speculation**
   A. fabrication
   B. prevention
   C. information
   D. supposition

689. **apparent**
   A. frequent
   B. negligible
   C. evident
   D. occasional

690. **remarkably**
   A. reasonably
   B. surprisingly
   C. commonly
   D. usually

691. **magnify**
   A. acclaim
   B. lower
   C. diminish
   D. enlarge

692. **extract**
   A. wait
   B. combine
   C. remove
   D. guess

693. **formidable**
   A. intimidating
   B. insignificant
   C. relevant
   D. specific

694. **objective**
   A. purpose
   B. experience
   C. observation
   D. source

695. **innovative**
   A. original
   B. traditional
   C. inept
   D. skillful

696. **tend**
   A. care for
   B. live for
   C. long for
   D. build for

697. **converge**
   A. come together
   B. break apart
   C. come forward
   D. spread out

698. **criterion**
   A. creativity
   B. alternative
   C. standard
   D. criticism

699. **provoke**
   A. doubt
   B. believe
   C. prevent
   D. incite

700. **manifest**
   A. demonstrate
   B. comply
   C. resist
   D. maintain

701. **fragile**
   A. strong
   B. decorative
   C. sturdy
   D. delicate

702. **inordinate**
   A. moderate
   B. excessive
   C. ordinary
   D. generous

703. **perpetuate**
   A. continue
   B. cease
   C. care
   D. concern

704. **anxious**
   A. happy
   B. fearless
   C. content
   D. worried

705. **arid**
   A. wet
   B. rigid
   C. dry
   D. heavy

706. **rigor**
   A. mildness
   B. kindness
   C. closeness
   D. harshness

707. **moreover**
   A. separately
   B. additionally
   C. independently
   D. unintentionally

708. **strew**
   A. gather
   B. scatter
   C. receive
   D. order

709. **tremendous**
   A. minute
   B. trendy
   C. huge
   D. minimal

710. **prestige**
   A. timidity
   B. lowliness
   C. faith
   D. status

711. **inflate**
   A. insert
   B. anger
   C. enlarge
   D. compress

712. **consistent with**
   A. in cooperation with
   B. in trouble with
   C. in contrast with
   D. in agreement with

713. **peril**
   A. comfort
   B. safety
   C. danger
   D. pleasure

714. **contract**
   A. condense
   B. predict
   C. stretch
   D. contain

715. **anarchy**
   A. disorder
   B. analysis
   C. harmony
   D. method

716. **devise**
   A. create
   B. destroy
   C. control
   D. balance

717. **likewise**
   A. vastly
   B. chiefly
   C. officially
   D. similarly

718. **complex**
   A. portion
   B. respect
   C. facility
   D. comment

719. **solely**
   A. truly
   B. warmly
   C. only
   D. richly

720. **objective**
   A. unknown
   B. unfair
   C. unbiased
   D. unjust

721. allegiance
A. knowledge
B. development
C. loyalty
D. experience

722. trauma
A. damage
B. calm
C. relief
D. shape

723. ephemeral
A. hidden
B. permanent
C. temporary
D. excellent

724. adequate
A. disturbing
B. inferior
C. helpful
D. suitable

725. disband
A. distract
B. dismiss
C. repress
D. design

726. expansive
A. liberal
B. spacious
C. significant
D. reserved

727. dramatic
A. dull
B. sharp
C. ordinary
D. significant

728. complex
A. proper
B. complicated
C. relative
D. dependent

729. restrict
A. break
B. expand
C. prohibit
D. fix

730. mounting
A. speeding up
B. slowing down
C. decreasing
D. increasing

731. dependable
A. sensitive
B. interested
C. misleading
D. reliable

732. anticipate
A. overlook
B. continue
C. expect
D. allow

733. shatter
A. destroy
B. fix
C. deflate
D. attach

734. attribute
A. clarity
B. attraction
C. characteristic
D. praise

735. revise
A. change
B. continue
C. corrupt
D. control

736. copious
A. meager
B. abundant
C. scarce
D. thin

737. anxiety
A. noise
B. ease
C. comfort
D. worry

738. comparable
A. competitive
B. incoherent
C. equivalent
D. balanced

739. explicit
A. obscure
B. obvious
C. observant
D. obsessive

740. essentially
A. extremely
B. apparently
C. basically
D. additionally

741. thrive
A. throw away
B. take back
C. do well
D. bring up

742. subjected to
A. limited to
B. guarded with
C. cover with
D. exposed to

743. detrimental
A. beneficial
B. harmful
C. favorable
D. valuable

744. negligible
A. major
B. insignificant
C. frequent
D. standard

745. collaborate
A. cooperate
B. disturb
C. follow
D. manage

746. indigenous
A. poor
B. rich
C. foreign
D. native

747. engraved
A. carved
B. buried
C. engaged
D. sharpened

748. trigger
A. block
B. transport
C. take
D. activate

749. embellish
A. decorate
B. enable
C. progress
D. recover

750. current
A. straight
B. present
C. curly
D. past

751. retrieve
A. give back
B. talk back
C. bring back
D. hold back

752. conversely
A. slightly
B. favorably
C. contrastingly
D. equally

753. hypothetical
A. supposed
B. authentic
C. genuine
D. evident

754. nevertheless
A. ever
B. never
C. forever
D. however

755. assert
A. deny
B. debate
C. declare
D. delude

756. commission
A. revoke
B. order
C. tailor
D. settle

757. hamper
A. manage
B. represent
C. understand
D. obstruct

758. decline
A. decrease
B. return
C. use
D. save

759. enduring
A. short-lived
B. lasting
C. momentary
D. fleeting

760. frankly
A. fluently
B. frequently
C. honestly
D. unfortunately

761. compensate
A. reimburse
B. compute
C. expand
D. concentrate

762. bombard
A. begin
B. attack
C. assist
D. protect

763. alternative
A. assistance
B. substitute
C. necessity
D. exception

764. intimate with
A. friend of
B. enemy of
C. unfamiliar with
D. familiar with

765. eccentric
A. elegant
B. unusual
C. insignificant
D. careful

766. merge
A. combine
B. divide
C. carry
D. remove

767. immune
A. immense
B. reliable
C. invulnerable
D. favorable

768. drastically
A. slightly
B. faintly
C. severely
D. clearly

769. excessive
A. moderate
B. reasonable
C. accessible
D. extreme

770. viability
A. complexity
B. modesty
C. vanity
D. feasibility

771. continuous
A. ongoing
B. outgoing
C. regular
D. disturbed

772. continual
A. temporary
B. constant
C. fleeting
D. eternal

773. thriving
A. impaired
B. scarce
C. failing
D. successful

774. prime
A. unworthy
B. inferior
C. superior
D. respectable

775. decisive
A. definitive
B. uncertain
C. problematic
D. extreme

776. hence
A. unnecessarily
B. subsequently
C. consequently
D. importantly

777. speculate
A. neglect
B. disregard
C. specialize
D. hypothesize

778. uniform
A. imbalanced
B. inconsistent
C. invariable
D. imperfect

779. primarily
A. additionally
B. mainly
C. secondarily
D. informally

780. exceed
A. surpass
B. follow
C. precede
D. acquire

781. chancy
A. careful
B. certain
C. risky
D. safe

782. counterpart
A. contrast
B. opposite
C. stranger
D. equivalent

783. evoke
A. conclude
B. arouse
C. result
D. unsettle

784. requisite
A. essential
B. unnecessary
C. optional
D. beneficial

785. dissipated
A. dispersed
B. attached
C. isolated
D. detached

786. cite
A. mention
B. bring
C. perform
D. withdraw

787. obtain
A. discredit
B. sacrifice
C. predict
D. acquire

788. halt
A. stop
B. begin
C. learn
D. affect

789. heritage
A. expression
B. limitation
C. hesitation
D. tradition

790. appreciably
A. appropriately
B. insignificantly
C. noticeably
D. briefly

791. duplicate
A. support
B. deliver
C. reproduce
D. indicate

792. reasonable
A. intolerable
B. sensible
C. accountable
D. unbearable

793. pristine
A. guilty
B. pure
C. stiff
D. alert

794. elongate
A. lengthen
B. shorten
C. command
D. request

795. link
A. allow
B. detach
C. connect
D. restart

796. facet
A. fact
B. center
C. branch
D. aspect

797. deviate
A. go straight
B. turn aside
C. move forward
D. travel far

798. assorted
A. broken
B. similar
C. alert
D. various

799. camouflage
A. uncover
B. hide
C. disclose
D. bare

800. presumable
A. apparent
B. extreme
C. impossible
D. uncertain

761A 762B 763B 764D 765B 766A 767C 768C 769D 770D 771A 772B 773D 774C 775A 776C 777D 778C 779B 780A
781C 782D 783B 784A 785A 786A 787D 788A 789D 790C 791C 792B 793B 794A 795C 796D 797B 798D 799B 800A

ACTUAL TOEFL VOCABULARY TEST | 273

801. **abnormally:** unusually, uniquely

802. **abolish:** eliminate, discontinue

803. **absorbing:** 1) learning, understanding
2) interesting, engrossing

804. **accelerate:** occur at an increased speed; precipitate

805. **accurately:** correctly, precisely

806. **adapt:** adjust, modify

807. **adept:** skillful, capable

808. **administer:** 1) manage, govern 2) distribute, provide

809. **adverse:** unfavorable, antagonistic

810. **affect:** influence, have an effect on

811. **aftermath:** result, outcome

812. **against:** 1) opposite to, adjacent 2) direct at, target

813. **aim:** goal, intention

814. **alarm:** surprise; upset

815. **allied:** related, united

816. **anonymous:** unknown, unidentified

817. **any given time:** any selected or chosen time

818. **apart from:** besides, except

819. **apex:** crest, top

820. **appraisal:** evaluation, judgment

821. **appropriate:** suitable, acceptable

822. **archetypal:** quintessential, most typical

823. **archive:** collection of records, annals

824. **arouse:** stimulate, excite

825. **article:** object, item

826. **artifact:** antique, remnant

827. **as well:** in addition, also

828. **ascendancy:** dominance, control

829. **assemble:** gather together, congregate

830. **assign:** specify; accredit

831. **assist with:** help with, aid

832. **astounding:** amazing, surprising

833. **astoundingly:** incredibly, extremely

834. **astute:** insightful, perceptive

835. **attest:** confirm, certify

836. **authoritative:** valid, reliable

837. **authority:** expert; power

838. **available:** convenient, feasible

839. **barrier:** obstacle, limit

840. **be accompanied by:** occur together, coincide

841. **be inclined to:** tend to, lean toward

842. **be incorporated in:** be part of, included in

843. **bias:** prejudice, partiality

844. **blossom:** flourish, mature

845. **boast:** 1) show off, pride oneself on 2) exhibit, possess

846. **boom:** 1) rapidly expand, prosper 2) prosperity, growth

847. **bound for:** going to, destined for

848. **bountiful:** plentiful, abundant

849. **breeding:** development, training

850. **brew:** 1) plan, contrive 2) beverage, blend

851. **buffer:** protect, cushion

852. **buildup:** accumulation, development

853. **burst:** 1) break, rupture 2) outbreak, surge
3) blast, explosion

854. **by and large:** for the most part, altogether

855. **calculatedly:** deliberately, intentionally

856. **candidly:** honestly, directly

857. **cargo:** shipment, baggage

858. **cast about:** seek, search

859. **cease:** stop, conclude

860. **chaotic:** disorganized, utterly confused

861. **characteristic:** 1) quality, trait 2) typical, distinctive

862. **circuitous:** indirect, meandering

863. **circumstance:** condition, situation

864. **circumvent:** evade; mislead

865. **classify:** categorize, organize

866. **coarse:** 1) crude, rude 2) rough, grainy

867. **coating:** layer, covering

868. **collision:** crash, accident

869. **colossal:** enormous, gigantic

870. **commemorate:** celebrate, honor

871. **commence:** begin, initiate

872. **commending:** admiring, praising

873. **compact:** condensed, firm

874. **comparative:** relative, approximate

875. **compatible:** consistent, agreeable

876. **competent:** adept, able

877. **complaint:** protest, grievance

878. **complement:** supplement, complete

879. **compose:** make of, form

880. **conducive to:** favorable to, in consideration of

881. **confidence:** certainty, belief in oneself

882. **confirm:** ascertain, validate

883. **conforming:** obeying, agreeing

884. **congeal:** solidify, coagulate

885. **conjuncture:** a combination of circumstances

886. **considering:** taking into account

887. **constricted:** narrow, tight

888. **contain:** 1) enclose 2) control, stop

889. **contemptuous:** scornful, arrogant

890. **contradictory:** inconsistent, conflicting

891. **cordial:** friendly, amiable

892. **core:** center, essence, focus

893. **correlate:** interact, compare

894. **costly:** expensive, pricey

895. **counterproductive:** harmful, contrary to what is necessary

896. **coupled with:** together with, along with

897. **course through:** flow through, rapidly travel

898. **cramped:** confined, overcrowded

899. **credible:** believable, dependable

900. **crush:** 1) pulverize, squash 2) defeat, suppress
3) crowd, mob

901. **dainty:** delicate, fragile

902. **damaging:** harmful, injurious
903. **debris:** fragments, litter
904. **deduce:** infer, figure out
905. **deeply ingrained:** firmly established, implanted
906. **deficient:** imperfect, incomplete
907. **deflect:** divert, change in direction
908. **dejected:** depressed, blue
909. **deliberate:** cautious, thoughtful
910. **delineate:** outline, describe
911. **deluxe:** lavish, fancy
912. **demonstrate:** 1) indicate, display 2) protest
913. **desert:** abandon, defect
914. **desolate:** 1) deserted, lonesome 2) destroy, devastate
915. **despite:** in spite of, regardless of
916. **despondent:** discouraged, wretched
917. **destitute:** poor, devoid of
918. **deteriorate:** decay, degenerate
919. **diligently:** carefully, persistently
920. **dimension:** size, measure
921. **discern:** detect, identify
922. **discernible:** noticeable, recognizable
923. **discharge:** release, dismiss
924. **disclose:** reveal, expose
925. **discount:** 1) deduct, lower 2) ignore, disregard
926. **disentangle:** extricate; unravel
927. **disparity:** inequality, difference
928. **displace:** force out, move
929. **display:** show, exhibit
930. **dispose of:** get rid of, dump
931. **disputable:** challengeable, debatable
932. **disrupt:** interfere with, disturb
933. **dissent:** oppose, disagree
934. **distant:** faraway, apart
935. **distinguish:** differentiate, individualize
936. **distribute:** spread, allocate
937. **diversion:** 1) redirection 2) recreation, pastime
938. **draw to:** attract, gather
939. **drive:** effort, initiative
940. **dubious:** unreliable, doubtful
941. **due to:** caused by, because
942. **dwelling:** living quarters, residence
943. **eager:** anxious, enthusiastic
944. **ease into:** slowly enter, slowly begin
945. **echo:** imitate, repeat
946. **eerie:** strange, spooky
947. **efface:** wipe out, erase
948. **efficacy:** effectiveness, productiveness
949. **eject:** force out, discharge
950. **elevate:** raise, lift up
951. **elicit:** obtain, draw out
952. **eliminate:** get rid of, remove
953. **elite:** upper class, best

954. **elucidate:** clarify, demonstrate
955. **emanate:** emerge, radiate
956. **embrace:** accept; hug
957. **emerging:** developing; appearing
958. **empirical:** observational, practical
959. **employ:** utilize, apply; hire
960. **encroach:** invade, intrude
961. **end:** 1) stop, completion 2) intention, goal
962. **endeavor:** effort, attempt
963. **engulf:** immerse, overwhelm
964. **enjoy:** 1) experience 2) appreciate, relish
965. **ensure:** guarantee, warrant
966. **entail:** involve, necessitate
967. **enthusiastic:** eager, excited
968. **entice:** tempt, allure
969. **episode:** event, scene
970. **equivocal:** ambiguous, uncertain
971. **era:** period, generation
972. **eradicate:** completely remove, destroy
973. **eroded:** worn out, disintegrated
974. **erroneous:** wrong, incorrect
975. **erupt:** explode, emit
976. **escalate:** intensify, amplify
977. **especially:** particularly, exceptionally
978. **evacuate:** remove; vacate
979. **evolve:** develop, progress
980. **exempt from:** free of, excused from
981. **expedite:** accelerate, rush
982. **expose:** make visible, disclose
983. **extinct:** died out, dormant
984. **extracted:** removed, obtained
985. **extreme:** 1) intense, severe 2) faraway, furthest
986. **exude:** release, give off
987. **fascinating:** extremely attractive, highly interesting
988. **fine tune:** adjust slightly, modify a little
989. **flag:** indicate, identify
990. **flatter:** praise, adulate
991. **flee:** run away, escape
992. **forerunner:** predecessor, harbinger
993. **forestall:** thwart, avert
994. **formulate:** develop, plan
995. **fortify:** strengthen, reinforce
996. **forum:** public meeting, conference
997. **found wanting:** judged inadequate, lacking
998. **fracture:** rupture, break
999. **friction:** conflict, disagreement
1000. **full-fledged:** well developed, mature
1001. **sweep:** 1) range, region 2) remove 3) move quickly
1002. **gear:** 1) adjust, adopt 2) material, equipment
1003. **genuine:** true, authentic
1004. **get rid of:** eliminate, remove
1005. **gigantic:** huge, enormous

1006. **graduate:** progress, advance

1007. **gratify:** satisfy, delight

1008. **groom:** clean, make ready

1009. **groundless:** unfounded, illogical

1010. **groundwork:** foundation, basis

1011. **hairline:** 1) thin line 2) slight, fragile

1012. **handy:** convenient, accessible

1013. **haphazard:** random, by chance

1014. **hasten:** accelerate, expedite

1015. **hasty:** hurried, speedy

1016. **head for:** go forward, progress

1017. **heighten:** increase, intensify

1018. **heterogeneous:** varied, diverse

1019. **heyday:** golden age, high point

1020. **hollow:** empty; meaningless

1021. **homogenize:** remove variation within, conform

1022. **hurdle:** 1) obstacle, difficulty 2) leap, surmount

1023. **ice sheets:** glaciers; large areas of ice over a region

1024. **identical:** same, equal

1025. **idiosyncrasy:** peculiarity, feature

1026. **immerse:** submerge; engage in

1027. **immobile:** unable to move, motionless

1028. **immutable:** unchangeable, permanent

1029. **impact:** 1) collision, crash 2) influence, effect 3) jolt, hit

1030. **impervious:** impermeable, resistant

1031. **implant:** insert, embed

1032. **implausible:** unbelievable, unlikely

1033. **implement:** 1) tool 2) start, achieve

1034. **implication:** suggestion; association

1035. **imprecise:** inexact, approximate

1036. **improbable:** unlikely, doubtful

1037. **improvised:** unplanned, makeshift

1038. **in conjunction with:** together with, along with

1039. **in place of:** instead of, in lieu of

1040. **inconclusive:** not definitive, ambiguous

1041. **incredible:** 1) unbelievable, absurd 2) extraordinary

1042. **infer:** conclude, speculate

1043. **infinite:** limitless; eternal

1044. **initiative:** self-motivation; strategy

1045. **innumerable:** countless, numerous

1046. **inspect:** examine, investigate

1047. **inspire:** motivate, encourage

1048. **install:** put in place, set up

1049. **intercourse:** exchange, communication

1050. **interpreted:** elucidated, explained

1051. **interrupt:** interfere, stop

1052. **intervening years:** between years, interceding years

1053. **invaluable:** precious, costly

1054. **isolate:** seclude, exile

1055. **jointly:** together, simultaneously

1056. **judiciously:** 1) wisely, logically 2) appropriately, properly

1057. **juncture:** turning point, crossroad

1058. **legendary:** 1) famous, renowned 2) mythical, fabled

1059. **legible:** readable; coherent

1060. **monumental:** massive, enduring

1061. **motif:** pattern; central theme

1062. **noteworthy:** important, extraordinary

1063. **notion:** idea, belief

1064. **novel:** innovative, new

1065. **obligation:** responsibility, duty

1066. **obsession with:** fixation on, attraction to

1067. **option:** choice, alternative

1068. **outcome:** result, consequence

1069. **outstanding:** remarkable, superior

1070. **overall:** 1) comprehensive, complete 2) in general, chiefly

1071. **overlap:** superimpose, have in common

1072. **overlook:** miss, disregard

1073. **owing to:** because, as a result of

1074. **pace:** speed, rate

1075. **peak:** height, summit

1076. **peculiar:** unique; strange

1077. **perceptible:** noticeable, discernible

1078. **periodically:** regularly, systematically

1079. **perishable:** decaying, decomposable

1080. **permanently:** forever, enduringly

1081. **permit:** allow, enable

1082. **perspective:** point of view, outlook

1083. **pervasive:** widespread, extensive

1084. **pillar:** column, post

1085. **pioneer:** 1) founder, developer 2) invent, develop

1086. **pitfall:** difficulty, hazard

1087. **pivotal:** central, essential

1088. **plague:** 1) trouble, affliction 2) annoy, bother 3) widespread disease, epidemic

1089. **plentiful:** abundant, generous

1090. **plug:** clog, seal

1091. **pore:** 1) hole, small opening 2) scan, examine

1092. **portable:** movable, able to be carried

1093. **portion:** part, segment

1094. **portrait:** picture, image

1095. **portray:** represent, depict

1096. **precede:** come before, anticipate

1097. **precious:** valuable, treasured

1098. **preclude:** prevent, rule out

1099. **preeminent:** foremost, most important

1100. **premise:** assumption, hypothesis

1101. **preposterous:** unbelievable, ridiculous

1102. **presuppose:** assume, surmise

1103. **prey:** victim, casualty

1104. **primordial:** primitive, earliest

1105. **principle:** basic method, standard

1106. **prize:** 1) value, appreciate 2) best, outstanding

1107. **prodigious:** massive, gigantic

1108. **proficient:** skillful, experienced

1109. **profuse:** abundant, plentiful

1110. **progressive:** increasing; advanced

1111. **prohibitive:** extreme, restrictive

1112. **prompt:** 1) efficient, precise 2) convince, provoke

1113. **promptly:** quickly, immediately

1114. **prone:** likely, susceptible

1115. **propagate:** multiply, reproduce

1116. **propel:** force out, throw

1117. **property:** characteristic, feature

1118. **proponent:** supporter, advocate

1119. **proportion:** percentage, ratio

1120. **proposal:** idea, suggestion

1121. **prowess:** exceptional ability, superior skill

1122. **proximity:** closeness, nearness

1123. **pursuits:** goals; activities, hobbies

1124. **puzzling:** difficult to explain, confusing

1125. **quality:** feature, aspect, value

1126. **quantify:** measure, count

1127. **quarters:** residences, homes

1128. **question:** challenge, investigate, doubt

1129. **questionable:** doubtful, uncertain

1130. **randomness:** lack of pattern, haphazard

1131. **range:** scope, extent

1132. **rapid:** accelerated, hasty

1133. **rapidly:** quickly, speedily

1134. **rapport:** bond, unity

1135. **rare:** very unusual, infrequent

1136. **rather:** instead, alternatively

1137. **ratio:** proportion, percentage, correlation

1138. **rational:** logical, realistic

1139. **ravage:** destroy, ransack

1140. **realm:** area, territory

1141. **recall:** remember, recollect

1142. **reciprocal:** mutual; corresponding

1143. **recompense:** payment, redemption

1144. **reconcile:** bring together, adjust

1145. **recurring:** repeated, persisting

1146. **reduce:** decrease, lessen

1147. **redundant:** superfluous, repetitious

1148. **reform:** remake, transform, improve

1149. **refrain from:** avoid, resist

1150. **refuge:** safety, shelter

1151. **refute:** disprove, discredit

1152. **regard:** consider, believe

1153. **regenerate:** renew, revive

1154. **regrettably:** unfortunately, grievously

1155. **reinforce:** strengthen, augment

1156. **relay:** transfer, deliver

1157. **release:** free, discharge

1158. **relentless:** cruel, merciless

1159. **relevant:** applicable, appropriate

1160. **reliable:** dependable, trustworthy

1161. **relish:** enjoy, cherish

1162. **relocate:** move, transfer

1163. **reluctant:** hesitant, unwilling

1164. **rely upon:** depend on, count on

1165. **reminisce:** recollect, remember

1166. **remote:** distant, faraway

1167. **remove:** eliminate, get rid of

1168. **renounce:** give up, reject

1169. **repel:** drive away, repulse

1170. **replicate:** reproduce, imitate

1171. **representative:** 1) characteristic 2) delegate, member

1172. **reproduce:** copy, duplicate

1173. **resolute:** firm, determined

1174. **respective:** particular, specific

1175. **resurgence:** comeback, revival

1176. **reveal:** show, make known

1177. **revolutionize:** fundamentally change, transform

1178. **revolve around:** focus on, center on

1179. **rim:** edge, border

1180. **robust:** healthy, strong

1181. **rough:** 1) coarse, irregular 2) unruly, belligerent

1182. **roundabout:** indirect, ambiguous

1183. **rupture:** break apart, split

1184. **sacred:** holy, blessed

1185. **saturate:** soak, drench

1186. **scanty:** insufficient, inadequate

1187. **scarce:** short in supply, limited

1188. **scatter:** distribute, diffuse

1189. **scenario:** situation, expected sequence of events

1190. **scope:** extent, range

1191. **score:** grade, outcome in game

1192. **scorn:** ridicule, contempt

1193. **scrupulous:** conscientious, careful

1194. **seamless:** perfectly smooth, flawless

1195. **secluded:** hidden, isolated

1196. **secure:** 1) safe, protected 2) ensure, obtain

1197. **sedentary:** settled, motionless

1198. **sediment:** deposits, dregs

1199. **seek to:** try to; inquire

1200. **segregate:** separate people by race; set apart

1201. **sensational:** 1) extraordinary, remarkable
                          2) shocking, scandalous

1202. **set:** fixed, definite

1203. **setback:** defeat, disappointment

1204. **sever:** cut off, disconnect

1205. **shape:** affect, influence

1206. **share:** portion, allotment

1207. **shortcoming:** disadvantage, weakness

1208. **shriveled:** dried up, wrinkled

1209. **signal:** communicate, indicate

1210. **simulate:** imitate, pretend, replicate

1211. **size up:** evaluate, analyze

1212. **sleek:** smooth, glossy

1213. **slightly:** somewhat, a little

1214. **solid:** fixed, substantial

1215. **solitary:** alone, isolated

1216. **somewhat:** to some degree, moderately

1217. **span:** extend across, stretch over

1218. **spark:** bring about, encourage

1219. **sparse:** scattered, rare

1220. **specifically:** specially, particularly

1221. **spectacular:** magnificent, wonderful

1222. **spectator:** viewer, observer

1223. **spectrum:** range, extent

1224. **spell:** interval, a certain period of time

1225. **sporadic:** occasional, irregular

1226. **sporadically:** infrequently, unusually

1227. **spot:** see, recognize

1228. **spur:** stimulate, incite

1229. **staggering:** overwhelming, shocking

1230. **stagnant:** inactive, motionless

1231. **stamp out:** eliminate, destroy

1232. **standpoint:** perspective, belief

1233. **startling:** surprising, frightful

1234. **state:** indicate, declare

1235. **status:** rank, position

1236. **steadily:** constantly, consistently

1237. **stem from:** originate from, come from

1238. **stockpile:** store up, amass

1239. **stratify:** layer, arrange

1240. **stream:** flow; supply

1241. **strenuous:** intense, difficult

1242. **stress:** 1) emphasize, accentuate 2) anxiety, tension

1243. **strictly:** rigorously, exclusively

1244. **string:** series, succession

1245. **stringent:** strict, rigid

1246. **stunning:** impressive, amazing

1247. **subordinate:** secondary, lesser

1248. **subterfuge:** trick, deceit

1249. **sue:** take strong legal action, bring legal charges against

1250. **sufficient:** enough, plentiful

1251. **sufficiently:** adequately, abundantly

1252. **suitable:** appropriate, acceptable

1253. **superb:** excellent, admirable

1254. **superficial:** not deep, shallow

1255. **superficially:** apparently, lightly

1256. **supplant:** replace, eject

1257. **sure:** certain, positive

1258. **surpass:** exceed, beat, outperform

1259. **surplus:** extra, leftover

1260. **susceptible to:** likely to be affected, vulnerable to

1261. **suspend:** dangle, hang from above

1262. **synthesis:** combination, fusion

1263. **tactic:** strategy, plan

1264. **tame:** 1) domesticated, compliant 2) pacify, subdue

1265. **tangible:** concrete, real

1266. **tantalizing:** teasing, tempting

1267. **temperate:** moderate, mild

1268. **tension:** strain, tightness

1269. **tentatively:** uncertainly; conditionally, provisionally

1270. **tentativeness:** hesitation, timidity

1271. **terrestrial:** land, earthly

1272. **to a great extent:** for the most part, generally

1273. **toxic:** noxious, poisonous

1274. **traditionally:** typically, customarily

1275. **transition:** change, alteration

1276. **transmit:** convey, send

1277. **transplant:** remove and place elsewhere

1278. **trespass:** invade, offend

1279. **trivial:** small, insignificant

1280. **turmoil:** unrest, chaos

1281. **unconsolidated:** loose, separate

1282. **undergo:** experience, endure

1283. **undisputed:** acknowledged, accepted

1284. **unthinkable:** inconceivable, incredible

1285. **unwieldy:** awkward, difficult to manage

1286. **urbane:** cultivated, civilized

1287. **vacate:** abandon, evacuate

1288. **variation:** difference, alternative

1289. **variety:** diversity, type

1290. **vehicle:** means, tool

1291. **venturesome:** bold, courageous

1292. **vital:** essential, crucial

1293. **vitality:** energy, vigor

1294. **vow:** promise, oath

1295. **wholesale:** extensive, widespread

1296. **wholly:** completely, entirely

1297. **with respect to:** with regard to, in terms of

1298. **withstand:** resist, endure

1299. **yearning:** longing, desire

1300. **yield:** produce, provide; bear

ANSWER
KEYS

Answer Keys

Chapter 1 Vocabulary

Warm Up   p. 10

1) subsequent   11) intervention
2) monotonous   12) vivid
3) unreasonable 13) spectacle
4) abstract   14) inscription
5) transmit   15) deflecting
6) forecast   16) construct
7) diagram   17) fidelity
8) bilateral   18) conceded
9) disabilities 19) chronology
10) derive   20) novelty

Quick Practice   p. 11

1) Ⓑ Because copyright laws ensure that an artist receives money for his or her work, we can deduce that they prevent *not approved* copying of a work of art.

2) Ⓓ If copyright laws "prevent unauthorized copying," they exist to make sure, or *promise*, that people "make money from their artistic expressions" without their ideas being stolen.

3) Ⓐ According to the passage, a person's work becomes his or her "intellectual property" *after* the person copyrights the work. *Henceforth* is similar in meaning to "After." The word with the closest meaning, then, is *Hereafter*.

4) Ⓒ Based on context, we can determine that "intellectual property" is defined as "an expression that has become a product." Thus, *that is* provides a transition between a term and its specific definition and therefore must mean *to be exact.*

5) Ⓐ "Copyright coverage extends for only a limited time" so "that cultural treasures…can be *feasibly* accessed." From this relationship, we can determine that the public can *easily* access material after the copyright runs out.

6) Ⓓ The last sentence states

that "copyright protection may vary…" due to "*disparate* circumstances"; the word with a meaning closest to *disparate* and "vary" is *different.*

7) Ⓑ The phrase "this *duration*" refers back to the "fixed terms," such as the 70-year fixed term for U.S. copyrighted material. Thus, *duration* is related to "terms" and "70 years," so *duration* must mean *span*, or a period of time.

8) Ⓒ If the answer choices are plugged in for the word *anonymous*, only *unidentified* is logical because copyright laws must be different if there is no one to assign the copyright to.

9) Ⓐ Initially, the rumba "did not catch on" because it "scandalized," or shocked, the public. The only hip movements that would shock people are ones that are *exaggerated* because such movements may infer sexuality.

10) Ⓒ Hyperbolic, or *exaggerated*, hip movements may infer sexuality, which would likely *shock*, or *scandalize*, the American public.

11) Ⓓ According to Paragraph 1, the rumba "has its roots in Afro-Cuban dances," so it likely originated in Cuba. Thus, "'Monsieur Pierre' went to Cuba to learn" the original, or *genuine*, version of the dance.

12) Ⓑ Because "Monsieur Pierre" was a dance teacher hoping to introduce the rumba to the rest of the world, it is likely that he was dedicated to learning the dance well, so he would have practiced *intensively*, which is a synonym for *strenuously.*

13) Ⓑ The root of the word *standardized* is "standard." When something is standard, it is the customary way. Similarly, the prefix *homo-* means

"same," another synonym for "standard." Thus, *homogenous* means uniform, or *standardized.*

14) Ⓐ Literally, a *cornerstone* is a stone that forms the base of a building. This can be determined from the passage because "a small group of dance specialists" created the *cornerstone* syllabus, so we can assume it gradually grew over time, but the original syllabus still provided the *foundation* "for teaching and competition."

15) Ⓒ Usually ballroom dancers hope to make their movements as smooth and natural as possible. Also, "steps are small," so a "*swaying* hip motion" is unlikely to be *tossing* or *jerking* because these words do not imply smoothness or small steps. Therefore, *swaying* must be closer in meaning to *rolling.*

16) Ⓓ If two people dance with each other, they are likely to face one another and move in coordination. Thus, *maintaining*, or *sustaining*, eye contact would be the best way to accomplish both of these.

17) Ⓓ We can determine that "fertile farmlands" caused settlers to move west. Thus, the "fertile farmland" must have been desirable and therefore *lured*, or tempted, settlers.

18) Ⓐ Because settlers were able to "gradually move inland along…rivers," we can conclude that the rivers could be easily traveled upon, so they were likely *accessible*, a synonym for *navigable.*

19) Ⓓ The passage implies that settlers *would have* gone to the Pacific Coast, except "they feared crossing rugged mountains" among other things. Because settlers would have gone there, we can determine that it was a *desirable*

location.

20) Ⓒ The word *rugged* is an adjective describing the mountains, and the best answer choice to characterize most mountains is *rocky*, which is a synonym for *rugged.*

21) Ⓑ Paragraph 2 states that the Gold Rush and the territories gained by a war "motivated people…to move" westward. Thus, these "Two events spurred, or *encouraged*, Americans to overcome their hesitation" and move west.

22) Ⓐ Because the Mexican-American War encouraged people to move westward, we can assume that the war resulted in the U.S. gaining territory from Mexico "that now constitutes [the U.S.] western states." If the U.S. gained territories, these regions must *comprise*, or make up, the western states.

23) Ⓑ Paragraph 2 claims that people "both *affluent* and poor" were drawn to California, forming a contrast between people who are *affluent* and people who are "poor." The opposite of poor is rich, which is a synonym for *prosperous.*

24) Ⓒ Because the Gold Rush attracted people from "Asia, South America, and many other regions of the world," we can infer that many people came to California. Therefore, to reflect this large number of people, *droves* must mean large groups, or *crowds.*

25) Ⓐ Paragraph 1 states that microwaves are "useful" because they are "*conducive* to transmitting information." Thus, *conducive* is related to microwaves' usefulness, meaning the microwaves are *suitable* for transmitting information.

26) Ⓑ The passage states that microwaves have "nonmilitary applications as well," one of

which it to "*convey* information."
If the answer choices are plugged
in for *convey*, the only choice that
is logical is that one of *microwaves' applications is to transmit
information.*

27) Ⓓ Because a magnetron
produces microwaves, we can
infer that it produces and then
directs them into a microwave
oven cavity, where they then heat
one's food.

28) Ⓒ *Haphazardly* means by
chance, or *randomly*. We can
infer this because the *haphazard*
activity of microwaves causes
food molecules to "bump into and
move other molecules," which
implies a reaction of *random*
movement between microwaves
and molecules.

29) Ⓓ In Paragraph 2, the
microwaves "*bombard* and penetrate" food molecules. In order
to penetrate something, you must
first make contact with it. The
only answer choice that implies
contact is *strike*.

30) Ⓐ *Poles* in this sense refers
to opposite *tips*, much like the
north and south magnetic *poles* at
the extreme end of Earth.

31) Ⓑ The molecules are
"pulled toward opposite electric
charges," which are located at
either end of the molecule. This
process causes the molecules to
pivot, or *rotate*, around in circles,
which provides heat in the form
of movement.

32) Ⓓ According to Paragraph
2, "the food's own water molecules cause the food to cook."
Therefore, if there are "more
water molecules in the food,"
then the food will cook faster, or
more *effectively*. Thus *efficacious*
is a synonym for *effective*.

33) Ⓐ Paragraph 1 describes
quilts as having practical and
artistic applications that are both
"functional" and "decorative."
These numerous uses indicate
that the quilt is a useful and
clever, or *ingenious*, product.

34) Ⓒ As a synonym for *flank*,
only *surround* makes sense in
context because insulation is
something that is generally contained. Therefore, the cloth must
surround the insulation.

35) Ⓓ Paragraph 1 indicates
that a quilt is *fastened* together

with "many tiny stitches." A
stitch is the result of one pass
of the needle when sewing, so
stitches must hold together, or
attach, pieces of cloth.

36) Ⓐ The final sentence of
Paragraph 1 describes a contrast
between *utilitarian* quilts and
quilts that "are highly prized as
art." The opposite of something
that cannot be used because it is
on display at a museum is *practical*, so *utilitarian* must mean
practical.

37) Ⓒ Paragraph 2 describes the
placement of "flowers, animals,
people, or symbols" onto a quilt.
Because these designs do not
help keep a person warm, they
must not be added for practical
reasons, so they are *decorative*.
To *embroider* is closest in meaning to *decorate*.

38) Ⓐ Paragraph 2 claims that
"quilts *commemorate* a…family
or historical event," meaning that
some sign of the event is depicted
on the quilt. To remember an
event as being important is to
honor it.

39) Ⓓ Because a quilt "honors
a *compelling* family or historical event," we can conclude that
the event must be important and
interesting to be worth honoring.

40) Ⓑ The passage as a whole
discusses general features of quilt
assembly. Thus, it makes sense
that quilts are *pieced together*, or
assembled, from "worn-out clothing" because the clothing can
replace the "cloth that flank[s] a
thick layer of insulation."

41) Ⓑ Because *fractures* are areas of land that have "slipped" or
"moved apart," we can conclude
that *fractures* are large *cracks*
underneath the ground.

42) Ⓓ The best hint for the
definition of *non-pliable* is in
Paragraph 2, where it states, "tension along the fault builds up like
a coiled spring." In order for tension to build up, one must have
a stiff, or *rigid*, material. Thus,
non-pliable is closest in meaning
to *rigid*.

43) Ⓐ Because the events that
may occur 25 million years from
now are impossible to predict
with accuracy, the best synonym
for *postulate* that expresses this
uncertainty is *hypothesize*.

44) Ⓐ The best hint for the
definition of *ruptured* is in
Paragraph 2, where it mentions
that "stored-up energy can cause
rock to suddenly crack and slide."
We can assume that this process
of cracking and sliding will occur
multiple times in the next 25 million years in California, meaning
that California may *rupture*, or
split completely.

45) Ⓑ Paragraph 2 contrasts
minute and "colossal" earthquakes. The passage claims that
"many earthquakes are *minute*,"
and because most earthquakes do
not cause much damage, we can
infer that "many earthquakes are
small."

46) Ⓒ Paragraph 2 contrasts
"minute" and *colossal* earthquakes. Because "minute"
earthquakes are small, *colossal*
earthquakes must be the opposite
of small, or *enormous*.

47) Ⓐ Minute/*small* and colos-
sal/*enormous* are indicators of
the *size* of an earthquake; thus,
magnitude must mean *size*.

48) Ⓒ Both *disorder* and *agitation* mean turbulence, but only
agitation fits in context because
an earthquake is an *agitation*, or
shaking, of the Earth's surface,
not a *disorder*, or lack of organization.

49) Ⓓ Paragraph 1 mentions
that Bishop "won *a myriad
of* awards," and while both
reputable and *exceptional* could
fit, the best answer is *numerous*
awards, as the Pulitzer Prize is
only one of many such awards.

50) Ⓐ The author indicates that
Bishop's *motifs* are more about
"deep emotional undercurrents"
than personal details of life. Thus,
we can conclude that *motifs* represent her main ideas, or *themes*.

51) Ⓓ An *undercurrent* is
something that is not apparent because it is indicated but not said,
and it is usually only discovered
after a careful analysis. Similarly,
a *connotation* is a deeper or
secondary meaning for a word or
expression.

52) Ⓓ In Paragraph 1, *swelling*
is closest in meaning to *rising*,
which can be determined because
swelling is being compared to
"spilling over," which occurs if a
water level *rises* too high.

53) Ⓐ The seal "in the water"
and the narrator being *immersed*
in [it] as well" implies that to be
immersed is to be surrounded, or
enveloped.

54) Ⓐ Because Bishop was
meticulous, she spent "years
revising a single poem." Thus, we
can conclude that Bishop spent a
lot of time ensuring that her work
was perfect, meaning that she
was very careful, or *fastidious*.

55) Ⓒ Paragraph 2 states that
Bishop "loved to travel," and
was able to do so because of "a
bequest from her father." This
bequest must have provided her
with the financial ability to travel
often, meaning a *bequest* is an
inheritance.

56) Ⓓ The author states that
"many of Bishop's poems" were
about the search for a feeling of
belonging. Thus, the topic that
she *dwelt on* was a major theme,
something that she *focused on*.

57) Ⓒ Paragraph 1 states that
Wind Cave "has not yet been fully explored." Thus, the *extensive*
cave must extend in all directions
and therefore be very *large*.

58) Ⓑ According to Paragraph
1, the "*drafts* of air" that "rush
out" of the cave led to naming
it Wind Cave. Thus, *drafts* are
related to "wind," so *drafts* is
closest in meaning to *currents* of
wind.

59) Ⓐ Paragraph 1 describes
the idea that the Wind Cave was
the *portal* between the world and
the underworld. Because a cave
connects the world's surface to
underground, a *portal* must be an
opening.

60) Ⓑ Because a "*gust* of wind"
supposedly "blew [the Lakota]
into the world," we can conclude
that *gust* has to do with wind.
Moreover, it would take a strong
wind to send someone from the
underworld to the surface of the
Earth, so a *gust* must be a *rush* of
wind.

61) Ⓑ Paragraph 1 implies that
the "gust of wind" was sent from
the underworld to the surface
of the Earth. Therefore, the gust
emanated, or *originated*, in the
underworld before coming to the
surface.

62) Ⓑ According to Paragraph
2, boxwork *adorns* the cave

walls, forming "complex geometrical" patterns. Therefore, it makes sense that "geometrical patterns" *decorate*, or *adorn*, the cave walls.

63) Ⓐ Because boxwork forms when minerals fill cracks in rocks, we can deduce that the minerals are *arranged* on the wall in the pattern of eroded rocks. Thus, *configurations* is closest in meaning to *arrangements*.

64) Ⓑ Although *decay* and *disintegrate* are similar in meaning, *decay* refers to the breaking down of organic, or living, material, whereas *disintegrate* means the breaking down of nonliving material. Because rocks are nonliving, *disintegrate* is the best synonym for *eroded* in context.

65) Ⓓ As the name implies, a "near-Earth object" is a space object that comes near Earth. Thus, its "*proximity* with Earth" must refer to its *nearness* to Earth.

66) Ⓑ Because NEOs come close to Earth, it makes sense that an NEO that may "collide with" Earth is one that may come too near to Earth and *crash into* it.

67) Ⓐ If scientists intend to mine NEOs for resources, they would have to *dispatch*, or *send*, a spacecraft to and NEO first.

68) Ⓑ A *depression* formed where "an asteroid struck [Earth] 65 million years ago," and we can infer that the asteroid made a large *hole*, so a *depression* must be the *hole* formed by an asteroid.

69) Ⓓ If an "*opaque* cloud" led to the extinction of "organisms, including dinosaurs," then we can conclude that this cloud was *impenetrable* by sunshine, leading to loss of plant life and food sources.

70) Ⓐ Because *opaque* means impenetrable, we can infer that sunlight could not penetrate such a cloud. Thus, a cloud that "*occluded* sunlight" *blocked* it out.

71) Ⓑ Paragraph 2 states that NEOs have either "landed in wilderness areas" or "*combusted* before" landing. Thus, we know that *combusted* NEOs do not reach land, but they would not disappear or melt because neither of those choices makes sense in context; so they must *burst* before they contact the ground.

72) Ⓒ According to Paragraph 2, an exploding NEO "*demolished* buildings and injured people." Thus, we can infer that *demolished* is similar in meaning to "injure." The answer choice closest in meaning to "injure" is *destroyed*, which fits in context.

73) Ⓑ We know that all the people of the Lost Generation were writers because the author begins by specifying "In the field of literature." Although both *novelists* and *writers* fit in context, *writers* is a better synonym for *scribes* because some of the people who were part of the Lost Generation were poets, playwrights, or essayists rather than novelists.

74) Ⓓ Because authors of the Lost Generation such as Ernest Hemingway and F. Scott Fitzgerald are very well known now, we can infer that their reputations "rose" to a high level, or they achieved *fame*.

75) Ⓓ Because the author gives a *list* of names shortly after mentioning the "Lost Generation *roster*," we can infer that *roster* means *list*.

76) Ⓐ The best hint for the meaning of expatriate is in Paragraph 3, when the author mentions that Hemingway wrote about "aimless young Americans living in Paris." Because Lost Generation writers "lived in Paris as *expatriates*," we can infer that an *expatriate* is someone living in *exile* from his or her home country, which was apparently America for many writers.

77) Ⓐ Words used to describe Lost Generation writers are *disillusioned*, "aimless," and of course "lost." The answer choice with the closest meaning to these adjectives is *disenchanted*, which is an appropriate synonym for *disillusioned*.

78) Ⓑ According to the author, Gertrude Stein supposedly invented and defined the phrase Lost Generation. Thus, *coined the term* is closest in meaning to *created the phrase*.

79) Ⓒ Although the author implies that Hemingway's book is not about a happy subject (aimless young Americans), the title is optimistic because a rising Sun is often a sign of hope. Therefore, the title *emphasizes* "Hemingway's hopeful view...."

80) Ⓐ Although Hemingway presents his generation as "aimless," the author states that he also has a "hopeful view" that they "will be *resilient*." Thus, *resilient* expresses an optimistic emotion about human character and is closest in meaning to *irrepressible*, or not possible to keep down.

Chapter 2 Referent

Warm Up   p. 27

1) they
2) all
3) it
4) him
5) which
6) their
7) the term
8) both
9) the former
10) several
11) it
12) whose
13) them
14) the other
15) its
16) emphases
17) a mistake
18) much
19) it
20) their

Quick Practice   p. 28

1) Ⓐ The pronoun appears in a sentence that basically says: the term describes people like this and *people* (*who are*) like that. Thus, the referent is *people*.

2) Ⓒ Because *Mexico, Central America, and South America* encompass a huge area with many different cultures, it makes sense to characterize them as having *diversity*, especially because the countries directly precede the highlighted word.

3) Ⓓ Often the words "one" and *another* pair together. Therefore, the noun phrase following "one" will apply to *another* as well, and it makes sense to say "*another reason for the large U.S. Hispanic population....*"

4) Ⓐ The sentence that begins with *These* continues the discussion of *areas that were once Spanish or Mexican* territories. Thus, it makes sense that *These* refers back to the areas that were discussed in the previous sentence.

5) Ⓒ Both the sentence that begins with *He or she* and the one that precedes it focus on characteristics of a *rap artist*. Thus, it makes sense to keep the subject consistent throughout the two sentences, meaning that *He or she* must refer to the subject of the previous sentence, the *rap artist*.

6) Ⓒ Like much of Paragraph 1, the sentence containing the pronoun *most* focuses on rap artist characteristics. Using "a strong beat, personal lyrics" refers to qualities of rap *artists*, so *most* refers back to *artists* mentioned in the previous sentence.

7) Ⓑ *Percussive breaks* is the closest plural noun phrase that precedes *them*, and it makes sense to say that DJs "used two turntables to extend *percussive breaks*."

8) Ⓓ Paragraph 2 states that DJs "isolated the percussive breaks, then used two turntables to extend them." Furthermore, the paragraph states that *This technique* "created a rhythmic base" for artists to rap over, indicating that it is a musical technique. From this, we can infer that *This technique* refers to *an isolation-and-extension method* because the other answer choices do not refer to a musical procedure.

9) Ⓒ *Water was present for life's origins* is the closest plural noun phrase that precedes *This assumption*, and it makes sense in context since water's presence on Earth millions of years ago is an assumption; no one was around to confirm the claim.

10) Ⓓ Because "break[ing] down organic matter into nutrients" is a *role* that an organism might have, it makes sense that *these* refers to *roles*, which is an applicable, plural, and preceding noun.

11) Ⓑ Because "break[ing] down organic matter into nutrients" is the nearest process that precedes the word *process*, we can conclude that *process* is standing in for *breaking down*.

12) Ⓐ In the final sentence, *researchers* are the only nouns mentioned that would be able to "deduce" anything. Thus, *they* must refer to *researchers*, which makes sense in context.

13) Ⓓ *Regular competitions* is the closest plural noun phrase that precedes *these*, and it makes sense to say "The most important and prestigious of [the] *regular* competitions...."

14) (A) The *many reasons* for athletic competitions show that there was a *convergence* [union] *of purposes* for people to attend these events. Therefore, *convergence of purposes* refers back to the *many reasons* listed in the previous sentence.

15) (B) *Contestants* is the closest plural noun that precedes *they*, and it makes sense to state "... as long as *contestants* were male, not enslaved, and ethnically Greek."

16) (A) *Competing in the nude* is the closest singular noun phrase that precedes *factor*, and it makes sense in context more than the other choices, since substituting "*competing in the nude*...[would lead] to married women being excluded from watching."

17) (C) Because the process of an "object that is orbiting [something] and then flies out of rotation" accurately describes *centrifugal force*, which can be considered a natural "phenomenon," it makes sense that *the same phenomenon* refers to *centrifugal force*.

18) (B) *Prehistoric people* is the closest plural noun phrase that precedes *They*, and it makes sense to say that "*Prehistoric people* nestled a rock in a leather pouch...."

19) (D) Centrifugal means "to flee from the center," and *centripetal* describes the process that opposes centrifugal force, so *centripetal* must be *the term* that means "to seek the center."

20) (A) The final sentence of Paragraph 2 discusses two ways that centripetal force works, which are 1) "because something is holding the *object*" on a curved path, or 2) "because something is stopping it." Thus, *it* refers back to the *object* that is either held in orbit or stopped from leaving orbit.

21) (B) *More connection* is the closest singular noun phrase that precedes *this*, and it makes sense to say that "as a consequence of *more connection*, society experiences...."

22) (D) A reflexive pronoun, such as himself, herself, or *themselves*, is generally used for em-

phasis and refers back to the noun or noun phrase that immediately precedes it, which is *workers* in this case.

23) (D) The clause containing *several* is discussing multilingual people who speak "their native language and at least one more [language]." Because "one more" refers back to "language," it makes sense that *several* also refers back to *other languages*.

24) (C) *Having a lingua franca* is the closest singular noun phrase that precedes *trend*, and it makes sense to say that *having a lingua franca* "is also leading to the extinction of thousands of languages...."

25) (A) *The House Committee on Un-American Activities* is the closest singular noun phrase that precedes the pronoun *its*, and it makes sense to say that "He turned *HUAC*'s attention...."

26) (C) The first sentence of Paragraph 2 describes the relationship between the *accuser* and Hiss. Therefore, it makes sense to say that "Hiss had passed secret government documents to the *accuser*" because *him* must refer to a male, and the accuser is the only male other than Hiss in the sentence.

27) (B) *It* refers to a crime that Hiss could not be tried for. Because *spying* is the only crime mentioned in the sentence, *it* must refer to *spying*.

28) (D) Because *there* is a demonstrative pronoun that refers to a place, and the *Soviet Union* is the only place mentioned in the sentence, *there* must refer to the "recently dissolved *Soviet Union*."

29) (B) "Some" and *others* are pronouns that often pair together. Therefore, if "some" refers to *characters*, and *others* pairs with "some," then *others* must also be referring to *characters*.

30) (D) "*Real humans*" is the closest possible referent for the pronoun *anyone*, since anyone generally refers to a person. Moreover, it makes sense to say that a "comprehensive photographic memory has never been proven in *humans*."

31) (A) Paragraph 2 discusses the ability of some children to

recall details of an image shortly after seeing it. Yet their memories were not completely photographic because, according to the passage, "after a few minutes passed, they remembered less of the *image*."

32) (A) Paragraph 2 focuses on the ability of *short-term photographic memory* present in some children. Because this is the only ability mentioned in the paragraph, *unusual ability* must refer to *short-term photographic memory*.

33) (C) Although *it* can refer to both the *Orsay Museum* and the *collection* contained within, the *collection* is a better choice because it more closely precedes the pronoun *it*, and people likely "flock to see the *collection*" rather than the building that forms the *Orsay Museum* itself.

34) (C) According to the passage, *the originals* are something that people pay a high price for, and Paragraph 1 states that "Impressionist and post-Impressionist paintings...are among the most highly valued." Therefore, *the originals* refers to *Impressionist paintings*.

35) (D) The *1870s* period is the only time frame mentioned in Paragraph 2, so *the time* must be referring to *1870s*.

36) (D) Monet's process of *applying fresh paint to wet layers* is the nearest applicable process to the phrase *the practice*, and it makes sense to say, "*Applying fresh paint to wet layers* resulted in soft, intermingled edges."

37) (B) *Dry farming* is the closest possible referent that describes a process for the phrase *the method*, and it makes sense to say that "*dry farming* will work in locations...."

38) (D) *Varieties* refers to something that is "deep-rooted and drought-tolerant," and *crops* is the closest plural noun that can be described as "deep-rooted and drought-tolerant."

39) (C) The pronoun *these* describes plants that are "good candidates" for dry farming, and the previous sentence states that "good candidates" are *deep-rooted and drought-tolerant [plants]*. Therefore, it makes sense that

these refers to such *plants*.

40) (A) The final sentence makes a comparison between dry farmers' *products* and "*those [products]* of wetter regions." In order to be logical, comparisons must compare two of the same thing, so *those* must refer to *products*.

Chapter 3 Fact & Detail

Warm Up   p. 43

1) O	6) F	11) O	16) F
2) O	7) O	12) F	17) O
3) F	8) F	13) F	18) F
4) F	9) F	14) F	19) O
5) O	10) O	15) O	20) O

Quick Practice   p. 44

1) (C) Froebel stressed "the impact of early childhood learning on later academic development," which means he recognized that *early learning improves subsequent achievement*.

2) (A) Paragraph 1 states that "children, like plants, need to be given time, nurturing, and resources...." Thus, "garden of children" indicates that *young children should be treated* like plants in a garden.

3) (D) Because kindergarten gave children "time for singing, dancing, gardening, and playing with toys," it allowed time for social interaction and *many hands-on activities*.

4) (B) According to Paragraph 2, Froebel trained kindergarten teachers, so *he trained teachers....*

5) (C) Before Spanish arrival, the fluid from rubber trees was used for "waterproof shoes," which is an example of *impermeable footwear*.

6) (A) Paragraph 1 states that *caoutchouc* is "a white fluid... from rubber trees." Thus, it is a *milky substance from a tropical plant*.

7) (B) Rubber becomes "sticky in hot weather and stiff in cold" weather, which means it is *not useful at temperature extremes*.

8) (C) Paragraph 2 states that "Goodyear worked for years," so *he persevered*, and "he discovered how to produce weather-resistant rubber" by accident. Thus, he also was *lucky*.

9) (B) EEGs measure "the con-

tinuous electrical activity of neurons [that] occurs in patterns," so it *detects cycles in electrical activity.*

10) Ⓑ Paragraph 1 claims that EEGs "provide information about both normal brain activity (*healthy functioning*) and about irregularities (*brain problems*)."

11) Ⓓ In Paragraph 2, "the frequency of the brain waves" is *how often* (frequently) *an electric pattern occurs.*

12) Ⓒ Because Paragraph 2 states that beta waves reveal "taxing mental activities" and alpha waves indicate "relaxing activities," clearly EEGs reveal a subject's *level of alertness or calmness.*

13) Ⓒ Because air pressure is a measure "of how much the air's weight is pressing down on the Earth's surface," we can conclude that air pressure is *how heavy the air is.*

14) Ⓑ The jet stream causes air molecules to either "pile up (*converge*)"or "radiate out (*disperse*)."

15) Ⓑ If "Rising air frequently forms clouds, and clouds are more likely to bring rain," then *when air molecules ascend, they form rain clouds.*

16) Ⓐ Paragraph 2 states that clouds "act as a shade during the day (*reflect solar heat*) and a blanket at night (*retain surface warmth*) for Earth."

17) Ⓒ According to Paragraph 1, "Humor is an inherently social phenomenon (*intrinsically communal*)," but it "is also contagious (*infectious*)."

18) Ⓐ A funny event requires "a non-serious context," which means *people perceive that it is lighthearted* rather than serious.

19) Ⓓ An event becomes comedic when "someone does or says something unexpected," so that event must be *inconsistent* with *expectations.*

20) Ⓒ Paragraph 3 states that "People in virtually all cultures value humor (*it is cross-cultural*).... Humans begin to laugh as infants (*it is socially innate*)," and "Apes also laugh when playing (*it is cross-species*)."

21) Ⓒ Paragraph 1 emphasizes that Holzer exhibits work "to a

wide audience (*a broad spectrum of people*) outside of museums through printed and electronic signs (*with written commentary*)."

22) Ⓐ Because conceptual artists "believe that an idea...is the principle element in an art object," we can conclude that they *place more emphasis on meaning* (an idea) *than on appearance.*

23) Ⓑ Because Holzer's work contains "truisms" as well as "clichés, philosophical sayings, and controversial comments," we can deduce that her artistic *statements and documents* [are meant to provoke] *thinking.*

24) Ⓓ Paragraph 2 mentions "*posters* with clichés," "*projected* declassified government documents," "inscribed silver spoons (*eating utensils*)," "marble benches (*stone seating*)," and "electric *LED lighting.*"

25) Ⓓ Paragraph 1 states that "infectious fluid" "can also become airborne (*breathing air around infected people*), and that *physical* "contact with an infected person" may also spread the virus.

26) Ⓐ Because "90 to 95 percent of the native population died from smallpox," we can conclude that smallpox had the effect of *depopulation.* The answer is not *genocide* because that entails the intentional rather than accidental killing of populations.

27) Ⓑ Paragraph 2 states that, because "bloodletting" was ineffective and dangerous, English colonists *asked others*, or "turned to Native Americans or Africans for home medicines."

28) Ⓓ Bloodletting was a means to cure "an imbalance of the body's *humors*, or fluids," by *reducing a fluid that was out of proportion* via draining it from the body.

29) Ⓓ Soil contains microbes, which "*produce* inorganic elements," and protozoa, which "eat bacteria," acting as *consumers.*

30) Ⓒ Microbes "digest organic materials (*organic waste*)...and produce inorganic elements," which "Plants depend on...for *nutrients.*"

31) Ⓓ In rhizosphere, plant "roots release nutrients for mi-

crobes" and "microbes mineralize nutrients for the plant." Thus, a system in which *microbes and plants benefit each other* is created.

32) Ⓐ Because "Herbicides... can usually be broken down quickly by microbes, but some pesticides...cannot" be broken down, we can conclude that *microbes can break down some more easily than others.*

33) Ⓐ Paragraph 1 describes feng shui as the "Chinese art of arranging a...space (*art of object placement*) to promote...happiness and health (*free energy flow*)" through good chi flow.

34) Ⓑ In Paragraph 1, "chi can be blocked or misguided in a space, which can be destructive"; so feng shui warns against *unbalanced or blocked* chi *energy.*

35) Ⓑ Feng shui has "five elements," an element being a *simple but essential material*, such as wood, or *phenomena*, such as fire.

36) Ⓓ Feng shui promotes balancing the major elements in a space by *recognizing an object's major element* and emphasizing *appropriate* "placement of an object" for maximum chi flow.

37) Ⓑ The author mentions that *King Kong* was released during the "financially devastating Great Depression," so we can conclude that *Americans were struggling economically.*

38) Ⓓ *King Kong* "was a smash success" because of "trick photography (*special effects*) and exotic settings (*intriguing locales*)."

39) Ⓐ In Paragraph 2, the film producer tells a member of the ship's crew that "the Beast's love for the Beauty made him 'soft.'" Thus, the producer indirectly advised *a tough sailor not to fall in love.*

40) Ⓑ Kong tries to rescue Ann by taking "her to the top of the Empire State Building," an action that *inadvertently endangers* Ann when Kong was seeking to protect her.

Chapter 4 Negative Fact

Warm Up   **p. 59**

1) C	6) B	11) C	16) D
2) B	7) C	12) D	17) B
3) A	8) A	13) C	18) B
4) A	9) C	14) A	19) C
5) C	10) E	15) D	20) E

Quick Practice   **p. 60**

1) Ⓓ Because Wood taught "people to read two to five times faster," we can conclude that she did not believe that *reading speed was immutable*, or unchangeable.

2) Ⓑ According to Paragraph 1, "faster readers actually retained more information," so one does not have to *sacrifice some amount of comprehension* for speed reading.

3) Ⓐ Bad reading habits include "'saying' each word mentally (*internally 'pronouncing' each word*)," "rereading a sentence or phrase (*needlessly looking back*)," and "stumbling on long words (*reading lengthy words with difficulty*)." But *skipping sections* is not mentioned.

4) Ⓒ Fast readers are known for "setting a purpose (*reason for reading*)," "focusing completely (*concentrating fully*)," and "looking at groups of words (*moving... between clusters of words*)." Reading *only the topic sentence* is not mentioned.

5) Ⓐ The author states that people "make decorative model ships for enjoyment (*to decorate the home* and *to divert oneself*)" and "to test designs (*to try out certain designs*)." Yet the author never mentions building ships *to keep a record.*

6) Ⓒ Ancient people used models for "toys (*play and amusement*)," "funerary offerings (*burial for the dead*)" and in "prayers for safe travel (*during prayer*)." Model ships were not used *to plan and navigate sea voyages.*

7) Ⓑ Model ships "range from matchbook-sized (*a few centimeters long*) to just large enough for a person (*can hold a person*)," and "Some are models of particular ships (*exact replicas of existing ships*)." But the author does not state they *are as big as regular vessels.*

8) Ⓐ Though the passage says that putting ships in bottles adds to the building challenge

of model ship construction, the author does not state that they *always require more…work than any other model.*

9) (B) In Paragraph 1, ethnography is described as the "study of a given community's customs and other aspects of its culture." Thus, such a broad field of study does not *mainly chronicle parenting strategies*, though that may be one facet of ethnography.

10) (A) Although ethnographers must "live with the group" that they study, the author does not claim that they must become *a leader of the community* that they are studying.

11) (C) Paragraph 2 claims that ethnographers must "maintain an objective viewpoint (*objectivity*)…, interact closely with the group's members (*empathy* and *impartiality*)," and balance "fact with interpretation (*factuality with elucidation*)." However, ethnography is not supposed to include *criticism*.

12) (B) Because ethnography "usually requires the researcher to live with the group," we can conclude that *studying a people's way of life without their knowledge* is not a practiced method.

13) (A) Compared to marine dolphins, river dolphins "have *smaller eyes*," have snouts "four times longer than…marine dolphins (*longer nose and mouth structures*)," and their "necks are flexible (*pliable necks*)." Dolphins' brains, however, are not mentioned.

14) (C) Threats to river dolphins include "dams (*constructed barriers*), pollution (*toxins*)… and noise (*sounds that interfere with hearing*)," but *competition from other species* is not mentioned.

15) (D) River dolphins live "in estuaries (*where the rivers and the sea meet*)" and "in waterways…bordered by vast human populations (*human populations are dense*)." The "*baiji* dolphin… is thought to be extinct (*a species disappeared*)," but the author does not mention a preference for *rivers that are equatorial.*

16) (D) According to Paragraph 2, river dolphins have smaller eyes and longer snouts than marine dolphins, so it is NOT true

that *they are indistinguishable from marine dolphins.*

17) (C) Because Bierce "took pride in being an outspoken cynic…," we can conclude that he did not *inspire many people with his hopefulness.*

18) (C) As a Union soldier, Bierce was involved in "violent battles (*took part in violence*)," possibly forged his cynical viewpoint (*became distrustful*), and wrote a story from "the view of a Confederate sympathizer (*able to imagine…opposing perspectives*)." However, the author does not mention *nostalgia for his youth.*

19) (A) Paragraph 3 mentions that Bierce was "editing a newspaper called the *Wasp* (*jobs that Bierce held*)." The passage also gives examples of "satirical word definitions" he published, but it does not talk about the literature he criticized.

20) (B) Because one of Bierce's definitions mocks both liberals and conservatives, and because the author makes no mention of Bierce's political affiliations, we cannot conclude that *Bierce was a political conservative.*

21) (B) Although the passage states that "physicists including Albert Einstein" established principles of physics, the author does not state that physics *originated with the discoveries of Albert Einstein.*

22) (B) Paragraph 1 says that sometimes particles "are depicted as dots," but not that physicists hypothesize that *forces…look like dots.*

23) (A) String theory postulates that "all matter and force come from different oscillations of tiny strings or loops." Thus, different vibrations determine particles' qualities, not *different types of strings.*

24) (D) According to the passage, these strings are *incomprehensibly slight* – very, very small – and move in 11 dimensions (seven more than we can perceive). Also, strings themselves are "one-dimensional (*neither two-dimensional nor three-dimensional*)." But the speed of their *oscillating movement* is not mentioned.

25) (C) Paragraph 1 states that Wisconsin is "known for its dairy (*milk and cheese*)," contains "lead in its southwestern hills (*large deposits of sought-after metal*)" that "brought the first wave of European settlement," so miners rather than farmers were the first to arrive. The author does not mention *mountainous terrain.*

26) (A) Because miners were given "the nickname 'badgers'" for their "solitary" lifestyle, we can conclude that they did not *bring their families and root themselves in one place.*

27) (B) The badger is "a solitary animal that sleeps in burrows (*sleeps alone in subterranean homes*)"; badgers "are brisk diggers (*expertise is…digging*)," and are known for "growling ferociously (*clamorous threats*)." Yet they are not characterized as *serene in temperament.*

28) (D) The badger was a symbol for lead prospectors, but not all *European-American colonists* were prospectors; thus, the badger does not stand for all European-American colonists, only the ones involved in lead mining.

29) (C) Titan is "orbiting the planet Saturn," so it is NOT *one of the moons of Jupiter.*

30) (B) Paragraph 2 states that the "probe parachuted down through the…atmosphere," so it was NOT *propelled to the surface with rocket technology.*

31) (A) Titan has "rains of liquid methane (*evidence of precipitation*)," "pale hills (*lighter-colored slopes*)," and "a dark plain (*dark…dry gullies*)." Paragraph 2 makes no mention of *nitrogen snow.*

32) (D) Paragraph 3 claims that "Titan's core is not solid," so it is NOT true that Titan *has a solid, rocky center.*

33) (D) Although "both [political] parties were divided within themselves over the issue of slavery," Paragraph 1 does not mention that *each faction found it impossible to negotiate at all.*

34) (A) Paragraph 2 states that "members of both major political parties were attracted to join" the Free Soil Party, so we cannot conclude that *it was mainly a*

disgruntled segment of the Whig Party.

35) (C) Although Paragraph 3 mentions that "Congress abruptly opened the door to slavery" in new western territories, it only elaborates on Republican reactions, NOT the reactions of *voters in the new western territories.*

36) (A) Paragraph 3 states that the Republican Party was formed by "all three parties," and they "opposed allowing slavery (*forced labor*) in new territories…[and] launched a successful presidential campaign when they nominated Abraham Lincoln." The passage does not mention that they *wanted land.*

37) (A) Paragraph 1 mentions that "People have set fires on high places for millennia," but it never specifies what these fires use for fuel, so we cannot conclude that the fires *were generally fueled by wood.*

38) (B) The Pharos "guided ships into the port at Alexandria," but the passage does not indicate that it *indicated treacherous seas.*

39) (B) Although the lighthouse in Boston had "a canon for auditory signaling in foggy weather," there is no indication that the candles in the lighthouse were *constantly obscured by atmospheric vapor.*

40) (D) According to the passage, "The Great Wall of China (*a barrier in ancient China*)…made use of beacons," "the Mayan people built shrines…that doubled as lighthouses (*in religious settings*)," and beacons "were commonly used in castles…in the British Isles (*regions of Great Britain*)." The author does not mention beacon use on Pacific trade routes.

Chapter 5 Coherence

Warm Up   p. 75

1) 2-1-3	6) 1-2-3
2) 3-2-1	7) 2-3-1
3) 3-2-1	8) 2-3-1
4) 1-2-3	9) 1-3-2
5) 3-1-2	10) 2-3-1

Quick Practice   p. 76

1) (C) The sentence after letter [B] gives examples of "obvious" sources of indoor air pollu-

tion. The added sentence adds information about *less noticeable sources*. Thus, the added sentence must be placed at [C] because it continues the discussion about examples of air pollution.

2) Ⓖ The added sentence contains the phrase *such substances can clog filter pores* but does not specify what *such substances* are. We must refer to the clogging substances identified as "large amounts of dust" mentioned after letter [F]. Hence, the added sentence should be placed at letter [G].

3) Ⓑ The added sentence discusses the electrical charges of systems with "an unequal number of protons and electrons," a discussion started after letter [A]. Therefore, we must place the added sentence at letter [B] to add information about electrons, protons, and ionization.

4) Ⓗ The sentence that follows letter [G] discusses the basic properties of baking soda. Because the added sentence adds information about the practical uses of baking soda, it is logical to have the added sentence follow these basic properties. Thus the added sentence should be placed at letter [H].

5) Ⓐ The main idea in Paragraph 1 focuses on specific reasons people might desire an object. The added sentence introduces this main idea using a non-specific example about *Marketing managers*, so the added sentence should introduce the paragraph and be placed at letter [A].

6) Ⓖ The sentence that follows letter [F] discusses the psychology of "easily attainable" items. The added sentence elaborates upon the concept of easily attainable items because something that *has already been given* to a person is easily attainable.

7) Ⓒ The end of Paragraph 1 discusses the origins of the Gothic style. The sentence that follows letter [B] discusses what people used to believe about the origins of Gothic style, but the added sentence contrasts this statement by showing what *Researchers now believe* about Gothic origins. Thus, the added sentence should come after the

idea that it contrasts.

8) Ⓕ The sentence after letter [F] discusses the benefits of an arched roof, and the added sentence explains how the arched roofs are so stable. Because how something works should come before its practical applications, the added sentence should be placed at [F].

9) Ⓓ Paragraph 1 gives specific information on eviction. The sentence after [C] describes first steps, while the added sentence describes more extreme procedures. We can deduce that the added sentence should follow the general eviction procedures and therefore should be placed at letter [D].

10) Ⓕ The sentence following letter [E] discusses the qualities necessary for a living space to be "fit for habitation." The added sentence directly contrasts these "fit" living conditions by describing an "*unfit*" living space. Thus, the contrasting added sentence should be placed at letter [F].

11) Ⓓ The added sentence explains the reason for the Fed's *unique structure*, which we can deduce, refers back to the Fed being "a combination of public and private sectors," as mentioned in the sentence following letter [C]. Therefore, the added sentence should follow at letter [D].

12) Ⓗ In the added sentence, *They* refers to the southerners, who "opposed the idea" of the Fed because, as the added sentence elaborates, *it would be unconstitutional*. Because the added sentence begins describing reasons that southerners opposed the Fed, it should be placed at letter [H], right after the idea of opposition is introduced.

13) Ⓐ The sentence that follows letter [A] explains one of the potential health benefits of poultices, but the general purpose of poultices is introduced in the added sentence's statement that poultices *increase healing to wounded...parts of the body.* Therefore, the added sentence should precede the explanation and be placed at letter [A].

14) Ⓔ The sentence following letter [E] begins, "When [patches] can be used...." Thus,

the added sentence should be placed before it at [E] to explain a limitation on their use.

15) Ⓒ The phrase *His character* in the added sentence indicates that it follows a sentence that included a singular, masculine noun. Mr. Punch, described in the sentence preceding [C], is the only noun that fits these qualifications. Thus, *His character* must refer to "Mr. Punch," and the added sentence adds to his description, so it must belong at letter [C].

16) Ⓔ The added sentence provides general, introductory information about the variable plots of Punch and Judy. Thus, the added sentence would best serve as an introduction to Paragraph 2, which discusses plot features.

17) Ⓓ Paragraph 1 describes the series of events that culminate in a heart attack. The added sentence states that *the patient may recover*, and the only thing one would need to recover from in Paragraph 1 is a heart attack. Therefore, the added sentence should conclude Paragraph 1.

18) Ⓖ The added sentence focuses on the future of heart treatment, which is only mentioned in the last sentence of Paragraph 2. Thus, [G] is the best place for the added sentence because it introduces general information about future technology that is elaborated upon in the final sentence of the paragraph.

19) Ⓑ In the added sentence the pronoun *Each* refers back to "The cells of plants...[and] the cells of animals." Therefore, the added sentence should follow the introductory sentence and be placed at letter [B].

20) Ⓕ The sentence that follows letter [F] begins with "The reactions," which refers back to the *resulting chemical reactions* mentioned in the added sentence. Therefore, for "The reactions" to have any meaningful context, the added sentence must be placed at letter [F].

Chapter 6 Inference

Warm Up   **p. 91**

1) B	5) B	9) B	13) B	17) A
2) A	6) A	10) A	14) A	18) B
3) A	7) B	11) A	15) B	19) A
4) A	8) A	12) B	16) A	20) B

Quick Practice   **p. 93**

1) Ⓑ Because it was the "geologist at the British Natural History Museum" who "presented scientific papers about the 'Piltdown man'" rather than amateur archaeologist Dawson, we can infer that Dawson used *an expert's reputation to validate his claims*.

2) Ⓓ Because "discovered" is placed in quotes, we can infer that he fabricated his second fossil find. Also, "public doubt seemed to dissipate" after his second fossil, so we can conclude that he *contrived a second find to quiet scientific challenges*.

3) Ⓒ A geologist studies the formation and history of the Earth, and the geologist mentioned in the passage misidentified every fossil sent by Dawson. Therefore, we can infer that the geologist *had little expertise in zoology*, or the study of animals.

4) Ⓐ Paragraph 2 states that "There was excitement that early human remains had finally been found in English soil." Because the author mentions that the excitement was centered around "English soil," the Piltdown Man was associated with England and likely generated *national pride*.

5) Ⓐ Although not mentioned in the passage, we can infer that a dog's sensitive sense of smell developed, or *evolved*, over many generations, making (A) the only safe assumption.

6) Ⓓ A dog's "olfactory lobe... is 40 times larger than that in a human," and a dog has well over 100 million more scent receptors. Because a dog's anatomy has evolved to contain large scent processors, we can assume these processors are *more effective than those in humans*.

7) Ⓒ Because dogs search for an animal's "den, nest, or waste materials," we can infer that they determine *where an animal has been even after it has moved on* based upon scents the animal left behind.

8) Ⓓ Dogs are able to locate

"whale feces," which are left behind after a whale has left an area. Thus, by locating whale feces, dogs can *indicate where a whale has been*.

9) **B** Wood was inspired to paint *American Gothic* after seeing a farmhouse "window that looked like…a Gothic cathedral window." Thus, it is likely that something about the contrast between the opulence of cathedral architecture and the austerity of farm life tied into his main idea.

10) **A** Wood was "recruiting his sister" for the painting, so we can infer that she was not a farmer by trade (a recruit is someone who is new at something), and the passage states that the man was based on Wood's dentist. Thus, neither *led the life that the painting depicts*.

11) **D** After newspapers printed Wood's painting, it garnered "a range of reactions," which implies that many people viewed the work of art. Moreover, "Wood went on to create many more… paintings," indicating that he was able to continue a professional painting career after the release of *American Gothic*. Thus, we can infer that the work *helped establish Wood professionally*.

12) **C** Paragraph 2 states that "Some art critics assumed" one thing about the painting's meaning, but "others believed" something else entirely. Moreover, the painting garnered "a range of reactions," meaning people *interpreted* the figures in the painting *in many ways*.

13) **B** America was experiencing "domestic and international conflicts" during the 1960s, and *Star Trek*'s plots involved solving problems such as "war or discrimination." Thus, we can infer that the themes of *Star Trek* involved issues that were *socially and politically relevant to Americans in the 1960s*.

14) **B** Because *Star Trek* only aired for three seasons, but "it was rerun frequently" in later years, which helped it earn a cult following, we can infer that many fans *were exposed to the show through reruns*.

15) **D** *Star Trek* addressed issues such as war and dis-

crimination, so it likely *increased optimism about peace*, and its characters were "international science professionals," so it *increased optimism…about international cooperation*.

16) **C** Paragraph 3 states that technologies like cell phones and Bluetooth technology resemble *Star Trek's* fictional technology, and "some inventors have said that…*Star Trek* gave them ideas for desirable…devices," so it is likely that "some inventors" purposely *set out to create devices they remembered from Star Trek*.

17) **C** The passage implies that many people believed in an "objective reality," or universal truths. Modernists rejected this convention by claiming everything is subjective. Thus, Modernists *questioned principles that had always seemed obvious*.

18) **D** Modernist painters "concentrated on how they… saw shape and color;" thus, we can infer that Modernist artists wanted to explore the world from their *unique perspectives*.

19) **A** Because "Postmodern artists and an art viewer are co-constructors of the viewing experience," we can infer that Postmodernists want to *be more interactive with the audience*.

20) **C** Postmodernism "emphasized multiple perspectives," which means that a postmodern work of art may draw inspiration from many cultures. Thus, a postmodern symphony would likely *incorporate music from many cultures*.

21) **B** Vespucci traveled "across the treacherous Atlantic Ocean," a journey that likely required him to *risk his safety*, to find "a lucrative trade route," which would *increase his trading opportunities*.

22) **C** Because Vespucci "studied the stars [and] estimated longitude" during his voyages, we can infer that he *applied astronomy and geometry to discern his ships' locations*.

23) **A** Paragraph 2 states that a major difference between Vespucci's and Columbus' letters was that "unlike Columbus, Vespucci realized that the land he was seeing was… another [new]

continent." Vespucci's letters included this revelation and outsold Columbus' journals. Thus, people likely read Vespucci's letters because they were *amazed that a large, unknown landmass existed*.

24) **B** Vespucci's letters claiming that there was a "New World" across the Atlantic Ocean had "created a sensation among Europeans," and thus we can conclude that the German cartographer was more *influenced* by these than by Columbus' journals.

25) **C** The manuscript recorded significant historical events such as battles and church affairs, so we can infer that eclipses were also *seen as important* for political or religious purposes.

26) **A** Paragraph 2 states that "the chronicle provides insights into the development of the English language," so we can infer that scholars use the chronicle for its *records of older forms of the English language*.

27) **A** Because the chronicle was "carried to different monasteries around the kingdom" and written by "monastery scribes," we can deduce that *most literature* at this time *was stored in monasteries*.

28) **D** The passage implies that the chronicles stayed within monastic circles and were continually updated for centuries. Because the manuscripts chronicle historical events and received little distribution, we can infer that copies were circulated to *increase the chances of preserving Anglo-Saxon history*.

29) **D** Roosevelt's efforts to "protect deer on the plateau from hunters" led to the deer starving "in huge numbers." Thus, Roosevelt did not properly protect the species, and we can infer that *his attempts to replenish a species were misguided*.

30) **C** The killing of "species at the 'top' of the food chain" caused the deer population to overinflate. Hence, we can infer that top predators regulate other species' population through predation, which means predators are *crucial to maintaining ecological balance*.

31) **A** According to Paragraph 2, orcas eat seals and otters,

which eat fish and urchins, which eat kelp. Thus, nothing eats the orca, so orcas must be *one of the top predatory animals of the North Pacific food chain*.

32) **B** Paragraph 2 states that the overharvesting of fish has occurred "in recent decades." Therefore, we can deduce that recent fishing technologies *enabled the fishing industry to overfish the North Pacific* because overfishing is not mentioned as an issue amongst more primitive peoples.

33) **C** If the enforcement of tariffs causes the price of imported goods to increase, we can conclude that *imposing tariffs discourages imports* because of the price increase for consumers.

34) **D** The example in Paragraph 1 states that free trade makes goods "less expensive to consumers" and provides everyone with more goods. Hence, we can infer that with more money and goods going to consumers, *free trade will increase consumers' standard of living*.

35) **B** If companies exhibit transparency and have to reveal their business dealings, it is likely that they will adhere carefully to *laws regarding production and trade* because they are publicly accountable for their business actions.

36) **B** If FTAs negatively affect, for instance, "small corn farmers" and union workers in "factory jobs," we can infer that these *farmers and labor unions* will oppose FTAs.

37) **D** Because Antigone believes that "it would be more serious to defy the gods than her uncle," we can infer that she fears the gods more than she fears her uncle, the king. If the gods are worthy of so much fear, they must *be dangerous if angered*.

38) **D** Creon is willing to punish his niece with a death sentence for disobeying his laws, and he believes that "there is nothing worse than disobeying the king's authority." From these pieces of information, we can infer that Creon is *resolute in his beliefs and decisions*, even when they harm those who he cares about.

39) **B** Romero was "distressed at the Salvadoran government's

violent repression" and spoke out against it. Because the government is characterized as repressive and violent, we can infer that the government, or *those in power*, sent Romero threats because *they wished to silence him.*

40) Ⓐ Because the government was likely involved in Romero's assassination in 1980, but now Romero is "celebrated as a national hero," we can infer that the country *has experienced much political change since Romero's era.*

Chapter 7 Purpose

1) Ⓑ Paragraph 1 states that "ideals associated with the Enlightenment" changed people's views towards punishment. Thus, "the Enlightenment" gives specific *background* information to show where these *new attitudes* came from.

2) Ⓓ The highlighted portion states that "In the centuries since, Western societies have been debating" prison structures. The sentence implies that the debate continues today, and therefore discusses *a societal issue that is still unresolved.*

3) Ⓐ Because the Walnut Street Jail was meant as "an enlightened form of correction" but was actually "horrendous," we can determine that the real, "horrendous" *consequences* contrast with the "enlightened" yet failed *plan.*

4) Ⓓ The majority of Paragraph 3 discusses the intended rehabilitating effects versus the actual effects of isolating prisoners. Thus, we can conclude that "isolating prisoners" is mentioned to *describe* a failed yet *extreme attempt to improve prisoners.*

5) Ⓒ The first sentence emphasizes that Banneker was known for "math-related achievements, including" his work on Washington, D.C. Thus, we can conclude

that the mention of Washington, D.C., is *an example of…math-related achievements.*

6) Ⓐ The passage states that African-American "children were not permitted to attend school with white children," so it is surprising that Banneker was allowed to attend school. However, he went to school with Quakers, "a sect that opposed slavery," which *explains how Banneker had the opportunity to go to school.*

7) Ⓒ Banneker's clock that "kept time accurately" is mentioned as "An early sign of his cleverness" in Paragraph 2. Thus, we can conclude that the clock is mentioned *to support the idea that Banneker was ingenious* (very clever).

8) Ⓒ Paragraph 4 states that "Banneker…was not afraid to make his abolitionist views public." Thus, we can infer that mentioning his letters to Thomas Jefferson emphasizes *Banneker's courage* because pointing out the hypocrisy of a powerful political figure is usually quite risky.

9) Ⓒ Because the phrase "For example" follows the definition in the first sentence, we can determine that a lengthier definition of how sound works will follow. Using this reasoning, the simple definition in the first sentence *introduces the more extended explanation that follows.*

10) Ⓓ In Paragraph 2, the main, relevant example to the discussion of sound waves is how sound travels through air. Thus, the mention of sound traveling through "the vacuum of outer space" serves to *contrast the paragraph's main example.*

11) Ⓐ The sentence compares the *viewpoints* of humans and underwater inhabitants concerning noise levels in water. Thus, it *compares different conceptual viewpoints.*

12) Ⓓ The highlighted noises in Paragraph 3 serve as examples of noises fish make. Hence, these examples reinforce *the statement that fish make sounds.*

13) Ⓓ When something is *empirical*, it is based on verifiable evidence or experimentation. Thus, the author precedes his or

her examples with the statement "Empirical research…has found" *to point out that the following statements are based on evidence.*

14) Ⓒ The highlighted clause in Paragraph 1 serves as a link in connecting gratitude to self-acceptance. Thus, the clause comprises part of a *cause and effect relationship between gratitude and other feelings*, namely self-acceptance.

15) Ⓒ Paragraph 1 discusses how science has helped prove the positive effects of gratitude, or *theorems* about gratitude; and Paragraph 2 focuses on "Clear examples" of this theorem in "many ancient traditions" (*ancient cultural practices*).

16) Ⓒ Whereas Paragraph 2 gives examples of thanksgiving customs in "many Asian cultures," Paragraph 3 only focuses on Vietnamese practices. Thus, Vietnam is mentioned to *introduce one culture's unique focus at harvest time.*

17) Ⓐ The author indicates, "Removing outer wear signaled vulnerability and deference" like "bowing or kneeling did." Thus, we can conclude that the author mentions the two practices *to illustrate similar means of demonstrating submission or yielding.*

18) Ⓑ The author gives two reasons for a knight to uncover his head: to allow for the other person to confirm his identity (the obvious reason for showing one's face) and to convey the knight's "peaceful intentions," which is *an underlying message that also showed respect.*

19) Ⓑ Paragraph 2 focuses on situation in which "dressing in one's best clothes…signals courtesy and respect…." Thus, the highlighted sentence that follows *supports the previous statement* (the introduction to Paragraph 2) *with a pertinent example* that involves hats, adhering to the focus of the passage.

20) Ⓐ Paragraph 1 describes situations in which removing one's head covering shows respect, yet Paragraphs 2 and 3 describe situations in which keeping a head covering on shows spirituality. Therefore, the mention of "spiritual humil-

ity" indicates that the author is *exploring a different facet of the importance of head covering.*

21) Ⓒ Caffeine acts as a defense because it "paralyzes and kills some insects," so plants that produce caffeine have an "evolutionary advantage of producing caffeine" over plants that do not produce their own pesticide.

22) Ⓓ In Paragraph 2, Omar is forced to roast coffee because he fears starvation. Omar is starving because he has been "exiled" from his home city. Thus, the mention of "exile" serves to *set up a story's plot.*

23) Ⓓ The phrase "What is certain" in the highlighted sentence indicates that the author is moving away from the mythology presented in Paragraph 2 and presenting factual information about coffee. Thus, the sentence implies that Paragraph 3 will present *facts about the history of coffee that are not based only on legend.*

24) Ⓐ Paragraph 3 indicates "coffee drinking…spread throughout the Islamic world," which led to the prominence of coffee houses. Thus, coffee houses are mentioned to *introduce a widespread cultural phenomenon that was spurred by coffee.*

25) Ⓑ Paragraph 1 gives general information about glucose consumption and briefly mentions the purpose of mitochondria; Paragraph 2 focuses entirely on mitochondria. Thus, Paragraph 2 *elaborates on…* [the] *description of how organisms use mitochondria.*

26) Ⓑ Paragraph 2 describes the process by which mitochondria turn sunlight into energy by relating the process to a campfire and to spending currency. Therefore, we can deduce that Paragraph 2's primary purpose is to *improve comprehension of a process using* the *imagery* of a campfire and currency.

27) Ⓐ Paragraph 3 states that "Most organelles are pockets surrounded by one membrane while each mitochondrion has two membranes." Therefore, discussion of the second membrane is *providing details* [about] *unique characteristics of mitochondria.*

28) Ⓓ The second half of Paragraph 3 identifies a potential reason for why "each mitochondrion contains its own genes," so the highlighted sentence introduces this discussion by providing *the basis of the scientific hypothesis that follows.*

29) Ⓒ Because the author mentions the "long hours" and "perilous machinery" involved in child labor, we can conclude that the author intends to criticize child labor because it *exploited vulnerable people* (children).

30) Ⓓ The first two pieces of information about "Mother Jones" are that she was "an unlikely leader" because she was "152-centimeters tall," which is fairly short. Thus, she is implicitly described as a *small person* who tackled the *giant problem* of worker rights during American industrialization.

31) Ⓑ In Paragraph 2, the mention of famine, familial deaths, and the loss of possessions indicate how Mother Jones may have become "fiery," "tough," "feisty," and "fearless," as well as unusually committed to a cause – the experiences thus *shaped an unusual personality.*

32) Ⓒ Because Mother Jones used the familial term of endearment "my boys" for miners in her union, we can conclude that she had a *strong emotional commitment to miners.*

33) Ⓐ The majority of the passage discusses dystopian literature, but the first two sentences describe a contrasting genre. Consequently, we can conclude the author begins the passage with a discussion of utopias in order to *contrast one genre of literature with its opposite genre.*

34) Ⓒ The author analyzes what dystopian writers "Frequently" do. Thus, the author is *defining a central component of most dystopian fiction.*

35) Ⓑ *Fahrenheit 451* explores a future where book censorship has been taken to an extreme. Hence, the author likely mentions a real-world occurrence of censorship in order to *give an example of a phenomenon that an*

author extrapolated.

36) Ⓑ Generally, book censorship entails restricting the information allowed in texts or banning certain texts from an area. Thus, the act of "purposely [setting] fire to the homes of book owners" serves to *describe a drastic form of censorship.*

37) Ⓒ Although Posada is introduced as a printmaker, Paragraph 1 emphasizes: "his main legacy today is his political cartooning" of "Mexico's dictatorial ruler." Thus, Paragraph 1 stresses *how a cartoonist gained historical prominence.*

38) Ⓐ One reason Posada's work became popular was that the "largely illiterate public" could understand the cartoons because they were "visual statements" rather than written ones. Consequently, the mention of visual statements shows that Posada conveyed *information without words.*

39) Ⓑ The highlighted sentence emphasizes the peculiar piece of information concerning Mexican culture's "familiarity with death and spirits," a feature that may seem unusual to a reader. Therefore, the sentence *explains a peculiarity about the region.*

40) Ⓓ Because the author states that "Posada had a major influence on his [Rivera's] artistic development," and Rivera became "internationally renowned," we can conclude that Rivera is mentioned to *describe one aspect of Posada's impact on art and culture.*

Chapter 8 Paraphrase

Warm Up   p. 127

1) A	**6)** A	
2) B	**7)** B	
3) A	**8)** B	
4) A	**9)** B	
5) B	**10)** A	

Quick Practice   p. 129

1) Ⓒ The highlighted sentence defines ontology and places it under the study of philosophy. Answer [D] limits its questions to the existence of life. The only answer choice that suitably defines ontology as *examining fundamental questions about being* is [C].

2) Ⓑ Essentially, the sentence states that materialism considers "matter and energy [to be] the ultimate reality." Matter and energy can be rephrased as *substantive elements*; their interaction (*interplay*) causes *life and other "real" things to come to be.*

3) Ⓒ The primary idea of the highlighted sentence is that, for idealists, "reality is immaterial," which can be rephrased as *reality is intangible.*

4) Ⓒ The focus of the highlighted sentence is that the Leakeys "unearthed fossils and footprints…illuminating important aspects of human evolution." Thus, the Leakeys are famous for *finding fossils and other clues that helped explain how humans developed.*

5) Ⓑ The main ideas in the highlighted sentence are that *apes have shared ancestors with humans*, which caused Leakey's "curiosity" (he *wanted to learn more*) about ape behavior.

6) Ⓒ The sentence never indicates that Leakey himself called Goodall an "angel," not does the sentence indicate that Goodall *telephoned Leakey*, so choices (B) and (D) are eliminated. Thus, (C) must be correct because it correctly states that *Goodall was a secretary.*

7) Ⓑ The main idea of the highlighted sentence is that Coriolis *examined machinery*, which helped him *develop the principle of "work."* The remaining answer choices misconstrue the relationship between machinery and work.

8) Ⓐ The highlighted sentence focuses on the existence of *stored, or potential, energy* and the effects of an *external influence* on an object at rest. Other answer choices misinterpret the conversion of potential energy by claiming that it comes from gravity and force or that it results in force.

9) Ⓓ According to the highlighted sentence, energy in billiards transfers from the player to the cue ball, then from the cue ball to the other balls. Only (D) correctly orders these events while the other choices incorrectly order either the source or

the distribution of energy.

10) Ⓓ The key points of the highlighted sentence are that Mary Shelly told a story about a man who creates artificial life. Other answer choices leave one of these elements out, or focus too much on the creation's appearance while missing other crucial points.

11) Ⓒ The highlighted sentence emphasizes that "the created man repeatedly tracks down Victor… and his friends" because he felt "wronged." This is restated with *the man…chases Frankenstein and his associates due to his anger at being an outcast.*

12) Ⓒ The phrase "readers still find relevance in the…novel" is restated as *People probably remain interested*, and the "ethical dilemmas" are rephrased as *the role of responsibility.* Thus, (C) is an accurate rewording of the highlighted sentence.

13) Ⓐ The correct answer rephrases the concept that the purpose of investigative journalism is, in many cases, to stop *wrongdoing* by making it public, or to "bring about change by exposing neglectful or exploitative behavior."

14) Ⓑ The key ideas from the highlighted sentence are that Sinclair worked as a meatpacker (*processing meat*), and he was "concealing his identity" to *secretly gather material*, which he "included in his novel (*for fiction writing*)."

15) Ⓐ The main qualities of the book described in the highlighted sentence are that it is "humorously acerbic," or *witty and blunt*; that it "presented well-documented facts," or was *thorough*; and it exposed the funeral industry for taking "advantage of grieving customers" by *documenting* the industry's *exploitative business practices.*

16) Ⓑ The sentence focuses on the knowledge gained by Chinese cartographers from Islamic maps, so the Chinese gained *a greater awareness of lands they had not yet explored.*

17) Ⓓ The highlighted sentence conveys that the "map no longer exists," but "mapmakers wrote that they used it as a resource," which is paraphrased as *Textual references…are the only present-day evidence of* the map.

18) (A) Essentially, Korea was given "prominent placement" in *the layout and design of the Kangnido* to reflect "pride and confidence (*optimism*) about [the mapmakers'] new dynasty."

19) (B) The two main ideas in the highlighted sentence are that RNs take doctors' orders, "but they also have some autonomy." The only answer that addresses both these points accurately states that *nurses follow doctors' orders, but also follow their own protocols*.

20) (D) The sentence says that "generalizations" (*overall statements*) "about the scope of the job are unfeasible" (*cannot be made with certainty*) "because nurses work in such diverse settings" (*a wide variety of jobs*).

21) (A) Because the statement "men make up a small and growing percentage of nurses" means the same thing as *imbalanced gender ratios in the nursing profession are beginning to change*, (A) is the best paraphrase of the highlighted sentence.

22) (A) The highlighted sentence emphasizes researchers' "astounding findings about the large capacity for thought" of certain birds, which is best summarized by describing the birds as *surprisingly intelligent*.

23) (C) *Sessions marked with noisy caws and distinct endings* is the best paraphrase of "a cacophony of caws…followed by sudden quiet," and *sharing specific information* is the best paraphrase of "Crows…vocalize quite specific ideas."

24) (D) The main idea of the sentence is that crows recognize and resent their captors, and only answer choice (D) mentions that the *Crows appeared to become hostile* [to those] *who had captured crows*.

25) (C) The statement that Jackson "still garners both passionate admiration and blistering criticism" is best paraphrased by *The extent to which Jackson's…career was successful is still debated* because this paraphrase implies both praise and criticism.

26) (B) The main idea of the highlighted sentence is that "Jackson redirected all federal deposits…causing the central bank to collapse." This is restated concisely with *Jackson's withdrawal of funds ruined the institution* (the central bank).

27) (A) Only answer choice (A) includes the information that Jackson did the opposite of his predecessors by *relocating Native American tribes*, and it is therefore the best paraphrase of the highlighted information.

28) (D) The highlighted sentence stresses that mirrors are an ancient and widespread discovery; the best paraphrase of the sentence includes this information by stating that mirrors are found at *many ruins* (indicating they are ancient) and found *in diverse places* (indicating they are widespread).

29) (D) While choice (C) is technically accurate, the highlighted sentence focuses upon *uses* for mirrors such as "reflecting light…, signaling someone…, or starting a fire." The best paraphrase includes all these uses: *flashing messages…, sparking flames, or illuminating interiors*.

30) (C) The best paraphrase condenses the information that "mirrors were thought to accomplish what evil spirits despised the most: make the spirits visible" into *evil spirits…would avoid objects that could reflect their images*.

Chapter 9 Summary

Warm Up   p. 145

1) 3	**3)** 1	**5)** 2	**7)** 3	**9)** 1
2) 2	**4)** 2	**6)** 1	**8)** 3	**10)** 2

Quick Practice   p. 147

1) 1, 3, 4 The correct answers all describe the BaMbuti "unique musical tradition." Paragraph 2 states that songs have "one or two callers (*solo singing*) eliciting… responses from other singers (*whole-group singing*)," and that BaMbuti songs "add layers of variations in melody or rhythm (*melodic and rhythmic complexity*)." Moreover, Paragraph 3 states: "They also have singing ceremonies to welcome forest spirits" and for conducting other forest activities (*music is referential to life in the forest*).

2) 1, 4, 5 The correct answers all involve ways Geisel's work helps children learn to read. Geisel created "cartoonish line drawings" of "pom-pom trees [and] tilting platforms," or *simple lines and…amusing settings*. His "'Beginner Books'…use a limited supply of simple words," or *a small number of basic words to build literacy*. And he used "outlandish situations to address familiar, real concerns," so he *used humor…to address subjects that children care about*.

3) 2, 3, 5 The correct answers all focus on how wind turbines "meet many human needs." Paragraph 2 states that the first windmill was built because "water power…was likely untenable in a theatre," so *the original windmill was a substitute*. "In about the ninth century, farmers…discovered how to use windmills to grind grain," in other words for *agricultural innovations using wind*. Finally, windmills today "convert the rotational energy into electricity," so *energy supply is the primary purpose*.

4) 2, 4, 5 The correct answers all focus on necessary speed, technique, or strength for pole vaulting. According to the passage, pole vaulters must "plant the pole in the ground" while "relying on skill,"or *know exactly how to plant a pole*; they "require lower-body strength" to "sprint for 40 meters," so *strong leg muscles propel pole vaulters*; and "they must have strong…abdominal…muscles," which help them *lift their lower bodies… over the bar*.

5) 2, 5, 6 The correct answers accurately summarize some effect of phytoplankton. Normally, phytoplankton "serve as the base of aquatic food chains," so they *benefit sea life* [under] *normal environmental constraints*. However, red tide's toxins can "accumulate in lethal concentrations" *within the bodies of water-filtering marine organisms*. And one type of algae "emits a brief flash of blue light" when it is jostled, so it *shine*[s] *briefly when* [it] *bump*[s] *into something*.

6) 2, 3, 6 The correct answers focus on accurate details about carnival masks. Paragraph 3 states that "There are many different styles of masks," so they *come in a variety of…styles*. Because "Wealthy Venetian merchants sometimes wore masks to conceal their identities," the *use of masks may derive from the practices of Venetian tradesmen*. Also, Paragraph 3 indicates that the masks are made from "*papier maché*," "porcelain," or "leather," but are "primarily white," or *usually uniform in color*.

7) 2, 4, 5 The correct answers accurately describe how Graham communicated through movement. According to Graham, "a fall expressed mortality, and rising represented renewal," so *falling and getting up…had great significance*. Also, Graham tried "to focus the audience's attention" with *a minimalist approach to apparel and set design*, according to the beginning of Paragraph 2. Finally, Graham's "'contraction and release'…[was] a form of breath control that" *provided a simple way to express emotion*.

8) 2, 3, 6 The correct answers detail how the LHC works and what it has discovered. Paragraph 2 states that "huge computer detectors…capture data," so they *record and examine the data… from crashing particles*. The LHC uses "enormous magnets to guide [particles] into small but powerful collisions," or *uses massive magnets to steer groups of protons*. And the LHC verified the field that "provides resistance to the particles that make up matter," so it *provided evidence of a field that provides resistance to certain particles*.

9) 1, 3, 4 The correct answers focus on results of the various studies presented in the passage. According to Paragraph 1, during a study "volunteers were placed in a room and told they had no choice but to administer electric shocks…," so *they were persuaded to apply electric shocks to someone*. Because "of emotional trauma," the prison experiment "had to be halted after just six days," so *the Stanford experiment* ended *prematurely*. Also, according to Paragraph 3, *the studies have been challenged* because "volunteer participants...knew that they were part of a research experiment."

10) 2, 4, 5 The correct answers are accurate statements about specific "beneficial physiological changes." According to Paragraph 3, "bipedalism did allow for adroit hand-motor skills to develop" because *hands were no longer used for locomotion*. Some people "claim that bipedalism developed so that hominids stood taller and could see predators in tall grasses," or *spot danger from further away*. Finally, bipeds "developed an arch in the foot to provide better propulsion," or *for better forward momentum when moving*.

Chapter 10 Organization

Warm Up   p. 163

1) Research: 2, 5, 8   Writing: 1, 3, 7
2) Canada: 4, 6, 8   Siberia: 1, 5, 7
3) Muscle: 3, 5, 7   Bone: 1, 6, 8
4) Synonym: 1, 4, 8   Antonym: 5, 6, 7
5) Coffee: 2, 4, 8   Tea: 3, 5, 7
6) Vaccine: 1, 4, 7   Medication: 2, 3, 6
7) Hurricane: 1, 4, 7   Snowstorm: 3, 5, 8
8) Mice: 2, 4, 6   Elephants: 1, 5, 8
9) New York: 1, 3, 8   Beijing: 2, 4, 7
10) Nonprofit: 3, 5, 8   Corporation: 1, 6, 7

Quick Practice   p. 166

1) Paradigm: 4, 5, 6
    Paradox: 3, 7
The passage states that a paradigm is "a way of seeing and thinking about reality," or *that which seems obvious to a person* as well as *a set of assumptions about what is true*. Also, a "paradigm can shift or suddenly change," which causes things that seem self-evident to be reassessed, so a paradigm *is most noticeable when it must change* to reflect new information. Because a paradox is "self-contradictory but not necessarily illogical," it *may be confusing at first glance*. The phrase *fighting for peace* is a paradox because "fight" and "peace" are opposites, so it should be impossible to fight to attain peace.

2) Mesopotamian: 1, 2, 6
    Norse: 3, 8

Chinese: 4, 9
The Epic of Gilgamesh proposes that Gilgamesh "will live on in literature," or *achieve a kind of immortality by the written word*. It claims that "a plant at the bottom of the sea...will grant... immortality," so one must *seek in the seas for...eternal life*. The passage also states that the epic is "one of the oldest surviving works of literature," so it dates *to a time of the earliest written documents*. In Norse mythology from "the 13th century (*recorded during the 1200s*)," "immortality is ultimately unattainable even for...Norse gods," so *even the gods cannot live forever*. In Chinese myth, immortality is linked to "a peach tree that produces one fruit every 1,000 years," or *a tree bearing fruit every millennium*; and a divine emperor "holds a banquet for the Eight Immortals," so *only deities can attend* [the] feast.

3) Bonobos: 2, 4, 7
    Chimpanzees: 5, 6
Bonobos "rarely have to compete over resources...[and] interact... in a gentle manner," so their *friendly, social behavior may stem from...ample nutrients*; "the region of the brain associated with empathy (or *compassion*) is exceptionally developed (*highly evolved*);" and a male's status "is determined by his mother's social standing," so *a male... relies on his mother's position*. Chimpanzees, however, "use tools to acquire sustenance," so they have *devised skillful ways to access food*; and they "form rigid intergroup hierarchies," so *ranking order in this group is inflexible*.

4) Classical mechanics: 1, 2, 4
    Quantum mechanics: 3, 7
Classical mechanics is deterministic when *predicting the course of a large flying... object*, "such as a rocket;" many theories for classical mechanics were developed by 17th-century "physicist Isaac Newton" *in the 1600s*; and "classical mechanics are inapplicable" when dealing with "miniscule objects," so it is *unreliable at the atomic level*. In quantum mechanics, on the other hand, "measurements are expressed as probabili-

ties," *so researchers must accept findings as likelihoods*; and "the laws of gravity...are inapplicable" in quantum mechanics, so *gravity is not necessarily an essential factor*.

5) Martin Luther King, Jr.: 1, 6
    Malcolm X: 2, 3, 7
King advocated a "society where people of diverse ethnicity live side by side," in other words that *the U.S. could become more fair*; he also "took inspiration from... powerful peaceful protests," so he *felt that peaceful protests...could sway public opinion*. Malcolm X felt "it was naïve to think that any political action would bring justice," so he believed that *victims of oppression should be cynical about change*. Later in life, "he became more optimistic about implementing change," or *modified his...extremist viewpoints*; and he "urged African Americans to defend themselves 'by any means necessary,'" (*defend themselves with force if attacked*).

6) Asperger's: 3, 5
    Savant: 2, 4, 7
People with Asperger's Syndrome "may not easily understand other people's social cues," so they *might not understand when someone has said something in a joking manner*. They have an "inclination toward restricted interests," so they may *focus on a narrow interest*. Savants, on the other hand, have an "astounding talent," or *an exceptional ability in one cognitive task*; they may have "central nervous system injuries," or *trauma to the central nervous system*; and their "astounding talent...is incongruous with an overall disability," so they *may demonstrate extreme poles of brilliance and disability*.

7) Tropical: 2, 6
    Temperate: 1, 3, 5
Tropical rainforests are located "near the equator," or where *the northern and southern hemispheres* meet; a "tropical rainforest has the largest biodiversity," or *the greatest number of different plant and animal species*. Temperate forests are "known for cool temperatures (*has brisk winters*)"; they are known for having "massive trees" and "mosses... [and] ferns," so *trees tower over*

ferns and moss; and they "have the largest biomass," or *greatest weight of organisms as a whole*.

8) Stephen A. Douglas: 1, 2, 5
    Abraham Lincoln: 4, 7
Douglas claimed that "the matter [of slavery] should be decided at the state or local level," so *each region should be self-determining on slavery*; Douglas "was running for re-election," so he *was seeking to win another term in office*; and he claimed that "changes in the economy would end slavery gradually," or that *slavery would become economically unfeasible*. Lincoln, however, feared that the "monstrous injustice" of slavery "would thrive and spread to the whole nation," so he *was concerned about conflicting moral policies* and he *condemned slave-owning*.

9) Magical realism: 2, 7
    Fantasy: 1, 5, 6
In magical realism, "supernatural elements seem a natural part of an otherwise mundane, real-world setting," so *this genre fuses the real world and the inexplicable*; the genre also "depicts absurdities in politics or society," so it often *comments on political leadership*. In fantasy, on the other hand, "supernatural phenomena... [are] important parts of the plot," so *protagonists confront or use magic*; in fantasy "the settings... tend to be imagined worlds," so *Alice in wonderland fits into this genre*. Finally, fantasy may include "savage monsters" and "humanoid hobbits [and] elves...," or *strange beasts or human-like species*.

10) John Chapman: 2, 5
    John Muir: 4, 6, 7
Chapman was later mythologized as "a barefoot traveler who carried only a bag of apple seeds," so he *walked about shoeless, with few goods*; also, his "notoriety as a roaming seed planter stems from a romantic account," so his *life story became exaggerated and idealized by others*. Muir, however, "wrote and spoke about his travels into the wilds," so he *described his backcountry experiences*. He wanted to "protect national forests for future generations, or *advocate on behalf of future generations*; and he was

an "influential conservationist," motivated to *preserve America's woodlands*.

Chapter 11
Actual Practice

Actual Practice 1   p. 178
1) D According to Paragraph 1, Troy has "impregnable walls guarded by the finest archers." Thus, one would need to somehow *penetrate* these walls to be able to "open the gates." *Infiltrate*, then, means *penetrate*.
2) B Paragraph 1 states that according to mythologies, the Trojan War begins when "a prince of Troy kidnaps the beautiful Queen Helen" of Sparta, so the war began when *a Trojan prince kidnapped the Queen of Sparta*.
3) C In Paragraph 2, *war* is the closest applicable singular noun to the pronoun *its*, and it makes sense in context to say "countless reinterpretations of the *war* and *the war's* outcome."
4) A Because Virgil traced a nation's historical roots using a possibly fictional character from the Trojan War, we can conclude that *attempted* is mentioned in order to emphasize that *Virgil's account is not necessarily historically accurate* because it is based off unverifiable events.
5) B According to the passage, "Menelaus rallies sworn confederates…[to help] reclaim his wife," so he did not want to *capture Troy's beautiful queen*, but rather wanted to reclaim his own wife and queen.
6) D Contextually, the author does not indicate why *two-decade-long* is mentioned. We cannot assume that it indicates a *normal time frame for a…dig*, or that two decades has anything to do with criticism or the origins of Troy. Thus, using the process of elimination, we can deduce that *two-decade-long* emphasizes *Schliemann's dedication* to *ancient Greek culture*.
7) B The sentence that comes after [B] recounts how Schliemann used dynamite to reach the bottom of the tell; he likely did this because he *assumed that the Troy of the*

Iliad was the first of these cities. Thus, the information following [B] elaborates upon the added sentence, and the added sentence should be placed at letter [B].
8) C Because Schliemann wanted to discover as much about Troy as possible, it is *Almost inconceivable*, or *Almost unthinkable*, that he destroyed much of the archaeological evidence at Hisarlik using dynamite.
9) A Because a *tell* is created by many cities stacked on top of each other, we can assume that there was a reason that people kept rebuilding over the same spot rather than move somewhere else. Generally, a piece of land is valuable because it is militarily or economically advantageous, so we can infer that the presence of many stacked cities means that *Troy once occupied an advantageous geographic position*.
10) C The two main ideas in the highlighted sentence are 1) Blegen "reconfirmed that nine cities were stacked atop each other," (he *reaffirmed previous research*) and 2) he "was unsuccessful in locating [Homer's] Troy" (he *was not able to locate the Troy of legend*).
11) C Because Korfmann "discovered bronze arrowheads and signs of conflict," we know [A] cannot be *this claim*, as a claim implies uncertainty. It is also certain that Troy VIIa is "a version of the city that existed (*was present*) during the 13th century BCE." Thus, the only uncertainty is "that Homer's Trojan War may have occurred" in Troy VIIa. Thus, *this claim* refers to the theory that *the Trojan War actually occurred at Troy VIIa*.
12) A The first archaeologist mentioned is Frank Calvert in the first sentence of Paragraph 4. His excavations occurred in the 1860s, before Schliemann's excavations. Therefore, *Frank Calvert* was the first to excavate Hisarlik.
13) Troy II: 6, 7
    Troy VIIa: 1, 3, 5
The author states that Schliemann found "a cache of gold and jewels" at Troy

II (*treasure was found*), and it has been determined that "what Schliemann located was Troy II," as he *was the first to excavate this site*. Troy VIIa, on the other hand, "existed during the 13th century BCE" (*the 1200s BCE*), Korfmann "discovered [bronze] arrowheads and signs of conflict within Troy VIIa," and "in 1988…Manfred Korfmann began excavating… Troy VIIa," so it *was excavated primarily by Korfmann*.

Actual Practice 2   p. 182
1) C According to Paragraph 2, the Prairie School "rebelled against the dominant Greco-Roman architecture styles," and it wanted to "establish a uniquely 'American' style of architecture." From this information, we know that the "dominant" architecture in America was not American, so *America lacked a strongly established architectural style*.
2) D Paragraph 2 states that the American Midwest has "abundant open space." Because *pastoral* also describes the American Midwest, we can infer that it is *rural*, or farm-like and containing much open space for crops.
3) D Wright wanted to "integrate…[his] works into their surroundings" and make them blend with the landscape. Often, something blends in if it does not draw overt attention to itself, which is accomplished with minimal *embellishment*, or minimal decorative details.
4) B Wright's Prairie-style structures "accentuate [in other words make more noticeable] the abundant open space of…[the] American Midwest," so they *reflect the American landscape*.
5) B The two main ideas in the highlighted sentence are that 1) concrete blocks are unappealing (*unattractive*), and 2) Wright "challenged himself" (*confronted the notion*) by using them in his architecture. Only [B] addresses both points without adding unsupported information or information from elsewhere in Paragraph 3.
6) D A *culmination* is the end

result of something. Therefore, the author states that Wright's organic style uses ideas from his previous architectural efforts, and therefore *each of Wright's styles builds upon the previous ones*.
7) A The phrase *Structures of this style* in the added sentence must refer back to the second sentence of Paragraph 4. Also, the mention of "Large balconies…[that] provide panoramic views" provides an example of a *space that integrates itself…into nature*. Thus, the added sentence should go at [A].
8) C A main idea of Paragraph 4 is that organic-style structures blend into their surroundings. Because *it* "blend[s] harmoniously with the landscape," and the organic *structure*, "Fallingwater," is mentioned in the same sentence, we can conclude the *it* refers to *the structure*.
9) A In Paragraph 5, the author emphasizes that Usonian houses catered "to a different audience than his past projects" by being "affordable," so we can infer that his previous styles were not affordable and *were built mostly for wealthy clients*.
10) C Usonian houses are "relatively small," yet contain "large living rooms." Because the living room is large, but the house as a whole is small, the "kitchen and bedrooms" must be *small*, or *diminutive*.
11) C In Paragraph 5, the author mentions that Wright created the word "Usonian" to refer "to the people and cultures of the United States," or *the traditions and artistic styles unique to the* U.S.
12) C According to the passage, Wright's architecture encourages "social interaction within the house" (*large spaces for socialization*), it "accentuate[s] the abundant open space of…[the] American Midwest" (*emphasizes the neighboring landscape*), and it "used minimal ornamentation and rustic colors" (*use earthy colors and little embellishment*). *Arches and columns* are not mentioned.
13) Prairie School architecture: 3, 6
    Textile architecture: 1, 4, 7

Usonian architecture: 5, 9
According to the passage, Prairie School uses "long, horizontal lines" to "accentuate...open space" and *blend with a flat landscape*, and many structures "are located in Illinois, the Midwestern state" (*mostly in the...Midwest*). Wright's textile structures "displayed complex geometrical patterns" (*intricate patterns*), he built them "primarily in Los Angeles," and they use the "unappealing... concrete blocks" for construction (*an unsightly construction material*). Usonian structures are "middle-income houses" (*for a particular economic demographic*), and they encourage "social interaction within the house" (*conducive to socializing*).

Actual Practice 3   p. 186

1) Ⓒ The phrase *Both works* in the added sentence refers to the play and film titled *Six Degrees of Separation*, so the added sentence should follow the sentence that mentions both these works. Thus, the added sentence belongs at letter [C].

2) Ⓑ Karinthy's story is "about characters...[who] try to connect themselves to any person on the planet...." Thus, Karinthy wanted to propose that *all people on Earth are closely connected* by writing a story.

3) Ⓒ Karinthy's characters wanted to use "a sequence of no more than five individuals" to connect themselves to others, so he proposed to *measure*, or *quantify*, human interconnectivity in his short story.

4) Ⓐ Social network theory focuses upon identifying relationships among seemingly unrelated people. Thus, the theory tries to find hidden, or *imperceptible*, relationships.

5) Ⓒ Paragraph 4 states that mathematical models "cannot take into account factors such as social class," so *societal factors limit the accuracy* of mathematical models.

6) Ⓑ The sentence containing *it* discusses the delivery of a letter. Because "send" is the verb that shows what *it* is doing, we can infer that *it* is the *letter*.

7) Ⓑ According to Paragraphs 3 and 4, determining levels of interconnectivity is "hindered by many personal circumstances," we can infer that one such "personal circumstance" might be a *subjective factor, such as the definition of 'acquaintance.'*

8) Ⓒ Paragraph 5 discusses the criticisms leveled against Milgram's experiments. Because the second sentence states that "Some *critics*" have one point of view, we can assume that *Others* refers to other *critics* of Milgram's experiment, as this deduction is consistent with the main idea of the paragraph.

9) Ⓐ According to Paragraph 5, many path lengths were "unknown" because most letters never reached their destination. Thus, some letters would likely have long path lengths, but were unrecorded because they never reached their destination, so *average path length...may have increased if every letter reached its destination.*

10) Ⓑ Often, the validity of a theory is determined by the theory's experimental results as well as who conducted the experiments. Thus, the author probably mentions *Columbia University* in order *to show that a reputable research institute also was interested in the theory.*

11) Ⓓ According to Paragraph 6, "nearly 400 emails...were successful" and were sent to one of the target individuals. It is NOT true that *400...emails successfully came back to the original volunteers* because the emails were supposed to be sent to "one of 18 people," not returned to the original senders.

12) Ⓒ The highlighted sentence creates a contrast between technologies that increase connectivity, and other factors that limit connectivity. Only choice [C] accurately summarizes this contrast without claiming that one will dominate the other.

13) 2, 4, 6 The correct answers reflected *attempts to determine* connectivity. In Milgram's experiments, people "attempted to get a letter to one of two specific strangers" by *using the postal system to relay messages.*

"Mathematical models...test for interconnectivity among large populations," or *theories about degrees of separation have been represented by mathematical models.* Moreover, according to Paragraphs 4 and 6, *letter and email-based studies have claimed quantifiable results.*

Actual Practice 4   p. 190

1) Ⓓ According to Paragraph 1, Washington "led the colonial troops to victory," but he "resigned his command" after the war, so he *gave up his role as military leader.*

2) Ⓓ Paragraph 1 states that Washington is known as the "'Father of His Country,'" but the passage does not indicate that *He wanted to be commemorated* as such.

3) Ⓐ Paragraph 2 states that "Washington's strength and integrity set a *precedent*" for the U.S. presidency. Because he demonstrated these positive attributes, rather than just talking about them, the best answer choice is that he "set an *example*" for future presidents.

4) Ⓑ Paragraph 2 emphasizes Washington's "integrity" as president and that he recognize "the bounds of his legal authority," so we can infer that he stuck to, or followed, the law. Thus, *adherence* to the rule of law is closest in meaning to *faithfulness* to the law.

5) Ⓐ Paragraph 2 claims that there are "very few examples of the ideal leadership skills needed for a president," but that Washington set a precedent partly because of his lack of "interest in seizing control of the government." Thus, we can infer that *Many leaders...have sought total control and power* because Washington was unusual in that he did not try to do so.

6) Ⓑ According to the title and the majority of the passage, the main idea is the Washington Monument. Thus, the first two paragraphs provide *reasons why the country wanted to honor Washington* based upon his contributions to the foundation of the U.S.

7) Ⓓ The main ideas of the highlighted sentence are that: "construction of the memorial" stalled because of 1) "the society's bankruptcy" and 2) the conflicts prior to and during the Civil War. Only [D] addresses these points without including false information about *shifting fundraising efforts* or the monument leading to *the increase in conflicts.*

8) Ⓑ Paragraph 5 basically claims that Congress wanted "to complete *the monument*...but *the project* stalled." Thus, *completing the monument* is the nearest preceding referent, and it makes sense in context.

9) Ⓐ Monument architect Mills believed that taking away the added "originally proposed design elements" made the monument "look '*like a stalk of asparagus*,'" which is not a flattering comparison for a giant monument. Thus, the phrase relays *the architect's disappointment in the final*, simplified *design.*

10) Ⓓ The added sentence provides information about the last step taken to complete the monument. Since the preceding sentences in Paragraph 7 discuss the monument's construction, the added sentence should be placed at letter [D] and serve as a concluding sentence.

11) Ⓒ According to Paragraph 7, "commemorative stones" line "the interior walls," but the passage does not indicate that *the building's peak* is built from *engraved bricks.*

12) Ⓑ According to Paragraph 7, the "*commemorative stones*" are meant to "honor Washington," so we can conclude that the author mentions such feature of the monument to show that this feature was meant to *honor or preserve the memory of a person.*

13) 2, 3, 5 Correct answers show how *Washington's legacy would be honored.* Paragraph 7 states that the monument exceeded, or *towered over*, all other buildings at the time, and Paragraph 7 also states, "a city law...limits the height of new buildings so that the monument's grandeur is maintained," so *a law regulates*

the maximum height of other buildings. Also, Paragraph 7 mentions that "In the interior walls, commemorative stones… honor Washington," so *carved stones…have been mounted inside the memorial.*

Actual Practice 5   p. 194

1) Ⓒ Paragraph 2 states that "Since…1921, Sherpas have been renowned for their mountaineering expertise," so they have *been known* since the 20th century, not the *19th century.*

2) Ⓐ Sherpas are described as having "extraordinary physiological abilities including… adaptation to the cold," so we can infer that these abilities may result from being *better adapted genetically* to mountainous environments.

3) Ⓒ The two main ideas of the highlighted sentence are that "Tenzing participated in two Swiss expeditions," which opened "up a new route." Only [C] addresses both points without including false information.

4) Ⓑ The main idea and conclusion of Paragraph 4 is that Hillary came "to regard Tenzing as the ideal climbing partner," so the paragraph primarily shows *why Hillary chose Tenzing as his mountaineering partner.*

5) Ⓓ The added sentence is an understated description of Hillary's experience when reaching the summit. Thus, it logically follows the statement that the climbers "finally" reached the summit, or at letter [D].

6) Ⓐ While this section of the trek is *infamous* and climbing it is *laborious*, the word *treacherous* is synonymous with danger or *peril*. Thus, the *treacherous* section has to be dangerous or *perilous.*

7) Ⓓ If something is *precious*, then it is highly valued. Therefore, we can conclude that *precious* describes oxygen because it is highly valued for *survival at that altitude.*

8) Ⓐ Much of Paragraph 5 describes the climbers' ascent to the summit of Everest by including details such as when they arrived and what they did once they reached the summit. Para-

graph 6 states that Hillary was knighted and Tenzing received the George Medal, both of which are *honors presented.*

9) Ⓑ Because Tenzing not being knighted created "a controversy that continues today," we can conclude that his *medal was a lesser award*, but the two climbers "insisted on equally sharing the credit" for summiting Everest, so they *saw themselves as a team.*

10) Ⓒ A feat implies that something notable has been completed, so "*his* feat" most logically refers to an *attainment*, something that has been achieved. *Attaining world stature* is the closest possible referent preceding the pronoun phrase "*his* feat."

11) Ⓒ Paragraph 7 states that Tenzing was "humbly born" (*came from humble roots*), he attained "world stature and world renown" (*His accomplishment… made him world famous*), and he served as "a bright portent" for Asians (*other Asians could achieve astounding goals*). Yet there is not mention of *greater economic opportunities.*

12) Ⓑ Paragraph 8 states that the reason the climbers' sons climbed Everest was "to celebrate…their fathers' accomplishment." Thus, the paragraph indicates that the *climbers' fellowship extended to the next generation.*

13) 2, 5, 6 The correct answers focus on summarizing Tenzing's *numerous attempts.* Paragraph 3 indicates that "in 1947 [Tenzing] became the sirdar," so *Tenzing was the sirdar….* He also participated in opening "up a new route during the trek" from "the Nepalese side," so he *helped start a new path to the peak….* And he "was a high-altitude porter for a 1935 British expedition," so he *started working for a British group…in 1935.*

Actual Practice 6   p. 198

1) Ⓒ The sentence containing *they* states that "a number of people…claimed" to have seen "mysterious" spacecraft that they assumed were "flown by extraterrestrials." Therefore, *they*

refers to "a number of people," or *people who said they had seen UFOs.*

2) Ⓐ If something is unauthorized, then it has not been given official approval. Thus, an "*unauthorized* press release" is one not sanctioned by the military, so *the officer did not get approval to issue the press release.*

3) Ⓓ Paragraph 1 gives general information about the Roswell reports, so it *introduces the phenomenon* of UFO sightings, and Paragraph 2 describes how the incident first gained media coverage, so it *shows how the story started.*

4) Ⓑ If something is *bogus*, then it is counterfeit or fake. Thus, the film *Alien Autopsy* is likely described as *bogus* to indicate that any autopsies performed in the film were *not genuine.*

5) Ⓐ As the "surveillance balloon" was designed to "track" something from above, we can conclude that it could also be called an *observation* balloon.

6) Ⓑ Because the author mentions that the balloon program was top secret "at the time," we can infer that by 1994 (decades later) the program was no longer top secret, so the military decided to *air the facts about the outdated program* to dispel suspicions of an alien cover-up.

7) Ⓓ Because no one has undeniably discovered an alien at Roswell, we can infer that the *alleged* aliens are *supposed* aliens, as all claims of alien sightings have been speculation.

8) Ⓒ The military claimed that people were "confusing… aliens with lifelike dummies" (*people began thinking that the test dummies had been aliens*), "people were experiencing transformed memories" (*Memories… had become distorted*), and people perpetuated "purposeful misrepresentations of incidents" (*Deliberate misinformation*). Yet the passage does not state that *secret information…could not be released to the public.*

9) Ⓒ The added sentence introduces the idea of dropping objects "from high altitudes," so it should be placed at [C] to pre-

cede the sentence that begins "In addition,…" and then elaborates on dropping objects.

10) Ⓑ According to Paragraph 7, "witnesses who saw the [test pilot]…stated…later that they had seen an alien." Thus, we can infer that time passed between them seeing the man and reporting their sightings, so *distorted recollections…may have impacted witnesses' perceptions.*

11) Ⓓ "Experimental *space probes*" is the nearest preceding noun phrase to *they*, and it makes sense to say, "*space probes* were dropped from balloons for testing purposes."

12) Ⓐ The main idea of Paragraph 8 is that "UFO enthusiasts…dismissed [military] explanations as "implausible" and "incompetent," which is best paraphrased as *UFO proponents believed that the military reports were inaccurate and poorly prepared.*

13) 1, 3, 4 The correct answer choices support the statement that *media attention increased.* Paragraph 4 states that an interview "in the late 1970s" caused the UFO events in Roswell to gain momentum, so *eyewitnesses came forward in the news to describe the space creatures.* Paragraph 4 also claims that UFO suspicions "gained…international attention through an article in the *National Enquirer*," which is *a popular tabloid.* And "further media attention fueled ongoing interest in" UFOs because *sensationalistic versions of the events* of Roswell were published.

Actual Practice 7   p. 202

1) Ⓒ In Paragraph 1, *These variations* refers back to *alleles*, which are variations of genes – in other words, they are *alternative forms of genes.*

2) Ⓑ Paragraph 1 states that "Genes are not identical from individual to individual" because of different allele combinations. Thus, an individual's genes differ *because of allele diversity.*

3) Ⓑ In Paragraph 1, *organisms* is the closest applicable, plural noun to the pronoun *their*, and it makes sense in context to

say "alleles that help organisms survive in [the] *organisms' environment.…*"

4) Ⓐ The first sentence of Paragraph 2 creates a contrast between the *environmental factors* of natural selection and the "randomness" of genetic drift. Therefore, the mention of *environmental factors* serves to show *how natural selection differs from genetic drift*.

5) Ⓐ A *paradox* is a seemingly self-contradictory statement. In Paragraph 4, the paradox is that there are more humans than primates, yet primates have greater genetic variance. Thus, *Paradoxically* is mentioned to *emphasize* that this information is a *surprising fact about human genetics*.

6) Ⓒ According to Paragraph 4, "humans have less genetic variance than their closest living relatives." Hence, we can reverse this statement to come to the conclusion that *modern primates have more genetic variance than humans*.

7) Ⓑ The phrase "For instance" indicates that the added sentence is providing an example of a previously mentioned concept. Because the example is about overhunting, and a population bottleneck is sometimes caused by overhunting, we can conclude that the added sentence should follow the definition of "population bottleneck," and therefore be placed at letter [B].

8) Ⓑ Examples of "*catastrophic* events" given in the passage include "flood, famine, or overhunting." All of these things are potentially harmful, or *ruinous*, to the populations of living species.

9) Ⓑ The main idea in the highlighted sentence is that "current (*modern*) genetic diversity" may come from "isolated groups…repopulating the Earth after the eruption." Only [B] provides an accurate restatement because other choices claim that modern diversity is the same as ancient peoples' diversity, or that small groups gathered together.

10) Ⓒ According to Paragraph 5, "volcanic ash blocked the Sun's light and killed much of

Earth's vegetation and animal population." Because humans rely on vegetation and upon animals that require vegetation, we can safely assume that *Most humans died out because of insufficient food supplies*.

11) Ⓐ According to the passage, different physical characteristics result from different alleles. If "people in various regions of the world have developed minor physical and genetic differences," then we can determine that these physical and genetic differences result from *Different alleles becoming dominant among disparate migrating populations*.

12) Ⓑ Paragraph 2 states that "environmental factors influence natural selection" whereas "genetic drift introduces an element of randomness." Thus, natural selection and genetic drift contrast, and *genetic drift* does NOT *work with natural selection*.

13) Population bottleneck: 3, 7
Founder effect: 1, 4, 6
A population bottleneck "occurs when a catastrophic event… causes a large decrease in… population" (*a destructive event greatly reduces…population*), and it is possible that "humans experienced a population bottleneck during the *Toba catastrophe*." A founder effect, on the other hand "occurs because a small population…splits from a main species group;" during the migration, a group's "genetic variance decreased compared to the main population," so there is *a very gradual decrease in genetic variance*; and the "gradual migration from Africa…beginning about 200,000 years ago" provides an *example of* the founder effect.

Actual Practice 8   p. 206

1) Ⓑ Because Paragraph 1 gives a brief chronology of NGOs starting with "the 18th century" and explaining their status "today," we can conclude that it *establishes a brief background* for NGOs.

2) Ⓐ According to Paragraph 1, the NGOs that are *subsidiary* to the U.N. are "valued advisors and partners in many U.N. pro-

grams." The answer choice with the closest meaning to "partner" and *subsidiary* is *affiliate*.

3) Ⓓ Paragraph 2 claims that NGOs "earn stellar reputations by collecting donations" from the rich, and giving the donations to the poor. Thus, we can infer that *Good publicity in wealthy societies is important* because that is where NGOs receive funding.

4) Ⓓ The main idea of the passage is that NGOs seek donations to provide services; there is no mention of them *earning profits for investors*.

5) Ⓒ In Paragraph 3, *cultural hegemony* is presented as the opposite of being "initiated by the affected community," so this *hegemony* must mean "initiated by the donors' community or *culture*." Thus, *cultural hegemony* is an example of *the domination of one culture over another* by deciding what is best for it.

6) Ⓐ Paragraph 3 states that "most NGOs…are not elected by the people whom they serve," which leads to some criticism and is therefore a *structural problem*.

7) Ⓑ The highlighted sentence emphasizes the contrast between "assistance" and being "overbearing," which is best described by the contrast of a *helping hand* versus being *controlling and interfering*.

8) Ⓓ The paragraph provides examples of ways an NGO "may upset a community," then summarizes criticism of NGOs as, "assistance can seem overbearing." *Such issues* likely refers to the overall concept of the paragraph, which is paraphrased as *helping in a way that is overbearing*.

9) Ⓑ The added sentence helps clarify why many NGOs have become "more transparent" in their financial accountability. Thus, the added sentence should precede any mention of "transparency" and be placed at letter [B].

10) Ⓐ Because "Haitian people were excluded from rebuilding their own county," we can conclude that *foreign construc-*

tion companies did the work of rebuilding the damaged country, generating criticism.

11) Ⓐ The sentence containing "reinvest" describes how some *profits*, or earnings, are spent on projects that will help the cooperative company in the future and local needs. Thus, the author mentions the word *reinvest* to describe that a cocoa farmer's cooperative *uses business earnings to improve the company and community*.

12) Ⓒ Because Paragraph 5 describes situations where NGOs simply alert customers that "farmers…earned a fair price and had good working conditions" for their goods, we can conclude that some NGOs try to give the farmers autonomy, which is an *attempt to avoid the problem* of fostering dependence.

13) 3, 4, 5 The correct answers focus on how NGOs "draw criticism" or "play a crucial role." Paragraph 1 states that NGOs "voice the needs of people who would otherwise not be heard," so they help those *whose interests are not well represented by their governments*. Paragraph 3 states that an "NGO may upset a community by trying to change hierarchical structures," so NGOs sometimes *make decisions on behalf of the communities that they serve*. And Paragraph 2 states that NGOs collect "donations from…affluent countries" in order to *serve worthy causes in developing countries*.

Actual Practice 9   p. 210

1) Ⓑ The end of Paragraph 1 states that "modern understanding for the potential of AI" is a "real *possibility*." The similar statement made in Paragraph 2 claims that "computer technology…has made dreams and fears of replicating human intelligence a *contingency*." Both *contingency* and *possibility* are used in the same context, and they mean nearly the same thing.

2) Ⓓ One difference in Paragraph 2 between brains and computers is that "humans can reflect upon actions and events," so *the*

human brain can make connections through self-reflection.

3) Ⓒ The main idea of the highlighted sentence is that "scientists must…understand how intelligence functions" to create AI. Only [C] also focuses on the need to understand the mind in order to *reproduce* it.

4) Ⓑ According to Paragraph 3, the *Blue Brain Project* is the "attempt to *reverse-engineer the human brain*," which is what *This project* is "a precursor" to. Because *This project* is a *precursor*, or something that comes before, it must be the smaller project of *simulating a rat's neocortical column.*

5) Ⓓ In Paragraph 4, "mind uploading" is presented as a speculative, futuristic technology. Thus, the author included "hypothetical" *to emphasize that "mind uploading" does not yet exist.*

6) Ⓒ The author states that "mind uploading" could "ensure the immortality of a human mind." Thus, *the human conscience* [could] *live forever* if "mind uploading" were successful.

7) Ⓓ To be coherent, the added sentence requires awareness of ASIMO's mobility (*performs choreographed dances*) and its ability to "respond to human gestures" (*understanding of voice commands*). Thus, the added sentence should be the conclusion of Paragraph 5.

8) Ⓐ According to Paragraph 5, ASIMO is "programmed to respond to human gestures" and is "designed to help individuals." Based on these quotes, ASIMO is programmed to fulfill certain roles, but it does not perform actions based off its own judgment, so it *is not capable of autonomous thought.*

9) Ⓒ From the word "However," and from the subsequent description of a dystopian novel, it is clear that besides "intriguing" people, as stated in Paragraph 1, AI also scares them, or *generates* "many fears and anxieties."

10) Ⓑ According to Paragraph 6, Dick's novel "questions what differentiates humans from machines," so it *challenges the*

---

distinction between biological and synthetic beings.

11) Ⓓ The author states that the androids are similar to humans because they "appear human and contain implanted memories," but they are different from humans because they *lack empathy.*

12) Ⓒ ASIMO is described as a "humanoid robot," and Paragraph 6 states that Dick's androids "appear human." We can infer that people imagine that *all machines with human-like characteristics have a human-like appearance.*

13) 1, 5, 6 The correct answers summarize the "potential benefits" of AI. Based on the theory of "mind uploading," people speculate that "an active biological brain" can be "relayed to a mechanical device," so a computer can possibly store *the memories and thought processes of an individual human.* Also, *replicating human intelligence may* help determine "how intelligence functions in humans." And robots like ASIMO *seem to see, talk, and walk* and were "designed to help individuals who have difficulty with mobility," or *people with disabilities.*

Actual Practice 10   p. 214

1) Ⓐ In Paragraph 1, the novel "*chronicles* the life of a main character," and usually novels *describe*, or record, the life of their characters. Therefore, we can conclude that *chronicles* means *describes.*

2) Ⓒ In Paragraph 1, *The Tale of Genji* is being compared to works created around the same time, thus *contemporaneous* likely refers to the time in which the novel was written. *Concurrent* is the only answer choice that indicates time, so *contemporaneous* must mean current, or *concurrent.*

3) Ⓑ According to Paragraph 1, because of the "believable interactions" of characters in the novel, "it outshines all other contemporaneous works…," so "*believable interactions*" is mentioned to show why the novel *is an enduring work of literature.*

4) Ⓑ Paragraph 2 states that

"aristocratic women were allowed to use kana and produced poetry…" in kana, so kana *provided a language with which… women could compose literature,* such as poetry.

5) Ⓐ Because the highlighted sentence reiterates that Chinese was political language in Heian-era Japan, we can infer that Chinese politics strongly influenced Japan, so *China was the dominant political force in Japan.*

6) Ⓒ The main ideas in the highlighted sentence are that 1) Murakashi composed in both Chinese and Japanese, and 2) using multiple languages adds to the realism of the novel. Only answer choice [C] addresses both these points without adding new information.

7) Ⓑ The sentence that follows [A] introduces the main character generally, and the sentence that follows [B] gives specific plot information. The added sentence should come in between, as it gives general information about the main character.

8) Ⓓ In Paragraph 4, the author states that Genji's relatives are involved in " a power struggle," but the passage does NOT mention their *status in the imperial court.*

9) Ⓐ Paragraph 5 mentions that Genji is romantically involved with many women, so *endeavors* must have something to do with involvement, or *efforts*, because an *effort* is an activity, or something a person pursues.

10) Ⓑ The main idea of the final sentence of the passage is that the use of "poems throughout the *novel*" contribute "to *its* beauty and timelessness." Once the sentence is paraphrased, we can see that *its* refers back to the *novel* mentioned earlier in the sentence.

11) Ⓑ Paragraph 5 states that "dialogue in the novel often includes traditional Japanese poems," so *Murakashi's characters incorporate poetry into conversations.*

12) Ⓒ The passage mentions that the novel "includes more than 400 minor characters" (*hundreds of characters*); an

---

unclear conclusion, as "the novel ends mid-sentence" (*an ambiguous ending*); and it "makes use of…kana…[and] switches to Chinese writing" (*Chinese and kana writing*). Though Genji is described as a virtuous character in Paragraph 4, the passage does not specifically describe *the virtues of aristocratic life.*

13) 1, 4, 6 The correct answers focus on how the novel provides an authentic view of old Japan. *The Tale of Genji* recounts "many assignations between Genji and his love interests" (*many conversations between Japanese men and women of the period*), it "makes use of…kana" but also "switches to Chinese writing" in order to *display female language restrictions*, and it provides "an in-depth look at daily life in the Heian court…." (*depicts everyday aristocratic life at the Japanese imperial court*).

Actual Practice 11   p. 218

1) Ⓓ Because whales' "*unfathomable* aquatic life inspired humans to speculate…," we can conclude that *unfathomable* has to do with mystery and speculation. Anything that requires speculation is unknown or *unknowable.*

2) Ⓑ In Paragraph 1, the highlighted phrase comes just after the author's mention that whales are "among the most intelligent animals on Earth"; therefore the highlighted phrase is likely giving *examples demonstrating whales' intelligence.*

3) Ⓐ Paragraph 1 states that our understanding of whales has improved because of "improved observation of whales in their natural habitat." The only way humans can hope to observe whales in the ocean is by use of *enhanced submersible recording technology.*

4) Ⓒ Paragraph 2 states that ambulocetids developed "the ability to swallow prey while submerged," so *they were able to consume food while underwater.*

5) Ⓓ The *primitive structures* mentioned in the highlighted portion "later evolved into baleen," so we can infer that the author mentions "*primitive*" to *emphasize that baleen in modern whales is more developed* because it has been evolving for millions of years.

6) Ⓑ Paragraph 3 states that "a branch of semi-aquatic mammals...developed into the fully aquatic *Basilosauridae* family." Thus, the *Basilosauridae* was the first completely aquatic mammal.

7) Ⓓ Essentially, the sentence states that sound waves "bounce off of *objects or animals*," which helps determine the location of those same *objects or animals*.

8) Ⓒ Though the added sentence would make sense if placed at letter [B], it fits better at letter [C] because the sperm whale provides an example of whales' use of "echolocation... [to] hunt deep in the ocean," and the added sentence discusses the sperm whale's diet, which is the main idea of the sentence directly preceding letter [C].

9) Ⓑ According to Paragraph 6, some whale species developed baleen to access small food sources. The only reason a creature would evolve to consume a different food source is if there is a great deal of, or an *abundance*, of that food source, so a "*profusion* of small organisms" must be an "*abundance* of small organisms."

10) Ⓒ According to Paragraph 6, baleen likely developed "because of a profusion of small organisms that were [otherwise] inaccessible;" in other words, baleen developed to *help some whale species access miniscule organisms for food supply.*

11) Ⓐ There is "a profusion of small organisms" for baleen whales to eat, and the enormous blue whale can consume several tons of food a day, so we can infer that the baleen whale suborder does not *face much competition for nourishment.*

12) Ⓒ According to Paragraph 6, a *blue whale* is a type of baleen whale, or *Mysticeti*, not a type of toothed whale, or *Odontoceti*.

13) *Odontoceti:* 3, 6, 7
Mysticeti: 1, 4
According to the passage, *Odon-*

toceti "hunt using echolocation," or reflected sound waves. One of the reasons why *Odontoceti* uses echolocation is because they "hunt deep in the ocean where light is minimal," or *where little light permeates.* "The prey of toothed whales varies greatly," so *this type of whale has a diverse diet.... Mysticeti*, on the other hand, includes the blue whale, "which is the largest creature to have ever lived" (*the largest creature on Earth*); a baleen whale feeds by "filter[ing] out water, and consumes only the small animals that are left...in its mouth" (*filter its sustenance from water*).

Actual Practice 12   p. 222

1) Ⓓ Although Paragraph 1 states that the Pueblos "suddenly moved away around 1280 CE," it does not state that they *disappeared for many obvious reasons.*

2) Ⓐ The highlighted sentence in Paragraph 1 recounts how the Ancient Pueblo received their Spanish name. Only [A] addresses all the main points by stating that *Pueblo...refers to the unique sites of the area's native people.*

3) Ⓓ Chaco Culture National Historic Park, which presumably contains the *Chaco Canyon* mentioned in the added sentence, is not mentioned until the end of Paragraph 3. Thus, the added sentence should come after this mention of the park.

4) Ⓓ Paragraphs 2 and 3 describe Ancient Pueblo housing as "partially sunken homes," and later as "above-ground dwellings," and as "larger complexes with different levels." All these descriptions indicate that Paragraphs 2 and 3 *describe the evolution of Ancient Pueblo dwellings.*

5) Ⓐ Among other things, the *celestial calendar* mentioned in Paragraph 4 was able to "track a lunar cycle" and indicates when a solstice was occurring. Thus, the *celestial calendar* is mentioned to show that Ancient Pueblos *predicted astronomical events.*

6) Ⓐ Paragraphs 4 and 5 focus

on the Pueblo people's precision in astronomy, their resourceful agricultural practices, and their involvement in a complex trade network. These are all indications that the author wants to emphasize *how advanced the Anasazi culture was.*

7) Ⓑ Although we could infer that [D] is true based on Paragraph 5, choice [B] is a more complete answer since it mentions that Pueblo "people relied more on farming than hunting [but] continued to hunt" despite the development of agriculture.

8) Ⓐ It makes sense that "*those* found in beams..." refers to *tree rings* because *tree rings* takes the verb "found" as well, and *tree rings* are certainly present in "beams used for dwellings," as the beams would be made from trees.

9) Ⓐ According to Paragraph 6, a "narrow ring growth" on a tree "indicates much less precipitation," so it is safe to infer that the opposite is also true. Thus, *in a wetter year* it is likely that *a tree is able to add a thicker band to its trunk.*

10) Ⓒ Although it may be true that the Pueblo people deforested the area, their intent was not to deforest but to collect "wood for roof beams and firewood." Thus, we can deduce that the *inadvertent* deforestation was *unintentional.*

11) Ⓐ The author mentions "forensic science" to specify how researchers found evidence of the Pueblo's disappearance. Because forensic science relies on using technology, we can infer that scientists used *technology to uncover evidence and determine what occurred.*

12) Ⓓ Possible factors for the "sudden migration of the Ancient Pueblo" include "drought" (*lack of rainfall*), "warfare with non-Pueblo groups" (*conflicts with other tribes*), and "overuse of resources" (*run through their supply of timber*). Yet no mention is made of *Spanish arrival*, which occurred much later.

13) Ⓑ Much of Paragraph 7 discusses factors that "would explain the rise...of defensible architecture," such as "food

shortages [that] led to political conflicts," or *difficult environmental factors* and *conflicts.*

14) 2, 3, 6 The correct answers focus on the pueblos' "successful agricultural techniques" or the outcomes of successful farming methods. Paragraph 5 states that the Pueblo "made use of reservoirs," so they *devised methods to store rainfall.* Paragraph 2 claims that Pueblo "began building above-ground dwellings...to store foods for longer periods," so *Housing changes indicated a need to preserve harvested goods.* And Paragraph 5 states that they eventually "relied more on farming than hunting," or *participated in fewer hunting activities.*

Actual Practice 13   p. 226

1) Ⓒ Because much of Paragraph 1 discusses sunlight's effect on Earth's surface, the author mentions in *all directions* to indicate that, though some sunlight reaches Earth, much of it travels elsewhere in space.

2) Ⓑ If the three types of radiation compose "sunlight," then they are visible all around humans nearly every day; they seem to be everywhere, or are *ubiquitous* and *pervasive* in our world.

3) Ⓒ Because "all electromagnetic radiation travels at the same speed of light," *oscillate* cannot mean *accelerate.* Thus, the only way that waves can carry more or less energy is if they move up and down at a greater rate, as in "their waves *fluctuate....*"

4) Ⓑ The conjunction *or* means that only one thing can be chosen. Therefore, the phrase *atom or molecule* is singular because it refers to one *or* the other, but not both. It makes sense to say "causing an *atom or molecule* to assume a positive or negative charge...."

5) Ⓐ According to Paragraph 3, "radiation that carries sufficient energy completely removes a particle...in a process called ionization." Therefore, ionization *separates a particle from an atom or molecule.*

6) Ⓑ The sentence after letter

[B] states that less UV radiation reaches the Earth's surface than leaves the Sun, which is introduced by the added sentence: *Earth's atmosphere blocks* "most UV" *radiation.* Thus, the added sentence should be placed at letter [B].

7) Ⓓ The main process described in the highlighted sentence is that a protein that stimulates the nerves causes sunburn pain. The passage never states that *UV radiation carries a protein into the body*, as [A] does, or that *a protein increases or absorbs UV radiation*, as [B] and [C] do. Thus, [D] is the only reasonable answer.

8) Ⓑ Paragraph 5 states that UV radiation "constitutes about 3 percent of the sunlight that reaches Earth's surface," but it does not say that *3 percent is ionizing.*

9) Ⓐ *Ionization energy* is "the amount of energy required to extract a particle from an atom," so ionization energy is a specific amount of energy, which is provided by radiation. For human tissue, the amount of energy required for ionization is provided by *high-frequency UV radiation.*

10) Ⓑ According to Paragraph 6, "bone molecules…have a higher ionization energy than tissue," so "the radiation becomes absorbed." Thus, *it takes more energy to ionize a bone molecule.*

11) Ⓒ Based on the information in Paragraph 6, x-radiation is high-frequency radiation that can "pose health risks." Thus, we can infer that x-radiation can *potentially ionize* [harm] *human tissue*, making overexposure to x-rays dangerous.

12) Ⓓ According to the passage, UV radiation is potentially ionizing whereas "visible and infrared radiation are entirely harmless" and therefore not ionizing. Furthermore, Paragraph 6 states that x-radiation "has a higher frequency than UV radiation." Thus, *x-radiation* has the highest frequency.

13) Non-ionizing radiation: 2, 4
Ionizing radiation: 3, 5, 7
Non-ionizing radiation excites

particles, so it *temporarily transfers energy to an electron*, generally without permanently altering the molecules structure. Thus, since "infrared radiation [is] entirely harmless," we can conclude that it must be *an example of* [non-ionizing] *radiation.* Ionizing radiation, on the other hand, "completely removes a particle," which *alters the composition of the atom or molecule*; the removal of a particle can "cause hazardous mutations," or *is harmful to living tissue*; and x-radiation, which "has a higher frequency than [ionizing] UV radiation" is used in x-ray machines, so an x-ray machine uses…[ionizing] *radiation for medical purposes.*

Actual Practice 14   p. 230

1) Ⓓ Paragraph 1 speculates that Poe "would be surprised by his renown today, as he led a *turbulent* life frequently mired in poverty." His *turbulent* or *relatively unstable* life and lack of financial success may not have portended his renown 200 years later.

2) Ⓑ According to Paragraph 1, Poe was "motivated to produce fiction that would sell," and his work was characterized by "dark sensationalism." Thus, we can infer that he wrote scary and *shocking* work, in other words containing "dark sensationalism," because *He believed that people would buy it.*

3) Ⓐ The main ideas in the highlighted sentence are that Poe rose to greater fame "After his death" because of his "innovations in entertaining genres." Only choice [A] addresses all these points without including superfluous details.

4) Ⓒ Although Poe wrote "irresistibly horrifying tales," the passage does not mention that he spent any time *living in various mansions that seemed eerie*; eerie mansions are a characteristic of his literature, not of his personal life.

5) Ⓓ Because the highlighted sentence discusses the general characteristics of the plots in Poe's detective fiction, we can infer that the purpose of this

sentence is to *identify a pattern in Poe's detective fiction.*

6) Ⓒ According to the conclusion of Paragraph 3, Poe's stories caused "the detective or mystery genre to expand…," so the paragraph primarily describes Poe's *impact on other* [mystery] *writers.*

7) Ⓒ Because Poe's stories *portend* future technologies, we can conclude that *portend* is mentioned in order to *explain that Poe's science fiction predicted several modern developments.*

8) Ⓐ "*Factual account*" is in quotes to emphasize that the novel was advertised as factual, but is really another one of Poe's science-fiction *hoax*[es] *that fooled readers.*

9) Ⓒ The added sentence introduces the term "Gothic fiction," which is elaborated on in Paragraph 5. Because the added sentence introduces the main term of Paragraph 5, we can infer that it is serving as the paragraph's introduction and therefore should be placed at letter [C].

10) Ⓐ At the end of the short story, the narrator and his friend "believe that they do see the sister standing at the door." Usher dies from shock at the sight, and the narrator runs from the house. Thus, the disastrous ending results from *the frightening arrival of an unexpected figure* (the sister).

11) Ⓑ Because Montresor is able to narrate his story, we can infer that *Montresor was never suspected* or brought to justice for the murder. In addition, because the tomb remained undisturbed, we can infer that *Fortunato did not escape.*

12) Ⓐ Paragraph 5 summarizes "the Fall of the House of Usher," while Paragraph 6 details *another prime example* of Poe's Gothic tales.

13) Gothic fiction: 3, 4, 8
Science fiction: 2, 6
Detective fiction: 1, 7
Gothic fiction is "set in gloomy places," or *a dreary setting with morbid events*; it is the genre of "The Cask of Amontillado," in which Montresor *calmly retells his…outrageous act* of

murdering a friend; and Gothic fiction uses settings such as burial "vaults" and "crypts," which may incite a *fear of ghosts* among readers. Science fiction is the genre of Poe's "only complete (*finished*) novel," and it includes "innovations that were hardly imaginable in his day," so it involved *speculating about technology that may be discovered.* Finally, detective fiction includes plots with "multiple layers of clues," *so readers try to solve a crime as they read.* In addition, Poe's protagonist, Dupin, "inspired the Sherlock Holmes series," and he *became a prototype for other characters.*

Actual Practice 15   p. 234

1) Ⓒ Although Paragraph 1 states that some hydrogen atoms have been fused into helium atoms within the Sun's core, it never states that *the Sun achieves an equal ration of hydrogen to helium atoms.*

2) Ⓑ *Hydrostatic equilibrium* is a process of pushing and pulling that stabilizes the Sun. Therefore, the *equilibrium* describes a *balance* and provides the referent for the phrase *this balance.*

3) Ⓐ According to Paragraph 2, a supernova occurs when a star "runs out of fuel" (comes to *the end of its lifecycle*) and "explodes," or *bursts.*

4) Ⓑ Paragraph 2 states that black holes form when "the inward force of gravity overpowers the outward force of…fusion," in other words when *gravity overcomes atomic fusion.*

5) Ⓑ According to Paragraph 1, fusion results when an increase in mass increases pressure and temperature. Because larger stars have more mass, we can infer that they have more pressure and higher temperatures than small stars. Thus, we can also infer that the larger stars use this higher pressure and temperature to *fuse* [larger] *elements together*, which is why a large star's center is so dense that it eventually forms a black hole.

6) Ⓑ The added sentence serves as a transition between Paragraphs 2 and 3. The sentence

works best as an introduction to Paragraph 3 because it introduces the main idea of Paragraph 3 – that black holes *cannot be directly observed*.

7) Ⓒ Black holes cannot be observed, and can be understood based on their powerful effects on nearby celestial objects and using math equations. Thus, we can infer that mathematicians must use highly *sophisticated*, or *complex*, math equations to determine what black holes are like.

8) Ⓒ Although *anatomy* usually refers to parts of a living body, it can refer more generally to the structure of anything, be it living or nonliving. Thus, the author mentions *anatomy* in order to *introduce the* structure, or *different components of…[a] black hole*.

9) Ⓒ Because black holes are distant and unobservable phenomena, the author compares them to an earthly event, a waterfall, to help illustrate a black hole's anatomy in *visual terms*.

10) Ⓓ Because anything that occurs within a black hole is unobservable, it is reasonable to assume that *scientists are unsure of what happens to matter that enters a black hole* because they have no way of viewing such matter.

11) Ⓑ The sentence as a whole discusses the idea that the biggest black holes "have consumed 'aeons' worth of mass," or whatever came near them over an unimaginably long time. Thus, they are extremely old, or *ancient*.

12) Ⓑ Large black holes are called *supermassive* black holes, indicating that they are categorized based on their *mass*. Moreover, Paragraph 5 mentions the average size of both stellar black holes and supermassive black holes, so we can conclude that black holes are categorized based on *their mass*.

13) 1, 4, 5 The correct answers describe why black holes are "amazing yet mysterious." Paragraph 4 states that "not even light can escape" an event horizon, *so any matter or energy that traverses an event horizon*

becomes trapped in the black hole. Paragraph 5 claims that "at the center of nearly every… galaxy sits a supermassive black hole," so *centers of galaxies contain…enormous black holes*. And physicists have had to use "byzantine mathematical equations," or *complex calculations*, to *determine properties of black holes*, according to Paragraph 4.

Chapter 12 Actual Test

Reading 1   p. 240

1) Ⓐ Because Tubman *covertly* led "more than 300 slaves to freedom" from a place "where slavery was legal," we can infer that *covert* means *secretive*, as these missions would have to be secretive in order to be successful.

2) Ⓑ Paragraph 1 gives *historical background* by introducing important terms like "Underground Railroad" and places Tubman's accomplishment in historical context. Paragraph 2 focuses on Tubman as she "grew up as a field hand," so it *describes her life before her escape*.

3) Ⓒ Because the Religious Society of Friends was involved in the Underground Railroad, which "helped escaping slaves," we can infer that the Society of Friends *were abolitionists, and some assisted fugitives*.

4) Ⓒ The Religious Society of Friends, also called Quakers, is the only community explicitly mentioned in Paragraph 4, so it is the clearest and most logical referent for *this community*.

5) Ⓓ Though Tubman's description makes it seem as if she was *euphoric*, the description does not describe her remembering *how she had transcended adversity*.

6) Ⓒ In the added sentence, the phrase *as a result* refers back to the 1850 law that stipulated that northern "law enforcement officials" had to aid in slave apprehension, so the added sentence should come after this information and be placed at letter [C].

7) Ⓐ We can assume that because the passing of the Fugitive

Slave Act brought about change that made slaves less protected, escaped slaves must have been more protected in free states before the law.

8) Ⓐ The main points in Paragraph 8 are, "Tubman became involved in the abolitionist movement," she "became an armed scout and spy" in the Civil War, and she led "an armed assault." Only choice [A] addresses these three key ideas.

9) Ⓒ During her involvement in the abolitionist movement, Tubman was "speaking at meetings and working with many of the leading figures," or in other words she *undertook activities with principal abolitionists and gave speeches at events*.

10) Ⓑ Because her job as a spy included conducting "espionage," which helped "in several Union victories," we can infer that *intelligence* is related to "espionage," or spy work that garners *secret information*.

11) Ⓐ The highlighted sentence states that Tubman's "raid resulted in the liberation of 700 slaves," so *The invasion freed hundreds of slaves*, and the raid also brought about the recruitment of newly freed men," so some freed slaves *enlisted to fight for the Union*.

12) Ⓓ Although Tubman's "raid…brought about the recruitment of newly freed men," the author does not state that she *trained* [these] *former slaves to become soldiers*.

13) 1, 2, 4 Correct answer choices focus on Tubman's courageous acts. Paragraph 1 states that Tubman made "covert trips…to lead more than 300 slaves to freedom," so she *assisted captives in surreptitious flights to safety*. Paragraph 8 claims that Tubman "provided intelligence that assisted in several Union victories," so she gained *inside information during the Civil War*. And Paragraph 6 mentions that, despite the Fugitive Slave Act of 1850, Tubman "continued to sneak into the South to help slaves," so *she continued liberating those in bondage*.

Reading 2   p. 244

14) Ⓒ According to Paragraph 1, neurons "are encased in a soft tissue within the brain," *not composed of a soft tissue*.

15) Ⓓ According to Paragraph 3, an octopus' "brain and its eight limbs" must work together to accomplish quick "full-body color changes." Thus, *synchronize* has to do with working together, so it must be similar in meaning to *coordinate*.

16) Ⓒ Paragraph 3 states that some octopuses "imitate venomous fish or sea snakes" in order to "scare off a specific predator," so they *mimic predatory animals to deter being attacked*.

17) Ⓐ Because octopuses have camouflage abilities and can "scare off a specific predator" through mimicry, we can infer that they have to hide or trick predators often, meaning that they *have well-developed defense behaviors*.

18) Ⓑ Paragraph 3 states that "about 60 percent of an octopus'…neurons are not located in the brain," and if 60 percent of neurons are located outside the brain, *40 percent of the animal's neurons* must be contained in the brain.

19) Ⓓ One example given in Paragraph 4 concerning octopuses' "manipulation of their environment" is their use of "shells to form temporary homes." Thus, octopuses use their environment in creative ways, so the author mentions *manipulate* to show *the extent to which octopuses interact with their environment*.

20) Ⓒ The sentence following letter [C] gives an example of an exceptionally large lobe in the human brain. Because the added sentence states that *some lobes have grown larger to support complex processes*, we can infer that the example involving the temporal lobe should come after the added sentence, which should be placed at [C].

21) Ⓐ Physically and socially, octopuses and humans differ in countless ways. However, the author introduces Paragraph 5 with a surprising similarity between the two species. Thus, *Like octopuses* is mentioned to

introduce a comparison between dissimilar organisms.

22) Ⓓ The first two sentence of Paragraph 5 describes humans as "a relatively defenseless species." Thus, *these frailties*, mentioned in the second sentence, must refer back to humans' *frailties*, or weaknesses, in the form of a *scarcity of natural defenses*.

23) Ⓑ According to Paragraph 5, the "temporal lobe may have developed as language became more complicated," in other words to *process an increasingly conceptual language*.

24) Ⓑ The correct answer choice presents the same main idea that the frontal lobe developed to support social interactions as the highlighted sentence, but it switches the order of clauses.

25) Ⓑ Because the frontal lobe grows large in animals that "must balance social relationships with survival needs," we can infer that animals without social relationships, or *solitary animals, rarely develop large frontal lobes*.

26) Octopus brain: 2, 5, 7
  Human brain: 3, 6
The brain of an octopus communicates with its "eight limbs," which have their "own nervous system," so the *brain communicates with multiple autonomous nervous systems*; "the optical lobes…are the *largest features* of the brain" of an octopus according to Paragraph 2; and the "coordination between…[its] brain and its eight limbs helps it…synchronize full-body color changes," in other words the *brain can regulate camouflage*. A human brain must "balance social relationship with survival needs," or *accommodate social interactions*; and its temporal lobe "developed as language became more complicated…," so human brains *may have evolved to process complex communications*.

Reading 3   p. 248

27) Ⓑ Paragraph 1 states that "the outside world knew little about surfing before the 20th century," so we can infer that *surfing techniques were not*

widely diffused until the 20th century.

28) Ⓓ In Paragraph 1, surfing is described as a "socioreligious practice," and according to Paragraph 2, missionaries tried to "discourage" such practices. Thus, *quell* must have a meaning similar to "discourage," or *repress*.

29) Ⓐ Paragraph 2 discusses three instances in which surfers from Hawaii traveled to other costal locations and put on early surfing demonstrations, in other words *how surfing spread outside of secluded populations*.

30) Ⓒ Paragraph 3 introduces *Gidget*, implying that the film merges surfing and romance. If *Endless Summer* "perpetuated this romantic image," then it *continued* to spread it.

31) Ⓒ The end of Paragraph 4 states, "The international success of some surf bands helped spread…[perceptions] of surfing," so surf music brought *international attention to a burgeoning surf culture*.

32) Ⓐ The highlighted sentence focuses on surfing's appeal "to teens and young adults" (*younger people*) through "relaxation" (*leisure*) and "excitement" (*exhilaration*). The other choices misinterpret the relationship between leisure and excitement or are too general.

33) Ⓓ *These practices* refers back to the "Hawaiian surf philosophies" (*Hawaiian* ideologies) and connection to nature (*embracing one's environment*) mentioned in the previous sentence.

34) Ⓒ Because "stoked" describes a "mixture" of emotions, we can infer that *apprehension* is an emotion related to but different from "excitement"; moreover, because surfing a large wave is likely intimidating, we can infer that *apprehension* means *anxiety*, or worry.

35) Ⓑ According to Paragraph 6, *fiberglass and foam* are materials that helped "create shorter and lighter boards," so *fiberglass and foam* are mentioned to *give examples of how surfboards became lighter*.

36) Ⓓ The phrase *Regardless*

of why people pursue the sport in the added sentence refers back to the "two camps [that] had formed amongst surfers." Because the sentence following [C] elaborates upon these two camps, the added sentence serves as a conclusion that wraps up the rapid popularization of surfing, and should therefore be placed at letter [D].

37) Ⓓ The sentence containing *others* provides a contrast between "some devoted surfers [who] dream of professionalism," and "*others* [devoted surfers who] maintain…."

38) Ⓒ Although "soul surfers" are described as "dedicated surfers" in Paragraph 5, the passage does not state anywhere that they are *generally considered the best surfers*.

39) 2, 3, 5 Correct answers focus on "factors" in popularizing surf culture. According to Paragraph 6, professional surfing "added an element of…sponsorship" to surfing, and some surfers "attained international stardom," *so sponsorship provides worldwide exposure*. According to Paragraph 4, "The international success of some surf bands," *such as the Beach Boys, spread surf culture*. And Paragraph 2 states that "island surfers traveled to the…United States and Australia" *to display the prowess of surfers*.

SIMPLE ANSWERS

Chapter 1
Warm Up

1-5: subsequent, monotonous, unreasonable, abstract, transmit

6-10: forecast, diagram, bilateral, disabilities, derive

11-15: intervention, vivid, spectacle, inscription, deflecting

16-20: construct, fidelity, conceded, chronology, novelty

Quick Practice

Practice #1 (1-8):
B D A C / A D B C
Practice #2 (9-16):
A C D B / B A C D
Practice #3 (17-24):
D A D C / B A B C
Practice #4 (25-32):
A B D C / D A B D
Practice #5 (33-40):
A C D A / C A D B
Practice #6 (41-48):
B D A A / B C A C
Practice #7 (49-56):
D A D D / A A C D
Practice #8 (57-64):
C B A B / B B A B
Practice #9 (65-72):
D B A B / D A B C
Practice #10 (73-80):
B D D A / A B C A

Chapter 2
Warm Up

1-10: they, all, it, him, which / their, the term, both, the former, several

11-20: it, whose, them, the other, its / emphases, a mistake, much, it, their

Quick Practice
Practice #1 (1-4):
A C D A
Practice #2 (5-8):
C C B D
Practice #3 (9-12):
C D B A
Practice #4 (13-16):
D A B A
Practice #5 (17-20):
C B D A
Practice #6 (21-24):
B D D C
Practice #7 (25-28):
A C B D
Practice #8 (29-32):
B D A A
Practice #9 (33-36):
C C D D
Practice #10 (37-40):
B D C A

Chapter 3
Warm Up

1-10:
O O F F O / F O F F O
11-20:
O F F F O / F O F O O

Quick Practice
Practice #1 (1-4):
C A D B
Practice #2 (5-8):
C A B C
Practice #3 (9-12):
B B D C
Practice #4 (13-16):
C B B A
Practice #5 (17-20):
C A D C
Practice #6 (21-24):
C A B D
Practice #7 (25-28):
D A B D
Practice #8 (29-32):
D C D A
Practice #9 (33-36):
A B B D
Practice #10 (37-40):
B D A B

Chapter 4
Warm Up

1-10: C B A A C / B C A C E
11-20: C D C A D / D B B C E

Quick Practice
Practice #1 (1-4):
D B A C
Practice #2 (5-8):
A C B A
Practice #3 (9-12):
B A C B
Practice #4 (13-16):
A C D D
Practice #5 (17-20):
C C A B
Practice #6 (21-24):
B B A D
Practice #7 (25-28):
C A B D
Practice #8 (29-32):
C B A D
Practice #9 (33-36):
D A C A
Practice #10 (37-40):
A B B D

Chapter 5
Warm Up

1-5: 2-1-3 / 3-2-1 / 3-2-1 / 1-2-3 / 3-1-2
6-10: 1-2-3 / 2-3-1 / 2-3-1 / 1-3-2 / 2-3-1

Quick Practice
Practice #1 (1-2): C G
Practice #2 (3-4): B H
Practice #3 (5-6): A G
Practice #4 (7-8): C F
Practice #5 (9-10): D F
Practice #6 (11-12): D H
Practice #7 (13-14): A E
Practice #8 (15-16): C E
Practice #9 (17-18): D G
Practice #10 (19-20): B F

Chapter 6
Warm Up

1-10: B A A A B / A B A B A
11-20: A B B A B / A A B A B

Quick Practice
Practice #1 (1-4):
B D C A
Practice #2 (5-8):
A D C D
Practice #3 (9-12):
B A D C
Practice #4 (13-16):
B B D C
Practice #5 (17-20):
C D A C
Practice #6 (21-24):
B C A B
Practice #7 (25-28):
C A A D
Practice #8 (29-32):
D C A B
Practice #9 (33-36):
C D B B
Practice #10 (37-40):
D D B A

Chapter 7
Warm Up

1-10:
PER, CR, DES, DES, PER / DES CR CR PER DES

Quick Practice
Practice #1 (1-4):
B D A D
Practice #2 (5-8):
C A C C
Practice #3 (9-12):
C D A D
Practice #4 (13-16):
D C C C
Practice #5 (17-20):
A B B A
Practice #6 (21-24):
C D D A
Practice #7 (25-28):
B B A D

Practice #8 (29-32):

C D B C

Practice #9 (33-36):

A C B B

Practice #10 (37-40):

C A B D

Chapter 8
Warm Up
1-10:

A B A A B / A B B B A

Quick Practice
Practice #1 (1-3):

C B C

Practice #2 (4-6):

C B C

Practice #3 (7-9):

B A D

Practice #4 (10-12):

D C C

Practice #5 (13-15):

A B A

Practice #6 (16-18):

B D A

Practice #7 (19-21):

B D A

Practice #8 (22-24):

A C D

Practice #9 (25-27):

C B A

Practice #10 (28-30):

D D C

Chapter 9
Warm Up
1-10:

3, 2, 1, 2, 2 / 1, 3, 3, 1, 2

Quick Practice
Practice #1: 1, 3, 4

Practice #2: 1, 4, 5

Practice #3: 2, 3, 5

Practice #4: 2, 4, 5

Practice #5: 2, 5, 6

Practice #6: 2, 3, 6

Practice #7: 2, 4, 5

Practice #8: 2, 3, 6

Practice #9: 1, 3, 4

Practice #10: 2, 4, 5

Chapter 10
Warm Up
1) Research: 2, 5, 8

   Writing: 1, 3, 7

2) Canada: 4, 6, 8

   Siberia: 1, 5, 7

3) Muscle: 3, 5, 7

   Bone: 1, 6, 8

4) Synonym: 1, 4, 8

   Antonym: 5, 6, 7

5) Coffee: 2, 4, 8

   Tea: 3, 5, 7

6) Vaccine: 1, 4, 7

   Medication: 2, 3, 6

7) Hurricane: 1, 4, 7

   Snowstorm: 3, 5, 8

8) Mice: 2, 4, 6

   Elephants: 1, 5, 8

9) New York City: 1, 3, 8

   Beijing: 2, 4, 7

10) Nonprofit: 3, 5, 8

   Corporation: 1, 6, 7

Quick Practice
1) Paradigm: 4, 5, 6

   Paradox: 3, 7

2) Mesopotamian: 1, 2, 6

   Norse: 3, 8

   Chinese: 4, 9

3) Bonobos: 2, 4, 7

   Chimpanzees: 5, 6

4) Classical mechanics: 1, 2, 4

   Quantum mechanics: 3, 7

5) Martin Luther King, Jr.: 1, 6

   Malcolm X: 2, 3, 7

6) Asperger's: 3, 5

   Savant: 2, 4, 7

7) Tropical: 2, 6

   Temperate: 1, 3, 5

8) Stephen A. Douglas: 1, 2, 5

   Abraham Lincoln: 4, 7

9) Magical realism: 2, 7

   Fantasy: 1, 5, 6

10) John Chapman: 2, 5

   John Muir: 4, 6, 7

Actual Practice
Actual Practice 1
1-5: D B C A B

6-12: D B C A C / C A

13: Troy II: 6, 7

   Troy VIIa: 1, 3, 5

Actual Practice 2
1-5: C D D B B

6-12: D A C A C / C C

13: Prairie School architecture:

   3, 6

   Textile architecture:

   1, 4, 7

   Usonian architecture:

   5, 9

Actual Practice 3
1-5: C B C A C

6-12: B B C A B / D C

13: 2, 4, 6

Actual Practice 4
1-5: D D A B A

6-12: B D B A D / C B

13: 2, 3, 5

Actual Practice 5
1-5: C A C B D

6-12: A D A B C / C B

13: 2, 5, 6

Actual Practice 6
1-5: C A D B A

6-12: B D C C B / D A

13: 1, 3, 4

Actual Practice 7
1-5: C B B A A

6-12: C B B B C / A B

13: Population bottleneck: 3, 7

   Founder effect: 1, 4, 6

Actual Practice 8
1-5: B A D D C

6-12: A B D B A / A C

13: 3, 4, 5

Actual Practice 9
1-5: B D C B D

6-12: C D A C B / D C

13: 1, 5, 6

Actual Practice 10
1-5: A C B B A

6-12: C B D A B / B C

13: 1, 4, 6

Actual Practice 11
1-5: D B A C D

6-12: B D C B C / A C

13: *Odontoceti*: 3, 6, 7

   Mysticeti: 1, 4

Actual Practice 12
1-5: D A D D A

6-13: A B A A C / A D B

14: 2, 3, 6

Actual Practice 13
1-5: C B C B A

6-12: B D B A B / C D

13: Non-ionizing radiation: 2, 4

   Ionizing radiation: 3, 5, 7

Actual Practice 14
1-5: D B A C D

6-13: C C A C A / B A

14: Gothic fiction: 3, 4, 8

   Science fiction: 2, 6

   Detective fiction: 1, 7

Actual Practice 15
1-5: C B A B B

6-12: B C C C D / B B

13: 1, 4, 5

Actual Test
Reading 1
1-5: A B C C D

6-12: C A A C B / A D

13: 1, 2, 4

Reading 2
14-18: C D C A B

19-25: D C A D B / B B

26: Octopus brain: 2, 5, 7

   Human brain: 3, 6

Reading 3
27-31: B D A C C

32-38: A D C B D / D C

39: 2, 3, 5

www.ingramcontent.com/pod-product-compliance
Lightning Source LLC
Chambersburg PA
CBHW081348280326
41927CB00043B/3317